IF NOT, NOT

*The Oath of the Aragonese and the
Legendary Laws of Sobrarbe*

IN. PACE.ET.IVSTITIA.REGNVM.REGITO
NOBISQ.FOROS.MELIORES.IRROGATO.

E.MAVRIS.VINDICABVNDA.DIVIDVNTOR
INTER.RICOSHOMINES.NONMODO.SED
ETIAM.INTER.MILITES.AC.INFANTIO-
NES.PEREGRINVS.AVTEM.HOMO.NIHIL
INDE.CAPITO.

IVRA.DICERE.REGI.NEFAS.ESTO.NISI
ADHIBITO.SVBDITORVM.CONSILIO.

BELLVM.AGGREDI.PACEM.INIRE.INDV-
CIAS.AGERE.REMVE.ALIAM.MAGNI.MO-
MENTI.PERTRACTARE.CAVETO. REX
PRAETERQVAM.SENIORVM.ANNVENTE
CONSENSV.

NE.QVID.AVTEM.DAMNI.DETRIMENTIVE
LEGES.AVT.LIBERTATES.NOSTRAE.PA-
TIANTVR.IVDEX. QVIDAM.MEDIVS
ADESTO.AD.QVEM.A.REGE.PROVOCA-
RE.SI.ALIQVEM.LAESERIT.INIVRIASQ.
ARCERE.SI.QVAS.FORSAN.REIPVB.IN-
TVLERIT.IVS.FASQ.ESTO.

SI.CONTRA.FOROS. AVT.LIBERTA-
TES.REGNVM. A. SE.PREMI. IN. FV-
TVRVM. CONTINGERET. AD
ALIVM. SIVE. FIDELEM. SIVE.IN-
FIDELEM.REGEM. ADSCISCEN-
DVM.LIBER.IPSI.REGNO. ADITVS
PATERET.

If Not, Not

The Oath of the Aragonese and the

Legendary Laws of Sobrarbe

RALPH E. GIESEY

PRINCETON UNIVERSITY PRESS

PRINCETON, NEW JERSEY

1968

Publication of this book has been aided by grants from the
Whitney Darrow Publication Reserve Fund of Princeton University
Press and the University of Iowa Graduate College

Printed in the United States of America
by Princeton University Press

FRONTISPIECE:

The "False Fueros of Sobrarbe" of Gerónimo Blancas,
from his *Aragonensium rerum Commentarii*
(Zaragoza, 1588), pp. 25-26, 28.

To J · M · K ·

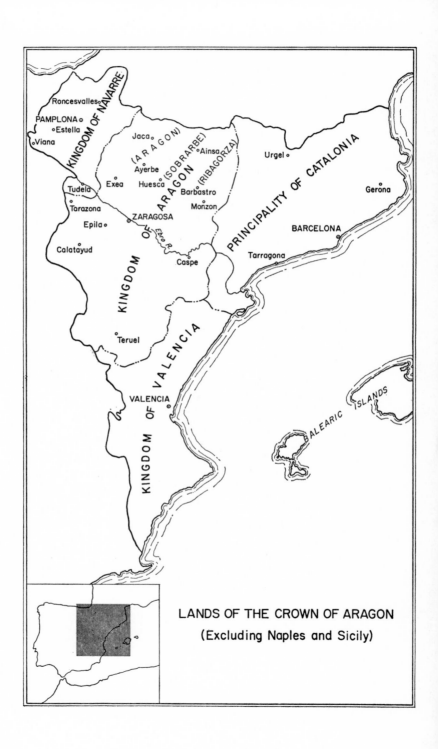

LANDS OF THE CROWN OF ARAGON
(Excluding Naples and Sicily)

Preface

𝒯he Oath by which the people of Aragon supposedly addressed their new king, opening with the proud claim "We who are worth as much as you . . . ," and, after stating the conditions of accepting him, ending with the open threat, "If not, not," has long been a stock item of history textbooks. If the Oath is accepted as an authentic practice, it is assigned to the Middle Ages, when indisputably the power of the king of Aragon was subject to special limitations. If believed to have been invented during the Renaissance, the Oath can illustrate the spirit of independence of the Aragonese people as their country became less and less important following the union with Castile under the Habsburgs, and culminating in the uprising of 1591-1592. In short, if old and authentic, the Oath epitomizes the Aragonese love of liberty; if recent and forged, it demonstrates the Aragonese penchant toward sedition.

Some five years ago, when preparing an edition of François Hotman's *Francogallia*, the Oath of the Aragonese was presented to me for the first time as a scholarly issue. Before then, when I had encountered the Oath in textbooks and the like, I had been amused and interested; now I had to make a learned evaluation of it. I consulted my friend, James M. Kingsley, Jr., of the University of Minnesota library, who is learned in Hispanic literature and history. He quickly discovered the century-old book by Xavier de Quinto in which Hotman was indicted as the forger of the Oath, and not long afterwards he came up with the 16th-century testimony of Giovanni Soranzo which fully exculpated Hotman. The actual origin of the Oath, however, remained an open question. The deeper I probed, the more it

became clear that the answer was to be found in the inter-
acting fields of late medieval law and Renaissance historiography, subjects of particular interest to me. For over a year
Mr. Kingsley gave generously of his time and talent to help
solve linguistic and bibliographical problems; I would like,
therefore, to dedicate this book to him in remembrance of
the many hours we devoted to scholarly detective work in
the University of Minnesota library.

This book was written during the year 1964-1965, when I
was a visiting member at the Institute for Advanced Study.
Among the permanent members who gave me counsel and
criticism, thanks are due above all to Felix Gilbert, who
read the entire manuscript. Daily conversations with his
colleagues, Marshall Clagett and Harold Cherniss, also influenced my conceptions in many ways, while the latter's
research assistant, Cynthia P. Gardiner (now my wife)
gave the work a thorough editorial examination.

Thanks must also be extended to two Spanish medieval-
ists, Angel Ferrari in Madrid and José M.ª Lacarra in Zaragoza, for helping me to procure films and transcriptions of
manuscripts; and to two American medieval historians,
Gaines Post and J. Lee Shneidman, who each gave the
manuscript an expert professional critique.

For the style and spelling of Spanish names, I have accepted as authorities the catalogues of printed books of the
Library of Congress, the British Museum, and the Bibliothèque Nationale, in that order. The Selected Bibliography contains complete references to all the books cited by
a short title in the body of the work, and indicates in which
footnotes they are to be found. The list comprises those
writings which have been most valuable to me (no matter
how seldom actually cited), and those which are most relevant to the topic (no matter how shabbily constructed).

RALPH E. GIESEY

Iowa City, Iowa
September, 1967

Contents

Abbreviations   2

I   *Introduction*   3

II   *The Oath in 16th-Century Writings*   18

    Giovanni Soranzo   19
    François Hotman and Other French Writers   20
    Antonio Pérez   24
    Gerónimo Blancas   26

III   *False Fueros I-IV*   31

    Sobrarbe: the Principality and its Fueros   32
    Sobrarbe and Tudela   34
    Sobrarbe and Navarre   41
    Navarre and the Prince of Viana   52
    The Prince of Viana and Blancas   57
    False Fueros I-IV   60

IV   *False Fueros V and VI: the Sagarra Story*   64

    The Justice of Aragon   65
    Cerdan's Letra intimada   70
    The Sagarra Story   75
    The Privileges of Union and Their Prohibition   87

V   *The Sobrarbe Legend and the False Fueros: 1450-1588*   102

    Tomic and Vagad   103
    Molino, Marineus, and Vasaeus   110
    The Nueva Compilación and Beuter   119
    Zurita, Garibay, and Blancas   131

VI   *Royal Oaths in Aragon and the Oath of the Aragonese*   158

    Supposed Ceremonial Circumstances of the Oath of the Aragonese   158
    Spanish Analogues to the Oath of the Aragonese   163
    Xavier de Quinto's Explanation of the Oath   176
    Dating the Oath of the Aragonese   181
    The Royal Jurisdictional Oath   186
    The Royal Jurisdictional Oath and the Oath of the Aragonese   216

VII   *If Not, Not: Slogan and Legend*   227

Appendices

   I: The Four Primary Versions of the Fictitious
      Oath of the Aragonese   247
   II: Diagram of the "False Fueros of Sobrarbe"   248
   III: Blancas' Sources for the "False Fueros
      of Sobrarbe"   249
   IV: Antich's Glossa on Daux's Observantiae   252
   V: The Kings of Aragon   255

Selected and Indexed Bibliography   257

Index   269

IF NOT, NOT

The Oath of the Aragonese and the
Legendary Laws of Sobrarbe

ABBREVIATIONS

ADA	*Anuario de Derecho Aragonese*
AHDE	*Anuario de Historia del Derecho Español*
BRAE	*Boletín de la Real Academia Española*
BRAH	*Boletín de la Real Academia de Historia*
CDIACA	*Colección de Documentos Inéditos del Archivo general de la Corona de Aragón*
CDIHE	*Colección de Documentos Inéditos para la Historia de España*
CHE	*Cuadernos de Historia de España*
FN	*Fuero general de Navarra*
RABM	*Revista de Archivos, Bibliotecas y Museos*

Chapter I · Introduction

$\mathcal{A}$lmost a century ago in Spain—a country where speech has not usually been free—the oratory of liberal and democratic intellectuals for a short while commanded the public scene. After the expulsion of the tyrannical government of Isabel II by a coup d'état in September 1868, the Cortes appointed a commission to draft a democratic constitution, and during many months of the following year this "Constituent Cortes" debated the articles of the proposed new constitution. One bone of contention, inevitably, was the nomenclature which should be used to designate the new government. The word "republican" was anathema to some and the notion of monarchy loathsome to others, but all professed adherence to the concept of democracy. Even the term "democratic monarchy" was possible. This meant that the nation—in effect, the people—was to be the receptacle of sovereignty, and that all power should flow from it. The chief derivative of the sovereign power was the monarch, but the people were represented, via universal suffrage, in the national Cortes. Of the three contemporary models of governance most frequently invoked in the debate—the United States, Switzerland, and Great Britain—the last was obviously considered exemplary of "democratic monarchy."

One of the vigorous exponents of "democratic monarchy" was the Catalan scholar and man of letters, Victor Balaguer. A romantic of good vintage, he believed that if democracy were to be viable in Spain it had to have been part of the country's own heritage, not just a product imported from abroad. And Balaguer found that democracy had indeed existed in Spain in its early centuries, most notably in Aragon. Before being amalgamated with Castile, he said,

3

Aragon had been a federated monarchy with kings as popular and "democratic" in their times as the present-day monarchs of England, France, and Belgium. The basis for this had been a compact by which the monarch of old Aragon had been bound to obey the laws. Because the monarch's powers were regulated from the outset, tyranny was not feared in medieval times, nor, argued Balaguer, should it be feared today if the same procedure be followed. He proposed that the draft constitution be amended to include the following sentence: "The form of governance of the Spanish nation is a democratic monarchy." Addressing the Assembly in defense of his proposal (and making particular reference to the republicans), Balaguer said:

A constitution is a pact between the monarchy and the people. They tell us here over and over again that we are going to vote for a monarchy when no monarch is recognized. What care I that I do not recognize a king? The pact, the law, the constitution: these are the things I strive for, these are the things upon which we rise or fall. Little care I for the monarch; he will appear in due time, when we want him, when we need him. And above all, in my humble opinion, the monarch should not be forthcoming until we have devised our constitution, until we can present the pact to him in the fashion of the old Aragonese formula: *if not, not*.[1]

The debate on the amendment was not a long one. The president of the draft commission, Salustiano Olózaga, re-

---

[1] "*La Constitucion es el pacto entre el monarca y el pueblo. Nos dicen y nos repiten aquí á cada momento que se va á votar una monarquía cuando no se tiene monarca. ¿Qué me importa á mí el no tenerlo? El pacto, la ley, la Constitucion es lo que yo quiero; el pacto, la ley, la Constitucion es lo que ha de salvarnos ó perdernos. Poco me importa el monarca: éste vendrá cuando convenga, cuando queramos, cuando lo necesitemos. Y sobre todo, en mi pobre opinion, el monarca no debe venir hasta que hayamos hecho la Constitucion, hasta que le podamos proponer el pacto por medio de la antigua fórmula aragonesa:* si non, non" (*Diario de Sesiones de la Córtes Constituyentes. Dieron Principio el Dia 11 de Febrero de 1869*, vol. I:3 [Nos. 58-74], p. 1944 [No. 74]). The debate in question took place on May 14, and covers pp. 1942-48. Extracts of Balaguer's speech are given by Danvila y Collado, *Libertades*, pp. 216-19.

sponded by rebutting the idea that a constitution was a pact between the king and people, asserting that the nation was the all-embracing concept, that the constitution was the system of its governance, and that the king was part of the constitution rather than a prerequisite for its existence. Olózaga also answered Balaguer in kind by referring to the *manifestación*, a famous Aragonese institution, equivalent to habeas corpus in Common Law. Olózaga pointed out that the substance of the *manifestación* had been inserted into the draft constitution; his commission had simply not felt the need to identify it by either its Aragonese or its English name. Thus Olózaga showed his proficient knowledge of old Aragonese history (he himself was a Castilian), while at the same time he chided his Catalan confrère for semantic quibbling.

Balaguer, in a short rejoinder, found a graceful way to claim that the substance of his ideas was indeed embodied in the draft constitution, as explained by Olózaga, and withdrew his amendment. In doing so, however, he had occasion to refer again to the idea of the compact. Of course, he said, all powers must emanate from the nation; indeed, at the establishment of the very first pact which is known in history, the nation said to the king:

We have a law, have a constitution, and this is the law and this is the constitution which we give you in order that you may be king; and if not, not.

As Balaguer wrote on another occasion, *Si no, no* was the key and substance of the political system of Aragon.[2]

The historical references made by Balaguer and Olózaga

[2] The remark quoted from the Cortes debate is found in *Diario de Sesiones*, p. 1948: *"Tambien allí al firmar el primer pacto que en la historia es conocido, se le dijo al rey: 'nosotros hacemos la ley, nosotros hacemos la Constitucion, y esta es la ley y esta es la Constitucion que te presentamos para que seas rey; y si no, no.'"* This is a free adaptation of Antonio Pérez's version of the Oath (see next note), which Balaguer believed belonged to the founding of Aragon in the 9th century. In 1896 Balaguer wrote: *"¿quién duda, quién puede dudar que el si non, non es la clave, y el organismo, y la esencia, y la substancia de todo el sistema político de Aragón?"* (*Instituciones y Reyes*, p. 43.)

would not have been lost on many members of the Constituent Assembly. *Si no, no* was a slogan which had been like a battle cry for Aragonese independence in centuries past. Many of the deputies may even have been able to quote the original context in which the phrase appeared in Renaissance literature:

We, who are worth as much as you, make you our King and Lord provided that you guard for us our fueros and liberties, and if not, not.[3]

Supposedly this "Oath" had originally been uttered by the people of the old kingdom of Aragon when they accepted a new king. But there was no consensus on whether this occurred as early as the 8th century, when Aragon began to take shape as a principality, or in the 13th and 14th centuries, when the kingdom of Aragon was one of the great powers of Europe, or as late as the 16th century, when the country was amalgamated with Castile to form a united Spanish nation. In fact, many refused to allow that the Oath was authentic at all. But the proverbial Aragonese spirit of independence as it showed itself in the 19th century could be proven to have its roots in mediaeval history; and no matter how dubious the authenticity of the Oath, everyone would accept it as a symbol of Aragonese pride in its past. To scoff at the Oath would only be to invite a score of other undeniable proofs of limits placed upon royal power in mediaeval Aragon.

The Oath of the Aragonese, and allied matters concerned with the ancient "Liberties of Aragon," had been the subject of acrimonious debate at the séances of the Royal Academy of History for some years before being broached in Parliament in 1869. Balaguer, who was both the *Diputado a Cortes* and an *académico*, provided a personal link between the two forums. Others probably held this double dignity also, and had heard the debate many times over the years. Our résumé of the dispute as it is found in historical literature of the 19th century must begin with one such

---

[3] This is Antonio Pérez's version of the Oath, the full text of which, along with other versions, is given below in Appendix i.

deputy-academician, D. Xavier de Quinto (1810-1860), the first to examine the historiography of the Oath.

When Quinto was admitted to the Academy of History in 1846, he gave as his inaugural address a discourse "On the Political Oath of the Ancient Kings of Aragon." Two years later he published the discourse in a much expanded form (referred to hereafter as *Juramento*).[4] Quinto's problem was exactly the same as that of the present monograph: to establish the origin of the "*Si no, no*" Oath. Quinto was a prodigious researcher, according to the standards of his age, and seems to have enjoyed considerable international repute; but he was a mediocre intellect by any standard. After examining all the texts at hand, he concluded that the earliest recorded example of the Oath occurred in François Hotman's *Francogallia* (1573). Quinto regarded the *Francogallia* as a seditious Huguenot tract aimed at undermining established monarchical authority, and its author as a polemicist without scruples who had foisted upon his times a lie about Aragonese history intended to justify rebellion in 16th-century France. The story of the Oath became rampant in France and quickly spread to Spain, where its potential for treason was obviously much more direct. The arch-traitor, Antonio Pérez (so goes the tenor of Quinto's argument), employed it in the 1590's in the service of rebellion. Since then naïve historians have accepted the Oath as authentic (according to Quinto), but critical scholars have either rejected or ignored it. Turning next to the facts

---

[4] *Del juramento político de los antiguos reyes de Aragon* (Madrid, 1848). The work also carries a primary title, *Discursos políticos sobre la legislacion y la historia del antiguo reino de Aragon*, by which name it is often called; but this can lead to serious bibliographical mistakes because this primary title is also used for another work by Quinto, *Del derecho de suceder les hembras á la corona de Aragon* (Madrid, 1840); see below, Ch. VI, n. 49. In effect, *Discursos políticos sobre . . .* is the series title, *Derecho de suceder* and *Juramento político* are the two "Discourses" which saw print. For a biographical sketch of Quinto, and a bibliography of his works, see Uriel's edition of *Bibliotecas antigua y nueva des escritores aragoneses de Latassa*, III, 7-9. This very important bio-bibliographical work, which I shall refer to as "Latassa²," is a thoroughly revamped and expanded version of the 18th-century original by Latassa, with the later articles—such as the one on Quinto—written by Uriel.

of mediaeval Aragonese history, Quinto spends nearly five hundred pages insisting that no evidence of such an Oath can be found. He then reverts to Hotman's Oath, demonstrating how, phrase by phrase, it was concocted by him from twisted readings of bits of laws from Visigothic times onwards.[5]

Quinto's *Juramento* soon found its critics. One of the first was the then noted essayist, Antonio Cánovas del Castillo, who substituted for his lack of scholarly prowess a "philosophical" defense of the Oath in terms of the contract theory of government. Cánovas' essay is exemplary of the "spirit of the times" argument, which invests the Oath with meta-historical truth as a way of transcending the seemingly insoluble problem of its historical validity.[6] Another protagonist of the Oath was Manuel Lasala, Aragonese soldier and civil magistrate. In 1849 Lasala published[7] the authentic text of one of the Privileges of Union (the more radical one), a charter of 1287 wherein the Aragonese king had acknowledged the right of his subjects to reject him and elect another king if he should violate certain privileges. A law of 1348 had condemned the charter to eternal oblivion, and its exact conditions were never made known until Lasala's publication.

[5] See Index, *s.v.* "Quinto," for specific references elsewhere in my text to the many items sketchily recapitulated in the foregoing paragraph.

[6] As Cánovas' essay appeared in his *Estudios Literarios* (Madrid, 1868), II, 477-520, it bears the prolix title *Breves Consideraciones acerca del Juramento Politico de los Antiguos Reyes de Aragon, escritas con ocasion del libro que dió á luz con este título Don Javier de Quinto.* I do not know what title this essay bore when it was printed for the first time (April 1849, according to the 1868 edition, p. 520, n. 20), nor just how it *"fué corregido y reformando despues"* (*loc.cit.*) for the second printing twenty years later. We might note that that second printing fell in the year of the Constituent Assembly to which I referred in the opening pages, and that Cánovas was a delegate with views close to Balaguer's. Cánovas was not quite so liberal in later years, however, when he became prime minister under the restored Bourbon monarchy of 1874. For over two decades thereafter he was the leader of the conservative and Catholic party; indeed, he was the outstanding Spanish statesman of the late 19th century.

[7] In his *Diario de Zaragoza*—a work I do not know—according to Danvila y Collado, *Libertades*, pp. 254-55.

Lasala had found a transcription of the Privileges of Union in a manuscript in the library of the Academy of History. Their contents were sufficiently remindful of the conditions of the Oath of the Aragonese to lend the latter some credence. A few years later Lasala discovered another manuscript of equal import for the Oath controversy: the autograph of a famous treatise on Aragonese institutions, *Aragonensium rerum commentarii* (1588), written by Philip II's royal historiographer, Gerónimo Blancas. Blancas' autograph contained, besides the text of the Privileges of Union (which he had copied from the same mediaeval manuscript as had Lasala), a transcription of the Oath in a context which clearly showed his belief in its authenticity.[8]

Here was ample ammunition for the Aragonese patriots stung by the slurs of Quinto's polemic against a cherished canon of Aragon's history: the implications of the Oath seemed to be fully confirmed by an authentic royal charter of 1287, and a very reputable Spanish scholar of the 16th century (who, Quinto had delighted to point out, said nothing about the Oath) was revealed to be an avowed believer. Topping it all, there was a sinister note pervading Blancas' work which set the pitch for the new chorus of champions of the Oath: Blancas had suppressed the texts of both the Oath and the Privileges of Union when he had published his *Commentarii* in 1588.[9] This clearcut evidence of purging historical works suggested that a vast conspiracy might have operated throughout the centuries to obliterate all traces of the ancient Liberties of Aragon. It would not be difficult to understand why the ancient *Si no, no* Oath went unrecorded until the 16th century once one saw how the Privileges of Union had been kept hidden for 500 years. Whether or not the Oath and the Privileges of Union were intimately related historically, they amounted to the same thing in terms of popular right of resistance. If one of them was known to have been suppressed the other most likely was, too. This, in sum, is the line of argument that Manuel

[8] Below, pp. 92-97 (esp. nn. 37, 40-42), I discuss the Academy of History MS and the autograph of Blancas.

[9] See below, Ch. IV, n. 37 and Ch. V, nn. 62, 93.

Lasala took in the following years, most notably in his three-volume work on the Aragonese Constitution published in 1868-1871.[10]

The question of the authenticity of the Oath had been involved ever since the 16th century with a set of "laws" known as the Fueros of Sobrarbe. Gerónimo Blancas had gathered fragments of these laws from mediaeval sources, and given the gist of them in his *Commentarii* (1588). He offered them as the laws which had been adopted by the founding fathers of the Aragonese nation, i.e. by the group of Christians who had fled from the Muslim invaders of the 8th century, assembled in the mountains of Sobrarbe (a region of modern Aragon), and established the first dynasty of kings on Aragonese soil. Two of these supposed Fueros of Sobrarbe carried notions of limiting the royal power which were congenial with the notions of the Oath.[11] The Oath therefore had an old spiritual ally in the Fueros of Sobrarbe, and the Privileges of Union joined with them in the 19th century to make a family of three. In this triangle the Oath was the most lively member, with its popular *Si no, no* slogan, but it lacked sound temporal roots and was difficult to relate in historical terms to the other two members. The Fueros of Sobrarbe and the Privileges of Union,

[10] As mentioned above in n. 7, I have not seen the earliest of Lasala's work which dealt with the Privileges of Union, nor have I located a copy of his *Reseña histórico-política del antiguo reino de Aragón* (Zaragoza, 1865), which would seem from its title to be relevant; but it is not likely that anything pertinent to our problem in these works would have been excluded from his three-volume *Exámen histórico-foral de la Constitución Aragonesa* (Madrid, 1868-1871). We should note that Lasala was also a deputy from Zaragoza to the Constituent Assembly in 1869, and spoke in the constitutional debate on the same day that Balaguer did, and on an allied topic; see the *Diario de Sesiones* (above, n. 1), pp. 1972-77. The judgments concerning Lasala's thesis have varied. López de Haro, *Justicia mayor*, p. 265, says that the work shows *"talento, erudición y trabajo"*; Haebler, "Fueros de Sobrarbe," p. 26, n. 1, calls it *"un escribo tendencioso, sin crítica, obra de un aficionado."* The latter is more correct, I believe; but many things can be forgiven when one remembers the bearing of Aragonese history upon the revolutionary events of mid-19th-century Spain.

[11] See Appendix III, items [v] and [VI] under the text of Blancas. Ch. IV below is devoted to these two "False Fueros of Sobrarbe."

on the other hand, seemed to dovetail very well. As the 19th-century champions of old Aragonese liberties saw it, the Privileges of Union of 1287 were actually a reconfirmation of the ancient Fueros of Sobrarbe. That is to say: the 9th-century Fueros of Sobrarbe had faded away (or been transferred piecemeal into other legal codes) by the time of the great revival of the 12th and 13th centuries, when the Privileges of Union clearly echoed and reasserted the ancient principles of resistance to tyranny.[12] In the 16th century Blancas had ingeniously reconstituted some of the Fueros of Sorbarbe, and had transmitted the precious Privileges of Union in the manuscript of his writings; moreover, he believed in the Oath. As we look back over the quarrels among 19th-century Spanish historians, we see that their arguments usually turned upon the printed and autograph writings of Gerónimo Blancas. And rightly so: Blancas will be the central figure of my study also.

During the 1850's and 1860's, the "liberal" position—upholding the glories of ancient Aragonese independence—dominated the scene. The Privileges of Union were reprinted many times.[13] The sin of the 500-year suppression of the document could not be explained in any honorable way, and must have been a special thorn in the sides of conservative thinkers anxious to defend the monarchy against the contagion of liberal ideas rampant everywhere in Europe. The high point of the pro-Oath cause probably came in 1868-1869, when Lasala was publishing his long treatise

[12] As we shall see later (Ch. v, n. 76), Blancas himself believed something like this. This belief, however, remained largely hidden from public view, since it was closely attached to Blancas' presentation of the Privileges of Union and was suppressed along with them when he published the *Commentarii* in 1588. Lasala gives the classical presentation of this argument.

[13] Danvila y Collado, *Libertades*, pp. 194ff, 254ff, gives the bibliography of the publication of the Privileges of Union up to his time (1881); see below, Ch. iv, n. 41. During the 1860's and 1870's there seems to have been confusion over the relationship of the Academy of History MS containing the Privileges of Union to Blancas' autograph transcription of them; Danvila y Collado resolved this by publishing these two versions in parallel, along with the Marichalar and Manrique version of 1868, and shows that they are virtually the same—i.e., they all derive from the Academy of History MS.

and Balaguer carried the issue into the Constituent Cortes. But the tide turned in less than a decade, when the first member of our family of three (i.e., the Fueros of Sobrarbe) was subjected to a devastating attack by Tomás Ximénez de Embún in an essay "On the Origins of Aragon and Navarre."[14] He exposed Blancas' Fueros of Sobrarbe as a fraud: they were not an ancient code of laws at all, but bits of different late mediaeval codes of law and juristic writings which had been assembled under a pseudonym. Blancas was not the sole culprit; he merely put the finishing touches on a legend-making process that went back to the late 14th century. Ximénez de Embún had little to say about the Oath itself; he considered it of the same ilk as the Fueros of Sobrarbe, and was satisfied with Quinto's earlier exposé.[15]

From our point of view, the fault of Ximénez de Embún lies more in what he failed to do than in what he did. He did not pursue all the byroads of the legend-making, and thus, though his treatise has few major misconceptions, it lacks a profound comprehension of the Sobrarbean laws and the Oath. This is quite excusable, however, on the grounds that Ximénez de Embún was primarily concerned to show that the "Kingdom of Sobrarbe" was a chimaera; demonstrating how Blancas had confected the necessarily false Fueros of Sobrarbe was only a secondary consideration.[16]

With the Fueros of Sobrarbe laid away by Ximénez de Embún, the Oath was left to draw what historical sustenance it could from the Privileges of Union. Victor Balaguer was still a champion of the Oath, and at the end of the year 1881, on the occasion of the reception of a new

[14] Tomás Ximénez de Embún, *Ensayo histórico acerca de los orígenes de Aragón y Navarra* (Zaragoza, 1878).

[15] See *ibid.*, pp. 123-24. Ximénez de Embún was aware of the presence of the Oath in the autograph of Blancas (see below, Ch. v, n. 93), but stresses that Blancas names Hotman as his source.

[16] Ximénez de Embún's treatise is a landmark in Spanish historiography because of the old errors which it exposed, although his own effort to establish the early dynasties of Navarre and Aragon has been considerably modified since; see Pedro Aguado Bleye, *Manual*, Ch. xxx, §2 (ed. 1963: I, 497-98); also below, Ch. III, n. 1.

member into the Academy of History, he fought doggedly for the losing cause. The new member was Antonio Romero Ortiz, and the title of his inaugural address was *"Las Cosas de Aragon,"* which assessed the impact of Ximénez de Embún's work upon the age-old problem of the Liberties of Aragon. Balaguer rose afterwards, however, and delivered a *contestación* which stressed the significance of the Privileges of Union as "proof" of the Oath. The dispute was aired in the newspapers, and Balaguer's speech was printed conjointly with Romero Ortiz' inaugural address.[17] But before the year was out, the supposed "democratic" Privileges of Union were subjected to a harsh evaluation in a monograph by the jurist Danvila y Collado, who argued that they were articles of a reactionary feudal movement which had to be quashed for the sake of the commonweal—an argument accepted by most scholars since then.[18] Somewhat the same line of argument was taken in several essays written later in the 1880's by Vincente de la Fuente. Because they help to fill in details of the Sobrarbe problem which Ximénez de Embún had only sketched in broad strokes, they are worth reading—if one can endure Fuente's childish railing against his foes.[19]

Another public airing of the quarrel occurred in the Academy of History in 1884. The introductory *discurso* on

[17] Ortiz and Balaguer, *Cosas de Aragón*; Romero Ortiz' address occupies pp. 5-34, Balaguer's *contestación*, pp. 35-57. The debate and public discussion is summarized in Danvila y Collado, *Libertades*, pp. 7-17. Balaguer's views can also be found spelled out in his *Instituciones y Reyes*, pp. 41ff.

[18] Manuel Danvila y Collado, *Las Libertades de Aragón. Ensayo histórico, jurídico y político* (Madrid, 1881). Danvila y Collado's opinion of the Union seems to have been expressed some years earlier by Emilio Castelar Ripoll, "D. Pedro IV y la Unión Aragonesa," in his *Estudios históricos sobre la Edad Media y otros fragmentos* (Madrid, 1875), pp. 23-154, to judge from the title of another work which refuted it: Serafín Olave y Diez, *La Unión Aragonesa y el pacto de Sobrarbe vindicados contra los desafueros históricos de don Emilio Castelar* (Pamplona, 1877). I have not seen these works, but the report of Dualde Serrano, "Pere el del Punyalet," p. 318, that they are preoccupied with the *"transcendencia política del levantamiento,"* makes me doubt that they have scholarly significance.

[19] Vincente de la Fuente, *Estudios críticos sobre la historia y el derecho de Aragón* (Madrid, 1884-1886), 3 vols.

this occasion came from the much-respected Bienvenido Oliver y Esteller, who attempted to salvage the battered pro-Sobrarbe, pro-Privileges, and pro-Oath positions. His tactic was to avoid arguing about historical particulars, and stress instead the "psychic element of the law"—a fashionable term of the day—which revealed the enduring principles of a nation's constitution. The constitution of Aragon, viewed from Oliver's castle in the air, had been based upon supremacy of the kingdom over the king ever since its beginnings in the mountains of Sobrarbe. Whatever legends about this that may have arisen do not alter the basic fact.[20] In effect, while one may doubt the temporal verity of some records of the Liberties of Aragon, the spiritual truth to which they testify remains indisputable. Such, it seems to me, is the general attitude of large numbers of scholars in the last few generations (especially outside of Spain) who have continued to quote the *Si no, no* Oath in history textbooks. And it is indeed tempting to utilize the Oath when one wants to characterize succinctly the spirit of independence of the Aragonese nation.[21]

[20] Oliver y Estellar's *discurso de ingreso* was entitled *La Nación y la Realeza en los Estados de la Corona de Aragón.* I know this work only through a half-dozen reviews and analyses by other authors, which are collected in *Análisis y crítica por historiadores y jurisconsultos nacionales y extranjeros de las obras de D. Bienvenido Oliver y Estellar* (Madrid, 1907), pp. 157-281. The first of these (pp. 157-99) is the *contestación* spoken by Pedro de Madrazo, who takes a conservative view of the Union similar to Danvila y Collado's; see above, n. 18. The second of them (pp. 199-210), by Eduardo Pérez Pujol, appeared first in a Valencian daily newspaper and so makes no mention of the Aragon-Catalan antithesis; what mattered to Pujol was the "free, independent and energetic spirit of the Iberian kings, not adulterated by Roman Caesarism" (p. 202). But from the third of the reviews in this collection, that by Joaquin Costa (pp. 218-32), we find that Roman and feudal elements make up the Catalonian character and account for its differing so greatly from the Aragonese character which is derived from Iberian and Gothic ancestry. This specific national partisanship shows up even today (see below, Ch. VI, n. 17), and in general it could be viewed as a minor episode of the centuries-old historiographical debate concerning "Gothic liberties."

[21] Among American authors, aside from Prescott in the 1830's (below, Ch. VI, n. 102), see Lea (below, Ch. II, n. 1), and Merriman, *Spanish empire,* I, 458-59. English authors: J. N. Figgis, *Studies of Political Thought from Gerson to Grotius, 1414-1625* (Cambridge,

Since the 1880's no relevant work of any great importance has appeared.[22] An apparent exception would be the handful of articles written in recent years by experts in Spanish mediaeval law on the Fueros of Sobrarbe. But these do not deal with the set of laws which we have been discussing; they deal with the *True* Fueros of Sobrarbe of the 11th century. How these may be related to Blancas' Fueros of Sobrarbe will be discussed later on. For the moment, the simple fact that there are True Fueros of Sobrarbe will explain why from now on I shall use the term "False Fueros of Sobrarbe" when referring to Blancas' inventions.

The labors of the last century on the False Fueros of Sobrarbe and the Oath were warmed by the fires of patriotism and political commitment, and to the extent that these things are absent today the issue must seem that much less vital. For scholarship's sake, however, the explication of the False Fueros and of the Oath may help to dispel the lingering air of mystery which still confuses modern historians.[23]

1956 [*ed. prin.* 1907]), p. 8, n. 12; M. V. Clarke, *The Mediaeval City State* (London, 1926), pp. 105-06; R. H. Murray, *The Political Consequences of the Reformation* (London, 1926), p. 197; H. J. Chaytor, *A History of Aragon and Catalonia* (London, 1933), p. 20 —who is, however, skeptical. German authors: Kern, *Gottesgnadentum,* and Wolzendorff, *Widerstandsrecht* (below, Ch. vi, n. 10). See also below, Ch. ii, n. 17, for older literature on the Oath.

[22] A short essay by Nicolás S. de Otto Escudero, *Especialidades políticas y civiles del antiguo reino de Aragón* (Barbastro, 1915), reviewed quite well the 19th-century debate over the Privileges of Union, and quoted some authors I was not able to use when doing the same. Escudero, like Lasala (above, n. 10), was a militant believer in the Liberties of Aragon. One very long work, Carlos López de Haro, *La Constitución y libertades de Aragón y el justicia mayor* (Madrid, 1926), will be quoted frequently hereafter because it addresses itself to almost all the problems with which we are concerned; but it is so muddle-headed that one wishes it had never been written. I would like to apply to it the criticism which Haebler made of Lasala's work, cited above, n. 10.

[23] In recent years Antonio Marongiu has written several pieces involving the Oath. In general, he holds to a modified Quintonian position. I had already finished composing the present monograph when I first encountered his 1965 article, "Nos qui valemos tanto como vos"; I criticized this quite harshly in "Nuevos puntos de vista sobre el juramento: 'Nos que valemos tanto como vos,'" published two years

The rôle of the Oath will be interpreted differently here, and the part played by the two False Fueros of Sobrarbe which Ximénez de Embún explained least well—the most radical ones, and the ones most apposite to the Oath—will be considerably recast. In both cases, the Privileges of Union, the only authentic member of our trio, will assume a major role. Because of their 500-year exile from the public domain, it has been assumed that they had no importance, when in fact the contrary is the case: exactly because they were not known they were mysterious and therefore provocative. But the principal reason for retelling the whole story, rather than just glossing its more obscure points, is to shun the polemics which have hitherto guided its presentation and to offer it in its abidingly instructive configuration: as a genre of historiographical legend-making which was an important part of the intellectual world of the Renaissance.

The bulk of the present monograph comes in Chapters III, IV, and V, which are devoted to the origin and development of the False Fueros of Sobrarbe. Before and after these are chapters on the Oath: Chapter II offers briefly the "primary" versions of the Oath—i.e., independent 16th-century renditions—so that the reader will be sufficiently informed to sense its affinity with the False Fueros of Sobrarbe before launching upon that tangled subject; Chapter VI reexamines the Oath in the reflected light of the False Fueros of Sobrarbe, and includes sidelights from late mediaeval and Renaissance Aragonese literature and history. Chapter VII, the conclusion, first of all considers briefly the origin of the famous *Si no, no* phrase, then takes up the

---

later. [N.B. In the title of this article, and on line 4 of p. 209, read *qui* for *que*; and in the title as well as on line 4 of n. 1, read *come* for *como*.] Since then I have been apprized of two more articles by Marongiu, one of which deals with the Oath peripherally ("Geronimo Zurita e 'Las Cortes' d'Aragona," 1962), and the other principally ("L'avvento al trono nella monarchia aragonese," 1966). Both of these are sounder than the 1965 article, but still they have its main errors of fact and interpretation. The index to the present book will allow the reader to locate my views on persons and issues with which Marongiu has dealt.

Aragonese rebellion of 1591-1592 (which involved several of the men and ideas with whom we are concerned), and finally reflects upon the significance and utility of this study from the point of view of Renaissance historiography.

Chapter II · The Oath
in 16th-Century Writings

$\mathcal{X}$avier de Quinto's contention that the Oath was a cunning and seditious invention by the French Huguenot François Hotman, in the early 1570's, can be defeated in a number of ways, even without using evidence inaccessible to Quinto himself. For instance, as we shall soon see, Hotman was perhaps not even the first Frenchman to set down the Oath in writing. Completely devastating to Quinto's thesis, however, was the uncovering of some new evidence a few years after his *Juramento* appeared, which showed that the Oath was known to an Italian diplomat several years before the time when Quinto said Hotman invented it. Thus the hundred-odd pages of the *Juramento* in which Quinto spins his web around Hotman—pages of dubious value even when written—were instantly made worthless. Blancas' manuscript, which also came to light not long after Quinto's work, had even more serious implications for Quinto's hypotheses, since it showed that the Oath had achieved considerable status in the highest circles of Spanish scholarship in the 16th century, upsetting Quinto's prideful claim that no respectable Spanish scholar had ever believed in the Oath. Quinto's thesis is so shaken by all these things that we will proceed more rapidly and directly if we drop his *Juramento* as a guide for our own study.

In the following sections, I will give a brief presentation of what I consider to be four independent renditions of the Oath: the first by the Venetian diplomat Giovanni Soranzo; the second by Hotman and other Frenchmen; the third by Antonio Pérez; the fourth by Blancas.

Giovanni Soranzo

"When they accept their king," wrote Giovanni Soranzo of the Aragonese people in 1565, "they use these exact and lofty words":

We, who are as good as you, swear to you, who are no better than we, as prince and heir of our kingdom, on condition that you preserve our laws and our liberty, and if you do otherwise we do not swear to you.

The people then bring forth the book in which their privileges, or *fueros*, are written, and the king swears to uphold them.[1]

In this *Relazione*, addressed to the Doge, Soranzo is contrasting the conduct of the Cortes of Aragon with that of the Cortes of Castile. According to him, the pith of the Aragonese Cortes is its obstreperousness. The tenor of the Oath is proof that the people are quite prone to rebellion, and the king hates to convene the Cortes because he must listen to innumerable grievances before securing a subvention. A few sentences later Soranzo discusses the recently held Cortes of Monzon (1563-1564), which confronted Philip for the first time since he had become king, and which was particularly tempestuous because of bitter feelings over the growing authority of the Inquisition in Aragon. Soranzo's account, therefore, treats the Oath as a contemporary practice, which may well have been sworn at the Cortes of Monzon just two years earlier.

An ambassador of the Republic of Venice had particular reason *not* to invent stories, but this does not mean that Soranzo's reports were necessarily true to fact. He had obviously heard about this Oath, and it probably struck him as so typical of the independent spirit of the Aragonese people that he decided to quote it exactly. We can conclude from Soranzo's report, therefore, only that the Oath was in

[1] The text is given in full below, Appendix i. The only historian I have found who has taken note of Soranzo's version, and remarked that it pre-dates Hotman's so that doubt is cast upon Quinto's thesis, is Lea, *Inquisition of Spain*, i, 229, n. 1.

existence before Soranzo wrote; how long before he does not say.

To speculate upon Soranzo as the source of all later versions of the Oath because he is the earliest known reporter of it would be to follow the treacherous path of Xavier de Quinto's accusing Hotman. Besides being feeble methodology, it would not allow proper weight to be given to the many bits of evidence from the older 16th-century sources which indicate that the story of the Oath was fairly widespread and entered the ken of different writers independently from each other. For our present purposes, therefore, it suffices to say that the oldest known record of the Oath comes from a person who was certainly not the inventor of it.

François Hotman and other French Writers

Xavier de Quinto was correct in one aspect of his accusation against François Hotman and his Huguenot confrères: they did make good use of the Aragonese Oath in their pamphleteering against French royal absolutism. In addition to Hotman, in his *Francogallia* (1573), Quinto's report also implicates the author of the *Vindiciae contra tyrannos* (1579).[2] He missed two other French writers of the 1570's, however, each of whom would have provided him with good copy: Jean Bodin, *Six livres de la république* (1576), whom Quinto would have been delighted to adopt as an ally of sorts because, being neither a *monarchomach* nor a Huguenot, he attributed little constitutional worth to the Oath; and Theodore Beza, the Calvinist chief himself, whom Quinto would as soon have dubbed the villain as Hotman, and who, given Quinto's own criteria of selection, was probably the chief French conspirator.

Theodore Beza's tractate *De iure magistratuum* was published anonymously in 1574, and its true authorship remained hidden until modern times. In it, the Oath in its "Spanish" form appears as follows:

[2] Quinto, *Juramento*, pp. 15-44, 96-105.

NOS QUI VALEMOS TANTO COME VOS, Y PODEMOS MAS QUE VOS, ELEGIMOS REY: CON ESTAS Y ESTAS CONDITIONES, INTRA VOS Y NOS, UN QUE MANDA MAS QUE VOS.

Although Hotman and Beza differ somewhat in their reports of the circumstances under which the Oath was uttered, their Spanish renditions of the Oath are identical. Thus one might be inclined to guess that they derived it independently from a common source. But their Latin translations of the Oath are also identical, making it almost certain that one borrowed from the other.[3]

It would be wrong to assume that Beza must have drawn the Oath from Hotman because his tract was published a year later than Hotman's. Archival evidence has revealed that Beza and Hotman had both completed their tracts in July of 1573, and that each of them had a very intimate knowledge of the other's work. Beza, in fact, was instrumental in persuading the Geneva Town Council to allow Hotman's *Francogallia* to be published, and Hotman returned the compliment by trying to get his friend's tract (which the Geneva Town Council thought too radical) printed in another city.[4] Had Xavier de Quinto been aware

[3] Below, Ch. vi, nn. 2-3, the Oaths of Beza and Hotman are quoted in full context, revealing their identicalness. In Hotman's *Francogallia*, the Oath is found in Ch. x of the first two editions (Geneva, 1573; Cologne, 1576) and in Ch. xii of the third edition (Frankfort, 1586); for Beza's version I have drawn upon *De iure magistratuum* (Lyon, 1580), pp. 71-72, and *Du Droit des magistrats* (Lyon, 1579), pp. 38-39.

[4] Archival information identifying Beza as the author of the *De iure magistratuum* was published from Scottish copies of Geneva records, dated 1573, by Thomas McCrie, *Life of Andrew Melville* (2nd ed., London, 1824), i, 427-30; and the full set of documents, from the Genevan archives, was utilized by H. Fazy, *La Saint-Barthélemy et Genève* (=Memoires de l'Institut national Genevois, xiv [1878/9]; Geneva, 1879), pp. 77-78, which shows the intimate relationship between Hotman and Beza and the efforts of each to help the other get his treatise published. See also Alfred Cartier, "Les idées politiques de Théodore de Bèze d'après le traité: 'Du Droit des magistrats sur leurs sujets,'" *Bulletin de la Société d'Histoire et d'Archéologie de Genève*, ii (1900), 187-206, who adds further documents of 1573. A concise summary of the printing of the *De*

of these facts, he would probably only have doubled his number of Huguenot villains; indeed, Quinto's thesis would have been enhanced by making the chief Calvinist theologian of the times a conspirator.

I am inclined to believe that Beza knew the story before Hotman. First of all, his leadership of the Calvinist movement put him in constant touch with Spanish reformers who could have imparted the story to him.[5] Secondly, there is the unusual fact that in the *Francogallia* the Oath story is the only one of some 800 quotations for which Hotman fails to indicate his source. This can be explained reasonably by the fact that his source, Beza's *De iure magistratuum*, was still unpublished and had been forbidden publication by the Geneva Town Council.[6]

While there are some differences between the accounts of Hotman and Beza in respect to the ceremonial setting in which the Oath was supposed to have been uttered, both of them give a primary place in the ceremonial to the Justice of Aragon, an official whom Soranzo does not even mention. This is proof enough that our French Huguenot writers did not get the Oath story from the Italian ambassador's report, but rather in the same manner which he did

---

iure magistratuum is given by A. A. Van Schelven in his introduction to Henri-Louis Gonin's recent English translation of the tract under the title *Concerning the Rights of Rulers Over Their Subjects and the Duty of Subjects Towards Their Rulers*, ed. by A. H. Murray (Capetown-Pretoria, 1956), pp. 1-3. See also the preface to the new Latin edition by Klaus Sturm (Neukirchen-Vluyn, 1965).

[5] There were many Spanish religious refugees in Geneva from the mid-1550's onward. They were involved, for one thing, in translating Reformation tracts into Spanish, having them printed, and smuggling them back into Spain. See John E. Longhurst, "Julián Hernández, protestant Martyr," *Bibliothèque d'Humanisme et Renaissance*, xxii (1960), 90-118; E. Droz, "Note sur les impressions genevoises transportées par Hernández," *ibid.*, pp. 119-32; Georges Bonnant, "Note sur quelques ouvrages en langue espagnole imprimés à Genève par Jean Crespin (1557-1560)," *ibid.*, xxiv (1962), 50-57. One famous Huguenot, known well to Hotman and Beza, had traveled in Spain: Hubert Languet.

[6] The prohibition of Beza's tract is fully attested by the sources cited above, n. 4. For more on this, and on the composition of the *Francogallia* (of which I am preparing a critical edition), see my "When and Why Hotman Wrote the *Francogallia*," *Bibliothèque d'Humanisme et Renaissance*, xxix (1967), 581-611.

(though in a variant form) from some other source—undoubtedly a Spanish one.

The *Vindiciae contra tyrannos* offers no problem: it derives its version of the Oath, along with much else, from Beza's *De iure magistratuum.*[7]

Jean Bodin published *Les six livres de la république* in 1576, three years before the *Vindiciae* appeared. The Oath itself he apparently derived from Beza, but he also mentions "a Spanish Knight," who gave him the additional information that the Oath was no longer used. Furthermore, after giving the Oath, Bodin remarks: "He deceives himself who wrote that the king at that time was elected by the people"—an accusation which would fit either Hotman or Beza.[8] In short, Bodin believed that the Oath, although it did have force once, cannot be taken as proof of elective kingship. When Bodin translated his famous work into Latin in 1586, he held to the same arguments, though for some reason he dropped the reference to the Spanish Knight[9]—a reference nonetheless precious to us for having

[7] *Vindiciae* (ed. 1579), pp. 100, 166, gives the Oath twice in Latin. The first rendition is condensed: "*Tantum valemus nos, quantum vos, at super nos ambos est (Iustitiam Aragonicam intelligunt), qui magis imperat, quam vos.*" But the second has perfect clausal—and, for the most part, also verbal—correspondence with the Hotman-Beza Latin versions: "*Nos qui tantum valemus, quantum vos, (ita enim fert idioma Hispanicum) & plus possumus, quam vos, regem vos eligimus, cum his & his conditionibus. Inter vos & nos unus imperat magis, quam vos.*" We can be fairly certain, however, that Beza was actually the source used by the author of the *Vindiciae,* because his description of the ceremonial circumstances of the Oath-taking compares very closely with Beza's (see below, Ch. vi, n. 2).

[8] Bodin, *République,* i, 8 (ed. Lyon, 1593, pp. 129-30): "Et quoy qu'on escrive du royaume d'Arragon, la forme ancienne qu'on gardoit envers les Rois d'Arragon, ne se fait plus, si le roy n'assemble les estats, comme j'ay appris d'un chevalier Espanol. La forme estoit que le grand magistrat, qu'ils appellent la Justice d'Arragon, dit au roy ces parolles, *Nos qui valemos tanto come vos, y podemos mas que vos, vos elegimos Re con estas y estas conditiones entra vos y nos, un que mande mas que vos.* . . . [A French translation follows, very close to the French version of Beza's tract.] Et quoy' s'est abusé celuy qui a escrit que le roy estoit alors esleu du peuple, chose qui jamais ne se fit."

[9] *De Republica,* i, 8 (ed. Frankfort, 1641), p. 131: "*Quae autem de regibus Aragonum initiandis traduntur, iampridem exoleverunt, sic autem acceptimus fieri consuevisse: Praetor maximus Aragonum, quem Iustitiam magnum appellant, regem sic affatur: Nos, qui nec*

been given once, because it shows a certain currency of the Oath among Spaniards several years before the Oath appears in print in Spain.

In 1586 François Hotman came out with a much-enlarged edition of the *Francogallia*. Although he did not change a single word of what he had already said about the Oath, he did add to this several pages of quotations concerning the office of the Justice of Aragon, drawn from recent histories of Spain. Since he offers no commentary on this additional material, we can conclude that he wanted simply to enhance the plausibility of the Oath (for which he could never cite a written source) by presenting proof that the role of resistance to royal power which the Justice had played throughout Aragonese history was not incommensurate with the role which he played in the supposed ceremonial Oath-taking. Hotman's quotations do not present a coherent picture of the office of the Justice, but by chance they include sources which do contain, in addition to many true things about the Justice, most of the elements of a complex legend which had been evolving for two centuries or more.[10] Hotman had simply picked up strains of it from contemporary Spanish authors without having any greater idea than they did about what was true, what false. Hotman, Beza, and the other French writers, like the Italian Soranzo, were not much more than gossip-mongers; none of them knew enough about Aragonese history to be able to assign the Oath a plausible place in it.

Antonio Pérez

Many Spaniards must have heard of the Oath as early as Soranzo did, and after 1573, with the many French publi-

---

virtute inferiores, & potestate superiores teipso sumus, regem te creamus, his conditionibus legibusque, ut unus aliquis plus habeat, quam tu potestatis ac imperii. *In quo fallit is qui scribit*, regem a populo creatum."

[10] Hotman's additions in the third edition of the *Francogallia* (ed. Frankfort, 1586), pp. 98-103, consist of the quotations from Vasaeus and Marineus which I cite below, Ch. v, nn. 30, 31, and several passages from Zurita's *Indices* (cf. below, Ch. v, n. 57) which have to do mostly with late mediaeval incidents involving the Justice.

cations of it, it would have been available to all Spanish scholars. Yet not until 1590 does there appear to have been even an allusion to the Oath in any Spanish publication, and only in 1591 was a text of it, copied from Hotman, included in a book published in Spain.[11] Neither of these works provided any new insights. But in 1593 a work by a Spaniard appeared which, though not printed in Spain, certainly circulated there and had great notoriety: the *Relaciones* of Antonio Pérez. It gave a version of the Oath which was to become the most famous of all because it adds for the first time the phrase *Si no, no*:

Nos, que valemos tanto como vos os hazemos nuestro Rey, y Señor, con tal que nos guardeys nuestros fueros, y libertades, y syno, No.

For the Aragonese, says Pérez, this was "the ancient manner of swearing to their King." He embellishes the circumstances of its utterance by having the king, uncovered, coming before the Justice of Aragon, covered, and, with his hand upon the Evangels and crucifix, swearing to uphold the fueros. The ceremonial of the Oath provides the background for only part of a complicated narration by Pérez of the power of the Justice of Aragon. The story is filled with fancy, but it could seem reasonable to an educated Spaniard, and it did have the high credential of coming from the pen of the one-time secretary and favorite of Philip II.[12]

Xavier de Quinto was convinced that Pérez had simply taken Hotman's text and played freely with it. But not only is the *Si no, no* phrase an extrapolation; other parts of the

[11] Portolés, *Scholia*, pt. III (1590), says simply *"Ottoman, in sua Franco-Gallia, fol. 75 in fi. et 76* [ed. Cologne, 1574], *ubi notabilia verba recenset, quibus uti fuerunt aragonenses eo tempore, quo primum Aragoniae Regem elegerunt"* without actually quoting the Oath; cf. Quinto, *Juramento*, pp. 77-79, 150-52, upon which I have had to rely since I have not seen Portolés' *Scholia*. The first printing of the Oath in Spain, it seems, was by Diego de Morlanes, *Alegaciones*, pp. 93-94, who quotes Hotman; cf. Quinto, *Juramento*, pp. 80-82, on whom I have had to rely for Morlanes. Cf. below, Ch. VII, n. 9.

[12] See below, Ch. VI, n. 5, where Peréz' allegation of the Oath is quoted in context.

wording are quite different, such as "*nuestros fueros, y libertades*" instead of the general "*con estas y estas conditiones*" of the Hotman-Beza version. Since the theory of French Huguenot invention has now been proven fallacious, and we know that the Oath was familiar to different unrelated people in the 1560's and 1570's, I see no reason why Pérez may not have had the Oath from oral tradition, just as Soranzo and Hotman-Beza had it. If so, Pérez' version may be more venerable than those of the Italian and Frenchmen, even though it was not set in print until many years after theirs. When, towards the end of our story, we return to a minute examination of the wording of the variants of the Oath, further arguments will be provided for the independent derivation of Pérez' rendition.

The *Relaciones* of Antonio Pérez has had the greatest role in propagating the Oath in later times. This was inevitable because Spanish historians have been most interested in the problem and, naturally, prefer their earliest "national" exponent of the Oath. Besides, only Pérez' version carries the value of a slogan—*si no, no*. On the other hand, Pérez' record of treason and the undoubted deceits which pervade the *Relaciones* (which he wrote in exile) have also allowed those who do not believe in the Oath to argue its falsity from the fact that Pérez alone of late 16th-century Spanish authors gave it credence.[13] Had there been known some other early Spanish writer of unquestioned loyalty and scholarly integrity who endorsed the Oath, the subsequent historiography of the problem would have been vastly different. We know today that there was such a person: Gerónimo Blancas.

Gerónimo Blancas

On the face of it, Blancas' rendition of the Oath in the autograph of his *Commentarii* would seem to have been drawn from Hotman. The opening sentence of the paragraph devoted to the Oath speaks of the "ancient and mem-

[13] One would have to except Diego de Morlanes (as above, n. 11) perhaps, but I have not seen his work and am not certain that he really believes in the Oath.

orable formula, so much used by our ancestors, and so celebrated by François Hotman, the serious French writer of our days." But then, after proclaiming the certitude of its authenticity, Blancas announces that he is going to record the Oath "in the same vulgar tongue, that is, in our vernacular way of speaking, by which here and there it is published."[14]

Here is Blancas' version of the Oath:

NOS TAN BUENOS COMO VOS, É QUE PODEMOS MÁS QUE VOS, TOMAMOS Á VOS POR REY: CON QUE HAYA SIENPRE ENTRE VOS, Y NOS UN QUE MANDE MÁS QUE VOS.[15]

The "one between ourselves and you who commands more than you" is certainly an allusion to the Justice of Aragon although nowhere in this paragraph does Blancas make an explicit reference to him. The Oath-givers are the barons. The "verses" of the Oath in Blancas match the successive phrases of Hotman in content, but the words are occasionally different, and grammatically it reads much better than any of the French versions. The significance of these verbal differences will be taken up later. For now, we shall assume that Blancas' version of the Oath should be classified as an independent rendition.

Since Blancas suppressed the Oath when he published the *Commentarii*, his version of it remained unknown until the mid 19th-century, when his autograph was examined and its deleted parts printed. By chance, Soranzo's version remained unknown for almost the same period of time. These two versions will prove even more helpful to us in unravelling the riddle of the Oath than the "standard" versions of Hotman (and other Frenchmen) and Pérez, which were the sole bases of knowledge of the Oath for almost 300 years. These four versions are the only ones we shall heed, because every other form of the Oath proves upon investigation to be a corrupt form of one of them. Usually the deviations took place when a modern Spanish author

---

[14] The full text of this statement is given below, Ch. v, n. 93.
[15] *Ibid.*

encountered a version of the Oath in some foreign tongue and re-translated it into Spanish.[16] The French translation in Moréri's *Dictionnaire*, based upon Hotman, and the English translation by Robertson in his *Charles V*, based upon Pérez, although proper themselves, were the chief springboards for "new" Spanish versions.[17] Needless to say, the problem of the Oath has been unnecessarily muddled by these spurious modern versions, and it has been the chief purpose of the present chapter to get our own researches off on the right foot by establishing the "pure" texts.

The Oath of the Aragonese has always been recorded as a spoken formulary and, because of its content, has usually been thought to fit the inauguration of the king. The Oath is not, however, to be found in surviving records of Aragonese coronations or in other manners of royal inaugurations.[18] Some also assert that the Oath was spoken at the

[16] The result of this over the centuries may be seen in the work of López de Haro, *Justicia mayor*, pp. 194ff. He found enough variants of the Oath in modern Spanish to set forth an imagined evolution of it over the centuries of mediaeval history, corresponding to an equally fanciful idea of the growth of liberty in Aragonese history.

[17] William Robertson, *The history of the reign of the emperor Charles V* (London, 1769), I, 153; Louis Moréri, *Le Grand dictionnaire historique* (Lyon, 1674—with a score of editions in the following century), *s.v.* "Aragon." In general, see Quinto, *Juramento*, pp. 66-76. Quinto is at his best as a researcher when showing the propagation of the Oath during the 17th and 18th centuries, although this section has the usual quota of his Quixotic tilting with imaginary foes. One early source Quinto seems to have missed is Louis Turquet de Mayerne, *Histoire generale d'Espagne* (Paris, 1608), also in English, *The generall historie of Spaine* (London, 1612); from the latter book (p. 1265) I quote the following version of the Oath, which, though drawn by the author avowedly from Pérez, inserts an extra clause (indicated in roman) which gives the king more status than we find in any other version: "*Nos que valemos tanto come vos, y vos tanto come nos, oz hazemos nuestro Rey y Sennor contal que nos gardeys nuestros fueros, y libertades, sy no, no.*"

[18] Already in the 16th century Gerónimo Blancas made a thorough investigation of the Aragonese coronations—a work which could well have been motivated by his own curiosity about the Oath—and his failure to locate any authentic document recording an historical instance of the use of the Oath has not been disapproved by anyone since. See below, Ch. VI, n. 8, for remarks on Blancas' *Coronaciones*; Quinto, *Juramento*, pp. 267ff, quotes passages from this work which he regards as especially telling against the believers in the Oath.

Cortes, yet this, too, fails to find confirmation in the historical record.[19] These negative facts naturally establish a firm basis for the position of the skeptics; likewise, they force those who remain credulous to seek less direct modes of argument.

The skeptics have not rested their case simply upon the silence of authentic mediaeval sources; they have tried to show that the Oath flatly contradicts those Aragonese practices which are recorded. Therewith the Oath becomes not only unattested but also demonstrably implausible. Against this stance of the skeptics, believers have had to find some location in Aragonese history where the Oath will not be incompatible with the historical record. This can be done generally in two ways. One is to say that the Oath was an ancient practice, going back to times for which the written record is always scarce, and that it had been discontinued before the times for which the historical record is quite complete—roughly, before the 12th century—but had survived orally. The other way is to assert that, whether or not the Oath is ancient, it was used in the later Middle Ages— say, in the 13th century or later—but was eradicated from official records because of the dangerous ideas it contained.

The skeptics' position has certainly been sound insofar as it has maintained that the Oath of the Aragonese is basically incompatible with the coronation and Cortes oaths of the Aragonese kings (the latter were quite within the traditional mediaeval practice of the king's swearing to uphold the laws and the people's swearing to obey the king), but their argument fails for another reason. A royal oath did exist in Aragon, which was neither a coronation oath nor a Cortes oath, but which is quite appropriate in spirit—and even somewhat in verbal and ceremonial respects—to the Oath of the Aragonese: the "royal jurisdictional oath."[20] Save for this, the usual arguments of the skep-

[19] Blancas also researched the manner of holding the Cortes, and his work on this, along with a complementary one by Gerónimo Martel, was published in the 17th century; see below, Ch. vi, n. 8.

[20] See below, Ch. vi, pp. 186-216.

tics based upon traditional oath practices may simply be overlooked.

Those who have believed in the historical authenticity of the Oath have, like the skeptics, been wrong most of the time; but patient and careful attention must nevertheless be paid to their arguments if one is to unravel the mystery of the Oath. Of the two schools of believers which I have delineated, the "ancient Oath, long-lapsed" school and the "recent Oath, but obliterated" school, the former has tended to link the Oath to the False Fueros of Sobrarbe supposedly promulgated in the 9th century, and the latter to link it with the Privileges of Union granted in the late 13th century. Since the full set of six False Fueros of Sobrarbe also embraces a disguised form of the Privileges of Union, the situation can be quite complicated with any given author. Moreover, the authors themselves, as often as not, have been quite unaware of the sources of their information.

It would be worthwhile for its own sake to sort out the strands of the legal-historical literature which culminated in the False Fueros of Sobrarbe, for this is an issue which has long vexed Spanish historiography. To the extent which this is done in the following chapters, however, the aim has only been to show that an understanding of the Oath of the Aragonese must itself be based upon a knowledge of the development of the False Fueros of Sobrarbe. After that it should be easier to appreciate how the "royal jurisdictional oath" may have stimulated the actual enunciation of the Oath of the Aragonese. In my judgment, the Oath could have come into being without the existence of the "royal jurisdictional oath," but would not have come into being without the prior existence of the False Fueros of Sobrarbe.

Chapter III · False Fueros I-IV

$\mathcal{T}$he "Diagram of the False Fueros of Sobrarbe" (Appendix II) shows the main stems of the genealogy of our problem. Quickly read, the six False Fueros
conjoined under the name of Gerónimo Blancas at the
bottom of the chart are seen to have two major lines of as-
cendants: the Navarre-Viana tradition and the Sagarra
Story. The roots of each of these can be traced back as far
as the 13th century, and they do not seem to be associated
with each other until the generation before Blancas. For
the purpose of our analysis, however, the moment in time
which will prove most useful as a divisional point is the
1450's, when, on the one side, Charles of Viana applied the
epigraph, preface, and first law of the *Fuero General de
Navarra* to the history of Aragon, and, on the other side,
Antich de Bages set forth the Sagarra Story in the form that
became traditional. In the present chapter we shall be concerned almost exclusively with the development of False
Fueros I-IV up through Charles of Viana. In Chapter V we
shall follow the story from there, showing the consortium
with False Fueros V and VI and the melding of the whole
code of the False Fueros of Sobrarbe.

At the top left of the chart in Appendix II have been
placed the True Fueros of Sobrarbe, enclosed within
brackets in order to indicate that they do not really belong
to the family history of the False Fueros of Sobrarbe. It
must be our first task to justify these brackets, and therewith to dispose ourselves ever after to regard the False
Fueros as a late-mediaeval phenomenon separate from the
True Fueros. Similarly, we must distinguish at the outset
between the Renaissance legend of the kingdom of So-

brarbe, which is intimately related to the False Fueros of Sobrarbe, and the actual history of this principality.

Sobrarbe, the Principality and its Fueros

Sobrarbe is a toponym identifying the mountainous region above the Arbe river (*Super-Arbe* in Latin), an area of about 40 by 50 miles in dimension lying on the southern watershed of the central Pyrenees, a western province of mediaeval Aragon near the border of Navarre. The term "mountains of Sobrarbe," in a general sense, is unambiguous, but when one begins to speak of Sobrarbe as a territory of precise boundaries, or as a constituted political entity, or even as a loose feudal agglomeration with distinctive customs, caution is in order. In the late 8th century the area was a dependency of the Duchy of Toulouse, along with its neighbors to the east, Ribagorza and Pillars. It became independent along with the others during the decline of the Frankish monarchy in the 9th century, and we know very little of it until it was incorporated into the kingdom of Navarre by Sancho Mayor in the early 11th century. From 1035 to 1037, it was given along with Ribagorza to a cadet son of Sancho Mayor, who bore the title of King; after that it passed over to Aragon, and ever since has been considered part of that kingdom. For only two years, then, could we say that Sobrarbe was actually a kingdom.[1]

[1] The growth of the legend of the kingdom of Sobrarbe is a major constituent of Ch. v, below. The history of Sobrarbe is part of the still much-studied history of the principalities of the Pyrenees in the 8th through the 10th centuries. The first landmark in the modern critical study was Ximénez de Embún's *Orígenes,* modified by Serrano y Sanz's *Noticias.* The development of the problem up to 1920 is reviewed by Ballesteros y Beretta, *Historia,* II, 295-310, and a concise summary up to our days is given by Aguado Bleye, *Manual,* Ch. xxx, §2 (ed. 1963: I, 497-98). The dynasty of Pamplona-Navarre in the 9th century remains in dispute. A fair summary of the status of the debate may be had by examining Ibarra y Rodríguez, "Estados pirenaicos," Lévi-Provençal, "Royaume de Pamplune," Lacarra, "Textos navarros," and Sánchez-Albornoz, "Navarra del siglo IX." Two works I regret not being able to consult are B. Estornés Lasa, *Eneko "Arista," fundador del reino de Pamplona y su época. Un siglo de historia vasca, 752-852* (= Biblioteca de Cultura Vasca, n. 53), Buenos Aires, 1959; and José M.ª Lacarra, *Orígenes del contado de Aragón* (Zaragoza, 1945). The latter author, however, edited the

The legendary kingdom of Sobrarbe, on the other hand, has a dynastic history dating back to the 8th century. The list of kings provided in Appendix v shows that the early dynasties of "Sobrarbe" consisted of the rulers of the principality which scholars now term the kingdom of Pamplona (or, in the older and still common usage, the kingdom of Navarre) from the late 8th to the early 11th century, and from 1035 onwards of the rulers of Aragon. Legendary "Sobrarbe," about which much will be said, is in fact proto-Navarre—i.e., a kingdom based in the city of Pamplona.[2]

Our attention will be focused chiefly on the Arista dynasty (see Appendix v). They were Basques, not long since Christianized, who recovered Pamplona and its environs from the Muslims in the late 700's. Most of the legends about the early laws of Aragon (i.e., Sobrarbe—i.e., Pamplona) revolve around the primogenitor of this dynasty, Iñigo Arista. The Aristas in actuality were followed by the Jimena dynasty in the early 10th century, but in the fabulous history of Sobrarbe the order was reversed; this is significant chiefly because the law-making at the time of Iñigo Arista appeared to take place after the reign of one whole dynasty of kings. It was very important to the legend-makers to know whether laws or kings came first in the founding of Aragon.

If the actual history of Sobrarbe is slight compared with the legend about the kingdom of Sobrarbe which grew up, the discrepancy is even greater between the True Fueros of Sobrarbe, which are scarcely knowable to us, and the

---

posthumous publication of his friend, Ramos y Loscertales, *Reino de Aragon*, which has a fine summary of how myths of Sobrarbe and early Aragon arose and are to be explained. For other bibliography, consult Ch. Higounet, "Chronique du Midi carolingien," *Annales du Midi*, LXVIII (1956), 69-75.

[2] Ernst Mayer, "Fuero de Sobrarbe," critically reviewed by Ramos y Loscertales (whose own works on the subject are cited below, n. 4) in *AHDE*, I (1924), 448-51; Mayer's riposte, "El origen de los fueros de Sobrarbe y las Cortes de Huarte," *AHDE*, III (1926), 156-67, ends on a distastefully condescending note. Ramos y Loscertales responded in "Un documento importante para los orígenes de la legislación aragonesa," *Spanische Forschungen der Görresgesellschaft*, I,1 (Münster, 1928), pp. 380-92.

False Fueros of Sobrarbe, which have played a great role in Aragonese historiography since the Renaissance. What we know about the True Fueros of Sobrarbe comes chiefly from some documents connected with the city of Tudela, the principal town of southern Navarre in the later Middle Ages. One of those documents is the 13th-century Fuero of Tudela, which definitely influenced the 13th-century Fuero of Navarre; the latter, in its turn, is the chief inspiration of the 16th-century False Fueros I-IV (see Appendix II). It appears, therefore, that the True and False Fueros of Sobrarbe are related. This is true at most on a nominal basis, however, and has no great historical significance.

Sobrarbe and Tudela

We may proceed by taking up four questions in turn: what are the True Fueros of Sobrarbe? what is their relationship to the Fuero of Tudela, with its "Sobrarbe Introduction"? how does it happen that the "Sobrarbe Introduction" of the Fuero of Tudela is found also in the Fuero of Navarre? how were the False Fueros of Sobrarbe derived from the "Sobrarbe Introduction" of the Fuero of Navarre? The last of these questions will be considered in some detail, but only after we have disposed of the first three questions as briefly as possible.

There has been sharp controversy for centuries about the True Fueros of Sobrarbe, but only in our century has scholarship transcended the partisanship which characterized studies of early national histories since the Renaissance. Modern critical study of the True Fueros of Sobrarbe may be said to have begun in 1919 with the thesis propounded by Ernst Mayer, and later modified by his countryman, Konrad Haebler,[3] which posited a full-blown Fuero of So-

[3] Konrad Haebler, "Fueros de Sobrarbe." Haebler based his thesis upon the Danish Royal Library MS of the Fuero of Tudela (below, n. 11), arguing that variants in it proved that the Fueros of Sobrarbe (mentioned in the Fuero of Tudela) were originally a royal charter of the late 11th century. Ramos y Loscertales, "Fueros de Sobrarbe," p. 66, n. 59, has cast doubt upon this. I have found another instance where Haebler based his argument on a spurious manuscript (see below, Ch. IV, n. 6).

brarbe of the 11th century as the *Ursprung* of many later codes in the Navarre-Aragon region. Opposed to this are the opinions of most Spanish legal historians, notably José M.ª Ramos y Loscertales[4] and José M.ª Lacarra de Miguel,[5] who hold that the original Fueros of Sobrarbe were just one among many sets of regional customary laws in the Pyrenees; that we have very little knowledge of their actual contents and can only be sure that they were limited in application to just one section of the nobility; and that the recollection of them in later centuries—and just a nominal recollection at that—was restricted to one locale: Tudela.

Every treatment of the problem of the Fueros of Sobrarbe must begin with an examination of three documents relating to the city of Tudela, a provincial capital in Southern Navarre. The earliest and the latest of these are official charters, and both of them speak explicitly of "Fueros of Sobrarbe."

The earliest is a charter of 1117, granted by Alfonso I of Aragon (el Batallador) to the towns of Tudela, Cervera,

---

[4] A bibliography of Ramos y Loscertales' works is appended to the necrology on him by Claudio Sánchez-Albornoz, in *CHE*, xxv-xxvi (1957), 377-80; to this should be added Ramos y Loscertales' review of Mayer (above, n. 2). Important for our problem are the following: "El diploma de las Cortes de Huarte y San Juan de la Peña," *Memorias de la facultad de filosofía y letras de Zaragoza*, i (1923); "Textos para el estudio del derecho aragonés en la Edad Media," *AHDE*, i (1924), 397-416, ii (1925), 491-523, v (1928), 389-411; introduction to his edition of the *Fuero de Jaca*; "Fueros de Sobrarbe." The last of these is the ultimate word on the True Fueros of Sobrarbe, although we regret not having the edition of the Fuero of Tudela which Ramos y Loscertales had projected.

[5] José M.ª Lacarra, "Fueros Navarros," esp. pp. 208-13. Worthy of note as supporting the contentions of the Spanish historians, against Mayer and Haebler, is the study of E. M. Meijers, "Fueros de Huesca y Sobrarbe." Meijers' special concern is to dissociate Aragon's laws from the supposed early code of Sobrarbe. A critical study of the Fueros of Sobrarbe, embodying the recent works mentioned in this and preceding footnotes, was in the process of being made by José Enrique Rivas Pérez and was scheduled for early publication, according to *ADA*, iv (1948), 601; but I am not aware that it has ever been printed. Nor have I seen the work by Francisco Salinas Quijada, *Temas de Derecho foral navarro* (Pamplona, 1958); but from the review of an earlier serialized version of the work (see *ADA*, viii [1956], 403) it seems that the author believes that the Fuero of Sobrarbe was the first law of Aragon.

and Gallipienzo just after he had captured them from the Moors. The vital part of the charter reads: "I give and concede to all the peoples of Tudela . . . [*et alia*] . . . those good Fueros of Sobrarbe, that they should have them just as [do] the better *infanzones* of my whole kingdom." It goes on to spell out quickly (in just fifty-odd words) certain exemptions from service and a few obligations.[6] The latest of the documents, an edict of the year 1330 modifying the Fuero of Tudela, makes reference in passing to "the city of Tudela . . . [and] other places where the Fuero of Sobrarbe prevails."[7] In the case of the 1117 charter, one is strongly tempted to say that the few exemptions and obligations which are cited should be understood as appositional to the Fueros of Sobrarbe mentioned immediately beforehand. If true, however, we learn little, because these exemptions and obligations concern only the king and one class of nobles, the *infanzones*; and at that they deal with stereo-

[6] ". . . , *dono, et concedo omnibus populatoribus in Tutela, et habitantibus in ea, ac etiam in Cervera, et Gallipienzo, illos bonos foros de Superarbe, ut habeant eos sicut meliores infanzones totius regni mei; et sint liberi, et soluti ab omni servitio, pedatico, usatico, petitione, vel aliqua alia subjugatione mei, et omnis generis mei in perpetuum excepta hoste, vel lite campale, vel obsidione alicujus castri mei, vel meis injuste obsidiantibus adversariis meis, quod sint ibi mecum cum pane trium dierum, et expensis. Expresius dico pro tribus diebus, et non amplius*" (Muñoz, *Coleccion*, p. 418). I do not know the full story of this document from the point of view of diplomatics, but there is one copy of it in the Archivio General de Navarra, made by a notary in 1501, which Messrs. Lacarra and Ramos y Loscertales (see previous note) have dealt with—and the latter doubts its authenticity. All this information, with appropriate bibliography, will be found in *Catálogo del Archivio General de Navarra*, ed. by José Ramón Castro, i (Pamplona, 1952), 74, No. 22. Note, however, that the document is erroneously dated 1124 in the *Catálogo*; the text of the document says 1155, which by the usual rule of 38-year error in Spanish mediaeval documents makes it 1117.

[7] ". . . *et qui quiere que de otro fuero usará en la villa de Tudela, ni en otros logares do el fuero de Sobrarbe corre*," says this charter, when giving an admonition, followed by a threat of penalty, against those not recognizing the "*fuero anciano original*" deposited in the cathedral church of the city (Muñoz, *Coleccion*, p. 425). Elsewhere in this document it is clear that the "*fuero anciano original*" is the Fuero of Tudela which is discussed below.

typed feudal relationships of the age of the *reconquista*.[8] On the other hand, it could be argued that the exemptions and obligations mentioned in the 1117 charter stand in supplementary relationship to the Fueros of Sobrarbe, thus revealing nothing about the nature of those Fueros themselves. In 1117, fueros as customary law were still being transmitted orally, so that Alfonso el Batallador did not need to spell them out. Those who would like to believe that the Fueros of Sobrarbe were at that time a complete code, covering all kinds of relationships with all classes of subjects, would almost do better to assume that the 1117 document does not give any details of that code, rather than to assert that the exemptions and obligations mentioned in fifty words are part of the Fueros of Sobrarbe.

The document of 1330 is even more ambiguous. It yields no clue to the content of the Fueros of Sobrarbe, but only acknowledges the influence of one "Fuero" in certain regions in and around Tudela. To say that the reference here is to the same Fueros of Sobrarbe mentioned in the 1117 charter means little without knowing the contents of them. Granted, the use of the singular "Fuero" in 1330 does seem to point to a code of law rather than to a miscellany or selection, which the term "good Fueros of Sobrarbe" used in 1117 implies. But it would also be possible to argue that the 1330 phrase, "where the Fuero of Sobrarbe prevails," meant no more than a territorial designation. The region around Tudela could have been known since 1117—and exactly because of the wording of that first city charter—as the region

[8] Ramos y Loscertales, "Fueros de Sobrarbe," pp. 35ff and *passim*, makes a telling case of this in respect to the Fuero of Barbastro, cited in a charter of Peter I of Aragon in 1100 (cf. Muñoz, *Coleccion*, pp. 354-56); the general pattern has the king affirming the customs by which the *infanzones* of the area handled relations between themselves—without spelling out in the charter any of those customs—and then adds a few rules which should apply in relationship with the king. It is exactly what one would expect in the age of rapid territorial expansion of the Christian kings. Later, with the consolidation of the area and the development of uniform administration and laws, these primitive city-county customs became relatively less and less important, and finally disappeared.

where the Fueros of Sobrarbe had force, but the laws of that region could have evolved to the point where they bore little or no relationship to the pristine Fueros of Sobrarbe.[9] In the 14th century the phrase "lands of the Fuero of Sobrarbe" could have meant simply the lands where the Fuero of Tudela held force, for the Fuero of Tudela should probably be considered at least a descendant of the Fueros of Sobrarbe. But the Tudelans in the early 14th century may have had no more idea than we do about the content of the Fueros of Sobrarbe which had been applied in their country on the morrow of its liberation from the Moors over two centuries earlier. They may have retained the name "land of the Fueros of Sobrarbe" purely for sentimental reasons, because their first city charter had distinguished their province in this particular way. Considering the enormous social, political, and economic development that took place during the 12th and 13th centuries, it is impossible to imagine that the Fueros which held sway in 14th-century Tudela would resemble very closely the "good Fueros of Sobrarbe" of two hundred years earlier. The most that can be said— and here we come to the core of the "pro-Sobrarbe" school of modern historiography[10]—is that the original Fueros of Sobrarbe had become interwoven in time with the new legislation in Tudela, and that the perspicacious historian should be able to sift out the old from the new. The net effect of the documents of 1117 and 1330, therefore, has been to focus great attention upon the actual laws of Tu-

---

[9] We should take note of the cautionary remarks of Lacarra, "Fueros Navarros," pp. 204f, that the "family of fueros" of Navarre do not bear names which correspond to the political boundaries of that country in later mediaeval times. The commonness of these early charters of the age of the reconquest was still known to early 15th-century jurists, but was then lost sight of until modern times. Cf. the remarks of Martin Didaci Daux, the Justice of Aragon who composed the *Observantiae* in the 1430's (below, Ch. IV, n. 18): "*Nota etiam, quod quando Civitates Aragonum fuerunt à Sarracenorum manibus liberatae, Reges Aragonum dederunt forum populatoribus, quod essent ita boni Infantiones sicut meliores totius Regni, ipsi & suae possessiones*"; *Observantiae*, Lib. VI, Tit. "De generalibus privilegiis totius Regni Aragonum: Interpretationes," §11, *Nota etiam* (ed. 1667, fol. 27).

[10] See esp. Haebler's thesis, cited above, n. 3.

dela, that is, upon the Fuero of Tudela compiled in the 13th century, in the hope of gleaning precise information about the pristine Fuero of Sobrarbe.

This brings us to our second question: the relationship of the true Fueros of Sobrarbe to the Fuero of Tudela, with its "Sobrarbe Introduction." The Fuero of Tudela is an anonymous "private" compilation, probably of the mid-13th century. It survives in at least three manuscripts, and although the contents have been frequently quoted and analyzed, the whole document has never been edited.[11] The main problem is this: the collection has borne for centuries the title "Fuero of Sobrarbe," and even some modern scholars believe that at least a large part of it is the very collection referred to in the 1117 and 1330 documents.[12] On the other hand, it can be argued that "Fuero of Sobrarbe" is a misnomer based upon a misinterpretation of the Introduction, which, though it does mention the Fueros of Sobrarbe and has other "Sobrarbe symptoms," should not be viewed as an integral part of the collection of laws.

The Sobrarbe Introduction consists of three elements.

[11] Two extant manuscripts are Real Academia de la Historia MS 107 (14th century) and Danish Royal Library MS Thott 328² (14th century), both of which I possess on film. Molho, *Fuero de Jaca*, p. 635, cites what I assume is the former under the number RAH II-2-6; he ascribes it to the 15th century. It differs from Thott 328 so greatly in organization and text, says Molho, that the two could hardly have come from a common archetype. Konrad Haebler, "Zwei Handschriften des Fuero von Sobrarbe in nordischen Bibliotheken," *Nordisk Tidskrift för Bok- och Biblioteksväsen*, XX (1933), 142-51, actually describes: 1) a copy of the *Fuero General de Navarra*, which is often labeled "*Fuero de Sobrarbe*" (see below, n. 17); and 2) Thott 328, which he does recognize as a redaction of the Fuero of Tudela. Now extinct is the copy of the Fuero of Tudela formerly located in the Facultad de Derecho de Madrid (16th century), but Professor José M.ª Lacarra possesses a film of it and very generously transcribed for me the initial paragraphs which contain the "Sobrarbe Introduction." Regrettably, Ramos y Loscertales never published the edition of the Fuero of Tudela which he planned (cf. Lacarra, "Fueros Navarros," p. 211), but his article, "Fueros de Sobrarbe," has a fine discussion of the place of the Fuero of Tudela in early Spanish law. Extensive quotations from the Fuero of Tudela (called Fuero of Sobrarbe) are given in Marichalar and Manrique, *Historia del derecho*, IV, 295-318.

[12] See below, n. 15.

First, the opening sentence speaks explicitly of the Fueros of Sobrarbe:

In the name of Jesus Christ, who is and will be our salvation, we begin this book by always recalling the Fueros of Sobrarbe, exalted in Christendom.[13]

Immediately following this is a long prologue which relates events in Spain from the Moorish invasion until the time when a band of Christian warriors gathered together in the mountains of Sobrarbe and Ainsa and decided to elect a king. Following the advice of other Christian nations, they adopted laws before doing so, and the Introduction goes on to relate these laws, presented in the form of conditions which the new king was sworn to uphold. The introductory apparatus concludes with a description of the ceremonial in which the new king was elevated.[14] It is important to note that the laws adopted were not called "Fueros of Sobrarbe." That term appears only in the initial sentence of the Introduction, and the precise wording of that sentence —"we begin this book by always recalling the Fueros of Sobrarbe"—makes an implicit distinction between the compilation at hand and the Fueros of Sobrarbe. Nevertheless, when one reads in the historical prologue about a Fuero adopted by an assembly in the Sobrarbean mountains, what conclusion is more logical than that this Fuero is none other than the Fueros of Sobrarbe mentioned in the opening sentences?

The skeptical view, on the other hand, has much to commend itself. We know that the Tudelans revered the Fueros of Sobrarbe. Should we be surprised then that the compiler of the Fuero of Tudela in the 13th century should invoke the remembrance of this old code, perhaps as an act

---

[13] "*En el nomne de Ihesu Christo qui est et sera nuestro salvamiento. Empecamos est libro por siempre remembramiento de los fueros de Sobrarbe et de christiandat exalcamiento*"; MS of the Facultad de Derecho (see above, n. 11), fol. 2ᵛ. The Danish Royal Library MS (fol. 9) varies only in orthography, but MS 107 of the Academy of History is significantly different, as is noted below, n. 22.

[14] These later parts of the introduction to the Fuero of Tudela are the same as the parts in the Fuero of Navarre quoted below in Appendix III.

of piety? If in fact he was giving the actual Fueros of Sobrarbe, why did he not come right out and say so? As far as I know, the label "Fueros of Sobrarbe" was put on the manuscripts of the Fuero of Tudela by later scribes, and therefore is meaningless *per se*;[15] the argument about the validity of this ascription, therefore, must always proceed from the interpretation that is given the introductory part of the document.

One way—perhaps the only way—to resolve the character of the Fuero of Tudela is to establish its relationship with the many other vernacular collections of law of the same epoch, with which it shares many passages. A critical edition of it, along with a comparative study of its contents, should establish its date of composition, at least in relationship to other Fueros of the age; therewith the plausibility of its being a very old code could be soundly argued.[16] Then we would find out definitely the answer to our third question: how does it happen that the "Sobrarbe Introduction" of the Fuero of Tudela is found also in the Fuero of Navarre?

Sobrarbe and Navarre

Like the Fuero of Tudela, the Fuero of Navarre is a private compilation, originally nameless; it was probably written in the mid-13th century.[17] Its character is somewhat

[15] On the Danish Royal Library MS Thott 328[2] the words *"Fueros de Sobrarbe"* are written faintly in the upper right-hand corner of the first page of the text (fol. 9), obviously in a different hand from the text of the manuscript. In Real Academia de la Historia MS 107 these words do not appear at all on the title page, but are probably found on the cover of the binding of the work. The words *"Fuero de Sobrarbe"* may appear as a heading on the MS of the Facultad de Derecho, but that manuscript is a Renaissance transcription. That the two oldest of the three manuscripts we know were originally transcribed without the label *"Fueros de Sobrarbe"* would seem to be decisive evidence that this label did not occur in the original redaction.

[16] Cf. Lacarra, "Fueros Navarros," pp. 208-11, which notes the complex relationships between the members of *"las familias de fueros navarros,"* in which he includes the Fuero of Sobrarbe; see also the remarks of Ramos y Loscertales, "Fueros de Sobrarbe."

[17] Concerning the date of composition of the Fueros of Navarre, see Schramm, "König von Navarra," p. 149, n. 77, which lines up the authors who favor a 12th-century date of composition as against

obscured by its having the same "Sobrarbe Introduction" which is found in the Fuero of Tudela, but after that there are repeated references to the king and kingdom of Navarre. There is almost no excuse, therefore, for labeling this document the Fueros of Sobrarbe, unless one believes that the kingdom of Navarre of the high Middle Ages adopted as its constitution the code of laws of a quondam duchy that had become part of the neighboring kingdom of Aragon. The many manuscripts of the Fuero of Navarre which bear the title "Fueros of Sobrarbe" on their spines or in their headings are, therefore, the products of scribes or librarians who knew less than they thought; they were seduced, no doubt, by the same tricky references to Sobrarbe that swayed the scribes of the Fuero of Tudela.[18]

Compared with the Fuero of Tudela, the Fuero of Navarre is only a secondhand source for the legend of Sobrarbe;

---

those who favor a 13th-century date. Haebler, "Fueros de Sobrarbe," pp. 26-27, upholds the earlier date, maintaining that the Fueros of Sobrarbe applied in both Navarre and Aragon until they split in 1134, and that at that time the Fuero of Navarre supplanted the Fuero of Sobrarbe in Navarre. Schramm himself follows those authors who argue for a 13th-century date of composition (e.g., Ramos y Loscertales and Lacarra, above, nn. 5-6), when almost all other national codes of law were being drawn up (in Spain, notably the *Compilación de Huesca* [i.e., Fuero of Aragon], and the *Siete Partidas*). The Fuero of Navarre is probably related to the advent of the Counts of Champagne to the throne of Navarre. Another reason for a post-1200 date is the likelihood that information for the prologue was derived from a chronicle of ca. 1200; see below, n. 25.

[18] A perusal of the *Inventorio general de manuscritos de la Biblioteca nacional* (Madrid, 1953ff), shows that almost every manuscript of the Fuero of Navarre bears on its binding the title *Fuero de Sobrarbe*. These titles are dated from the 16th to the 19th centuries: (see MSS Nos. 188, 279, 280, 707, 761). Even such a modern critical scholar as Ernst Mayer, "Fuero de Sobrarbe," p. 252, has read the epigraph as an announcement that the document to follow is the Fuero of Sobrarbe; see the remark of Haebler, "Fueros de Sobrarbe," p. 26, n. 23. On the other hand, as early as the 17th century the fact that the Fuero of Sobrarbe (i.e., Tudela) was not an ancient document, and that it was constantly being confused with the Fuero of Navarre, was stated by Arnauld d'Oihenart, *Notitia utriusque Vasconiae* (Paris, 1638), Lib. 2, cap. 9; cited by Uztarroz in his edition of Blancas' *Coronaciones, ad finem* (signature S, 5ᵛ). In this place Uztarroz cites several early works on the Fueros of Sobrarbe that I have not been able to consult.

but of these two Fueros, that of Navarre was by far the more important for the legend-makers. The reason is simple: whereas the Fuero of Tudela passed out of usage in the later Middle Ages and survived in only a handful of manuscripts, the Fuero of Navarre was augmented, broadcast in scores of manuscripts, and finally published in the 17th century and twice since then.[19] Most important of all, however, is the fact that Navarre was an independent kingdom for some time in the later Middle Ages, so that the Sobrarbe apparatus at the head of the Fuero of Navarre acquired far greater prestige than it could ever have gained had it remained solely at the head of the Fuero of Tudela.[20]

The Fuero of Navarre was originally a compilation of various regional *costumbres*; Tudela was a principal city of Navarre; the Fuero of Tudela had an historical introduction which was general enough to apply to all of Navarre: by some simple kind of reasoning such as this one can account for the Fuero of Navarre's expropriating the Sobrarbe Introduction from the Fuero of Tudela. For our purposes, however, it is not as vital to know why as it is to know how

[19] None of the three printed editions of the *Fuero General de Navarra* (1686, 1815, 1869) is in any way a critical edition. (Because I am ignorant of its contents, I exclude from consideration the 1614 *Recopilacion de todas las Leyes del Reyno de Navarra*, listed in the British Museum catalogue under "Navarre, Spain. Laws.") All my references are to the edition by Pablo Ilarregui and Secundo Lapuerta (Pamplona, 1869). If there had been an incunabular or early 16th-century edition, which would have represented the living law of Navarre before that region was completely welded into the Habsburg monarchy, then the numerous manuscripts of the Fuero of Navarre might not have been tampered with by early modern scholars and we would have been spared the confusion that has arisen by the indiscriminate labeling of them as the *Fueros de Sobrarbe* (see previous note). At the time that the Navarrese tried to get Philip II to authorize an official edition of their Fueros in 1583, they pleaded on the basis of textual variations in the manuscripts (cf. Ximénez de Embún, *Orígenes*, pp. 117-18); confusion still reigns.

[20] See also below, Ch. vii, n. 3, for some remarks about the general question of prefatory apparatuses affixed to mediaeval lawbooks. Ximénez de Embún, *Orígenes*, pp. 113ff, discusses at some length the introductory parts of the Fuero of Navarre, which he had examined in many manuscripts; he attacks vigorously the erroneous conceptions which they have propagated due to the "*autoridad incuestionable, supersticiosa*" (p. 115) which they have had among historians.

this was done. This brings us to the last of the four questions posed earlier: how were the False Fueros of Sobrarbe derived from the "Sobrarbe Introduction" of the Fuero of Navarre?

The "Sobrarbe Introduction" in the Fuero of Tudela divides itself naturally into three parts, as we have seen. In the Fuero of Navarre this tripartite division is realized in the formal organization of the work: first comes the epigraph (the remembrance of the "good Fueros of Sobrarbe"); then the prologue (the invasion of the Moors, the assembly of Christian warriors in Sobrarbe, the decision to elect a king after drawing up a Fuero); and finally Book I, Title 1, Chapter 1 of the Fuero of Navarre itself (referred to hereafter as *FN* I,1,1) which contains the fueros to be sworn and a description of the ceremonial elevating of a new king. This ceremonial section is well-known in modern historiography by the name *alzar el rey*, and much has been made of the practice it describes of elevating the new king on a buckler and acclaiming him thrice: *Real! Real! Real!* In late mediaeval and Renaissance legend-making, however, this ceremonial plays no role at all, and so we may ignore it, at least for now. The sentences immediately preceding it, on the other hand—the first half of *FN* I,1,1 where the fueros are spelled out—provides the raw material for False Fueros I-IV (cf. Appendix II). The epigraph and the prologue are crucial, of course, in providing the reason for identifying *FN* I,1,1 as a Sobrarbean practice.

In the Fuero of Navarre, the epigraph is somewhat more ample than the equivalent parts of the Fuero of Tudela:

Here begins the first book of the fueros which prevailed in Spain as soon as the mountain peoples won the lands, even without a king. In the name of Jesus Christ our Saviour, we begin by always recalling the fueros of Sobrarbe exalted by Christendom.[21]

[21] "*Aquí comienza el primer libro de los fueros que fueron fayllados en Espaynna assi como ganavan las tierras sin rey los montaynneses. En el nombre de Ihesu Crispto, qui es et será nuestro salvamiento, empezamos pora siempre remembramiento de los fueros de Sobrarbe de cristiandad exalzamiento*" (ed. Ilarregui, p. 1).

One of the three manuscripts of the Fuero of Tudela contains a variation of this form of the epigraph, so that we cannot be certain whether this form was part of the original, later dropped in some copies, or an addition to the original made by a copyist.[22] If, however, we assume that it is in all manuscripts of the Fuero of Navarre, which was the primary source for the legend-making in later times, we really need not bother ourselves about its ultimate validity. It was written there, and so it was believed. Its importance can be stated very quickly: this form of the epigraph positively supports the notion that the book of laws which follows will be the Fueros of Sobrarbe, something which the introduction to the Fuero of Tudela had not done. The Fuero of Tudela differentiates between the collection at hand and the Fueros of Sobrarbe: "We begin *this book* by always remembering the fueros of Sobrarbe . . ."; the Fuero of Navarre epigraph almost destroys the distinction by interposing a long phrase: "[Here begins the first book] of the fueros which prevailed in Spain as soon as the mountain peoples won the lands, even without a king [. . . we begin by recalling the fueros of Sobrarbe]." What reader, seeing this and then reading the prologue's account of the Fuero drawn up by the mountain people of Sobrarbe before they elected a king, could doubt that the text that followed was actually the Fuero of Sobrarbe? The fact that many specific laws in the collection speak about the king or kingdom of Navarre may be evidence for today's scholars that something is wrong with the epigraph; but for scholars of the Renaissance, who took documents like this at face value, it only

---

[22] Real Academia de la Historia MS 107, fol. 5, begins in this way: "*Aqui conpieça el libro del primer fuero que fue trobato en Espania come ganavan les montaños [. . .] tierras sines Reies. Liber Primer. En el nombre de Ihesu. . . .*" Saying, as it does, "the book of the first fuero which was found in Spain," implies something different from the words of the Fuero of Navarre, "the first book of the fueros established in Spain"; but I cannot see how one would have given more impetus than the other to the conviction of the reader that the collection which followed was the Fueros of Sobrarbe, although, to be sure, both of them worked more in this direction than the version of the epigraph found in the two manuscripts of the Fuero of Tudela quoted above, n. 11.

indicated that the Fueros of Sobrarbe were observed in the kingdom of Navarre.[23] As we shall see, the legend-makers —especially the Aragonese ones—had many reasons quite unrelated to legal documents to believe that the "first fuero in Spain" or the "fuero which prevailed in Spain as soon as the mountain people won the lands" could be none other than the Fuero of Sobrarbe.

We have given an inordinate amount of attention to the epigraph because it is the only place in the text of the Fueros of Tudela and Navarre where the words "Fuero of Sobrarbe" are expressly set down. But even without the epigraph, these collections would eventually have come to be called the Fueros of Sobrarbe because they contained the historical prologue.

In the Fuero of Navarre, the prologue appears in the following fashion, which is not significantly different from its rendition in the Fuero of Tudela:

Prologue. By whom and for what reasons Spain was lost, and how the first king of Spain was raised up. [There follows a short résumé of the dissolution of Spain following the Moorish invasion, and the reducing of Christian control to northern mountainous retreats, from the Asturias to Sobrarbe.] And in these mountains a few people resisted, and taking to foot they made forays and they captured horses, and they divided the goods amongst the strongest of their number until there were in these mountains of Ainsa and Sobrarbe more than 300 mounted men, none of whom had more of the booty than another. And envy developed among them, and disputes over the booty, and they came to send envoys to Rome to seek the advice of the *apostóligo Aldebano,* and also to Lombardy, whose people were notable for their justice, and to France. And they received the answer that they should have a king to rule over them; but first they should have their laws sworn to and written. And they did as they were advised, and they wrote down their laws with the counsel of the Lombards and the Franks, since these people had been better able than themselves to

[23] See below, Ch. v, n. 36 *et sqq.*

win against the Moors; and then they elected as king Don
Pelayo, who was of Gothic lineage, and an Asturian warrior against the Moors in the mountains.[24]

So much of this "history" is either improperly drawn from
early chronicles of Spain or downright phantasmagorial,
that we must accord its author a failing grade in History,
his talents as a jurist notwithstanding. A quite complete
account of affairs up to the meeting of the assembly (the
part epitomized in brackets in the above quotation) is
found in the *Chronicón Villarense*, the first national chronicle in the vernacular, dated not long after 1200.[25] The ref-

[24] "*Prólogo. Por quien et por quoales cosas fué perdida Espaynna,
et cómo fué levantado el primer rey Despaynna.* [¶] *Por grant traycion
quoano moros conquirieron á Espaynna sub era de DCC.*os *et dos
aynnos por la traycion que el rey D. Rodrigo fijo del rey Jetizano
fezo al conde D. Julian su sobrino que se li jogó con su muger, et ovo
enviado el su sobrino á los moros; et despues por la grant traycion,
onta et pesar que ovo el Conde D. Julian, ovo fabla con moros con
el Miramomelin rey de Marruechos et con Albozubra et con Alboalí
et con otros reyes moros, et fezo sayllir á la bataylla al rey D. Rodrigo
entre Murcia et Lorqua en el campo de Sangonna, et ovo hy grant
mortaldat de Crisptianos, et perdióse hy el rey D. Rodrigo qui á
tiempos fué trobado el cuerpo en Portogal en un sepulcro, et avya
hi escripto que ailli iacia el rey D. Rodrigo. Entonz se perdió Espayna
ata los puertos, sinon Galicia, las Asturias, et daquí Alava et Vizquaya,
et de la otra part Baztan et la Berrueza et Deyerri et en Ansso, et
sobre Iaca et encara en Roncal et Sarasaz et en Sobrarbe et en Aynssa.
Et en estas montaynas se alzaron muyt pocas gentes, et diéronse á
pié faciendo cavalgadas, et prisiéronse á cavayllos, et partiéronse los
bienes á los más esforzados ata que fueron en estas montaynas de
Aynsa et de Sobrarbe mas de CCC.*os *á cavayllo, et no avia ninguno
que ficies uno por otro sobre las ganancias et las cavalgadas. Et ovo
grant cavalgada et envidia entre eyllos, et sobre las cavalgadas
barallavan, et ovieron su acuerdo que enviassen á Roma pora con-
seyllar cómo farian al apostóligo Aldebano que era entonz, et otrossi,
á Lombardia que son ombres de grant iusticia, et á Francia. Et estos
enbiáronles dizir que oviessen rey por qui se caudeyllassen; et primer-
amente que oviessen lures establimientos jurados et escriptos; et
ficieron como los conseyllaron, et escrivieron lures fueros con conseio
de los lonbardes et franceses, quoanto eyllos meior podieron como
ombres que se ganavan las tieras de los moros; et despues esleyeron
rey á D. Pellayo qui fué del linage de los godos et guerreó de las
Asturias á los moros et de todas las montayanas*" (ed. cit., pp. 1-2).

[25] Also called the *Liber Regum* from the name of the manuscript
in which it is found. The few paragraphs which correspond to the
section in the prologue ("*Por grant traycion quoano moros . . . iacia
el rey D. Rodrigo*") are found on p. 208 of Serrano y Sanz's edition

erence to the *apostóligo Aldebano* (or *Aldebrano*[26]) has
given rise to many serious speculations, the sum of which
elicits a smile. On philological grounds, a reasonable guess
would be that Aldebano refers to Hildebrand, Pope Gregory VII. This would make a mockery of the prologue's claim
to be relating 8th-century history, but would suit those
modern scholars who argue that the Fuero of Sobrarbe
(which they believe is ultimately the subject of the prologue) was composed as a full-blown code in the 11th century. On the other hand, if one assumes that the word
apostóligo bears the error, then the reference could be to
the 8th-century king of the Lombards, Hilpranco (or Hil-
debrando), which would uphold the chronological accuracy of the prologue. But allow me to refer to a passage in
the *Villarense*—ca. 1200 and, as we have seen, likely to have
been a source of the prologue—which speaks of "Pope
Aldebrando" as "apostle in Rome" at the time of the Gothic
crossing of the Danube in the 4th century![27] In short, by the
measure of the *"apostóligo Aldebano"* it is hard to take the
historical prologue very seriously.

The item which betrays the fantasy of the prologue's history most surely, however, is the reference to Don Pelayo,

---

and, although the assembly of the knights and the seeking of advice
from the Pope and others are not in the *Villarense*, Don Pelayo is
there as the first Asturian king. In effect, then, the prologue of the
Fuero of Navarre interpolates the deliberation of knights in the
mountains of Sobrarbe into a story that otherwise is to be found *in
extenso* in the *Villarense*.

[26] The Faculty of Law and Academy of History MSS of the Fuero
of Tudela read *Aldebrano*, the Danish Royal Library MS, *Altebrano*.

[27] *Villarense*, ed. Serrano y Sanz, p. 207: *"E movieronse doltras
flum de Danubium e passoron mar e vinieron gastando por tierra de
Roma. Et era apostoli en Roma el Papa Aldebrando."* The letters in
roman are ones which Serrano y Sanz provided; since the manuscript
he used is unique and only a copy, we are hampered in knowing
what scribal error may have been operative. The Aldebrando=Hilde-
brand equation seems to go back to José de Moret, *Investigaciones
históricas de las antigüedades del reyno de Navarra*, II, 11, § 30
(*ed. prin.*, 1665; ed. Pamplona, 1766, pp. 527f), while the Aldebrando=
Hilpranco equation is given in Marichalar and Manrique, *Historia
del derecho*, IV, 281f; the literature (including a long quotation from
Moret) is reviewed in López de Haro, *Justicia mayor*, pp. 187ff.
See also below, n. 37.

first king of the Asturias (718-737), the genearch of León and therefore of Castile. In the "Sobrarbe" prologue, however, Don Pelayo appears as just a warrior of the Asturias, who became the first king in the region of Sobrarbe. We may sympathize with the author's wish to have an important personage for Sobrarbe's first king, but stealing Don Pelayo from the Asturias is going a bit too far.

Despite its historical fantasies, the prologue is an important document. It made little difference to later generations who the first king was (the error of the prologue in this respect could be corrected[28]), nor did it matter who gave the first assembly advice on how to organize the nation (good sense would have sufficed[29]). The fact of lasting importance was that an assembly had taken place, and that it had drawn up laws before electing a king. The notion of "laws before kings" is found in several places in the "Sobrarbe Introduction." In the epigraph to the Fuero of Navarre it is stated most clearly: "the fueros which prevailed . . . even without a king." This was probably composed with an eye on the historical events recorded in the prologue, which made a point of the equality of the 300 knights assembled in the mountains, and emphasized the advice given to the assembly, and followed by them, to make laws before electing a king. In Renaissance times, when the legend of the kingdom of Sobrarbe and its False Fueros was fully developed, the notion of "laws before kings" was the hub of the idea that a compact between the king and the people was the basis of the Aragonese nation; and the prologue to the Fuero of Navarre helped foster this idea among Aragonese jurists.[30]

The last part of the Fuero of Tudela's "Sobrarbe Introduction" appears in the Fuero of Navarre as Book I, Title 1, Chapter 1 (*FN* I,1,1), and it begins immediately after the closing words of the prologue:

[28] It was Iñigo Arista, of course, who became the king elected by the "Sobrarbe assembly" according to late mediaeval historiography; how this happened will be shown in the next few pages.

[29] The pith of the story of Justice Cerdan in the early 15th century; see below, Ch. IV, n. 9.

[30] See below, Ch. V, n. 39.

Title 1. Concerning Kings and Armies, and
things that bind Kings and Armies.
Chapter 1. How they [the people] should
elevate a King in Spain, and he
should swear to them.
And first it was established as a Fuero in Spain
always to elevate a king. . . .[31]

These title and chapter headings belong to the Fuero of
Navarre alone; they are not included in the Fuero of Tudela.[32] That they should be construed as part of the apparatus of the prologue is evident when we hark back to the
words of its opening sentence: "By whom and for what
reasons Spain was lost, and *how the first king of Spain was
raised up.*" In effect, the compiler of the Fuero of Navarre
or some later copyist chose to cut the prologue short and
make the latter part of it into *FN* 1,1,1. What was meant to
be a relation of distant historical events therewith became
part of the current law of the kingdom of Navarre. That it
still related events "in Spain," and was not changed to read
"in Navarre," may show the scribe's faithfulness to his
source, but it clearly sets off *FN* 1,1,1 from all the rest of

---

[31] The text is given below in Appendix III.

[32] The oldest version, Danish Royal Library MS Thott 328², fol.
9-10ᵛ, has the epigraph as a separate incipit, and makes the prologue
into Chapter I (with a title, squeezed in by a later scribe: "De
quando moros conqueron España") and Chapter II ("De como deve
el Rey ser alcado"), which corresponds to the division in the Fuero
of Navarre between the prologue and *FN* 1,1,1. Academy of History MS 107, fol. 5ʳ⁻ᵛ, is the most complicated. First of all, it has its
own special "incipit" as noted above, n. 22. After that, all the historical parts of the introductory apparatus are subsumed under Book
I. The epigraph becomes Chapter I, the narration up to the mention
of the gathering in the mountains of Sobrarbe and Ainsa becomes
Chapter II, the rest of the narration up to the mention of Don Pelayo
becomes Chapter III, and the equivalent of *FN* 1,1,1 (without its
title and chapter headings, however) becomes Chapter IV. The MS
of the Facultad de Derecho, fols. 2ᵛ-3, is the simplest. Under the
heading of the Fuero of Sobrarbe, the epigraph and the prologue
appear in separate paragraphs just as they do in the Fuero of Navarre;
then, under the heading "De como debe ser el Rey alcado," the
equivalent of *FN* 1,1,1 is given (without its title and chapter headings). These are the facts, but only a critical edition of the texts
will reveal their significance.

the compilation because thereafter (in fact, as soon as *FN* 1,1,2) the reference is always to the "king in Navarre."[33]

In sum, *FN* 1,1,1 appears to be the equivalent of a coronation *ordo*. That such an *ordo* should be part of a mediaeval code of law is, in itself, strange. Coronation *ordines* are a special category of mediaeval document, as much religious as secular because the coronation was usually accompanied by consecration. But the king-making in *FN* 1,1,1 is more an elevation than a coronation; it is certainly not a consecration. As an *ordo* of the installation of a king it is, therefore, *sui generis*. It is entirely a secular ritual between the king and the people (the barons, particularly), with emphasis upon their mutual oaths. This provided the basis upon which later interpreters construed the origin of the kingdom and the powers of the king in purely secular, and essentially contractual, terms. We should not assume that the 13th-century author of the prologue (including *FN* 1,1,1) himself thought in philosophical categories of social contract. He only needed to have interpreted past events in terms of the facts of his own day; namely, that to be a king one had to be ceremonially inducted, and that this always involved the taking of an oath. These contemporary conditions were simply applied to the first king, since no one in the 13th century would have the slightest idea of the original ceremonial (if, indeed, there was one at all). To have an oath, however, one needed to have conditions agreed upon beforehand that would become the substance of what was to be sworn. Thus, by logical deduction, there must have been some "laws" before the first king was initiated. According to a simple scheme such as this, I dare say, the historical introduction to the Fueros of Tudela and Navarre was com-

---

[33] Cf. Fuero of Navarre, ed. Ilarregui, p. 2: "*Capítulo II.—En quoal logar se deve alzar el Rey en Navarra, et qué moneda deven echar, et quoantos dias.*" Despite the titular phraseology "how to elevate the king in Navarre," this chapter does not conflict with the *alzar el rey* conditions in *FN* 1,1,1. *FN* 1,1,2 is brief, and speaks only of the church in Pamplona where the ceremony should take place, and then about matters of coinage. The actual Navarrese practice when elevating a king is discussed below, pp. 175-76.

posed, the author of it being entirely oblivious to the radical doctrine of a secular compact of government which it implied.

We have not yet looked at the contents of the "fueros" embodied in *FN* i,1,1, and we shall postpone this still further while we continue to pursue the question of how our historical introduction, which speaks of events "in Spain" but locates them in the mountains of Sobrarbe, was made to apply to the kingdom of Navarre and finally to the kingdom of Aragon. It is clear from our analysis that if the historical introduction were to acquire credentials of validity in Spanish historiography it would have to be cleansed of its palpable errors. The *apostóligo Aldebano* would have to be changed, at least, and either the locale moved from Sobrarbe to the Asturias or else someone other than Don Pelayo found to be the first king. Different solutions to these problems could, and would, appear in time. But the re-ordering of the events of the historical introduction which was to prove most influential was done by a single man, a very celebrated personality, in the mid-15th century.

Navarre and the Prince of Viana

Charles, Prince of Viana, the luckless heir to the throne of Aragon, has won enduring fame in history as a man of letters and patron of the arts. He wrote just before the age of printing, and so could not see to the publication of his works; but there is ample evidence that the work which concerns us, his *Chronicle of the Kings of Navarre*, was known in manuscript form to scholars of every generation during the four centuries between its composition and its printing.[34]

[34] *Crónica de los Reyes de Navarra*, ed. by J. Yanguas y Miranda (Pamplona, 1843). The standard work on Charles is G. Desdevises du Dezert, *Don Carlos d'Aragon, Prince de Viane* (Paris, 1889); the *Crónica* is discussed on p. 409. See also P. Kehr, *Papsturkunden in Spanien II: Navarra und Aragon* (Abhandl. der Gesellschaft d. Wiss. zu Göttingen, phil.-hist. Kl., N.F., xxii:1; 1928), pp. 8f, on the merits of Charles of Viana and other early historians of Navarre. For a full bibliography of the works of Charles of Viana, see José M.ª Azcona, "Notas bibliográficas. El Príncipe de Viana. Escritos del Príncipe. Fuentes históricas. Iconografía," *Príncipe de Viana*, ii

By the time that Charles of Viana composed his *Chronicle* in the 1450's, the basic chronology of the 8th and 9th centuries in the Navarre-Aragon region had been much more elaborately—if not noticeably more accurately—worked out than it had been for the compiler of the prologue of the Fueros of Tudela and Navarre two centuries earlier. Two major chronicles upon which Charles of Viana drew in reconstructing the early dynasties of Navarre and Aragon were the *Chronicon* of Rodrigo Ximenez de Rada, Archbishop of Toledo, written ca. 1250, and the *Crónica de San Juan de la Peña* (*Pinatense*) composed in the 1340's.[35] It was natural for Charles of Viana, himself heir to the throne of Navarre through his mother and to the throne of Aragon through his father, to conflate the histories of these two kingdoms. It is not always easy to distinguish the two states in the early Middle Ages, and from the 11th century onwards they were united on several occasions. Charles of Viana's historiographical fusion of the two regions in the 9th century was, however, quite arbitrary. This is especially noticeable in his adaptation of the prologue and *FN* i,1,1. The following translation starts near the end of Charles' fifth chapter, where he appropriates the prologue of the Fuero of Navarre (at the point where it takes up the assembly of knights in the mountains) and goes through the opening parts of Chapter vi (which duplicate *FN* i,1,1):[36]

(1941), 55-83. The existence of this journal bearing Charles' title is sufficient evidence of the fame which he enjoys today.

[35] Ximenez de Rada's *Chronicon* is found in Schott, *Hisp. illust.*, ii, 121-246. The *Pinatense* is called by different names, as is evident from the title of the modern edition of it: *Historia de la Corona de Aragón (la más antigua de que se tiene noticia), conocida generalmente con el nombre de "Crónica de San Juan de la Peña"* (Zaragoza, 1876). Sánchez Alonso, *Historiografía*, i, 245, n. 58, observes that Peter IV (who was possibly the author, or at least sponsor, of the *Pinatense*) called it in Catalan *Cróniques dels reys d'Aragó e comtes de Barcelona*.

[36] *"En este tiempo los navarros é aragoneses, por cuanto habian entre si algunas disensiones sobre reparticion de sus vitorias é ganancias, deliberaron de mandar consejo al papa Adriano, é a los lombardos, por que eran gentes astutas é sabias, que los aconsejasen lo que debian facer, é aconsejaronles que levantasen rey; pero que*

In these times the Navarrese and the Aragonese, because they were having dissensions between themselves over the division of the spoils and booty, decided to ask the counsel of the Pope Hadrian,[37] and the Lombards, because they were astute and wise people, to advise them what should be done. And they advised them to elect a king, but that they draw up their fueros and laws first; and that they not allow a foreign king, but that they elect one of themselves; and that he should [not] be of the mayores because the menores would despise him, not of the menores because the mayores would hold him in small regard. And, having had this counsel, the said Navarrese and Aragonese, joined together in Sobrarbe, made their fuero, and following is its tenor. [¶] *CHAPTER 6.* [¶] *This is the first chapter which the Navarrese and Aragonese established in their fuero general.* [¶] We the *ricoshombres*, knights, and *infanzones* and men of the cities of Navarre and Aragon . . . establish first as a fuero to raise up a king for all time . . .

The "who, where, what, and when" of this passage each provide an interesting deviation from the Fuero of Navarre account.

---

formasen, é ficiesen primero, sus fueros é leyes; é que no se diesen á rey estraño, mas que lo esleyesen entre si; é que no fuese de los mayores, por que á los menores non menospreciase, ni de los menores por que los mayores non lo tobiesen en poco. E, habido este consejo, los dichos navarros é aragoneses, juntados en Sobrarbe, ficieron su fuero, el qual es del seguient tenor. CAPITULO 6.º Este es el primer capítulo, que, los navarros é aragoneses, establescieron en su fuero general. *Nos ricoshombres, cabailleros é infanzones, é hombres de buenas villas de Navarra é Aragon, . . . establescemos primerament, por fuero de levantar rey para sempre . . ."* (ed. Yanguas, 37-38). The rest of Chapter vi is given below, Appendix iii.

[37] Charles found an easy way out of the enigma of *"apostóligo Aldebano"* (above, n. 27) mentioned in the prologue (above, n. 24) by checking his chronology and finding that the Pope who would best fit the time (8th century), and yet come close to this name, was Hadrian I (772-795). Blancas had a solution that would be perfect, if true: it was decided *"ut per legatos Adrianum II. Pont. Max. (quem prisca nostra monumenta Apostolicum Aldebrandum vocant) ac Longobardos consulerent"*; see the full text, quoted below in n. 44. Blancas had this assembly occur during an interregnum, in the 9th century, which explains his fixing upon Hadrian II (867-872).

Who was involved in this assembly? Nowhere did the Fuero of Navarre give the names of any people: it was an event of Spanish history. Charles of Viana nationalizes the event, making it specifically the action of the Navarrese and Aragonese, so-named three times in the passage just quoted. Where did it occur? The Fuero of Navarre had said "in the mountains of Ainsa and Sobrarbe," Charles simply "in Sobrarbe." This is but a small step toward a clearer conception of the region, yet it is significant because the word "Sobrarbe" falls quite close to the word "fuero": "the said Navarrese and Aragonese, joined together in Sobrarbe, made their fuero." What had transpired, according to the Fuero of Navarre, was the making of the first *"Fuero en Espaynna"* (first sentence of *FN* 1,1,1), but Charles calls it the *"fuero general"* made by the Navarrese and Aragonese, gathered together in Sobrarbe. Now, since the full technical name of the Fuero of Navarre is *Fuero General de Navarra*, Charles was technically correct in referring to a "general fuero"; and Sobrarbe was the actual location. It is the mention of the Aragonese that is gratuitous, although this was amply justified in Charles' mind since Sobrarbe was now part of Aragon. In any event, the stage was set for the Fuero of Navarre story to be applied to the national historiography of Aragon.

Charles never uses the term Fueros of Sobrarbe, even though he must have known it from the epigraph of the Fuero of Navarre. But his readers could easily conclude that the "general fuero" drawn up "in Sobrarbe" might be called the "Fuero of Sobrarbe"; and indeed some later authors did just that. Thus the epigraph's "remembrance of the good Fueros of Sobrarbe" was not a necessary passage for the creation of the False Fueros of Sobrarbe, derived in part from the Fuero of Navarre; Charles of Viana's *Chronicle* was sufficient.

One very important step in Charles' "nationalization" of the prologue and *FN* 1,1,1 is not evident from the passage quoted above: Don Pelayo is removed from the scene, and a genuine Navarrese folk hero, Iñigo Arista, is made the first elected king. Don Pelayo was put where he belonged,

as King of the Asturias, a generation or more before the
assembly in Sobrarbe, at the end of Chapter v. Iñigo Arista
appears in Chapter vii as the first king elected by the assembly described in Chapter vi.

When all the borrowings are sorted out and arranged,
Charles' technique emerges as follows. He drew upon the
14th-century Aragonese chronicle, the *Pinatense*, for the
period from the Moorish conquest up to the point where
the first new king, who happened to be Garci Ximenez, is
mentioned.[38] Charles, preferring Iñigo Arista to be first king
of Navarre, switched to the 13th-century chronicle of
Ximénez de Rada, in which this tradition is firmly fixed.[39]
To make this transition from the *Pinatense* to Rada, Charles
adopts some of the apparatus of the Fuero of Navarre: viz.,
the last half of the prologue and all of *FN* i,1,1. Such obvious errors as the appearance of Don Pelayo and the use of
the wrong Pope's name are eliminated, and a vague episode
of "Spanish" history becomes an exact national event. All
the historical imprecision of the Fuero of Navarre is recti-

[38] Fuente, *Estudios*, iii, 315ff shows, by means of a comparison of
the *Pinatense* with Charles of Viana, the extent of the latter's borrowing and the exact point of his departure from the former; Ximénez de
Embún, *Orígenes*, pp. 27-28, notes the borrowing from the Fuero of
Navarre. Cf. *ibid.*, pp. 18-21, on the role of the *Pinatense* in deter-
mining early Aragonese dynasties. Later, Serrano y Sanz, *Noticias*,
p. 169, showed that Garci Ximenez belonged in the 10th century, a
century after Iñigo Arista; and this is the position held by recent
historiography (see above, n. 1). But it is far less important for our
purposes to know which mediaeval sources were right and which
wrong concerning the first king, than to observe the facility with
which facts regarding one were transferred to the other, and the
gross legend given stimulus; in Ch. v many instances of this will be
given.

[39] Cf. Ximenez de Rada, *Chronicon*, v, xxi, "De ortu et genealogia
Regum Navarrensium" (ed. Schott, ii, 91): ". . . *vir advenit ex
Bigorciae Comitatu . . . qui Enecho vocabatur . . . & post ad plana
Navarrae descendens . . . unde & inter incolas regni meruit princi-
patum.*" For Ximenez de Rada's role in the legendary history of
early Navarre-Aragon, see Ximénez de Embún, *Orígenes*, pp. 13-17;
also Serrano y Sanz, *Noticias*, pp. 146-47; and, if anyone wishes to
see how the Iñigo Arista–Garci Ximenez problem was aggravated
by a Renaissance forger, he may consult the detective work by
Suzanne Honoré-Duvergé, "Études d'historiographie navarraise. La
Chronique de Garcia d'Euguí, Évêque de Bayonne," *Bulletin Hispanique*, xliv (1942), 17-39.

fied, and the agglomeration of facts is well-ordered and fitted into a plausible historical situation. It was undoubtedly Charles' intent to improve his source by giving it a more solid historical mooring, and in this he succeeded admirably. Subsequent generations always had to contend with Charles' account because it was so reasonable, and frequently found themselves accepting it *in toto*. This would not have mattered very much if it had been simply a question of who first bore the name of King. What did matter was the idea of a compact between the ruler and the ruled, an idea which was probably an innocent contrivance of the author of the prologue, but became an issue of national history.[40] After Charles fixed it as the pivotal event of early Navarre-Aragon history, however, it acted as a magnet for any notions of primeval popular liberties. Indeed, the idea of the compact became so widely accepted that it could be applied to whomever a given chronicler preferred to name as the first king—such as Garci Ximenez. During Renaissance times, when historians became sophisticated enough to confront and attempt to resolve contradictory sources, they argued keenly over whether Garci Ximenez or Iñigo Arista was the first king of Aragon (i.e., Sobrarbe —i.e., Navarre), but usually accepted without question the proposition that from the outset there had been, as it were, a "constitutional assembly." Charles of Viana, if not solely responsible for this, was a most important agency in giving it effect.

The Prince of Viana and Blancas

Between Charles of Viana and Gerónimo Blancas there came many authors who influenced the shaping of the Sobrarbe myth, and Blancas knew these authors, besides knowing the Fuero of Navarre and Charles of Viana di-

---

[40] It may be worth noting that Charles buttresses the idea of a compact in two ways: 1) by adding to the prologue's account of the advice given by the Pope and others the special condition that the king should not be of too high or too low a station; 2) by opening his Chapter VI with the more legalistic words "We the *ricoshombres*, knights and *infanzones* . . . establish that . . ." in place of the construction of *FN* I,1,1: "It was established. . . ."

rectly. It will, however, do no injustice to the rhythm of
development of our problem to ignore these intermediate
authors for the time being, and to examine briefly Blancas'
arrangement and presentation of the facts concerning the
assembly in Sobrarbe and the drawing up of the first fuero.

By Blancas' time, the notion of "laws before kings" was
widely known, and considered to be peculiarly Aragonese.[41]
If Blancas was sensitive to the political overtones which his
presentation of early Aragonese history would inevitably
have—and it is hard to imagine that in the 1580's he could
have avoided such feelings—he was saved from having to
take an outright stand by being able to utilize a relatively
new version of early Aragonese history which proposed a
dynasty of four kings, beginning with Garci Ximenez,
which had died out and brought on an interregnum at the
end of which Iñigo Arista had been elected king. Blancas
placed the assembly of knights during the interregnum, so
that the code of laws which it adopted post-dated kingship
itself but was still made exclusively by the barons. The
compact theory is fully matured in Blancas' account, although in a more Lockean than Hobbesian manner. The
motive for the original founding of the kingdom under
Garci Ximenez was, in the first place, not dissension over
booty but greater efficiency in fighting the Moors.[42] The
process of re-founding the monarchy after the interregnum
is presented as a model of deliberate, wise, and peaceful
procedure. At first "our people"—the term by which Blancas
refers to the Sobrarbeans and Aragonese jointly[43]—tried to
live without a king, and elected instead "twelve of the principal magnates, into whose expert hands was given the direction of public affairs during the interregnum." After a
while, the delights of liberty were offset by the difficulties

[41] See below, Ch. v, n. 39.

[42] Cf. ed. Schott, III, 581: "*Garsiam autem hunc non Ducis, sed
Regis nomine insignitum fuisse, vetus, ac constans opinio est; a
nostrisque propterea id consulto factum, ut & sibi ipsi novae dignitatis
tuendae novus stimulus adderetur, Maurosque Regalis nominis maiestate maior timor invaderet.*"

[43] E.g., *ibid.*, III, 586: "*Atqui nostros quotiescunque dico, & Aragonenses, & Suprarbienses intelligo.*"

of stable rule, and another meeting was held, which led to the consultation with the Pope and the Lombards and the advice to establish laws and elect a king. Blancas' closing words, prior to taking up the "Fueros of Sobrarbe," are worth comparing closely with the text of Charles of Viana at the corresponding juncture:[44]

(Charles) And, having this counsel, the said Navarrese and Aragonese, joined together in Sobrarbe, made their fuero, the tenor of which follows.

(Blancas) Our people, content and satisfied with this response [from the Pope and Lombards], without loss of time instituted the ancient fuero of Sobrarbe.

Thus we see the full arc of the legendary assembly and primitive law-making: originally "Spanish," coincidentally in the mountains of Sobrarbe, and applying to Don Pelayo,

[44] The text from which the foregoing summary has been made, ending with the quotation about to be given, is found in Schott, III, 588: "*De reliquo tamen haud cessabant prospicere, & consulere omnium fortunis: maxime ea consilia exquirentes, quae ad bene statuendam Rempub. pertinebant. Cumque eorum animi in deliberando in contrarias partes distraherentur, ut sit, ne fortasse dum in bonorum consiliorum cursu cunctabantur, quid caperet Resp. detrimenti, Duodecim primarios Viros, ut prisca nostra monumenta testantur, selegerunt, quibus, Interregno huiusmodi durante, tota fuit ipsius administrandae Reip. cura commissa. . . . Et haec publicae rei gerendae ratio diu viguit. Veruntamen nequaquam videbatur, premente tanto Arabum incursu, stabilis, nec firma permansura. Nihilominus dulcedine capti libertatis, Unius se subiici imperio formidabant: quoniam quidem proventuram inde credebant servitutem. Omnibus denique rebus circumspectis, rationibusque subductis, perciti, ut proditur, ab Aragonensi Comite Fortunio, demortui Comitis filio, inque ipsius locum suffecto, hanc fecerunt suorum omnium consiliorum summam: ¶ UT per legatos Adrianum II. Pont. Max. (quem prisca nostra monumenta Apostolicum Aldebrandum vocant) ac Longobardos consulerent: Quem modum ad diuturnitatem imperii magis aptum statuendum esse censerent. A quibus responsum perhibent: ¶ UTI certo Iure, ac legibus praestitutis, praeviaque Iurisiurandi religione praecautis, Unum sibi Regem praeficerent. Peregrinum vero dominium repudiarent. Isque qui ab eis Rex cooptaretur, caverent, neve ex superioribus, neve ex inferioribus esset; ne, si superior, inferiores premeret; neve, si inferior, a superioribus derideretur. Cui consilio ac sententiae nostri acquiescentes, antiquum inde Suprarbiensem Forum condiderunt.*" There follows immediately the chapter "De Antiquo Iure, Suprarbiensi Foro Nuncupato," as in the next note.

it was transformed into the founding of the kingdom of Navarre and then became the central event in the re-founding of the kingdom of Sobrarbe-Aragon.

False Fueros I-IV

Less time need be spent upon analyzing the contents of False Fueros i-iv than we have just spent in discussing the context in which they arose; for, although they constitute the "original" part of the False Fueros of Sobrarbe, they do not have the revolutionary suggestiveness of False Fueros v and vi which were later joined with them.

In Appendix iii, I have arranged the three texts in question in parallel. There is no commentary necessary on Charles of Viana's adaptation of *FN* i,1.1: Charles was no jurist, so the changes he made in wording contain no subtle alterations of the law. With Blancas, however, the situation was quite different: he was trying to present the elements of the pristine constitution of Aragon, and he was very much aware of the controversial aspects of his subject. The first problem he had to resolve was whether to render the laws in Latin, the language of his treatise. They would be more pleasant to the ear, he states, if presented in the "proper old language" in which they were written, but they have been so severely corrupted by time, surviving only fragmentarily in the writings of Charles of Viana and others, that he is reduced to rendering them in Latin.[45]

---

[45] I give the entire section between the text given in the previous note and Blancas' presentation of the False Fueros (see Appendix iii): "De Antiquo Iure, Suprarbiensi Foro Nuncupato, Deque Magistratus Iustitiae Aragonum Institutione. *Siquidem iuxta responsum datum decreverunt omnes, Unum aliquem virtute praestantem, Regem sibi constitui oportere. Sed tamen ne Regum arbitria, quemadmodum in aliis Provinciis, apud nos etiam pro legibus futura essent: quasdam tulerunt leges in primis, quibus huiusmodi incommodo mederentur. Has leges postea, Suprarbiensem Forum nuncuparunt. Cuius seriem libuisset hoc loco late persequi, & annotare prisco illo germano, ac genuino idiomate, quo conditus fuit; in eo enim plus venustatis, ac leporis contineret. Temporum autem iniuria factum est, ut eius cognitio, aliarumque rerum antiquarum, maxime scitu dignarum, apud nos penitus iaceat sepulta. Quaedam tantummodo fragmenta exstant ab ipso Carolo Principe, nonnullisque aliis scriptoribus observata, quae hoc loco a nobis summatim perstringenda erunt. Sunt enim*

Blancas rendered the False Fueros in the style of the *XII Tabulae* of the Romans.[46] One reason for this was to give them greater pomp; another to suggest an analogy—in the favored fashion of Renaissance historians—between the first laws of the Romans and the first laws of a modern nation. Grammatical considerations were certainly heeded: the future imperative mood in the third person which Blancas uses, in addition to being a more forceful construction than the future indicative of Charles of Viana or the subjunctive of *FN* i,1,1, is the construction proper to legal documents used throughout the *XII Tabulae*. Another trick employed by Blancas to give his Fueros a semblance of antiquity and monumentality was to print them in extra-large capital letters, and to divide the words from each other by the use of periods (see Frontispiece). Although this was a standard

---

quasi prima Reip. nostrae elementa, in seque continent Magistratus Iustitiae Aragonum institutionem, quod est instituti nostri praecipuum. Itaque initio illius Fori praecautum fuit: ¶ UTI *futurus Rex, quandoquidem ad eum ultro, ac sponte Regnum iam e Mauris eripi, ac promoveri coeptum deferebatur, de legibus observandis, ac libertate Regni tuenda, tum iurisiurandi religione, tum etiam ipsarum legum vi, ac potestate premeretur. Ipsae vero leges huiusmodi fuere"* (ed. Schott, iii, 588).

[46] The attempt to reconstruct the *XII Tabulae* from fragmentary mentions in surviving Roman law and literature was begun in the early 16th century by Aymar du Rivail, *Civilis Historiae Iuris* (1515); we might notice a similarity between this "antiquarian" project and Blancas' effort to recover the scattered Fueros of Sobrarbe of his own country (see text quoted in previous note). Blancas calls the Fueros of Sobrarbe "Tabulae" repeatedly: cf. ed. Schott, iii, 718, line 57; 719, 19; 723, 43; 725, 7. The tradition of similitude of the Fueros of Sobrarbe and the *XII Tabulae* goes back at least to the 17th century, when the story arose that an Aragonese charter of the 12th century contained the Fuero of Sobrarbe, written in Latin in the style of the *XII Tabulae*. Lupiano Zapata, *Reyes de Sobrarbe* (1663) propagated the story, and several scholars later combed his *Nachlass* looking for the proof (see Quinto, *Juramento*, pp. 183ff, for a summary—recapitulated later, in a garbled fashion, by López de Haro, *Justicia mayor*, p. 185). Quinto, *Juramento*, p. 124, makes the comment that Blancas composed the [False] Fueros of Sobrarbe in the *"elegante y nervioso latin de las XII tablas de los primeros Romanos,"* and further compliments him by noting that the *Commentarii* in general were composed *"principalmente en la lengua de Tácito"* (*ibid.*, p. 122). See also the remarks of Charles de Tourtoulon, *Jacme Ier le Conquérant* (Montpelier, 1863-1867), ii, 174-75.

convention of Renaissance typography when rendering inscriptions in general, for the printing of legal texts, from Renaissance times to the present, it has been the style reserved almost exclusively for the *XII Tabulae*.[47]

The Latin language invites verbal economy, and thus well-suited Blancas' desire to be brief and "monumental." He makes short, separate laws out of the long compound sentences of Charles of Viana, whose syntax hardly deviates from *FN* I,1,1. Thus Blancas' Fueros I and II are drawn from the first sentence of the oath, Fueros III and IV from the third. He entirely ignores the second sentence of the oath, which concerns the contingency of a foreigner's becoming king.[48] Fuero I has the only passage which is not directly related to the texts of Charles or the Fuero of Navarre: that the king shall rule the kingdom "in peace and justice." Yet the glorification of *pax* and *iustitia* is so commonplace that beginning the Fuero of Sobrarbe with these lofty sentiments seems too obvious to warrant commentary. What is notable is something in *FN* I,1,1, which Blancas either altered or omitted completely: the status of the *ricoshombres*, the highest class of Aragonese noblemen. Had he been true to his sources, Blancas would have mentioned them in False Fueros II, III, and IV; in fact, he mentions them only in False Fuero II, and at that he twists the wording so as to depreciate them. Whereas the Navarre-Viana texts had listed the *ricoshombres* as one of a series of

[47] In the first edition of the *Commentarii* (Zaragoza, 1588), only inscriptions are given in capital letters identical to the False Fueros. I base my remark about the perennial custom of reserving capital letters for the *XII Tabulae* upon perusal of standard reference works, such as dictionaries; but probably the best proof of this practice is the authoritative work of C. G. Bruns, *Fontes Iuris Romani Antiqui* (7th ed., Tübingen, 1909), 2 vols. One of the inscription-like False Fueros did finally become an inscription in the 20th century: on the monument erected in 1904 by the Diputación de Zaragoza to honor the Justice of Aragon, and located in the main square of the city of Zaragoza, False Fuero v (see below, Ch. IV) is inscribed in letters of bronze; cf. *Fueros de Aragón*, ed. Parral y Cristobal, I, 364; also, pp. 311f for further remarks, and p. 588 for a sketch of the monument.

[48] This may well be related to the issue of the *virey extranjero* which was beginning to trouble the Aragonese; see below, Ch. VII, nn. 11-12.

three noble classes, Blancas opposes the *ricoshombres* to the other two by the use of adversative particles: "not only . . . but also . . . ," which tends to enhance the status of the knights and *infanzones*. That this was deliberate is supported by False Fueros III and IV. Where the original texts specify the *ricoshombres* as the unique counselors of the king, Fuero III says "an assembled council of his *subjects*"; where the original had spoken of war and peace as not being decided "without the counsel of 12 *ricoshombres* and 12 elders of the land," Fuero IV says simply "except by the favorable consensus of the elders." This down-grading of the *ricoshombres* by Blancas may well have been politically motivated.[49] It probably contributed to the failure of scholars for so long to recognize the source of Blancas' Fueros I-IV, for, whereas the stress in *FN* I,1,1 and Charles of Viana falls regularly upon this one group of barons, Blancas almost writes them out.

The content of Fueros I-IV is not radical; their ideas are common to mediaeval political thought. They may speak of the king's obligation to seek counsel in conducting the affairs of state, but they do not mention the right of resistance. That subject does not come up until Fueros V and VI, around which the intense controversy over the Sobrarbe legend, and indeed all Aragonese history, inevitably revolves.

[49] And related to the issue referred to in the previous note.

Chapter IV · False Fueros V and VI:
The Sagarra Story

$\mathcal{G}$erónimo Blancas' False Fuero v asserts that the office of the Justice of Aragon was founded in the ancient kingdom of Sobrarbe as a counterweight to royal authority; and False Fuero vi, that the people had the right to depose their king and elect another, even a pagan. The genesis of these two False Fueros goes back almost as far as that of False Fueros i-iv, but in an Aragonese rather than a Navarrese setting. I have given False Fueros v-vi the label "Sagarra Story" (see Appendix ii) because Martin Sagarra is the oldest known source of them. The pivotal figure in the transmission of the story, however, is the mid-15th-century jurist, Antich de Bages; and the main task of the present chapter is to assemble the elements of the early history of False Fueros v and vi and examine closely his presentation of them. For it is primarily through Antich de Bages' work—the least well-understood of all the important elements of our problem—that we can discover the key to the Sagarra Story itself and therewith uncover the wellspring of the radical elements of the False Fueros of Sobrarbe and thus provide the basis for our explanation of the *Si no, no* Oath.

The Justice of Aragon will be the first object of attention. It must be made quite clear, before dealing with the legend about him contained in False Fuero v, that he was indeed an officer of unusual authority. As with the Fueros of Sobrarbe so with the Justice of Aragon we must separate the true from the false. Special attention must be given to one of the most important of all the incumbents of the office, Juan Jiménez Cerdan, for his deeds provide a perfect example of the power of the Justice to resist royal authority. But we are interested more in his writing, in what he has to say about the history of his office. From there we move easily into the Sagarra Story itself, and to an examination of the work of Antich de Bages.

The Justice of Aragon

The office of the Justice of Aragon originated in the 12th century, although the national designation, "of Aragon," was preceded by other titular names, such as *juez supremo*, *juez mayor* and—most important of all—*juez medio* (*judex medius*) which survived into the late mediaeval period.[1] The office must have been instituted by the king, because he always had the unquestioned authority to name the incumbent.[2] The name of the Justice became prominent only

[1] Some modern authors believe the term "*Justicia de las Montañas*" to be one of the early variants of the title. This locution was loosely used in the 17th century by Domingo La Ripa, according to Danvila y Collado, *Libertades*, p. 354 (likely referring to La Ripa's *Corona Real del Pirineo, establecida y disputada* [Zaragoza, 1685-1688] 2 vols.), and when inserted into the legend of Sobrarbe insinuates some connections between "Mountains of Sobrarbe" and "Justice of the Mountains." In fact, the office of "*Justicia de las Montañas*" was instituted in 1585 as a separate jurisdiction to deal with brigands; cf. Pidal-Magnabal, *Perez*, I, 96.

[2] The modest origins of the Justice are given in proper historical perspective by Eduardo García de Diego, "Historia judicial de Aragón en los siglos VIII al XII," *AHDE*, XI (1934), 76-210; see esp. pp. 114ff. See also Adolfo Bonilla y San Martin, *El Derecho Aragonés en el siglo XII* (Huesca, 1920), pp. 31-33. The singular thesis of Julián Ribera y Tarrago, *Orígenes del Justicia de Aragón* (Zaragoza, 1897), that the office has its roots in Arabic institutions, has not been accepted. There does not seem to be a recent work devoted to the Justice alone, to which the reader can be sent for a sound and comprehensive analysis of the office. The work by López de Haro, *Justicia mayor*, is comprehensive, if the number of pages be the criterion; but it is deplorably organized and has only trivial documentation. Danvila y Collado, *Poder Civil*, I, 333-34, has some sound observations on the role of the Justice; in fact his whole section on the constitution of mediaeval Aragon (I, 314ff) is worth reading. The essay of Giménez Soler, "Poder judicial," has some good pages (cf. 57-69) showing the place of the Justice in the Aragonese constitution; other articles of his, especially those on specific Justices (see below, nn. 8, 18), are also important contributions. In English, Merriman, *Spanish Empire*, I, 463-71, gives a good general summary of the office of the Justice and its powers; also worthy of mention is

in late 13th-century legislation. Many of the "Liberties of Aragon" which were later canonized in juridical thought came into being during the reigns of James I (1213-1276), Peter III (1276-1285), and Alfonso III (1285-1291), especially in the legislation of the Cortes of Exea in 1265 and the General Privilege promulgated at the Cortes of Zaragoza in 1283. In both of these, the Justice performs an important function in guaranteeing the rights of the people. Indeed, in a third charter of these times the Justice seems not to be one of the king's officers, but rather a foil used against him. This occurs in the Privileges of Union, a double charter of 1287 which was extracted from the king by the baronial group known as the Union, and in which the Justice was allotted unusual powers to adjudicate disputes between the king and the barons.

As a rival to the king, the Justice's prospects were dim, and it is not surprising to find that when the Union subsided in the late 13th and early 14th centuries, the Justice assumed the status of an important arm of royal authority. We should, perhaps, think of him as an Officer of the Crown rather than as an officer of the king; for in this way we can understand the usual state of harmony that existed between the king and the Justice by reason of their common devotion to the administration of justice, and yet appreciate how they might be thrown into opposition at times when the king's political policy seemed to contravene established privileges which the Justice of Aragon was bound to defend. In the 1340's, during the revival of the Union, the interests of the king and the Justice remained identical. And

---

Lea's *Inquisition of Spain*, ɪ, 244ff, 439ff, 450f. The Justice of Aragon should not be compared with the justiciar in England, even though both offices came into being in the 12th century: first of all, the justiciar was powerful from the beginning, but disappeared by the mid-13th century, whereas the Justice of Aragon grew in power only in the late 13th century and remained an important official until early modern times; secondly, the justiciarship was always "the king's alter ego whose office met the need for an extension of the king's person and power" (Francis J. West, *The Justiciarship in England, 1066-1232* [Cambridge, 1966], p. 1), whereas the Justice of Aragon developed as a kind of super ego of the king.

when the Union was crushed on the battlefield and the Privileges of Union condemned to eternal oblivion, the position of the Justice was nevertheless assured in the extensive
legislation which was promulgated by the king, Peter IV,
in the Cortes of Zaragoza in 1348. The Justice of Aragon
remained the chief guarantor of the liberties of the people,
and it is safe to say that he was a more powerful official in
the later Middle Ages than he had been in the heyday of
the Union.

The status of the Justice was not similar to that of a judicial body such as the *Parlement* in France. The Justice was
not the pinnacle of the hierarchy of royal authority, but an
autonomous unit. His power, however, was as vast as that of
any judge in a mediaeval kingdom, because in certain instances he could assert his authority to the exclusion of all
others. By the 15th century this extraordinary power had
become crystallized under two headings: the *manifestación* and the *firmas de derecho*. Under the *manifestación*,
with its elements of English habeas corpus and "due process," the Justice could remove to his own jurisdiction, in the
Prison of the *Manifestación*, any individual who had been
apprehended by another judicial authority, in order to assure that the accusation was just. The *firmas de derecho*
were "special guarantees which were granted by the Justice
to those who demanded them, and which protected their
lives and their property from judgments contrary to the
law."[3] Only in extreme situations, where he was for some
reason at odds with the other judicial authorities, and at
the same time was inclined—or pressured by public opinion
—to be the champion of a popular cause, did the Justice
exercise these two powers, thus exposing the might of his

[3] Merriman, *Spanish empire*, I, 470. The *firmas de derecho* that
become peculiar to the Justice's competence come from much earlier
laws; see Antonio Ballesteros y Beretta, *Origen de la firma de
derecho ante el Justicia de Aragón* (Univ. thesis; Madrid, 1904).
The earlier term used was *fianza de derecho*; see below, n. 32. The
manifestación, however, is much later than many realize; the term
may belong to the 14th century, but the *carcel de manifestación*,
which was the main instrument of removing a person from royal authority, was built only in the later 15th century.

office in operation. These situations were few in history; but they were sufficient to give substance to the popular conceptions of the potentiality of his power which fostered the legends that grew up around his office.

A sober analysis of the history of the Justice of Aragon reveals that his power passed its peak in the course of the 15th century.[4] Although life tenure was achieved in 1441, the office became hereditary and inevitably associated with the established powers. The unification of Spain in the 16th century probably resuscitated the prestige, if not the power, of the Justice. The separatism of the Aragonese, and their frustration in trying to thwart the "Castilinization" of their government after the accession of Philip II, caused them to exalt the faded authority of the Justice. The result of this stance, the revolt of the 1590's, would be an historical farce had it not been so tragic for the Justice involved. Our chosen task, however, is to understand the legend about the Justice that had grown up over the span of almost two centuries, and then flowered in the decades preceding the revolt.

One of the things which made Blancas' False Fuero v so radical was its assertion that some other officer existed be-

---

[4] The position of the Justice vis-à-vis the "Liberties of Aragon" during the 15th century is the main subject of A. Giménez Soler, "Libertades." On the notable limitation of the Justice's power established in 1467, called the Inquisition of the Office of Justice of Aragon, see, *inter alia*, López de Haro, *Justicia mayor*, pp. 545ff. It will suffice, in order to prove the exalted position which the Justice of Aragon has had or has claimed, to cite some of the appellations— as often as not sarcastic—which have been given him over the centuries: *"una especie de divinidad olímpica"* (Fuente, *Estudios*, ii, 80); *"una ley divina"* (Danvila y Collado, *Libertades*, p. 352); *"Papa de Aragón"*—a mocking appellation among Castilians (Fuente, iii, 327). At least one famous Castilian, Juan de Mariana, spoke highly of the Justice of Aragon, likening him to the tribune of Rome and asserting that in concord with the laws and people he "has thus far held the regal power bound by sure limits"; *De Rege et regis Institutione* [1600], i, viii (trans. by G. A. Moore [Washington, 1948], p. 157). The greatest scholarly glorification of the Justice came from Gerónimo Blancas in his *Commentarii* of 1588 (see below, Ch. v, n. 62 *et sqq.*), to whom the famous Spanish humanist, Antonio Augustin, wrote in 1584: *"Ni los éforos á Sparta, ni á Roma la potestad de los tribunos, fueron más gratos, ni más útiles, que á esa ciudad la pública proteccion del justiciado"* (letter cited below, Ch. v, n. 66).

fore the king, and that this officer had the specific function
of checking royal arbitrariness:

> But lest damage and harm befall our laws and liberties,
> there shall be a certain *judex medius* to whom it shall be
> right and proper to make appeal from the King if he will
> have injured anyone, and [to whom it shall be right and
> proper] to check injustices if perchance they will have
> arisen in the Republic.[5]

This, according to Blancas, was decided upon by "our people" before they elevated Iñigo Arista to the throne. To the
extent that elements of the *manifestación* and *firmas de
derecho* are implied in False Fuero v it is valid. Clearly
false is the notion that the office of the Justice existed in
the 8th or 9th centuries, and that it was created by an assembly in the absence of any royal authority. Here we
touch again the idea of the compact, which was inherent in
the Navarre-Viana tradition of "laws before kings."[6] Now,
however, it is a matter of "the Justice before a king." It is not

---

[5] Translated from the text given below, Appendix III.

[6] See above, Ch. III, nn. 30, 40, for the Navarre-Viana evidence, and
below, Ch. v, n. 39, for the 16th-century introduction of the principle "laws before kings" into the *Nueva Compilación* of the Fueros
of Aragon. At the present juncture, however, we should perhaps correct a misconception, recently given high scholarly authority, that
the idea of "laws before kings" was current in 13th-century Aragonese
jurisprudence. Haebler, "Fueros de Sobrarbe," p. 28, adduces evidence from Lasala, *Constitución Aragonesa*, II, 350, to the effect that
the 13th-century redactor of the first books of the Fueros of Aragon,
Vidal de Canellas (Vidal Mayor), had said that the Fueros of
Sobrarbe existed before there were kings in that region. Haebler
based an important part of his argument about the early Fueros of
Sobrarbe upon this evidence, although he could not confirm it beyond Lasala; thus Haebler fell prey to the sin of ever believing
Lasala, for which he had castigated E. Mayer (Haebler, "Fueros de
Sobrarbe," p. 26, n. 21). There is no doubt that Lasala was referring
to MS 7391 of the Biblioteca Nacional de Madrid, a 17th-century
copy of Vidal Mayor's *In excelsis Dei thesauris* (a variant form of
his compilation of the Fueros of Aragon), in which Vidal's own first
prologue had been replaced by the prologue from the *Nueva Compilación* of the Fueros of Aragon of 1551. Thus, a mid-16th-century
source—fabulous in its own right—was applied in the 17th century to
the manuscript tradition of a 13th-century author. The key to the error
is manifest in the description of MS 7391 by Gunnar Tilander, *Vidal
Mayor*, I (=Leges Hispanicae Medii Aevi, IV) Lund, 1956, p. 16.

philosophical, but institutional—nay, personal. Or, if something philosophical is to be seen in it, it is a radical tone of right of resistance which is akin to the *Si no, no* Oath. Indeed, it might even be said to suggest a kind of dyarchy, which would be even worse in the eyes of a monarch. It is one thing to speak of the "king beneath the laws," which was a cherished principle of mediaeval political thought quite in tune with the idea that some law—at least Divine and Natural Law—preceded kingship itself, but quite another to say that in a nation where kingship had lapsed a fuero was promulgated which created an officer primed to enforce justice against the king, before kingship itself was reestablished and a new dynast elevated.

The ancestry of False Fuero v goes back to the first half of the 15th century, into the region of Aragonese legal literature, where it divides into two branches. One of them, the shorter of the two, leads us to a famous epistle written by a retired Justice of Aragon, Juan Jiménez Cerdan, in the year 1436. The other—the "Sagarra Story," in which False Fuero v and False Fuero vi are united—goes back at least to the later 14th century. The Sagarra Story is by far the more complicated to unravel, and ultimately the more important of the two in the development of the myth of Sobrarbe and its False Fueros. On the other hand, the Cerdan story has a much more noble pedigree, due to the dignity of the genearch, and became widely known at a much earlier date than the Sagarra Story, which lived an obscure life for generations in the writings of minor jurists.

Cerdan's Letra intimada

Juan Jiménez Cerdan succeeded his father as Justice of Aragon in the year 1391, and retired (under pressure) in 1424. Two others succeeded him for short terms, and in 1434 the office was filled by Martin Didaci Daux. Daux's five-year stint was one of the stormiest in the history of the office, and ended with Daux's being incarcerated and dying shortly afterwards. Daux is important for his own writings on Aragonese custom,[7] and also as the recipient of a long

---

[7] The famous *Observantiae*, which is discussed below, n. 18 and *passim*.

Letra intimada written to him by his septuagenarian predecessor, Cerdan, in 1436. In the *Letra intimada* Cerdan related the origin of the office of Justice of Aragon, enumerated its incumbents, and set forth its prerogatives. Although composed as an occasional piece to help Daux preserve the power of the office from its detractors, the *Letra intimada* turned out to have a spectacular history as part of the public law of Aragon. Starting with the second printing of the *Fori Aragonum* in 1496, the *Letra intimada* will be found as an appendix to almost all editions of the Fueros.[8]

The *Letra intimada* gives a unique version of the conduct of the founding fathers of the kingdom of Aragon, and the following portion of it merits extensive quotation:

The office of the Justice of Aragon (according to the opinion of all the ancients) was founded in this manner. Inasmuch as certain peoples had conquered part of the kingdom from the infidels, in the mountains of Sobrarbe, and there were communities that did not have a governor or ruler, so that many complaints and quarrels developed between them, it was proposed by some, in order to escape these troubles so that they might live in peace, that they should elect a king to rule over and govern them. Others said they should not do this, lest there happen to them what befell the Jews who had elected a king against the will of the prophet Samuel [I Samuel 8] who warned that the king once elected would take their wives, children and goods, and they would repent their action but it would be too late to retract it; although they [the Jews] heard this, nevertheless they demanded that they have a king, saying: "unless we have a king to govern us constantly we shall rob

[8] Andrés Giménez Soler, "Cerdán," gives a good scholarly résumé of Cerdan's career, stressing the circumstances of his resignation forced by Alfonso V in 1420. Fuente, *Estudios*, III, 211ff, attacks the Cerdans, father and son, as "Romanizers" of Aragonese law (the father, it is true, was a "Latinizer" of the law, being the translator of the Fueros from the vernacular into Latin), and charges them wildly as the spiritual progenitors of the Sobrarbe myth and even of the *Si no, no* Oath (*ibid.*, p. 221). On numerous other occasions Fuente makes extravagant misrepresentations of Cerdan's ideas and influence—see, e.g., below, Ch. v, n. 39. Concerning early published versions of the *Letra intimada* (1496 and afterwards) see Ureña y Smenjaud, "Fueros de Aragón," pp. 209, 217, 235.

and murder one another." So the Aragonese had a great quarrel and deliberation amongst themselves, and they were induced to act finally by the grace of the Lord and by taking heed of the following example drawn from Valerius Maximus, in the title *de moderacion* [*Fact. et Dict. Memorab.*, IV, 1, Est. 8]. It seems that Theopompos, King of the Spartans, wanted to bring the rule of justice into his land but realized that he alone was not equal to the task. Although he held his kingdom up to then freely and "absolutely," he elected two wise men with whose counsel (and not without it) he and his successors should execute the dictates of justice. When his wife and son heard this, they were irate and upbraided him for what he had done. He answered them that although henceforth he and his kin would not possess the kingdom freely and absolutely as before, they would hold it more securely and lastingly; for the kingdom would be more lasting and more firm because justice and reason held sway, even as kingdoms that are ruled against reason and by force are not lasting. *Quia nullum violentum perpetuum.* For this reason, the said conquistadores of the kingdom of Aragon agreed to elect a king, but also to have a judge between him and themselves, who should have the name of Justice of Aragon. And it is the opinion of some that before they elected the Justice there was no king, and that on that condition they elected him. In all times since then, there has been a Justice of Aragon in the kingdom, and he has cognizance of all cases which touch the lord King, of claims upon him as well as defense against him.[9]

[9] The *Letra intimada* is so widely available that I have not deemed it worthwhile to give the Spanish text, except to insert in the translation a few key phrases parenthetically. The last sentence, however, is vital for all transmission of False Fuero v: "*E por aquella razon, los sobreditos Conquistadores del Regno de Aragon acordaron de esleyr rey, pero que huviessen un judge entre el e ellos, que hoviesse nombre justicia de Aragon. Es opinion de algunos, que antes eslieron al justicia, que no al rey, e que de aquella condicion lo eslioron. De alli avant, toda vegada ha hovido justicia de Aragon en el regno, e conosce de todos los feytos tocantes al senyor rey, assi demandando como defendiendo*" (*Fori Aragonum*, fol. xlix^v in pre-1551 editions).

The general setting of the events bears a resemblance to the prologue of the Fuero of Navarre: the reconquest in the mountains of Sobrarbe, the dispute among the people, the decision to elect a king. Cerdan probably knew the prologue, but his version is finally so different that speculation about borrowing seems fruitless. Cerdan does not name the king who was actually elected by the baronial assembly, neither Don Pelayo of the Asturias nor any other. Everyone would know, however, that the events related must have taken place in the 8th or 9th century. When Cerdan speaks at the outset of the conquest of "a certain part of the kingdom from the infidels, in the mountains of Sobrarbe," he comes sufficiently close to saying "the kingdom of Sobrarbe" to give impetus to that conception; but later on when he speaks of the "*conquistadores* of the kingdom of Aragon," and of a "Justice of Aragon in the kingdom," we can only conclude that he simply was not thinking in precise historical terms. This we can say: the very vagueness of Cerdan's terminology allowed his story to be fitted into almost every later account of early Aragonese history.

Cerdan differs markedly from the prologue of the Fuero of Navarre in the essential parts of the story: how the assembly reached its decision; and what its decision was. In place of the embassy to the Pope, the Lombards and the Franks, Cerdan invents a dialogue between two factions based upon a pair of examples drawn from Scripture and an ancient author. The decision is the same: to elect a king. But where the Fuero of Navarre speaks of fueros being drawn up at the same time, Cerdan mentions no fueros, but only the decision to appoint a Justice to mediate between the king and the people.[10] Thus it was very simple for anyone who believed that the prologue of the Fuero of Navarre and the *Letra intimada* of Cerdan were both correct to assume that the Fuero of Navarre was simply negligent in not

[10] I would like to insist upon this point, for it is important in appreciating the separate stages of the growth of the myth and the False Fueros to note that the 14th- and 15th-century Aragonese jurists do not speak of an early fuero, let alone a Fuero of Sobrarbe; even modern writers err in assuming this (see, e.g., Fuente, *Estudios*, III, 313-15).

mentioning the Justice, whereas Cerdan on his part had neglected to mention the fueros simply because the *Letra intimada* was intended only to explain the origin of the Justice. The obvious solution when dovetailing the two accounts would be to construe the creation of the Justice as having been a separate fuero. Thus it is easy to see how Cerdan's story would be transmuted into False Fuero v.

Cerdan's account of the dialogue is obviously a literary fancy, but a rather nice one: kings can be tyrannical, but the wise king who installs officials to defend the people's rights builds a lasting rulership. The Aragonese, therefore, were wise *for* the king, and before electing him, they established an officer who should always mediate between the king and themselves. Cerdan qualifies himself by saying "it is the opinion of some" that the Justice existed before the king, but obviously he is basing his argument chiefly upon a reasonable conjecture such as: if judges must exist in a stable kingdom—as Theopompos demonstrated by creating them to assist him—then why can it not be true that a modern kingdom may have instituted such judges at the outset? The same line of reasoning, we have hypothesized, probably motivated the author of the prologue of the Fuero of Navarre when he posited the existence of laws before the first king was elevated. Neither that author nor Cerdan was consciously promoting the theory of a compact between ruler and ruled as the basis of government, but what they said was thoroughly compatible with such a view. If Cerdan could return to us, he would probably be quite disturbed to see how his charming tale about the prophet Samuel and the king Theopompos had been turned into False Fuero v of Sobrarbe, and he would be righteously indignant at the indictment of him by modern authors on the grounds that he had forged this story in order to foment resistance against royal authority. The fact is, the story of the creation of the Justice had already been invented by an earlier Aragonese jurist, Martin Sagarra, and Cerdan probably got the basic notion from him.[11]

[11] In the diagram of the descent of False Fuero v (Appendix II) I have made a dotted line between Sagarra and Cerdan, because it

The Sagarra Story

In what I have chosen to call the "Sagarra Story," False Fueros v and vi appear together. At the time of the election of Iñigo Arista (who, according to different traditions, was the first king of Aragon [Sobrarbe] or the first king after the interregnum), the office of the Justice of Aragon was created (False Fuero v) and there was established the right of the people to depose a king who did not uphold the fueros (False Fuero vi). My treatment of the Sagarra Story is incomplete because I believe that manuscripts exist, which were not available to me, containing additional information, or at least better readings than the manuscripts I have been able to consult. The root of the problem is that we know very little about Martin Sagarra.

According to the *Fasti* of the Justices of Aragon, drawn up by Blancas in the 1580's—and incorporated into his *Commentarii*—Martin Sagarra was a Justice of Aragon sometime between 1276 and 1296. Blancas was quite tentative in assigning this *floruit* to Sagarra, but later historians have found no good reason to question it.[12] I am convinced,

---

scarcely seems possible that any commentary upon the Aragonese law of the later 14th century, such as Sagarra's, would not be known to the Justice of Aragon, Cerdan, who bridged the turn of the century; but Cerdan's rendition of the Justice story is so different that it must stand alone.

[12] Blancas' reasoning was quite simple: (1) the list of Justices was fully known after the year 1291, when Pedro Martinez Artasona II acceded to the office; (2) the last date Blancas could verify was 1276, when Fortun Ahe acquired the office; (3) he believed that Martin Sagarra had been a Justice (but see below, n. 44); (4) *ergo*, Martin Sagarra could easily fit into this fifteen-year hiatus. In several places Blancas warns the reader that this is hypothetical. In the section on James I (ed. Schott, III, 657) he asserts his uncertainty about Sagarra in these words: "*Martinus autem Sagarra, vix affirmare possum, an sub eodem hoc Rege, vel sub Petri III illius filii imperio Iustitiatum obtinuerit. Adhuc enim certam huiusce rei rationem neque studio assequi potui, neque industria; tametsi ipsum Sagarram in haec tempora incidisse comperio.*" At the end of the section on Fortun Ahe (ed. Schott, III, 799) Blancas says that he will put Sagarra next because he believes that Sagarra must precede Salanova (see next note). And at the end of the section on Sagarra himself (ed. Schott, III, 799) he admits that he has no specific dates for Sagarra, and does not try to guess what they were. Blancas' theory became firmly rooted

however, that Sagarra lived in the later 1300's and that, although he was certainly a jurist of some note, he was not a Justice of Aragon but, at most, a Lieutenant Justice. These contentions will be supported when we come to analyze the text of the Sagarra Story and the context in which it has been transmitted to us.

Fully a century ago the role of the Sagarra Story in the formulation of the False Fueros of Sobrarbe was stated by Ximénez de Embún, who had located a manuscript which bridged the gap between Sagarra and Blancas: Antich de Bages' legal treatise of the mid-15th century. In his treatise Antich quoted Martin Sagarra; and in the margin of Antich's manuscript there was a note in the hand of Blancas himself.[13] In addition to Antich's account of the Sagarra Story, I believe that an entirely independent version of it is to be found in the well-known and often reprinted legal treatise, the *Repertorium*, by Miguel del Molino, composed just after 1500. I have chosen to treat Antich and Molino separately, as narrators of the Sagarra Story, rather than simultaneously; later on we can attempt to judge which is the more reliable.

---

by its incorporation into the authoritative *Bibliotheca de escritores aragoneses* of Latassa (Latassa², III, 95), and seems to be corroborated by the evidence of other authors cited by Latassa. Especially noteworthy, it would seem, is the mention of Sagarra by Bernardo de Monsoriu, *Suma de todos los fueros y observancias del reino de Aragon*, which Latassa elsewhere (Latassa², II, 342) dates 1525, considerably before Blancas' time. But Monsoriu's work was in fact written in 1587 (cf. Sánchez, *Bibliografía*, I, 188-89 [No. 133, pointing out Latassa's error] and II, 371 [No. 679, giving the correct date]), and thus is contemporaneous with Blancas' *Commentarii*. As for the other authorities whom Latassa cites in his article on Sagarra, they are all of the 17th and 18th centuries and surely are based on Blancas and Monsoriu. Unfortunately, I have not been able to locate a copy of Monsoriu. See further below, n. 20.

[13] I record this note in the apparatus of the text of Antich de Bages, given below, Appendix IV, n. 5. The parting remark of this note, "*M. Sagarra longe ante Salanovam Iustitiam fuisse credo,*" may be compared to what Blancas said about Sagarra in the *Commentarii* (ed. Schott, III, 799): "*cum Salanovam antecessisse.*" See Ximénez de Embún, *Orígenes*, p. 26, esp. nn. 3 and 4, a terse and true, but not well-expounded view of the relationship between Sagarra, Antich, and Blancas.

Johan Antich de Bages has not been a well-known figure up to now, and what facts have been gathered about him have been obfuscated by confusing him with his son who bore the same name. Only the father, to our knowledge, was a writer; he, not his son, was the author of the two books which go under the name Antich de Bages: a genealogy of the kings of Sobrarbe and Aragon (apparently extinct), and *Observantiae fororum regni Aragonum*.[14] The title of the latter work is exactly the same as that of a much more famous treatise by Martin Didaci Daux, and not without reason: Antich's *Observantiae* is a gloss upon Daux's *Observantiae*, and Antich (unhappily for later bib-

[14] On this score Ximénez de Embún, *Orígenes*, made one of his few errors. In his Appendix A (pp. 136-37) he tried to distinguish between "Antich de Bages el historiador" and his son by use of an archival document of 1508. This document (see next note) records payment to Johan Antich de Bages, "son of Johan Antich de Bages, who had been secretary of Alfonso V, who had composed the 'Genealogía y árbol de los reyes de Aragon' upon the order of Alfonso V." This establishes beyond doubt the father's authorship of the Genealogy; but for some reason Ximénez de Embún concluded that the son must have been the author of the *Observantiae* (i.e., the *Glossa*—see next note) and that it was written in the time of Ferdinand and Isabella. There is no doubt, however, that the *Observantiae* was written between 1450 and 1455, and therefore by the father. (See further below, next three notes.) A few years after Ximénez de Embún wrote his treatise, Miguel Gomez Uriel, the editor of Latassa[2], tried to integrate this archival information on the younger Antich by making a new entry under that name (cf. Latassa[2] [1884], I, 90), and the result was that father and son were confounded even worse than by Ximénez de Embún. Latassa's original entry is correct, as far as it goes, and Uriel's additional entry— actually the first under the name Antich, bearing an asterisk—should be ignored. Further information on Antich de Bages is given by Uztarroz, the 17th-century editor of Blancas' *Coronaciones*. On p. 117, marginal n. D, explicating Blancas' version of the coronation *ordo* of Peter IV, Uztarroz tells us that Antich had translated this *ordo* from Latin into *"lenguage antiguo"*—i.e., Spanish. Then, at the end of the *Coronaciones*, where Uztarroz describes the manuscript sources which he had used to make his edition of the work, there is cited a manuscript in the Archiv de la Deputación in which Miguel Molino says of Antich: *"muchas personas curiosas le tienen en esta Ciudad en sus librerias, la nuestra no carece de sus escritos."* Uztarroz goes on to report that in 1471 Antich began to copy the original Privileges of Zaragoza, a task continued later by Miguel Anchias (up to 1547, apparently) to the number of ten folio volumes. Another work by Antich is mentioned in the next note.

liographers) chose to begin his work by citing the title of the treatise he was going to gloss. One bibliographer has given Antich's work the title *Glossa de Observantiis Regni Aragonum*. I shall refer to it as the *Glossa*.[15]

In the opening pages of the *Glossa*, in which Antich justifies writing this treatise, he gives us some autobiographical information. He was currently a secretary and scribe of Alfonso V (who died in 1458) but had earlier served in the entourage of Alfonso's wife, Maria of Castile. Sometime before Maria's death (in 1450), Antich had been sent from Barcelona to Zaragoza, but at the time he was writing, she was dead. Therefore, the *Glossa* was composed between 1450 and 1458.[16] From the time he arrived in Zaragoza— probably after the demise of Martin Didaci Daux, and therefore in the early 1440's—Antich had been engaged in an extensive study of Aragonese customs. He had already been educated in Roman and Canon law, and his new duties seem to have been chiefly in the field of law. He grew increasingly discontented because he found that the au-

[15] The title *Glossa de Observantias* [*sic*] *Regni Aragonum* is given the work in Latassa², I, 90, which says there are many versions of it, and describes the copy known to us as Bib. Univ. Zaragoza MS 95 (see below, Appendix IV). Latassa² gives 1437 as the date of composition, which is wrong (see next note); the error is probably due to a hasty reading of the opening sentences of Antich's work, where he refers to Daux's *Observantiae*, which is dated 1437. Latassa² also records another work by Antich de Bages, "*Ordenanza* del Rey D. Pedro IV de Aragon, y la compilacion é ilustracion de los Privilegios Reales concedidos á la Ciudad de Zaragoza," which allegedly is conserved in the Archives of Zaragoza. The *Ordenanza* is probably the same as the document appended to Antich's *Glossa* in MS 95 just cited, and the "*compilacion . . . de los Privilegios Reales*" is probably the work to which Uztarroz refers (see above, end of previous note).

[16] The following words are the full proof of this: "*Cumque ego Antiquus de Baies eiusdem Domini Regis Secretarius et scriba noviter fuissem per Illustrissimam Dominam Reginam Mariam eiusdem Domini regis Alfonsi consortem et locum tenentem generalem* memoriae praeexcelsae et dignae *a civitate Barchinonae ad civitatem Caesaraugustam translatus.*" (I have romanized the words which show that Queen Maria was dead when Antich wrote.) Antich adds immediately the gratuitous information, "*et in matrimonio collocatus,*" which indicates 1440 as a *terminus post quem* for the birth of his son; cf. Bib. Univ. Zaragoza MS 95, fol. 1ᵛ; or the same in Madrid, Bib. Nac. MS 747, fol. 1ᵛ.

thoritative text on Aragonese usages and practices—although it was not false—was not true enough to the rich traditions of Aragonese jurisprudence. That authoritative text was the *Observantiae* of Martin Didaci Daux, composed in 1437; Antich, in effect, composed his *Glossa* in order to enrich Daux's *Observantiae*.[17]

It is very doubtful whether Martin Didaci Daux would have appreciated Antich's work had he lived to see it. In effect, Antich was denying the validity of Daux's *Observantiae*. This work had been composed by Daux, along with several notable collaborators under royal commission, in order to winnow the chaff from a century or more of writings by Justices and lesser officials on Aragonese "Observances and Practices," and to bring forth a succinct and well-ordered résumé of the germinal usages which had to be understood in conjunction with the Fueros themselves. This necessitated suppressing, or at least condensing, the bulk of earlier writings. Antich found himself quite agitated by Daux's codification: he was a true antiquarian (his other treatise on Genealogy also suggested this), so that the formless mass of Aragonese legal usages which Daux had deplored, and therefore had revamped, was beloved by Antich as a museum of riches to be guarded. Aragonese jurisprudents, however, accepted Daux's *Observantiae* with little criticism. The *Observantiae* became an adoptive twin of the Fueros, and appears along with the Fueros in the first printed edition of Aragonese laws in 1476 and in almost all printings thereafter. In fact, the usual term for the Aragonese law today is the *Fori et Observantiae*.[18]

[17] Antich takes pages to explain this, in monotonous style, but the matter is fairly well summed up in part of one sentence: ". . . *dicta antiquorum et modernorum foristarum in viam apparatus scripsi pro earum intellectu has notas sive apparatum formam glossarum tenentes*" (MS 95 Bibl. Univ. Zaragoza, fol. 2ᵛ [Madrid, Bib. Nat. MS 747, fol. 2]); cf. fol. 4 [Madrid, fol. 3] for Antich's remarks about his legal education.

[18] The early printed editions of the *Observantiae* are spoken of frequently by Ureña y Smenjaud, "Fueros de Aragón," but the best testimonial to the durability of Daux's work is that it survived the 1551 revision of the *Fori Aragonum* (see below, pp. 120ff) and was printed in each of the six editions of the *Nueva Compilación* (known

Antich de Bages' *Glossa* on the other hand, though never published, was not ephemeral. Several manuscript copies of it are known, and it was cited by legal scholars into the 16th century.[19] An oft-quoted passage in Antich's *Glossa* occurs in the prologue, where he reports the older sources which Daux had used in compiling the *Observantiae.* Seven writers are listed. In the first group of four, whom Antich identifies as Justices of Aragon, Martin Sagarra is the first named; but, whereas the other three are authenticated incumbents of that office during the 14th century, Martin Sagarra has not been verified as a Justice by any source other than Antich, and by him only in this one statement. Sagarra should probably have been included in Antich's second group of sources, three persons who are identified as Lieutenants of the Justice in former days.[20] In any event, these seven ancient scholars of Aragonese law provided the substance of Antich's *Glossa.* For lawyers who felt that Daux's *Observantiae* was too skimpy on a given topic, Antich's *Glossa* could provide a handy directory to the older literature. The history of Aragonese law may well prove indebted to Antich for having preserved at least the fragments of some writers who otherwise would have become extinct. In the present state of knowledge, Martin Sagarra must be put in this category.

---

to me) that appeared in succeeding centuries from 1551 to the present. For a sketch of Daux's career see Giménez Soler, "Diez de Aux."

[19] See above, nn. 14, 15; also below, Appendix IV, for remarks about the manuscripts which I have examined.

[20] In his sketch of Sagarra, Blancas gives the passage from Antich which lists the seven sources used by Daux (see Blancas, *Commentarii* [ed. Schott, III, 799; ed. Hernandez, 411]). Many scholars have not realized that the details we have about the compilation of Daux's *Observantiae* come to us from Antich's *Glossa,* and the worst confusion on this matter comes out in Latassa's entry (*s.n.* Diez de Aux: Latassa[2], I, 390) which gives Daux's *Observantiae* a 100-word title based upon the information provided by Antich about the contribution by Sagarra. Evidently some scribe, anxious to be helpful, composed this long description and affixed it to the front of a manuscript of Daux's *Observantiae.* Later writers then took it for the official title of the work. Fuente, *Estudios,* III, 330, draws upon Latassa[2]. In a word, Daux nowhere credits Sagarra as his source; this is Antich's doing.

To understand Antich's quotation of Sagarra, which contains the germ of False Fueros v and vi, we must understand the passage of Daux's *Observantiae* which Antich was glossing when he quoted Sagarra. The *Observantiae* is divided into nine books. Book vi is concerned with the *infanzones*, the broadest class of the nobility, being essentially those born of knights. The second title in this book is "Concerning the Privileges of Knights and their Descendants," and the twelfth paragraph of this title, which is cited in older literature by its incipit, "*Item de omnibus causis*," deals with the question of adjudication between *infanzones* and the king:

[*Item de omnibus causis*] Item, in all suits which the lord king has with the *infanzones*, the Justice of Aragon is the judge; likewise in all suits which the *infanzones* have against the king, according to the ancient Fueros and the Fuero of Exea. Nevertheless, use has it that appeal can be made to the king from the sentence of the Justice, on the part of the king or of the *infanzones*, and in that case the king will appoint a judge.[21]

The first part of this statement records one of the fundamental aspects of the office of Justice of Aragon, that of the *judex medius* (*juez medio*), a title often given the Justice. The source which Daux alleges, the Fuero of Exea (1265), says as much: "in suits between the kings and the *Ricoshombres, hijosdalgos* and *infanzones*, the Justice was the judge."[22] The other major notion, that appeal may be had from the Justice, is not documented; but it, too, conforms to the Fueros.[23] Daux's *observantia* on this question, there-

---

[21] "*Item de omnibus causis quas dominus Rex habet cum eis, est iudex iustitia Aragonum, idem de causis quas ipsi habent contra Regem iuxta Foros antiquos, & Forum Exeae. Appellari tamen potest de usu ad Regem a sententia Iustitiae pro parte Regis vel Infantionum, & Rex delegabit Iudicem*" (pre-1551 eds., fol. xxvi^v).

[22] The text of this is given below, Appendix iv, n. 3.

[23] Antich de Bages, glossing Daux, makes the relevant allegation to the Fueros; see below, Appendix iv, n. 3. The power of the king to appeal cases involving himself, and decided adversely by the Justice of Aragon, to another judge appointed by the king, would seem to load the case against the king's adversary. However, we should

fore, is quite orthodox. We have no problem understanding it, except to wonder what he meant by "according to the ancient Fueros." Since he follows these words with a specific allegation of the Fuero of Exea of 1265, he implies that "the ancient Fueros" were older still. The vagueness of this remark opened the way for Antich's gloss.

Antich de Bages' gloss upon Daux's observance "*Item de omnibus causis*" may be divided into five separate sections, according to five different phrases within the observance which he chooses to gloss. Of these five, the first three and the last one are quite straightforward: in them, Antich makes brief cross references to other relevant observances in Daux's own work, and he gives the full reference to book, chapter, and paragraph of the Fuero of Exea to which Daux had referred. We shall not translate these parts of the gloss (the full Latin text is given in Appendix iv), but only the fourth part of the gloss, a long digressive comment upon the words *juxta foros antiquos*, which adds substantially to Daux's notions. Remember that Antich was trying to explain the role of the Justice of Aragon as judicial mediator between the *infanzones* and the king, a position clearly stated at least as early as the Fuero of Exea in 1265, but also, according to Daux, practiced "*juxta foros antiquos*." This is how Antich glosses these words:

According to the ancient fueros this thing was secured to the kingdom by its people at the time of the election of Iñigo Arista, commonly called the fifth king of Sobrarbe,

---

regard the fact that the king could appoint a judge to decide royal cases as an advanced state of legal development indicating limits upon royal authority. Only in the 13th century, it seems, did the notion arise that "*Rex aut Imperator non cognoscunt in causis eorum*," (Andreas of Isernia, *In usus feudorum commentaria*, on Feud. II, 55 ["De prohibita alienatione feudi"], n. 84 [Naples, 1571, fol. 281r-v]), and consequently the practice, which is very close to our Aragonese example, that "*Imperator causas suas non ipse cognoscit: sed iudices alios facit*" (Cynus de Pistoia, *In Codicem*, on *Cod.* 6, 23, 19, n. 1 [Frankfurt, 1578, fol. 276v]). For this problem, see the remarks of Ernst H. Kantorowicz, "Kingship Under the Impact of Scientific Jurisprudence," in *Twelfth-Century Europe and the Foundations of Modern Society*, ed. by M. Clagett, G. Post, and R. Reynolds (Madison, Wisc., 1961), p. 93; reprinted in Kantorowicz, *Selected Studies* (Locust Valley, N.Y., 1965), pp. 155-56.

Ribagorza and Pamplona, as the tree of genealogies of the
kingdom of Aragon is called; and it is recounted in the gloss
on Book x, Fuero 1 of the Fueros, where the Privilege
of Union was abolished and cut out; and also Martinus de
Sagarra recites it in his Observances and Practices, in the
chapter "The Origin of Liberties"; in which places it is said
that the Aragonese swore to him and created him [king]
on the condition that he and his successors are held to
create—thus to make at once—one of them into a judge who
would adjudicate and be the judge between him and his
vassals; and that he would take cognizance of and hold court
in whatever suits and complaints there were between the
king and them, as much in pleading as in defending; and
that the aforementioned king should preserve the established fueros for him [the Justice] and his successors in perpetuity; and that if he should not so preserve them, that
they could strip him and elect another in his place as king,
even a pagan. And this was the Privilege of Union which
they renounced at the time of the lord King Peter, in the
year 1348, as it is said in the aforementioned Book x, Fuero
1; and in place of which, it is said, there followed, and still
does follow, the restraint *de facto* of the *firmas de derecho*
and the *manifestación*, as it is seen in our time and is said
in the Observance of said lord Martinus de Sagarra, which
has been introduced through the gloss of said Book x, Fuero
1 of the Fueros, as carefully by the letter as by intent of the
law, where the most important things are related which are
the liberties of this realm.[24]

The opening sentence gives three sources: (1) "this
thing" (*hoc*)—presumably the privileges being discussed—
had been acquired at the time of Iñigo Arista; (2) "it is recounted" in the gloss on Book x, Fuero 1 of the Fueros; (3)
Martinus de Sagarra "recites" (with no direct object, but
presumably there shall be understood, "the same thing")
in his *Observantiae*. Antich then goes on: "in which places
it is said that the Aragonese swore to him and created him
[king]. . . ." There are a number of exasperating ambiguities
in this statement. First of all, are the words "*juxta foros*

antiquos" to be understood as simply identificatory of the words in Daux which Antich is glossing, so that the passage should be read: "This is my comment upon Daux's words: *Juxta foros antiquos*. This was acquired by the people . . . "; or should we read the words *"juxta foros antiquos"* as part of Antich's own sentence, thusly: "According to the old fueros, this was acquired by the people . . . "? It makes a great difference which reading one assumes. If the first alternative, then *foros antiquos* has necessarily nothing to do with the beginning of the kingdom, and the events which are mentioned must be taken as mere historical happenings, and not laws. With the second alternative, *foros antiquos* is promoted to the status of a primary source—"lost laws," as it were—which immediately makes the specific legal allegations (i.e., the gloss on Book x, Fuero 1 of the *Fori Aragonum* and the *Observantiae* of Sagarra) become simply corroborative. In this event, the words which follow, *"in quibus locis dicitur,"* must be taken to refer to *three* different places where the details of the story which follows are to be found. And if one does this, then the narrative that follows—". . . in which places it is said that the Aragonese swore to him and created him [king] on condition . . ."—must be construed as directly related to the earlier remark about the "election of Iñigo Arista"; therewith, the creation of the Justice seems to be a fuero established at the founding of the nation. But—to repeat—if the opening words *"juxta foros antiquos"* are regarded as simply an identificatory phrase taken from Daux's text, a precise reading would not allow the automatic conclusion that there were fueros established at the election of Iñigo Arista. There is no reason to assume that Antich held such a belief. His opening reference to "this privilege [of the Justice] obtaining at the beginning of the kingdom" was only a reiteration of what everyone already knew from the *Letra intimada* of Cerdan; he simply embellished it by making specific reference to the first king, as one might expect the author of a genealogy of the kings of Aragon to do.[25]

[25] See above, n. 14, concerning Antich's work on Aragonese genealogy.

We must remember that we are dealing with the source of an erroneous conception of the Fueros of Sobrarbe, and the error grew from misconceptions and misreadings. Antich does not use the phrase *Fuero de Sobrarbe*, and we should not attribute to him conceptions that were not fully developed until a century after him. But in later times, anyone who read Antich and construed the passage from the words *"juxta foros antiquos"* to *"etiam paganum"* as a unity, and who also believed that there was a lost code called the Fuero of Sobrarbe, would jump to the conclusion that here he had found the first part of that Fuero. This is the story, *in nuce*, of the creation of False Fueros v and vi.

There is additional evidence to suggest that Antich's story was not derived from ancient sources. All earlier commentators have been content to quote the passage only up to the words *"etiam paganum."*[26] This is a natural tendency, because at this point the subject changes abruptly from the founding of the kingdom in the 8th century to events in the 14th century. Antich's procedure looks like an idiosyncrasy, or perhaps an instance of the phenomenon commonly found in legal writers of piling allegations on top of one another without intending to establish causal relationships. But in this case, I believe, the true understanding of what Antich says about the origin of the kingdom comes only by knowing the 14th-century events which he introduces so suddenly and proceeds to explain.

The "8th-century" portion ends with the words *"etiam paganum"*; Antich then goes on to say: "and this was the Privilege of Union which they renounced at the time of the lord King Peter, in 1348."[27] What, we ask ourselves, could Antich possibly mean by this? Surely he knew that the Privilege—really, Privileges—of Union was a document of the

[26] This is true of Blancas, Lasala, and Ximénez de Embún; see below, Appendix IV, n. 9.

[27] It is the best indication of the ignorance, or sloppiness, of the scribes who provided the transcriptions of Antich's work that they wrote *"regis primi"* instead of *"regis petri"*; they were still thinking about the origin of the kingdom dealt with in the preceding sentences; see below, Appendix IV, n. (1).

year 1287, granted by Alfonso III to the barons, which said nothing about the creation of the first king of the Aragonese nation, and could not possibly have mentioned the election of a pagan king. Still, aside from these erroneous implications or assertions, Antich's statement has essential truth. The first Privilege of Union does exalt the position of the Justice as mediator between the king and the nobles, and it does allow the nobles to reject Alfonso as king if he should not uphold the conditions of the Privilege. Reft of its mythical notions about the founding of the kingdom— which includes the *etiam paganum* notion, since it would make sense only in the context of the first days of the *reconquista*—Antich de Bages' gloss on the words "*juxta foros antiquos*" relates the terms of two quondam (and in the eyes of many, only quasi) fueros: the Privileges of Union.

The relationship between these "ancient fueros" and the Privileges of Union becomes even more evident when, after Antich tells us what consequence the renunciation of 1348 had as far as the Justice is concerned, he again alleges the *Observantiae* of Martin Sagarra and tells us that this had been inserted as a gloss to Book x, Fuero 1 of the Fueros of Aragon. When he first mentioned the gloss on Book x, Fuero 1, he had mentioned it in addition to Sagarra; now we find out that the gloss is *drawn from* Sagarra. There is, then, only one specific source in Antich's gloss: Martin Sagarra. He had written some *Observantiae* on the Fueros of Aragon; one section was devoted to the "Origin of Liberties"; parts of that section had been adapted as a gloss to Book x, Fuero 1, of the *Fueros de Aragon*; Antich had the text of Sagarra, and he had a glossed version of the Fueros; these sources, which are one and the same, provided Antich with the material for his own gloss upon Martin Daux's *Observantiae* on the powers of the Justice of Aragon.

The *Observantiae* of Sagarra itself seems to be lost. I have seen one glossed version of the Fueros of Aragon which refers to Sagarra in the margin opposite Book x, Fuero 1, but the substance of Sagarra's comment is not quoted.[28] So we are stymied in trying to confirm the accuracy of Antich's rendition of the Sagarra Story. But the pursuit should not end here, for the question remains: why would the Sagarra Story be attached to Book x, Fuero 1, of the Fueros of Aragon in the first place? Indeed, Antich himself, in addition to mentioning twice the gloss upon the fuero, also refers once to the fuero itself. This occurs when he speaks of the renunciation of the Privileges of Union in the time of Peter IV in 1348, "as it is said in the aforementioned Book x, Fuero 1." One would have to have a pre-1551 edition of the *Fori Aragonum* in order to know what this reference is (although the scholars of Aragonese law should readily guess it): it is the renunciation of the Privileges of Union by Peter IV himself, *De prohibita unione.* Something in this fuero, dated 1348, struck a jurist later on as being relevant to something Martin Sagarra had said, and so he alleged Sagarra in the gloss to the fuero. A quick review of the Privileges of Union, and Pedro IV's abolition of them, will make the situation clear.

The Privileges of Union and Their Prohibition

Of the two distinct documents which comprise the Privileges of Union, both issued by Alfonso III on December 28, 1287, the one that is traditionally cited as the First Privilege concerns us chiefly.[29] In large part it reads the same as the

[28] Biblioteca del Escorial MS Lat. P. II. 3, fol. 96; the text of this marginal gloss is given below, Appendix IV, n. 7. It is only by chance, when perusing the apparatus that Tilander used for his edition of the Fueros of Aragon, that I discovered that the Escorial MS refers, in its title, to the gloss of Martin Sagarra; see *Los Fueros de Aragón*, ed. Gunnar Tilander (=Skrifter Utgivna av Kungl. Humanistiska Vetenskapssamfundet I Lund, xxv) Lund, 1937, p. xxiii. One wonders, of course, if this barren citation of Sagarra's writing on the "Origin of Liberties" is not the entirety of the gloss to which Antich refers. One would have to check all the manuscripts described by Tilander which include Book x (see *ibid.*, pp. vii-xxxi), and even then one cannot be sure that there are not others which either escaped Tilander's notice or have become extinct.

[29] It will be well to remind the amateur of Aragonese history at this point that the Privileges of Union of 1287 must be clearly separated from the General Privilege of 1283, even though they both belong to the history of the Union. The General Privilege is an extensive list of "Liberties," which were reaffirmed by succeeding

Second Privilege, including the affirmation of peculiar powers of the Justice of Aragon, as follows:

Neither we nor our successors who may rule in the kingdom of Aragon, nor any person operating under our mandate, shall mutilate or execute or imprison for civil matters the nobles . . . and citizens of the city of Zaragoza, or incarcerate any nobles of the kingdoms of Aragon, Valencia and Ribagorza without the sentence given by the Justice of Aragon in the city of Zaragoza with the express counsel or approval of the Cortes of Aragon assembled in Zaragoza.[30]

Both the First and the Second Privileges of Union also contain the same sanction that might be applied against the king, to the effect that he would forfeit sixteen royal castles (which are offered as a kind of bond) if he should contravene the Privileges. After naming the castles, both the First and the Second Privileges allow that these may be given up to "any other king or señor," but then the First

---

rulers and finally entered the Fueros of Aragon under Peter IV; the Privileges of Union were two very short and special charters, whose legality has always been disputed and which were finally damned forever under Peter IV. A full treatment of all these documents, along with the texts, is given by Danvila y Collado, *Libertades* (below, nn. 30, 31) but, of course, almost every one of the modern works I have used deals with the Union, and discusses the various Privileges which were extracted from the kings. American readers may consult with profit an unpublished thesis (Washburn Prize Essay, 1937) at Harvard University: Alan Breck Calvert, "The Liberties of Aragon, 1283-1348." A brief, but interesting, comparison of the General Privilege of the Aragonese—plus other Spanish documents of a similar character—with the English *Magna Carta* is given by Rafael Altamira, "La Magna Carta y las Libertades medievales en España," *Revista de Ciencias jurídicas y sociales,* I (1918), 151-63.

[30] "*Que nos ni los nuestros successores . . . ni estemos, ni matar, ni estmar mandemos, ni fagamos, ni preso ó presos sobre fianza de dreyto detengamos, ni detener fagamos agora, ni en algun tiempo alguno ó algunos de nos sobreditos Ricos omens, Mesnaderos, cabelleros, Infanzones . . . sines de sentencia dada por la Justicia de Aragon dentro en la ciudad de Çaragoça con conseyllo é atorgamiento de la cort de Aragon ó de la mayor partida clamada é ajustada en la dita ciudad de Çaragoça.*" (Text in Blancas, *Comentarios* [ed. Hernandez, 1878], p. 164, n. 1; also in Danvila y Collado, *Libertades,* p. 235, and Näf, "Privilegien," p. 3.)

Privilege goes on to add another sanction which is even more drastic:

If—God forbid—we or our successors should contravene these articles in all or in part, it is our wish and express command that from that moment neither we nor our successors in the kingdom of Aragon should be taken or held anymore as kings and lords; and without any failing of faith and loyalty you may make another, whomever you wish, king and lord, and give to him said castles and even give yourselves to him as vassals.[31]

The provisions regarding the Justice of Aragon which are found in the Privileges of Union are far from unique: in many other Aragonese documents of this and later times, as well as in the annals of other Spanish kingdoms, comparable powers are allotted the chief justice of the land.[32] What gives the Privileges of Union their special sting are the threats against royal power embodied in the sanctions. The final clause quoted above, allowing that the reigning king may even be abandoned and another ruler elected in his stead, cannot be matched by any other official document to which any king lent his signature in the Middle Ages.

[31] *"Porque si lo que dieus non quiera nos ó los nuestros successores contraviniesemos á las cosas sobreditas en toto ó en partida, queremos e otorgamos y expressament de certa sciencia assi la ora como agora consentimos que daquella ora á nos ni á los successores ni [leg. en] el dito Regno de Aragon non tengades ni ayades por Reyes, ni por seynnores en algun tiempo, ante sines algun blasmo de fe e de layaldat podades façer y fagades otro Rey é seynnor cual querredes e don querredes"* (Danvila y Collado, *Libertades*, pp. 237-38; also in Näf, "Privilegien," p. 34, and Blancas [ed. Hernandez, 1878], p. 165, n. 1). Both the First and the Second Privileges of Union have another sanction (the only sanction in the Second Privilege) which involves surrendering the castles and allowing the barons to deliver them if they wish "to another King or Señor."

[32] The *"fianza de derecho,"* for example (see n. 30), will be found in Article ix of the pact of 1188 between Alfonso IX of León and his subjects; in Book ii, Title 1, Law 1, of the *Fuero Viejo* of Castile; in the Privilege of 1270 given by Don Enrique of Navarre to Laguardia; and in "ley XC de Sobrarbe"—i.e., in the Fuero of Tudela of the 13th century (see above, Ch. iii, n. 11). All these places are mentioned by Marichalar and Manrique, *Historia del derecho*, v, 40-41, when commenting upon the Privileges of Union.

Alfonso III may have thought that he was giving concrete expression to the theory of *rex sub lege*, a respected principle of rulership, but in fact he was trafficking in questions of legitimacy by offering his crown, as well as his castles, as surety for his own good conduct.

It is quite understandable that the Privileges of Union were odious to the kings of Aragon. The First Privilege was not renewed by immediately succeeding kings, although the Second (lacking the right of deposition clause) was reconfirmed by James II in 1300. By the end of James II's reign (1327), however, the Union had deliquesced and the Privileges of Union had fallen into desuetude. Twenty years later, however, the Union re-formed in opposition to Peter IV when he tried to tamper with the law of succession to the throne, and forced him to summon a Cortes and allow the Privileges of Union to be reinvoked. Peter had to put sixteen castles in surety, and he became virtually a captive of the barons. Time ran on the side of the legitimate monarchy, however, and within a year Peter was able to gather loyal forces and rout the opposition at the Battle of Epila (1348). At the next Cortes the king wreaked his vengeance on the parchment upon which the Privileges of Union were inscribed, as he performed his famous deed of cutting the odious articles from the register with a knife. From this deed he acquired his sobriquet, "Peter the Dagger."[33]

What concerns us is the official condemnation of the Privileges of Union which Peter published at this time. This edict of 1348, known by its incipit *De prohibita unione*, is a rare example of a *damnatio memoriae*, as the following excerpt shows:

Further we wish that the aforementioned privileges and confirmation, along with all the *processus*, books, register, seal, concessions and other things whatever deriving by

[33] M. Dualde Serrano, "Pere el del Punyalet," provides an exemplary examination of the matter: the known events leading up to the Cortes of 1348; the attribution of the *"el Punyalet"* agnomen in historiography from the 16th century onwards; and three new documents which prove that Peter himself did cut the leaves from the register and smash the seal of the Union.

chance from them and dependent upon them, and also the transcriptions of all these things, authentic or otherwise, and even the copies of them—that all these should be torn up, destroyed and burned, so that henceforth the remembrance of them may not be had or cannot be had at any time in the future. Adding further that whoever may possess said privileges, confirmation and book of the union, and its seal, should deliver it to us at once. Indeed, those who may possess the *processus* and other books, registers, concessions and whatever other things by chance derive from them or are dependent upon them, relative to the cause of the union and its assembly, as well as the transcriptions of all these things, authentic or otherwise, and even copies of these things—these people should be bound to bring these things forth and surrender them to us or to the Justice of Aragon within two months of the publication of the present constitution. And that who may do otherwise shall have deemed himself to have incurred a penalty of 500 *morabitinos* of gold chargeable to our treasury.[34]

The edict *De prohibita unione* became the first fuero in the new book (Book x) which Peter IV added to the Fueros

---

[34] "*Imo volumus quod privilegia et confirmatio praedicta cum omnibus processibus, libris registris, sigillo, concessionibus, et aliis quibuscumque occasione ipsarum subsecutis, et dependentibus ex eisdem, necnon et transumpta ipsorum et ipsarum tam autentica quam alia et etiam copie eorundem et earundem lacerentur, destruantur, et comburantur, taliter quod deinceps memoria de ipsis non habeatur nec haberi possit aliquo tempore in futurum. Adicientes insuper quod quicumque dicta privilegia, confirmationem, librumque unionis, et sigillum eiusdem tenuerit, die presenti nobis restituat et restituere teneatur. Qui vero processus aliosque libros, registra, concessiones, et alia quecumque occasione ipsarum unionis et colligationis subsecuta et dependencia et eisdem et transumpta ipsorum et ipsarum tam autentica quam alia, et etiam copias eorundem et earundem tenuerint infra duos menses a tempore publicationis presentis constitutionis ipsos et ipsa teneantur nobis vel iusticie aragonum revelare et tradere. Quod qui contra fecerit, penam quingentorum morabetinorum auri nostro erario applicandorum ipso facto se noverit incurrisse*" (pre-1551 eds., fol. LVI; post-1551 eds., fol. 178r·v). A vernacular rendition of this can be had in Jesus Bergua Camon's edition of the *Fueros de Aragón* from a 15th-century manuscript (Bib. Univ. Zaragoza, MS 207), *ADA*, VI (1952), 501-02.

of Aragon, and thus it was enshrined in the law of the land.[35] From one point of view it was not effective: at least two copies of the Privileges did survive. From another point of view, Peter's proscription had amazing success: not until the 19th century did the exact terms of the Privileges of Union become public domain. The latter fact interests us the most, because I will argue that the suppression of the exact terms of the Privileges of Union created the conditions under which wild notions about them sprang up. The adventures of one manuscript, perhaps the only one that existed between 1350 and 1550, will illustrate the aura of mystery that hung over the Privileges for centuries after Peter IV condemned them.

Gerónimo Zurita, the first official royal historiographer of Aragon (1512-1580), gave a clear and full summary of the Privileges in his *Anales,* published in 1562.[36] This résumé is so complete that we might judge that Zurita violated the spirit of *De prohibita unione.* In another respect he certainly violated the letter of the law: he possessed a manu-

[35] Book x of the old compilation of the Fueros is the most important statutory document for the Liberties of Aragon; for, after proscribing the Privileges of Union in Fuero 1, Peter IV went on, in the host of succeeding edicts of 1348 and following years which make up the rest of Book x, to grant new rights and guarantee almost all the rights which had been embodied in the General Privileges of 1283; see, e.g., below, pp. 187 *et sqq.* The 1348 legislation is well summarized in Marichalar and Manrique, *Historia del derecho,* v, 108-29. Aragonese historians have long argued over the significance of Peter IV's acts. Liberals such as Manuel Lasala (cf. his *Constitución Aragonesa,* II, 164ff) argued that Peter IV destroyed the liberties by his edict *De prohibita unione,* while others (e.g., Danvila y Collado, *Libertades,* pp. 273ff and Fuente, *Estudios,* III, 129ff) view this edict as the necessary step to destroy reactionary oligarchic elements, and as the prelude to the true development of liberty in Aragon represented by Book x of the Fueros.

[36] Zurita, *Anales,* Primera parte, Lib. IV, xciv (ed. 1562, I, 225-26). Zurita does not repeat the details of the Privileges of Union in his *Indices,* published in 1578 (see below, pp. 134-36). In the following account of the history of the manuscripts of the Privileges of Union, I rely chiefly upon Danvila y Collado, *Libertades,* pp. 194-255, who derived much from Marichalar and Manrique, *Historia del derecho,* v, 32-33 (cf. below, n. 41); some things mentioned in the introductory chapter above will be reiterated, viz., the role of the Privileges of Union in the context of the 19th-century political debate over the Liberties of Aragon.

script copy of the Privileges, which he gave to his friend Gerónimo Blancas who later succeeded him as royal historiographer. Blancas himself reports this in the autograph of his *Commentarii*:

Some time ago our friend Zurita presented us with a copy of these documents which today are so scarce. In our opinion, and in that of many others, they well deserve the honor of publication. For as among the stages of life old age has a good reputation [here follow a dozen lines crossed out] so also in remote events, the knowledge of the ancient privileges, especially of those buried in oblivion, not by the work of distant centuries, but obliterated from our monuments by law, remained completely erased from the memory of our colleagues. Here, then, to the letter is the text of these famous privileges. . . .[37]

Blancas then set down an exact transcription of both Privileges, thereby clearly violating the law. But between the writing of his manuscript and the publication of the *Commentarii*, Blancas had a change of heart. He decided to suppress the Privileges; he also dropped the paragraph just quoted, in which he implicated Zurita in the transmission of the documents to him. Instead, he said that he had seen a copy of the documents "today exceedingly rare" among the papers of the Archbishop of Zaragoza. Blancas would have liked to give the full text, "but willingly I obey the public law by which it has been made a crime to do this."[38]

[37] This English translation has had to be made from the Spanish translation of the Latin autograph of Blancas' *Commentarii* which Hernandez executed in 1878. It is unfortunate that Hernandez did not also provide the original Latin text of the suppressed passages. The manuscript used by Hernandez in 1878 was in the possession of D. Marcial Lorbés; Hernandez says (p. 164, n. 1) that this particular suppressed passage is located on fol. 158, line 5ᵃ of the manuscript. More of this passage is quoted below, pp. 143-44.

[38] Hernandez' edition does not tell us exactly what passages in the printed *Commentarii* replace the suppressed passages (see previous note), but the following sentences (ed. Schott, III, 662) counterdistinguish themselves quite clearly from the suppressed sentences: "*Eorum exempla, quae vix ulla reperiuntur, in praefati Excellentiss. Archiepiscopi monumentis annotata inveni. Atque illa ego libenter adiunxissem huic meae propositae narrationi. Continent enim, quam*

He probably transferred the copy which Zurita had given him to the archives of the Archbishop of Zaragoza, so that he was not prevaricating when he said that he had seen a copy of them there; in the meantime, however, the transcription which he himself had made in the manuscript of the *Commentarii* constituted a second copy of the Privileges.

In succeeding centuries, some scholars must have seen one of these two known copies of the Privileges, but the prohibition against publishing them remained a law of the land.[39] In the late 17th century, the Marqués de Risco, Juan Luis Lopez de Tarba, recorded them in an antiquarian work on Aragon, *Aragoniae Gentis, et Regni Vinditiae*, drawing upon the manuscript of Zurita; but this work was so rare that a Spanish historian of the 19th century, Fuente, could not procure a copy of the book and had recourse to a handwritten transcription of it provided by a friend. And even at that, the most radical part of the Privileges was probably not included.[40] In 1849, several scholars fi-

---

initio expressimus, Fori illius Suprarbiensis seriem, ac de Iustitiae Aragonum potestate non pauca. Expresse enim cavebatur: ¶ Ne contra Iustitiae Aragonum interdictionem, quam nos Iurisfirmam vocamus, Regem in quosuis animadvertere liceret. Quod si fieret, dabatur nostris libera illa, quae fuerat in Suprarbiensi Foro, optio delata. Sed libentius publicae legi parebo, qua id facere nefas est decretum: mihique ab ea re omnino temperabo, ne illa videar nunc velle me inducere, quorum memoriam, cum vestigio exempli, maiores nostri sapientissime quidem non ex patrio more, atque institutis solum, sed ex privatis etiam literarum monumentis delendam, uno omnium consensu, legeque publica ea de relata, decreverunt."

[39] See below, p. 183, where I attach considerable importance to the renewal of *De prohibita unione* in the revision of the Fueros of Aragon made in 1551. I have the impression that some Spanish authors even today are less than candid about the Privileges of Union. For instance, the very influential *Manual de historia de España* by Pedro Aguado Bleye, when summarizing the Privileges of Union in the text, says nothing about the royal disclaimer (but mentions only the promises about the Justice and the Cortes), and when quoting the résumé of the Privileges from Zurita's *Anales* (above, n. 36) emasculates the force of the disclaimer by employing ellipses; cf. 8th ed. (Madrid, 1959), II, 743, 899, n.

[40] Fuente, *Estudios*, III, 118-19, relates this story and then quotes the Marqués de Risco's remarks (copied for him from the *Aragoniae Gentis* by his friend, D. José Duaso). I offer them here again, since

nally started publishing the Privileges, using either Zurita's copy, which had found its way into the library of the Academy of History, or Blancas' manuscript version of his *Commentarii.*[41] The publication was motivated in part by Quinto's monograph of 1848: Aragonese patriots wished to demonstrate against Quinto that there was some basis for the idea of the *Si no, no* Oath. In the following decades the argument over Aragonese liberties waxed warm, as was shown in the introductory chapter. The suppression

---

they show how the suppression was fully in effect in the 17th century: "*. . . Cum igitur illorum temporum invidia ob quam ex Regni Regestis aboleri ea privilegia iussa sunt, vetitumque ea retinere, jam contabuerit, maximeque pro Regis et Regni retinenda maiestate intersit, ut quae tunc abolita fuerunt nunc respiciantur, operae pretium duxi ea Privilegia ex M. S., antiquis insignis Hieronimi Zuritae resarcire, et Historiae Regni restituere.*" From Latassa[2], II, 163-66 (*s.n.* Lopez y Martinez), we find that the *Aragoniae Gentis* was written after 1694 (when the author acquired the dignity of Marqués de Risco which is mentioned in the long title of the work) and was published in the year of his death (1732) by his son, Juan Luis Lopez Mesia (*ibid.,* II, 167; *s.n.* Lopez Mesia). The text of the First Privilege which Fuente (*Estudios,* III, 119-23) reproduces from the *Aragoniae Gentis* shows itself to be a transcription of the modern-day Academia de la Historia MS M. 139, fol. 101ᵛ *et sqq.* (cf. the text of the latter given by Danvila y Collado, *Libertades,* pp. 234-39); but this transcription is deficient in a most glaring fashion, for it omits the famous line: "*Antes sines algun blasmo de fe e de layaldat podades façer y fagades otro Rey é seynnor cual querredes e don querredes.*" Besides the Academy of History MS, the other extant mediaeval copy of the Privileges of Union is found in Barcelona, Archivo de la Corona de Aragón, Reg. 75, fol. 43ʳ⁻ᵛ and 45ᵛ-46, transcriptions of which are given by Borafull y Sartorio, *CDIACA,* XXXVIII (Barcelona, 1870), 369-73, and in Näf, "Privilegien," pp. 33-44.

[41] Although Danvila y Collado did not know of the 18th-century publication of the First Privilege of Union by the Marqués de Risco, we may still agree with him—having observed that Risco's rendition is very faulty—that the first full publication of the First Privilege of Union was by Manuel Lasala (*Diario de Zaragoza,* 1849), who then gave the text to Marichalar and Manrique for their monumental *Historia del derecho* (9 vols., Madrid, 1861-1872). They in turn published it along with the Second Privilege (known before then only by extracts from Gerónimo Borao, *Diccionario de voces Aragonesas* [Zaragoza, 1859], pp. 55-56—who gives, however, all of the First Privilege, pp. 52-55) in vol. v (1868). These are the "firsts" as recorded by Danvila y Collado, *Libertades,* pp. 194f, 254f, who also gives other, less important renditions of the 1850's and 1860's.

of the Privileges of Union over the centuries was interpreted by some ardent liberals as evidence of a vast conspiracy that had worked against knowledge of the Aragonese heritage, and, by implication, against self-expression in the Spanish empire.

If the text of the Privileges of Union was scarcely known in Renaissance times, we can infer that the same held true in the later Middle Ages. Blancas believed that he had the only surviving copy; he was not far wrong, for only two mediaeval copies of it are known today.[42] We can well imagine the curiosity about the contents of the document, if for no other reason than to learn what had occasioned the wrathful decree of Peter IV. Its provisions must have been an object of enquiry for every Aragonese interested in public affairs. Jurists, in particular, must have felt some mortification if they could not comment intelligently upon *De prohibita unione* because they did not know what had been prohibited. And ultimately, those whose office it was to enforce the law must have been in a quandary over how to prosecute violations of *De prohibita unione* if they did not themselves possess an authentic copy of the Privileges of Union with which to compare any seized document purported to be the Privileges. All these conditions combined to foster the growth of an acceptable common opinion about

[42] The present-day Academia de la Historia MS 139, fols. 101ff, is the one possessed by Zurita, known to Blancas, and then printed in the mid-19th century. This is perhaps the best place to clear up a confusing reference to the "*Fueros de la Union*" which is found in the *Letra intimada* of Cerdan. When giving short sketches of his predecessors in the office of Justice, Cerdan says about Galacin de Tarba: "*E aqueste traslatò partida de los Fueros de la union, de romanz en latin, segund parece por tenor de aquellos, creo que fue poco tiempo Iusticia*" (pre-1551 eds., fol. L^v). Blancas (ed. Schott, III, 811) devotes much space to Galacin de Tarba, who was president of the Cortes of Zaragoza in the famous assembly of 1348 that passed much of the liberal legislation which compensated for the ruthless *De prohibita unione*. Blancas quotes five edicts which were adopted (all of them later part of Book x of the Fueros of Aragon), implying that they were the work of Galacin de Tarba. These, therefore, may be the "translation of the *Fueros de la Union* into Latin" to which Cerdan refers; that is to say, they are a salvaging and reissuing of some privileges granted during the period of the Union, not to be confused with the Privileges of Union of 1287.

these documents of which the law forbade exact knowledge. This explains the true nature of the gloss of Antich de Bages on the words "*juxta foros antiquos.*"

We may review the whole situation in this manner. Martin Daux, in his *Observantiae* of 1437, saw the Justice of Aragon as a powerful intermediary between the king and the nobles. Antich de Bages, glossing this *Observantiae* in the 1450's, strove to explain specifically the *fori antiqui* to which Daux alluded. Martin Sagarra had narrated the origin of the Justice, and his story had been adapted by someone glossing the Fuero which prohibited the Privileges of Union. Exactly what Sagarra or the glossator said is unknown, and so we cannot be sure for what portion of the myth they are responsible. However, since (according to Antich) the title of Sagarra's writing on the subject was the "Origin of the Liberties," we suspect that Sagarra did connect the origin of the Justice with the origin of the kingdom. We will assume this to be true, and therefore declare Martin Sagarra to be the oldest known source of the most important element in the legend of Sobrarbe, False Fueros v and vi.

When did Martin Sagarra live? Specifically, when did he write—before 1348 or afterwards? If before 1348, then his "Origin of the Liberties" had not been written with reference to *De prohibita unione*, but was found by later jurists to be pertinent to that edict because it explained the powers of the Justice which were embodied in the prohibited Privileges of Union. Traditionally, the *floruit* of Sagarra is said to be the 1270's, a notion propagated by Blancas because Blancas believed that Sagarra had been Justice of Aragon but found no gap in the *Fasti* of the Justices wherein to place Sagarra after the 1270's.[43] But it is very doubtful that Sagarra was a Justice[44]; and if he was not,

---

[43] The sources for this have been given above, n. 12.

[44] The only passage which refers to Sagarra as a Justice of Aragon is the oft-cited place in Antich de Bages (above, n. 20). In none of the other "old" sources where his name is mentioned is this found, viz., Antich's two references to him in the "Sagarra Story" passage (below, Appendix iv); in Molino's *Repertorium, s.v.* "Contributio" (ed. 1533, fol. 75ᵛ); and in *ibid., s.v.* "Probatio" (*ed. cit.*, fol. 265ᵛ).

then the weight of the circumstantial evidence about his writings locates him in the last half of the 14th century.

The references to Martin Sagarra which Antich de Bages makes in his gloss on *juxta foros antiquos*, if taken literally, indicate that Sagarra lived after 1348. After mentioning Peter's denunciation of the Privileges of Union in 1348, Antich says: "and to this place, it is said, there followed and still does follow the restraint *de facto* of the *firmas de derecho* and *manifestación*, as it is seen in our time and it is said in the observance of said lord Martinus de Sagarra. . . ."[45] In other words, the powers of the Justice were altered as a result of the abolishment of the Privileges of Union. And, Antich says in concluding this paragraph, "[in the observance of said lord Martinus de Sagarra] which has been introduced through the gloss of said Book x, Fuero 1, of the

---

Blancas, in his sketch of Sagarra (*Commentarii*, ed. Schott, III, 799), deceives us greatly by quoting the last-named place from Molino in this fashion: ". . . *quaedam Observantia Domini Martini Saguarra, Iustitiae Aragonum*"; Molino himself says ". . . *domini martini de Saguarra iu. ara.*" Nowhere does Molino abbreviate *Justicia Aragonum* by "*iu. ara.*"; always he abbreviates it as "*iusti. arag.*" Therefore, *iu. ara.* stands for *iudex aragonum*, an office entirely separate from the *Justicia Aragonum*. We may refer to an edict of 1348 by Peter IV, entitled "Quod dominus rex teneatur duos milites," which begins "*Cum secundum forum antiquum Aragonum unius iudex aragonum qui forum Aragonum sciat continue curiam domini regis sequi debeat*," and then provides that the *curia regis* shall be henceforth expanded to include two knights, ". . . *necnon et duos iurisperitos, qui sciant foros, privilegia, libertates, usus, et consuetudines dicti regni*" (*Fori Aragonum*, Book x; pre-1551 eds., fol. LIX). We see from this that there was always one *iudex aragonum*, and that after 1348—when we believe Sagarra lived—there were others learned in the laws who were part of the *curia regis* and who probably also carried this title. If Sagarra was part of the bureau of the Justice of Aragon, he probably held only the title of Lieutenant Justice; Ximénez de Embún, *Orígenes*, p. 26, n. 3, terms him thusly and dates him in the late 14th century, but gives no reasons for doing so. Finally, Martin Sagarra could have been an official in the Catalan chancellery of the Crown of Aragon, if we can make any inference from the fact that Antoni Rubió y Lluch, *Documents per l'historia de la cultura catalana mig-eval* (Barcelona, 1908-1921), records a Berengarius Sagarra and a Bartomeu de Sagarra in Barcelona in the late 1300's, the former a *scriptor regis* (II, 148, 267 [*an.* 1363 and 1383]) and the latter a student of law (I, cviii [*an.* 1370]).

[45] See above, p. 83.

Fueros, as carefully by the letter as by the intent of the law, where the most important things are related which are the liberties of this realm."[46] Grammatically, the "most important things" may refer to Sagarra or to the gloss, or to both of them. The soundest conclusion seems to be that everything concerning the Justice which is found in the gloss, and related here by Antich de Bages, is to be found in the disquisition by Martin Sagarra upon the "Origin of the Liberties." Therefore it was composed, and Sagarra flourished, sometime after 1348.

If Martin Sagarra lived after 1348, and his commentaries upon the Liberties of Aragon were composed with an eye upon the edict *De prohibita unione*, then the elements of False Fueros v and vi found in the Sagarra Story must be related to the provisions of the first Privilege of Union. These False Fueros are, so to speak, generalized versions of the provisions of the First Privilege of Union, applied to the founding of the kingdom. Just how this came about cannot be determined from the information currently available. But I do not subscribe to the school that is content to call it a conspiracy against royal authority or an effort of the Justices to glorify their office by aggrandizing its ancestry.[47] Even if the Justices, and other jurists, had known the exact provisions of the Privileges of Union, they still would not have believed that the drastic statements about the office of the Justice and the right to depose the king were "invented" in 1287: such fundamental notions must have long been the custom in Aragon. If Alfonso III bound himself and his successors to specific legal procedures, and submitted himself and his successors to the sanction of deposition, then these principles must have been inherent in the constitution of the country from the first. These were not recorded rights until perhaps the 13th century; and none of the early juristic writers claimed that the power of the Justice or the right to depose the king were fueros—but they must have been understood as common law from the outset.

[46] *Ibid.*
[47] Cf., e.g., Francis D. Swift, *The Life and Times of James the First . . . of Aragon* (Oxford, 1894), p. 155, n. 1.

Great issues must have great beginnings. The Fuero of Navarre had adopted a prologue by the 14th century which spoke of the conditions that prevailed at the founding of the nation. It is not at all implausible, therefore, that Aragonese jurists should magnify the story of the Justice and the right to depose the king. They were kept ignorant of the exact truth by the edict of Peter IV; upon that ruler, therefore, more than upon anyone else, should fall the blame for the Sagarra Story.

The only part of the Sagarra Story which is pure invention is the phrase, "*etiam paganum.*" It had already struck 16th-century writers as repulsive and unacceptable (as we shall see later on[48]), and has naturally been the special target of those modern scholars who believe the Sagarra Story is pure invention. In order to support my contention that it grew out of misconceptions and romanticization of the Privileges of Union, some roots of the *etiam paganum* phrase should be found in the wording of those Privileges. Perhaps the phrase represents a twisted recollection, or explanation, of the words "*blasmo de fe*" that appear in the phrase which allows for the selection of another king.[49] But speculation is almost useless, and the answer may lie in some ludicrous misreading of Sagarra's little treatise, *Origo Libertatum*, which some day may be recovered.

I have resisted the temptation to fit the paleographical evidence of the lawyers and chroniclers into a coherent pattern of political motivation. It goes without saying that

[48] See below, Ch. v, nn. 15, 54, 90.

[49] See above, n. 31. The reader should be warned about a reference to "infidel or pagan king" which has been attributed to Bertran de Born (ca. 1190) and then affiliated with our legends about Aragonese liberties. Victor Balaguer, in his *Historia . . . de los Trovadores* (Madrid, 1878), i, 331, gives the following translation of lines 33-36 of Bertran de Born's poem "Pois lo gens terminis floritz": "*Por mi parte, prefiero un rey infiel ó pagano à aquél de quien hube de sufrir la traición el día mismo que le presté servicio.*" He repeated this translation in his *Instituciones y Reyes*, pp. 153-54, where he gives the impression that this is related to False Fuero vi. The original words of Bertran de Born, however, are as follows: "*pretz mais sa cort e son atur, / non fatz cella don fui trahitz / lo jorn qu'el fon per mi servitz*" (ed. H. Stimming, Halle, 1879).

the baronial element always strove to maintain its privileges, and the Justices of Aragon likewise; but of the trio of Sagarra, Cerdan, and Antich, only the middle one was clearly moved by prejudice. The first and the last of them could just as well have been fastidious scholarly jurists trying to clarify the law. What counts, in the final analysis, is not their motives in writing what they did, but the predispositions of those who read those writings later on.

Chapter V · The Sobrarbe Legend and the False Fueros: 1450-1588

$\mathcal{A}$ll that Gerónimo Blancas needed to compose his "False Fueros" of Sobrarbe in the late 16th century was extant more than a century earlier, in the Chronicle of Charles of Viana and the Sagarra Story. And Blancas knew both of these sources firsthand. Still, in the intervening century many others had concerned themselves with the origins of the Aragonese nation, and Blancas' peculiar synthesis can be fully understood only by reference to the "modern" treatment of the problem. If nothing else, these writers evidence how deeply the legend of Sobrarbe had been absorbed into popular historical notions by the time of Blancas; so that his thought was conditioned by an historiographical tradition from which his better antiquarian knowledge could never quite escape. More important for our study, we must prepare the ground for the consideration of the Aragonese Oath, which Blancas was the first Spaniard known to have recorded. The Oath is not found in later mediaeval writers, nor in Renaissance Spanish literature, yet we know that it was "in the air" in Spain during the 1560's.[1] When Blancas finally came to speak of it, he linked it with the apparatus of the Fueros of Sobrarbe, for it seemed to him that the Oath was a natural correlative of the Sobrarbe lore. In large part, I agree with him. Only in the environment of the Sobrarbe legend could the Oath have survived, no matter what its proper genesis may have been; therefore, the story of the growth of the legend before Blancas is most important. Blancas completes the

[1] This can be inferred from Giovanni Soranzo's account of the Oath; see above, pp. 19-20.

legend-making, and by his greater antiquarian abilities transcends the earlier authors.

The account of the period after 1500 must necessarily be incomplete. Although some printed works, post-incunabula but pre-Blancas, do exist, I was unable to obtain them; and many original Renaissance manuscripts dealing with Aragonese history, if extant, could not be located.[2] For all that, I am confident that the main line of development can be shown in works that are quite well-known, and which I shall treat *seriatim*, in four groups: Tomic and Vagad; Molino, Vasaeus, and Marineus; the *Nueva Compilación* and Beuter; Zurita, Garibay, and Blancas.

Tomic and Vagad

The chronicles of Pedro Tomic Cauller and Fabricio de Vagad were printed for the first time in the 1490's, and both enjoyed considerable reputation and authority for more than a century thereafter. Tomic's *Historias* had been written in the 1430's,[3] and a comparison of it with Vagad's

[2] One manuscript, contemporary with Blancas's, that might bear investigation is Madrid, Bib. Nac. MS 901 (cf. *Inventorio*, III, 19): "Martin Cleriguech de Cáncer, Opispo de Huesca. Discurso de las leyes, privilegios y libertades del Reyno de Aragón, en forma de questiones escholásticas." Cáncer died in 1593 (cf. Latassa², I, 339). Aguado Bleye, *Manual*, II, 9, cites several manuscript works of the 16th century dealing with the genealogy and history of Navarre which may contribute to the Sobrarbe legend. Also, many manuscripts are included in the list of source materials on the origin of Aragon given by Sánchez Alonso, *Fuentes*, Nos. 1695-1825, which is the best bibliographical aid for our problem. The titles of other, possibly relevant printed works not accessible to me are given below, n. 27.

[3] *Historias, e conquestes dels reys de Arago e Comtes de Barcelona* (Barcelona, 1495) is the title of the first printed edition (Sánchez Alonso, *Fuentes*, No. 1724), although it has a slightly different name in the manuscript form in which it circulated before this time, and different titles in printed editions of the 16th century and later (cf. Cirot, *Histoires d'Espagne*, p. 27, n. 3). Sánchez Alonso (*Historiografía*, I, 331) reports that the work was written in 1436, while Cirot (*ibid.*) notes a dedicatory letter dated 1438; but even the latter date is too soon after the composition of Cerdan's *Letra intimada* to have allowed this letter to influence Tomic. There is a Catalan chronicle which pretends to be written ca. 1400-1420 which, if it were authentic, would throw all that I am about to say concerning the legend of Sobrarbe and the False Fueros into a cocked hat. I refer to the *Libre de Feyts d'Armes de Catalunya* by "Bernat Boades,"

Corónica, composed over a half-century later, reveals in large measure the transition from mediaeval to Renaissance historiography.[4] In some ways, of course, Vagad is much more valuable, since he draws upon a larger body of source materials than Tomic; but in terms of the problem of the origin of the Aragonese nation, Vagad marks a step backwards in "scientific history." Faced with overlapping traditions about the earliest history of northern Spain, Vagad improvised a factual account of the founding of Aragon which he embellished with imagined speeches by the chief characters. But, deplorably casual with facts and verbose though Vagad may be, his work is grist for our mill, since he contributed significantly to the growth of the Sobrarbe legend.

First, however, a word about Tomic. His work draws chiefly upon earlier chronicles, and we find no influence of juristic writings such as the Sagarra Story in his account of the founding of the Aragonese nation. His genealogical recipe is essentially that of the Chronicle of San Juan de la

---

who is actually a 17th-century Catalan writer named Roig y Jalpi, according to the widely accepted demonstration by Giménez Soler; cf. Sánchez Alonso, *Fuentes,* No. 1865 (ed. 1952, I, 267), which gives the literature. The matter-of-fact way in which Boades speaks in his Book IX about the kingdom of Sobrarbe and the Fueros of Sobrarbe makes me certain that he knew Blancas' work; cf. the edition of Boades by Enric Bagué (Barcelona, 1930-1945), II, 6-17.

[4] *Corónica de . . . [los . . . reys . . . de Aragón]* (Zaragoza, 1499), is the title which Sánchez Alonso gives Vagad's work (*Fuentes,* No. 1712), and it seems from the Vatican copy of the work which is now readily available on microfilm (St. Louis University Microfilms, Series 17, Reel 9) that there is no proper title for it; see also Cirot, *Histoires d'Espagne,* p. 57, n. 1. By his classical allusions as well as his rhetorical flourishes, Vagad shows himself to have a humanist's disposition; but his verbosity—*"irrefrenada verbosidad"* Sánchez Alonso calls it (*Historiografía,* I, 385)—undoes what elegance he achieves. Vagad enjoyed the title *cronista mayor* given him by Ferdinand the Catholic, and the *diputados* of the realm commissioned the *Corónica* in 1495; but historiographers still prefer to call Zurita the first *Cronista del Reino de Aragón* because the Cortes awarded him that title in 1547; see Cirot, *Histoires d'Espagne,* p. 57. Cirot gives Vagad an important place in Spanish historiography exactly because of the "moral" view he adopts and the harangues he puts in the mouths of his actors in order to explain the whys and wherefores of great historical events (*ibid.,* pp. 56-61.)

Peña: Garci Ximenez the first king, Iñigo Arista the fifth. For the election of the latter, however, he also adopts elements of the story of Ximénez de Rada. For our purposes the importance of Tomic lies chiefly in the ingredients of Sobrarbe which he adds to the story. About the first king, Garci Ximenez, he says ". . . *se subiuga totes les muntanyes dessus dites de Subarbia e de Ribagorca, et daquelles muntanyes se intitula Rey*," thus suggesting that the original royal title was "King of the mountains of Sobrarbe and Ribagorza"; the second king, then, is referred to as Garcia Eniego *"de Navarra e de Subarbia e de Ribagorca,"* and after he died *"de Navarra e de Subarbia fou rey son fill, appellat Fortunyo."*[5] None of these "Sobrarbe symptoms" is found in the *Pinatense*. Finally (drawing, he says, upon Ximénez de Rada), Tomic has Iñigo Arista elected king by the *"Navarresos e Aragonesos."*[6] Neither Rada nor the *Pinatense* mentions Aragon in this connection, but the same formulation would be used twenty years later by Charles of Viana. I have already argued that Charles of Viana developed the "Navarrese and Aragonese" formula on his own, when interpreting the prologue to the Fuero of Navarre; I see no reason to change this.[7] But, if it was only coincidental that two authors of the 15th century, one of Navarre and one of Aragon, each spoke of the Navarrese and Aragonese together electing Iñigo Arista, this oddity would not be without significance in the 16th century because it allowed the two traditions to be fused quite easily by the synthetic historiography of the Renaissance.

The rather tentative, almost sly "Sobrarbizing" of Aragonese history by Tomic swelled to colossal proportions in the work of Vagad, so that all Aragonese history is subsumed under Sobrarbe history. There are undoubtedly intermediate steps in this process, between the 1430's and the 1490's—and one of them may well be the extinct work by Antich de Bages on the genealogy of the kings of Sobrarbe and Aragon[8]—but Vagad certainly completes the process.

---

[5] *Historias* (ed. Barcelona, 1886), pp. 37, 40.
[6] *Ibid.*, p. 40.   [7] See above, pp. 52ff.
[8] See above, Ch. IV, n. 14.

Vagad adopts the genealogy of Tomic—which henceforth is almost standard—but from the first he calls all kings "kings of Sobrarbe." Every chapter is devoted to one king, and every king is denoted by his Sobrarbe succession in the chapter heading: "*Garci Ximenez Rey Primero de Sobrarbe*," "*Garci Ynigo Rey segundo de Sobrarbe*," "*Don Inigo Arista Rey .V. de Sobrarbe*,"[9] and so forth, up to Don Ramiro I, who was the first king of Aragon. During the course of the chapter on Don Ramiro, the title "First King of Aragon" appears in the running head along with "Tenth King of Sobrarbe";[10] and for succeeding kings the chapter titles always give first the king's number in the Sobrarbe succession, followed by his number in the Aragonese and other successions (e.g., for Alfonso III: "*Del rey .XX. de Sobrarbe y .XI. de Aragon, y .III. de Valencia y Mallorcas y menorcas, y primer conquiscador dessa isla: don Alfonso el III, llamado don Alfonso el Franco*").[11] By making Sobrarbe the primary element in the style of later Aragonese kings—an unpardonable sin from the point of view of diplomatics—Vagad is allowed to break through the dynastic jumble of the early kings and attach Aragonese history directly to the election of Garci Ximenez. Thereby, what was at best just a place name in the 8th century had become a full-fledged legendary kingdom by the 15th century.

Later writers would not go as far as Vagad in "Sobrarbizing" Aragonese history; but by the same token never again

[9] *Corónica*, fols. i, x^v, xiiii; fols. viii^vff, defend the view that Sobrarbe is older than Navarre. The humanistic prejudice of Vagad shows itself very clearly in his devious analogy with the founding of Rome by Romulus and Remus.

[10] The running heads of the *Corónica* were perhaps not Vagad's doing, but the style they employ contributed to the "Sobrarbe" aspect of the book. For example, in treating Don Ramiro, the running head for the first pages of the chapter is "*Don Ramiro el Primero / Rey .X. de Sobrarbe*" (fols. xxvi^v-xxvii *et sqq*); but when the narrative in the course of this chapter comes to Ramiro's accession to the throne of Aragon, the running head changes to "*Don Ramiro primero .I. rey de Aragon / y .X. de Sobrarbe*" (fols. xxix^v-xxx). "*Rey de Sobrarbe*" is finally dropped from the running heads during the chapter on James I (fol. lxxxi), but it remains until the end of the book as the first item of chapter titles (as in the example identified by the next note).

[11] *Ibid.*, fol. cxvii.

could "Sobrarbe history" be easily divorced from Aragonese history. Normal procedure later on was to consider the early dynasties of Sobrarbe as forerunners of the Aragonese nation, and to drop the name of Sobrarbe when Don Ramiro became king. This still allowed the early history of Aragon to be invested with anything connected with Sobrarbe, and above all the elusive Fueros of Sobrarbe. This, then, is perhaps the greatest importance of Vagad's *Corónica*: by his simple genealogical trickery he set the stage for a tremendous expansion of the legend of Sobrarbe.

Vagad marks another important milestone in our story: he introduced into Aragonese historical writings the elements of False Fueros v and vi which had developed in juristic literature. We can easily see through Vagad's verbiage, and identify the traditions with which he was working. The story of the Justice of Aragon (False Fuero v) he had from Cerdan's *Letra intimada*. It will be remembered that Cerdan claimed that the Justice came into being along with the first king, but he did not name that king; Vagad's chronology called for Garci Ximenez to be the first king; *ergo*, the Justice must have been elected at the time of Garci Ximenez "to be as if a third party between the people of the kingdom and the king" (*como tercero entre los del reyno y su reys*).[12] The story of Theopompos, King of the Spartans, is the telltale trace of Cerdan in Vagad, although the tale is freely adapted. Where Cerdan has the Aragonese deliberating the question of how to limit the king and remembering the history of Sparta, Vagad has Garci Ximenez already elected and delivering an inaugural address in which Theopompos appears as a model ruler because he

---

[12] The vital passage (*ibid.*, fol. iii) reads: "*escogieron juntamente y de un golpe mismo, al magnanimo varon don Garci Ximenez, godo real, y de sangre de reyes godos venido, y al official que llamaron despues justicia de Aragon, para ser como tercero entre los del reyno y su rey, y entre el rey y los del reyno; non que el podiesse por si mismo regir, mas segun las leyes por el rey y el reyno ordenadas, que el poder fazer leyes en el rey y reyno quedo.*" Cánovas, *Estudios*, II, 485ff, devotes some pages to defending Vagad's account of the election of Garci Ximenez and Iñigo Arista against the criticism of Quinto (*Juramento*, pp. 107-15); but both Cánovas and Quinto were grinding political axes of their own day.

created Ephors, just as Garci Ximenez himself confirms
the election of the Justice of his land because it conforms
with right-ruling.[13]

The other main juristic element of the Sobrarbe legend,
that the king could be deposed and another elected in his
stead (False Fuero VI), must have come to Vagad through
a version of the Sagarra Story.[14] In the Sagarra Story, we
recall, the first king was Iñigo Arista, and both False Fueros
V and VI were linked with his accession. But Vagad's chronology called for Iñigo Arista to be the fifth king, and besides he had already "created" the Justice under Garci
Ximenez, and thus had accounted for False Fuero V. The
solution was really quite simple for a romanticizing historian of the ilk of Fabricio de Vagad: just before the accession of Iñigo Arista, he omits all mention of the Justice of
Aragon and has the assembled nobles decide that the new
king must "swear the privileges, fueros, and liberties of
the realm." Iñigo Arista is then given a flowery acceptance
speech (quite similar to Garci Ximenez's inaugural address) which concludes with the ruler-elect's offering the
people a chance to elect another person king "even a pagan,
if there is no Christian." The Aragonese do not accept this—
the idea of a pagan king is quite abhorrent, of course—and
so the whole *etiam paganum* notion is given the aspect of
a rhetorical gesture by the new king-designate to show how
deeply he feels his obligation to rule rightly.[15]

[13] The inaugural speech by Garci Ximenez runs from fols. iv to vii[v].
The Theopompos example occurs on fol. vii; Aristotle, Cicero, and
other classical authors, not to mention scriptural sources, are also
adduced in this painfully long-winded discourse. When Garci
Ximenez confirms the election of the Justice (fol. vii), he makes it
very clear that the Justice is not the maker of the law: ". . . *el fazer
de las leyes, al rey y reyno solamente pertenece.*" By "*reyno*" Vagad
seems to mean the Cortes, for in the same context he refers to the
power residing "*en el rey, y en los quatro braços del reyno*" (fol.
vii[r-v])—a fact we should note for later reference.

[14] By the end of the 15th century, besides Antich de Bages' version,
there was an "anonymous" rendition of the Sagarra Story given *in
extenso* by Molino in his *Repertorium* composed in 1507 (see below,
n. 22).

[15] *Corónica*, fols. xvi-xvii[v]. To make Iñigo Arista a king of
Sobrarbe, when all sources indicated that he was Count of Bigorra

When he treats Alfonso III and the Union, Vagad is similarly devious. Whatever "right of resistance" notions were involved on this occasion he makes out to be almost facetious. If Vagad knew the exact terms of the Privileges of Union, he does not show it; but the idea of deposing the king does appear. (This much was traditionally known to be the core of the Union.) In Vagad, the barons outnumber the king; they have grievances, but they are ill-advised. They bind themselves together against the king according to a certain "loyalty":

This certain loyalty is such that they could depose their king, and with his consent choose another king.

The king allowed this because he had obligated himself by his initial capitulation to them. The barons apparently regretted this, because they soon affirmed Alfonso as their ruler; and, as Vagad then says *ad nauseam*, it could not have been otherwise, for Aragon is the best-ruled nation there ever has been, etc., etc.[16]

Vagad apologizes at every stage for what seems to him to be elements of disharmony in Aragonese history. He sees the good will of all parties operating *au fond*. To this extent he does not contribute to the clash of interests and *quid pro quo* contracts between the king and barons in the Aragonese past which would be the basis for arguments of

---

before becoming King of Navarre, Vagad employed a fanciful etymological argument centering upon the territory of Ribagorza, a territory joined to the "kingdom of Sobrarbe" during the rule of the kings of the dynasty of Garci Ximenez: "*Ribagorça ya por algun tiempo (como atestiguan algunos) se llamo Riba de gurria, que es conforme de alguna manera con begorra*" (fol. xvi). The vital passage regarding the pagan king reads: "*Fue luego mucho contento el esclareçido rey don yñigo arista de les otorgar quanto pidian; y ahun por los mas animar, les otorgo poder y licencia de escoger nuevo rey, e ahun pagano, si cristiano falleçia, do caso que los el agraviasse o quebrantasse lo prometido; esto bien que lo el otorgasse, los aragoneses no lo recibiero, assi que escoger rey pagano en algun caso no lo tenian por bueno*" (fol. xvii).

[16] *Ibid.*, fols. cxviii^v-cxix, with the quotation from the latter page: "*Esta llamad llaltad esta, que podieron deponer a su rey, y el consintiendo, pudieron escoger otro rey.*"

resistance during the Renaissance. Still, Vagad does include in his history the gist of all the elements that contentious historiography would be based upon in the generations that followed.[17]

Molino, Marineus, and Vasaeus

The most important treatise on Aragonese law composed in the 16th century was Micer Miguel del Molino's *Repertorium fororum et observantiarum regni Aragonum*, which is as near to being an encyclopedia of Aragonese law as anything that has ever been written. Molino wrote this work (he tells us) in 1507, to provide lawyers with an alphabetical guide to the body of Aragonese jurisprudence—a companion, as it were, to the *Fori* and *Observantiae*.[18] Molino ranges widely through the corpus of unpublished *Observantiae* and legal records, just as Antich had done, giving us a wealth of information about Aragonese law of the late mediaeval period that cannot be found in any other place. Since the entries often take the form of essays, and

[17] The chief element missing from Vagad is the account of Charles of Viana. The omission seems to have been deliberate because of the consistent effort by Vagad to separate Sobrarbe's—i.e., Aragon's—history from Navarre's. There is no basis, as far as I know, for the statement of López de Haro, *Justicia mayor*, p. 582, that the Fuero of Navarre prologue was used to narrate the election of Garci Ximenez.

[18] *Repertorium fororum et observantiarum regni Aragonum, una pluribus cum determinationibus consilii iusticie aragonum practicis atque cautelis eisdem fideliter annexis* (Zaragoza, 1513, 1533 [from which I quote], and 1554—all identically paginated), also see Sánchez, *Bibliografía*, Nos. 51, 189, 357. The 1585 edition (*ibid.*, No. 638) has the same pagination, but contains marginal additions to bring it up to date with the *Nueva Compilación* of the Fueros of Aragon (see below, pp. 119ff). The 1589 edition was revised, and translated, by Bernardo de Monsoriu under the title *Suma de todos los fueros y observancias* (*ibid.*, No. 694); see above, Ch. IV, n. 12. The maintenance of identical pagination in the early editions of the *Repertorium* matches the practice of the *Fori et Observantiae* themselves. This was practical because Molino had cited the 1496 edition of the *Fori* by page references, and also, not coincidentally, because Molino was the editor of the 1517 and 1533 editions of the *Fori*. Thus Molino was chiefly responsible for the very impractical word-for-word, page-for-page tradition of publishing the Fueros which was a main complaint of the revisors of the *Fori* in 1551; see below, n. 35.

the author has a sense of the changing practices of Aragonese law, the *Repertorium* often comes close to being an historical treatise.

By the time that Molino's *Repertorium* was published, the *Letra intimada* of Cerdan had already been printed in conjunction with early editions of the Fueros, and, through the chronicle of Vagad, Cerdan's notions about the creation of the Justice had entered into the chronicle tradition about the origin of the kingdom. Molino, in the opening words of his essay on the Justice of Aragon, refers the reader to these two sources for an account of the origin of the office of Justice, and also to a third source, another essay by Molino himself, incorporated into the *Repertorium* under the heading "*Libertates Regni.*"[19] This third source, it turns out, is a version of the Sagarra Story. Molino names no author, but he claims to be giving a verbatim account as he found it "in old writings of the Aragonese." It would be very tempting to assert that Molino was quoting the *Observantiae* of Sagarra itself, which would mean that we have a version of the story as good as, if not better than, the one provided by Antich de Bages' paraphrase. That Molino did know the *Observantiae* of Sagarra is certain, since he alleges it specifically in at least one place,[20] but this fact makes it all the more difficult to argue that he drew the Justice story directly from the *Observantiae*: for why, then, would he have said vaguely "old writings of the Aragonese" instead of identifying the precise source? Molino, it should be recalled, was a jurist, characteristically precise in identifying his sources.

The essay on "Liberties of the Realm" is quite long: it runs to ten folio columns and is divided into three parts. The first part, proceeding directly from the rubric without a subtitle, gives a general definition of the liberties of the realm. The last part lists many specific liberties, under the

---

[19] *Repertorium*, ed. 1533, fol. CC, *s.v. Justicia Aragonum*: "*Justiciae aragonum officium qualiter a quibus, et quando fuit inventum et de creatione et origine huius officii: vide in littera intimatoria Joannis Ximini Cerdan . . . et vide etiam in cronica aragonum; et vide infra in verbo libertates regni, versu libertatum aragonensium origo etc.*"

[20] See above, Ch. IV, n. 44.

subtitle *"De libertatibus regni et aragonensium, in quibus consistant."* The middle part, which interests us, concerns the vicissitudes of "liberties" during the history of the kingdom, involving chiefly the status of the Justice; we could call it the "historical" aspect of the problem.[21] A proper subtitle for this section would have been *"Origo libertatum,"* but instead we find the curious subtitle: *"In antiquis aragonensium scripturis, sequens capitulum reperitur."* The only sensible explanation for the use of this uninformative subtitle is that Molino wanted to make it very clear that what followed was not his own invention, but something extracted—presumably verbatim—from some other writer or writers. Here, then, is how the text begins:

In Old Writings of the Aragonese, the Following Chapter is Found. The origin of the liberties of the Aragonese in the first conquest; from ancient writers I have learned that the Aragonese, out of their ranks of equals and comrades in arms, elected as their king Iñigo Arista, or else, according to the chronicle of Aragon, he was called Garci Ximenez, who was of Gothic origin. And at the same election, or on the same day, they elected one of themselves as Justice of Aragon, who would be a judge between the king and his subjects regarding all those things which the king should do or demand against them, or vice-versa. And they made the power of the king conditional upon this: that unless he and his successors ruled according to the existing and future fueros, that they could elect for themselves a king, even a pagan. And by this he conceded to the Aragonese the privilege which on the last occasion of the Union was renounced and canceled after debate had been held, for otherwise the Aragonese were unwilling.[22]

---

[21] The section on *"Libertates Regni"* is one of the longer of the 474 entries in the *Repertorium*, running from fols. ccvii^r to ccx^r, with the middle essay, quoted in part in the next note, on fols. ccvii^v-ccviii^v.

[22] *Repertorium, s.v. "Libertates Regni"* (ed. 1533, fol. ccvii^v), subsection *"In antiquis aragonensium scripturis, sequens capitulum reperitur"*: *"Libertatum aragonensium origo in prima conquesta antiquis didici. Quod aragonenses de seipsis paribus et sociis in armis peditibus elegerunt in regem suum enecum de ariesta, alias secundum cronicam aragonum vocabatur don Garci Ximenez* [fol. ccviii^r] *qui*

The use of the first person singular, in the opening sentence of a text entitled "A Chapter Found in Old Writings of the Aragonese" seems to denote a direct quotation from some earlier author—whom we, knowing that the substance of the passage that follows is the Sagarra Story, could well assume was Sagarra himself speaking. But careful reflection upon what is said in that first sentence proves that the "I" is Molino himself; in other words, although he prepares the reader for a direct quotation from some older source, he immediately reverts to indirect relation in the first person of what older sources contain.

The clue is the reference to Garci Ximenez who, "*secundum cronicam aragonum*," is said to be the king under whom the Liberties of Aragon originated, as opposed to other sources that claim it was Iñigo Arista. This *Chronica Aragonum* could easily be assumed today to refer to the *Crónica de San Juan de la Peña* (the *Pinatense*), which in modern times at least has acquired the title of the *Crónica de Aragón*.[23] The *Pinatense* was written in the mid-14th century, so that Martin Sagarra could well have quoted it. But the reference is not to the *Pinatense*. The second sentence of Molino's text makes it clear why this must be so. The problem posed is: under which king, Iñigo Arista or Garci Ximenez, was the office of Justice founded? The *Pinatense* says nothing about the creation of the Justice. But another "Chronicle of Aragon" states that the Justice

---

fuit de genere gotorum. Et in eadem electione sive die elegerunt unum de seipsis in iusticiam aragoniae, qui esset iudex inter regem et subditos suos super omnibus hiis que rex faceret vel peteret contra eos, vel econtra. Et condicionarunt potestatem regis quod nisi ipse et sui successores regerent iuxta foros datos et dandos quod possent sibi eligere regem etiam paganum, et de hoc concessit privilegium aragonensibus quod tempore unitatis [leg. fortasse: *unionis*] *ultime renunciatum extitit et cancellatum prehabito tractatu alias nolebant aragonenses renunciare.*" Blancas, *Commentarii* (ed. Schott, III, 721), quotes this entire passage, and as much again of the continuation of it, from Molino. The later parts of it go into an explication of the powers of the Justice according to the Fueros of Aragon, and are clearly the work of Molino himself or some other author of the later 15th century, not part of the "*scripturae antiquae*" which he began this section by quoting.

[23] See above, Ch. III, n. 35.

of Aragon was created at the same time that Garci Ximenez was elected: Fabricio de Vagad's *Corónica de Aragón*
of 1499. This indeed is the only source we know that ties
the creation of the Justice in with the election of Garci
Ximenez; all others relate the Justice to Iñigo Arista's election. It is the very precision with which Molino's narrative
specifies the "Chronicle of Aragon" as the source for the
simultaneous election of the Justice and of King Garci
Ximenez that identifies that chronicle as Vagad's.[24] We
should note at this point, however, that Molino prefers the
Sagarra Story tradition, i.e., Iñigo Arista as the king under
whom the Justice was created. This is an important fact,
since the Sagarra Story had not been printed before, and
in the meanwhile Vagad had recast the events. Had Molino
preferred Vagad's account, and had the relationship between the election of Iñigo Arista and the election of the
Justice remained as an obscure manuscript account, then
those who followed Molino would not as easily have connected the Sagarra Story (Justice *cum* Iñigo Arista) with
the Charles of Viana story (Navarrese-Aragonese "fueros"
cum Iñigo Arista), and the growth of the whole Sobrarbe
myth might have been stunted.

Having established that the Molino version of the Sagarra Story is not verbatim, as it might seem to be, we must
conclude that we are no nearer to the original of that story
than we were with Antich de Bages' *Glossa* rendition of it.
Both renditions are at least potentially of equal validity,
so that we may assume in advance that the differences between them can lead to very limited conclusions. One thing
is obvious, however: the Molino presentation has much
cleaner lines than the Antich versions (for which I have been
forced to use corrupt manuscripts). For example, the statement in Molino's version that the election of the Justice
took place on the same day as the election of the king (*in*

[24] For Vagad's account, see above, n. 12. That Molino refers to
Vagad's *Corónica de Aragón* is also borne out by the other passage,
quoted above, n. 19, which gives the *cronica aragonum* as a source
for the origin of the Justice. This cannot be the *Pinatense*, which
does not mention the origin of the Justice; it must be Vagad, who
wrote the first "Chronicle of Aragon" to mention this subject.

eadem electione sive die elegerunt . . .) makes the thorny phrase in Antich *"sic fecit tunc in continenti"* much more explicit[25]; and the statement in Molino that the king's power was "conditioned" (*et conditionarunt potestatem regis*) by the fact that he must uphold the fueros "now given and to be given in the future" is much clearer than the complicated construction in Antich *"quod ille rex serveret ipsi et suis successoribus in perpetuum foros dandos."*[26]

I have given the text of and analyzed only the first three sentences of Molino's long subsection *"In antiquis aragonensium scripturis, sequens capitulum reperitur."* After mentioning the revocation of the Privilege, Molino goes on to discuss in considerable detail the changing position of the Justice vis-à-vis the king, and he guesses better than Antich had done what privileges Peter IV had abolished. Molino did not have a copy of the Privileges of Union, or surely he would have given the date and precise wording of the power of the Justice which both Privileges mention; but he had scraped together considerable information out of the *"antiqui foriste,"* as he repeatedly calls his sources. It is clear that among those old legal writings there was considerable difference of opinion as to the jurisdiction of the Justice of Aragon. If Molino had identified and dated his sources, we might be able to relate the arguments to the tempestuous history of the Justice of Aragon in the late 14th and 15th centuries—a story quite well-known to modern scholarship. As it is, we only derive the general impression from Molino's essay—but it is quite appropriate to our problem—that the Justice had had vaster powers under the Union than he enjoyed after its prohibition. This notion,

[25] Molino may here have been influenced by the *"golpo mismo"* notion of Vagad—see above, n. 12. It should be made clear that while Molino's version of the Sagarra Story differs sufficiently from Antich's to indicate a separate derivation, Molino was acquainted with the writings of Antich; see above, Ch. IV, n. 14, *ad finem.*

[26] The verb *conditionare* is rare. Indeed, Charles Du Cange (*Glossarium mediae et infimae latinitatis*, ed. Frankfort, 1710, p. 1271) cites as the only example of its use the very passage of Molino with which we are dealing. For some inexplicable reason, Du Cange chose not to explain the meaning of this passage in Latin, but to translate it into French: *"Id est,* Ils bornerent le pouvoir du Roy."

which is essentially incorrect, now became rooted in Aragonese juridical and historical thought.

To trace the growth of the Sobrarbe myth and the False Fueros during the three generations of writers from Molino to Blancas is potentially much easier to do than to trace it in the earlier period. Almost all the elements of the story existed by the early 1500's; and much of it was in print, and therefore readily accessible to the learned world. This learned world grew increasingly large during the 16th century, of course, and historical studies, both scholarly and popular, enjoyed an extraordinary vogue. Not all the treatises relevant to our subject written during this period were printed, however, and some of those that were are now very rare; but I do not think that the main lines of our story will be blurred by this inability to present the full bibliography.[27] The stages in the growth of the Sobrarbe myth are clearly reflected in the writers I do know.

[27] Ximénez de Embún, *Orígenes*, p. 29, gives a list of the 16th-century writers who adopted the *Pinatense* genealogy, beginning with Garci Ximenez, and applied it to Navarre-Sobrarbe. But Ximénez de Embún does not say whether these authors adopted Charles of Viana's version of events at the time of Iñigo Arista (fifth king according to the *Pinatense*); nor does he tell us whether they claimed that the history they were setting forth should be taken as part of Aragonese history proper. I cannot, therefore, tell where these authors fit into our story, unless I happen to have been able to consult them. They are: Marineus (see next note); Beuter (below, n. 41); Pedro Miguel Carbonell (presumably his *Chroniques de Espanya* [Barcelona, 1546]—Sánchez Alonso, *Fuentes*, No. 1726); Sancho Albear (unknown to me); Francisco Tarafa (*De origine, ac rebus gestis Regum Hispaniae liber* [Antwerp, 1553], also in Schott, I, 518ff—cf. pp. 548-549, where Garci Ximenez and his successors are called kings of Sobrarbe, but no mention is made of the Justice, of fueros adopted, or of any issue vital for our legend); Fr. Alonso de Venero (unknown to me); Martin Viciana (presumably his *Chronica de . . . Valencia*, 4 vols. [Valencia, 1564(?)-1566]—see Sánchez Alonso, *Fuentes*, No. 1989); D. Fernando de Aragon, Archbishop of Zaragoza, d. 1575 (probably his *Historia de los Serenisimos Reyes de Aragon*, 2 vols., MSS, listed in Latassa[2], I, 122); Juan Vaseo (below, n. 29); Fr. Gonzalo de Illescas (presumably his *Historia Pontifical y Católica* [Salamanca, 1594]—Sánchez Alonso, *Historiografía*, II, 85); and Ambrosio de Morales (*La Coronica general de España* [Alcalá, 1574-1586], 3 vols.). In addition to these, the early 17th-century antiquarian, Juan Briz Martinez, who was himself one of the great proponents of the kingdom of Sobrarbe (see his *Historia*

As has been suggested, the introduction of the Fuero of Navarre—Charles of Viana element into Aragonese historical legend is the crucial step to watch for in the years after Vagad and Molino. We might consider first, however, the writings of two men who, though they had nothing substantial to add to Vagad and Molino, gave considerable publicity and authority to the version which the latter had propagated. These two authors, Lucius Marineus Siculus (Lucio Marineo Sículo) and Johannes Vasaeus (Juan Vaseo), both happened to have been born outside of Spain, but each devoted himself to the study of the history of his adopted country. Together they represent fully the impact of humanistic style upon Spanish historiography. Marineus, an Italian by birth, came to Spain in 1484 and spent the last fifty years of his life there. In 1509 he composed a brief treatise, *De primis Aragonie regibus*, which became very widely known after 1530, when he incorporated it into his compendious *Opus de rebus Hispaniae memorabilibus*.[28] Vasaeus, a Fleming by birth, came to Spain in the 1530's, and his great work, *Rerum Hispanicarum Chronicon*, was published in 1552.[29] Vasaeus, even more than Marineus, adhered to the canons of Italian humanist historiography which had been laid down by Flavio Biondo in the 15th century, and were widely copied elsewhere—in England and France, especially—in the early 16th

---

de la fundación y antiguedades de San Juan de la Peña y de los Reyes de Sobrarbe, Aragón y Navarra [Zaragoza, 1620], pp. 26-125), lists in one place (*ibid.*, p. 27) seven sources which "*confiessan la antiguedad deste Reyno.*" I have considered three of them (Tomic, Vagad, and Beuter); another three I have not been able to identify (Aclot, Catalanes, and the Coronista de los Reyes Catolicos); the last of them, of which I am also ignorant, sounds the most intriguing: "*y en particular en una historia antiquissima manuscrita, que vio en el Real y famoso archivo de Barcelona.*" Other manuscripts perhaps relevant to our problem are cited above, n. 2.

[28] Sánchez Alonso, *Historiografía*, I, 375-77, implies that the work on Aragon was written in Castilian and published in 1523; but this is only a translation of the Latin work of 1509; see Sánchez, *Bibliografía*, I, 54-58, No. 28. Cirot, *Histoires d'Espagne*, pp. 76-89, gives a good analysis of Marineus' life and works.

[29] Sánchez Alonso, *Historiografía*, II, 19-22; Cirot, *Histoires d'Espagne*, pp. 158-68.

century. The art of history quickened more than the craft of history under the pens of this school, so that notions that were not *prima facie* unreasonable were seldom questioned.

By putting the brief accounts of Marineus and Vasaeus alongside one another, we can readily see how the latter followed the former and how both drew upon Vagad and Molino:

Marineus	*Vasaeus*
Ennucus Arista . . . princeps à Navarris et Aragonibus eligitur, propositis tamen nonullis conditionibus, ut in eos aequis legibus uteretur, à quibus etiam iudex qui medius inter eos esset, petebatur, et Aragoniae Iustitia vocatur. His concessis conditionibus, cogitans quibus signis et armis uteretur, ei divinitus revelatum est, ut ubi in aere crucem videret, illic consisteret.[30]	*Ennucus Arista populari suffragio electus rex, unctus et coronatus, primusque rex Navarrae, sed certis conditionibus, appellatur nimirum ut in eos aequis legibus uteretur, atque ut iudex esset medius inter regem et populum, si quid controversiae oriretur, isque Aragoniae Iustitia appellaretur.*[31]

In Marineus' account, the final sentence, in which divine grace is imparted to Iñigo Arista by the sign of the cross in the sky, shows the influence of Vagad's *Corónica*[32]; but the *iudex medius* phrase and several less apparent parallels reflect Molino's *Repertorium*. Vasaeus' version could have been drawn totally from Marineus', except for his "*iudex . . . medius inter regem et populum*," which is closer to Molino's phraseology than to Marineus'.

Indicative of the persistently inchoate conception of the earliest days of Aragon's history is the contrariness of nomenclature between Marineus and Vasaeus. Marineus lists the early rulers as dukes of Navarre, with a parallel dynasty

---

[30] *De rebus Hispaniae memorabilibus opus*, lib. viii; ed. Schott, I, 364.

[31] *Chronicon, sub anno* 839; ed. Schott, I, 710.

[32] Cf. Vagad, *Corónica*, fol. xvii.

of the counts of Aragon (Sobrarbe being cited only once—and as a place name, not as a political entity) until Iñigo Arista is elected *"princeps"* by the Navarrese and Aragonese jointly; the fifth ruler after him, Ramiro I, becomes the first king of Aragon.[33] With Vasaeus, however, Sobrarbe occupies a much more prominent position. The first four rulers, Garci Ximenez and his descendants, are each entitled "king of the Sobrarbeans in Navarre" (*Suprabrorum in Navarra rex*); Aragon is not mentioned at all until the *Iustitia Aragoniae* is elected simultaneously with the "first king of Navarre," Iñigo Arista. We are not told why Iñigo Arista is called king "of Navarre" instead of "Sobrarbeans in Navarre" as his predecessors had been.[34] Our humanist authors suavely gloss over the problem, but native Aragonese scholars for generations—even centuries—thereafter would feud bitterly about it.

The Nueva Compilación and Beuter

In the year 1551, the two mainstreams of the myth of Sobrarbe were at last brought together by two different and independent works. One of them is a prologue to the *Nueva Compilación* of the Fueros of Aragon which had just been revised. This prologue is valuable not because, as might be guessed, it records the Sagarra Story (there is not even a mention of the Justice) but because it adopts the "Fueros of Sobrarbe" as a familiar phrase to describe the country's early law, and thus links current law to Navarrese law in terms of mythical antecedents. The other work that appeared in 1551 was Pedro Beuter's *Corónica general de toda España* where, for the first time that I know, Charles of Viana's version of Navarre's foundation is made into the history of Aragon and, therewith, the apparatus of Book ɪ, Chapter 1, Title 1 of the Fuero of Navarre becomes (and is exactly so entitled by Beuter) the Fuero of Aragon. It would be difficult to say which of these two works of the year 1551 caused more mischief in later Aragonese historiography.

[33] *De rebus Hispaniae*, lib. viii; ed. Schott, ɪ, 363-66.
[34] *Chronicon, sub annis* 758, 815, 839; ed. Schott, ɪ, 704, 707, 710.

We have already made several observations about the problems that the corpus of Aragonese law faced over the centuries. The original 13th-century compilation, ordered by James I, was divided into eight books, shaped along rational topical lines. Succeeding kings added new books, recording new legislation as it was promulgated without heed to the subject. In the glosses and *observantiae* of the 14th- and 15th-century jurists, cross references were made between the original code and later legislation on like subjects, which helped lawyers to find their way through the growing bulk of disorganized law. The *observantiae*, being supplementary to the Fueros and unofficial in their nature, could be revised regularly; Martin Daux's famous revision of the 1430's is the best example. But the revision of the Fueros themselves could not be accomplished except with the cooperation of the Cortes. The confusion became greater, naturally, as legislation became more prolific. The legislation of John II and Ferdinand the Catholic, the last two pre-Habsburg kings, was as great in bulk as the body of Aragonese law to which it was appended. At the same time, of course, more and more of the earlier Fueros became archaic. By the 16th century an anomalous and very troublesome situation had come to pass: the very early books of Aragonese law were well-organized but had become largely obsolete, while the later Aragonese law, vaster in quantity and more vital in content, was totally without topical organization.

With the accession of the Habsburg line and the unification of Spain, the need to reform Aragonese law could no longer be ignored. The Cortes of 1533 started the process, and the Cortes of 1542 appointed a commission of twenty-one jurists to revise the law. This commission self-consciously adopted the form of Justinian's *Code*, selecting the minimal number of edicts which would embrace the needs of the law and arranging them in nine books whose topics paralleled as much as was feasible Books I-IX of the Code of the *Corpus Juris Civilis*. The project was completed in 1551, and in that year there was printed the *Nueva Compilación* (the name usually applied to the new redaction in order to distinguish it from the original compilation).

The prologue to the *Nueva Compilación* recounts at some length the history of the travails of the Fueros of Aragon from James I to Philip II, as if the members of the commission were trying to justify their task.[35] But they do more than this: they also tell us about Aragonese law *before* James I; they tell us the story from the very beginning, from the times of the Arab conquest. Without being precise about dates or names of rulers, the authors still give a rational explanation of how laws first came into being in Aragon. The content of no single law is given, but the name of the first code—the "Fueros of Sobrarbe"—is mentioned several times:

At the time that the infidel African Arabs came into Spain, the country was ruled by Gothic kings and governed by Gothic laws, for the Roman law had been abolished and forgotten. After the Christians had been expelled from Spain and the country occupied by the Moors, the land submitted to the Mohammedan sect until the time that the Christians—who meanwhile withdrew to the northeastern part of Spain, in rough and rugged places such as dense woods, caves and the like—having recovered their spirit and prowess, with the aid of God took arms and entered into the mountains of Ainsa, in the part of it called Sobrarbe; there they had many clashes with the Moors and captured the castles, towns and villages of that region which had been in the hands of the infidels, and, taking command in these places, returned them to the holy Catholic faith; and they did this by their own sheer power, without the aid of any Prince, or other person who was descended from the royal line of Goths, who could have claimed the right of succes-

[35] Ed. Parral y Cristobal, II, 6-8; this account stresses the disorganization of the Fueros much as have I in the preceding paragraph. Another complaint of the commission was the practice of page-for-page identicalness of the printed editions of the *Fori* which Miguel de Molino had instituted in order to standardize legal references. Obviously, the grouping of laws into Books and the numbering of laws within each Book was a much more practical device from the printer's point of view.

sion in Spain (as did Don Pelayo, Duke of Cantabria, of the royal line, who retired into the Asturias, round about Oviedo, from whence he began to conquer Spain proper as legitimate successor and natural lord of it); wherefore the Aragonese *conquistadores* made laws with which the land and provinces won by them and freed from the perfidious sect of Mohamet were governed; and they instituted the Fueros of Sobrarbe, so that in Aragon there were laws before kings; and they lived under these laws at that time as well as later when they did elect a king from among themselves, always adding to them other laws which seemed fitting to the king and the people of the kingdom. And for a long time the Navarrese also used this Fuero under the name of the Fueros of Sobrarbe, accepting them as just, honest and reasonable.[36]

[36] *"En el tiempo que los Arabes infieles Africanos entraron en España, era dominada por Reyes Godos: y governada con Góticas leyes las Romanas abolidas y del todo olvidadas. Despues que los Christianos fueron de España espelidos, por los Moros ocupada, la enseñorearon y sometieron a la secta Mahometana, hasta en tanto que los Christianos que se recogieron a la citerior España en los Montes Pirineos, en partes asperas y fragosas, en espesuras y cuevas, y otros lugares secretos, recobrando animo y esfuerço, con el ayuda de Dios tomaron armas y descendieron a las Montañas de Ainsa, a la parte que se dize Sobrarbe: donde huvieron muchos rencuentros con los Moros, y les ganaron los Castillos, Villas y Lugares, que en aquella partida estavan en poder de los infieles, y aquellas dominadas y reducidas a la santa Fe Catolica, con proprias fuerças, sin ayuda de Principe alguno, ni otra persona q[ue] descendiese de la linea Real de los Godos, que pudiesse pretender drecho de sucession a España (como lo fue don Pelayo Duque de Cantabria de la linea Real, que se retraxo en las Asturias de Oviedo, de donde començo a Conquistar la ulterior España, como sucessor legitimo y señor natural de aquella) los Aragoneses Conquistadores hizieron leyes, con que la tierra y Provincia por ellos ganada, dexada la perfida secta de Mahoma, fuesse governada, & instituyeron los Fueros de Sobrarbe. De manera que en Aragon primero huvo Leyes que Reyes: con las quales, aun despues de elegido de entre ellos Rey, vivieron, añadiendo siempre a aquellas las que al Rey y a los del Reyno parecian convenientes. Y de aquel Fuero usaron los Navarros so el mismo nombre de Fueros de Sobrarbe por muchos tiempos, como leyes justas, honestas, y razonables. Favoreciendo Dios á su pueblo, el poder de los Christianos prevalescio al de los Moros, y descendiendo de las Montañas de Sobrarbe a lo llano, aunque en diversos tiempos, y so diversos Reyes, ganaron muchas Ciudades, Villas, Fortalezas y Lugares, y assi tomaron titulos de Reyes de Aragon y las Leyes que hizieron de*

Then, in one breathtaking sentence that speaks of the gradual prevailing of Christians over Moors, the assumption by the kings of the mountain region of the title King of Aragon, and the natural change of title of the Fueros to the Fueros of Aragon, the authors bring the reader to the city of Huesca in 1247 and the compilation of law adopted by the Cortes in that year under James I.

Besides the one indirect reference to the Fuero of Navarre, there are other traces of its introductory parts in the text which prove that it was a major inspiration of this account of early Aragonese law; for example, the epigraph of the Fuero of Navarre speaks of the "remembrance of the Fueros of Sobrarbe" and the prologue to the Fuero of Navarre speaks of the assembly "in the mountains of Ainsa and Sobrarbe." Don Pelayo "of Gothic lineage," who is mentioned in the prologue to the Fuero of Navarre as the first king to be elected, also occurs in the *Nueva Compilación*, but now as an antitype of the first Aragonese king.[37]

Even the most celebrated passage of this text, the line "in Aragon there were laws before kings," has some roots in the prologue to the Fuero of Navarre. The latter, reporting the result of the embassy to the Pope, the Lombards, and the Franks, says that counsel was given to draw up laws before electing a king. Charles of Viana had altered this account

---

voluntad de los Aragoneses se dixeron Fueros de Aragon, aunque volumen ni libro dellas no tenemos, hasta que el invictissimo Rey de Aragon don Iayme el primero . . . ganó . . . en las Cortes . . . de Huesca el año 1247" (ed. Parral y Cristobal, II, 5-6). In the first edition this preface was apparently written also in Latin (Quinto, *Juramento*, p. 185, cites part of it in Latin); but in the later editions that I have been able to consult (1576, 1624), no Latin text is found. The practice of the *Nueva Compilación* is to give fueros originally in Latin in that language along with a Spanish translation, but not to give a Latin translation of fueros originally in Spanish.

[37] When the authors of the *Nueva Compilación* deny that their own first king was of Gothic lineage, they seem to reject Garci Ximenez as the first king (for, according to the tradition at least as old as Tomic [*Historias*, c. XII; ed. 1886, p. 36] and much stressed by Vagad [*Corónica*, fol. 2], Garci Ximenez was of Gothic descent), and they thereby accept Iñigo Arista implicitly as the first (no one says he was a Goth). This again shows a preference for the "Navarre" tradition, which always names Iñigo Arista as the first king.

to say that it was the "Navarrese and Aragonese gathered together in Sobrarbe" who had drawn up this Fuero.[38] Therefore, when the authors of the *Nueva Compilación* report that there were "laws before kings," they are reflecting more closely notions found in the Navarre-Viana tradition than they are the idea found in Cerdan's *Letra intimada*, that the Justice existed before the king.[39] If I am not mistaken, therefore, the slogan so famous in modern Aragonese legal history, "In Aragon there were laws before kings," is not an Aragonese juristic invention of the later Middle Ages, but a mid-16th century derivative of the Fuero of Navarre. We should not be surprised at this, of course: by the mid-16th century the myth that the first

[38] See above, Ch. III, n. 36.

[39] See above, Ch. IV, n. 9, for Cerdan. Among the claims that one encounters that the notion "laws before kings" existed before the mid-16th century, I find one worth citing. Lasala, *Constitución Aragonesa*, p. 151: "Antes de pasar á elejir Rey (*decia la Diputacion del Reino á uno de nuestros Monarchas*) quisieron los nuestros hacer leyes con que despues los gobernáran, y asi hicieran los que llamaron fueros, quedando por notorio aquel axioma, que en Aragon primero fueron las leyes que los Reyes." I suspect that this unidentified "quotation" is a paraphrase of the words of the preface to the *Nueva Compilación* of 1551. Lasala cites many witnesses to this concept, but the only two who lived before 1551 are Cerdan, whom we have just excluded, and Molino, whom we have not found to express the idea of "laws before kings" unless it is inferred from his rendition of the Sagarra Story (above, n. 22). Fuente, *Estudios*, II, 82-90 berates the idea of "laws before kings" in his usual extravagant fashion, contributing some color but no new substance to the historiography of this problem. One is tempted to relate this Aragonese saying to the Castilian maxim, "*Alla van leyes o quieren reyes*," which was widely known by the mid-13th century; see below, Ch. VI, n. 19. The Aragonese saying, however, refers to a definite historical event, whereas the Castilian maxim enunciates a timeless principle. On the other hand, I would be greatly swayed by any evidence which supported the idea that the Aragonese dictum came into being as a riposte to the Castilian one. More humdrum, but still a respectable hypothesis, is the possible influence of the *lex regia*. In Roman history, according to the theory of the *lex regia* (certainly known to Spanish jurists by the 13th century), the *Imperium* was conferred by the people, and, obviously, laws existed before the first emperor came to rule: "*cum lege regia . . . populus ei et in eum omne suum imperium et potestatem conferat*"; *Dig.* 1,4,1 (also in *Inst.* 1,2,6, where "*conferat*" is "*concessit*"). This refers, however, to a change in form of government, and not to the original foundation of the kingdom on which the Aragonese were always speculating.

kingdom of Aragon was called the kingdom of Sobrarbe was so engrained in Aragonese thought that the Sobrarbe strains in the history of Navarre and in the Fuero of Navarre could be appropriated with complete good faith.

We wonder, of course, why the *Nueva Compilación* does not speak of the content of any of the Fueros of Sobrarbe. It implies that the content is lost, except for what may have survived in the compilation of Huesca of 1247. We may even surmise that the authors of the *Nueva Compilación* believed that some of the Fueros of Sobrarbe were embodied in the Fuero of Navarre—they must have had something like this in mind when they report that the Fueros of Sobrarbe were used also in Navarre "for a long time . . . as just, honest and reasonable [laws]"[40]—but they may have hesitated (as Blancas and others did not) to say just which Sobrarbe laws had survived. In any event, their aim was to give a rapid summary of the general outline of Aragonese legal development, not to expound on particulars. The absence of details does not weaken the main point which the *Nueva Compilación* makes: that Aragon's first laws were called the Fueros of Sobrarbe. This alone gave a tremendous boost to the growth of legend, because it vouchsafes the existence of a "Constitution," as it were, for the kingdom of Sobrarbe. It would not be long before someone would identify specific Fueros of Sobrarbe. Indeed, this was being done by an historian in Valencia in the very same year that the Commission for Reform was drawing up the *Nueva Compilación* in Zaragoza.

Pedro Antonio Beuter's *Corónica* is a composite work. It started as a history of Valencia, the first part of which was

---

[40] Briz Martinez, *Historia*, p. 30, quotes this sentence verbatim as it is found in the preface of the *Nueva Compilación* (above, n. 36, near the end: "*Y de aquel fuero . . . honestas y razonables*"), alleging Morlanes (probably *Alegaciones* [Zaragoza, 1591]), who doubtless copied it from the *Nueva Compilación*. Briz Martinez goes on to say, however, that "*Lo mismo confiessa el Principe don Carlos en su historia de Navarra*," and he alleges lib. i, cap. ii. I do not find the reference at this juncture, nor at any other place in Charles of Viana's *Crónica*, unless the passages in Charles' Chapters v and vi, discussed above, Ch. iii, n. 36, can be understood in these terms.

published in Valencia in 1538, and the remainder in 1546. Together these form the *Prima parte de la corónica general de toda Espana.* The *Segunda parte etc.* was finished in 1550, according to the *explicit*, but the title page bears the date 1551. It is this second part which interests us.[41] It is important to stress that Beuter was a Valencian, and that in the second part of his chronicle he was trying to give a general history of the entire northern region of Spain. The breadth of his point of view helped him to see valid inter-relationships between separate national histories—especially those of Aragon and Navarre—but also led him at times to scramble those traditions into a woeful mess. In the case of the early history of Aragon, it is easy to see his mistake: he accepted Charles of Viana as the primary source of Aragonese history for the events around the accession of Iñigo Arista, and thus brought into Aragonese history a large body of lore that Charles had taken from the prefatory apparatus of the Fuero of Navarre.[42]

Beuter was very concerned to make the early history of Aragon quite distinct from the early history of Castile, yet parallel and analogous to it. For this reason, Garci Ximenez is posed as a contemporary and equal of Don Pelayo,

[41] See Cirot, *Histoires d'Espagne*, pp. 149-57, for a résumé of Beuter's work. The chronology of Beuter's writing shows that he was working on his version of early Aragonese history at the same time that the authors of the *Nueva Compilación* were composing their preface. There is no evidence that one knew of the other's work and, indeed, the superficial similarity of their respective "Navarrizings" of Aragonese history seems to be only coincidental when weighed against the differences between them.

[42] Cirot, *Histoires d'Espagne*, pp. 150f, notes that Beuter was a great plagiarizer. In the case of Charles of Viana, Beuter at least names his source, but the reader has little idea when Beuter is copying verbatim and when he is paraphrasing or even extrapolating from other sources. Ximénez de Embún, *Orígenes*, p. 125, notes that, besides Beuter, Pedro Luis Martinez utilized the account of Charles of Viana when narrating his history of Aragon. I assume that this refers to Martinez' *Anales de la Corona de Aragón con la suma de la vida de sus reyes*, Bib. Nac. MS 6742, still unpublished; see Sánchez Alonso, *Fuentes*, No. 1746 (ed. 1952, p. 254). Martinez probably wrote about the time of Blancas (cf. Ch. VII, n. 12, for a work by him written in 1591); so it would be interesting to know just how his use of Charles of Viana stands in relation to Blancas', especially in light of speculations such as the one made below, Ch. VI, n. 26.

though not as his rival. Don Pelayo, says Beuter, simply was not able to give assistance to the embattled Christians led momentarily by Alznar, Count of Aragon, and so the people of that region were forced to elect their own king. They chose Garci Ximenez, of Gothic lineage.[43] The word Sobrarbe does not appear, even as a region or a mountain range, until Garci Ximenez becomes king. Beuter adopts the popular etymology that Sobrarbe got its name from an apparition of a cross above a tree (*sobre árbol*) which Garci Ximenez then took as his device. Since Garci Ximenez did not want to appear as a contestant for the title King of Spain, which was commonly attributed to Don Pelayo, he took his kingly title from his cross-above-a-tree device and called himself King of Sobrarbe.[44] The story itself is trivial, but it served a particular purpose for Beuter. "Sobrarbe" becomes a purely artificial designation for the re-

[43] *Coronica general*, ii, 5 (ed. 1604: ii, 20-22).

[44] *Loc.cit.* (*ed. cit.*, ii, 22): "*Por este milagro fue llamada aquella tierra Sobrarbe, quasi encima de arbol, do se vio la cruz, y haziendo el Rey por armas en un escudo dorado un arbol verde con una cruz colorada, intitulose Rey de Sobrarbe, no queriendo entrar en quistiones con el Rey Pelayo, que se dezia de España por algunos, y Rey de Asturias por otros.*" Vagad had used the cross-above-the-tree device in a section of the shield used as a frontispiece for his *Corónica*; it is conveniently reproduced in Konrad Haebler, *Early Printers of Spain and Portugal* (London, 1897), frontispiece and pl. xviii, and was used for the dust jacket of this book. The small cross-above-the-tree device reproduced above on this page is from Blancas' *Commentarii* (as reproduced in Hernandez' edition), where it is presented as the shield of several early Kings of Sobrarbe.

gion of Aragon, so that whenever the reader encounters the name Sobrarbe, he should understand it to mean actually Aragon. So, Garci Ximenez was first of all king of Aragon, though he called himself king of Sobrarbe. During his lifetime, other names were added: Ribagorza by conquest, and also Pamplona after Navarre had transferred its allegiance to him from Don Pelayo. As Beuter recounts the first four kings, he shifts the title repeatedly: "Sobrarbe, Ribagorza, Pamplona"; "Navarre, Sobrarbe, Ribagorza"; and finally, with the last of Garci Ximenez's line, "Sobrarbe, Ribagorza, Aragon and Navarre."[45] Then came the interregnum, and here Beuter takes up the narrative of Charles of Viana.

We have seen how Charles explained that dissension among the leaderless mountain folk (in Beuter, the suddenly kingless kingdom) led them to send an embassy to Pope Hadrian II, the Lombards, and the Franks (no Franks in Beuter), upon whose advice "the Navarrese and Aragonese, gathered together in Sobrarbe, made their Fuero." Beuter relates this story almost verbatim, until he arrives at the sentences where Charles had ended his Chapter v and begun Chapter vi. These sentences Beuter changed in a very drastic fashion:[46]

Charles of Viana	*Pedro Beuter*
[. . . le tobiesen en poco.] E habido este consejo, los dichos navarros é aragoneses, juntados en Sobrarbe, ficieron sa fuero, el qual es del seguient tenor. Cap. 6º. Este el primer capitulo que los navarros é aragoneses, establescieron en sa Fuero general.	*[. . . le tuviessen en poco.] Por lo qual establecieron un fuero y ley general en el qual escrivieron el primer capitulo que es del seguiente tenor.*
Nos ricoshombres . . . etc.	*FUEROS DE ARAGON Nos los ricos hombres . . . etc.*

[45] *Coronica general,* ii, 5 (*ed. cit.* ii, 23-25).
[46] The text of Charles of Viana is given above, Ch. iii, n. 36; Beuter's text occurs in his *Coronica general,* ii, vi (*ed. cit.,* ii, 26). Beuter copied all of Charles' Chapter vi, including the ceremonial *alzar el rey.*

By this device Charles of Viana's persons (the Navarrese and Aragonese), place (Sobrarbe), and thing (*fuero general*) are transformed by Beuter into the momentarily king-less people of the kingdom of Aragon (remember: Sobrarbe is just an armorial synonym for Aragon), drawing up the Fueros of Aragon. The text that follows (*"Nos ricoshombres . . . etc."*) is identical; that is, all of Charles' Chapter VI (i.e., *FN* 1,1,1), which contains the substance of False Fueros I-IV, is presented by Beuter as the Fueros of Aragon.

Beuter did not end here, however; after he finishes transcribing Charles of Viana's Chapter VI, he goes on to give another fuero which he had found elsewhere and which he believed must also belong to the first code of Aragon:

They ordered also that they should have a judge intermediate between themselves and the king, so that it might be judged whether the king upheld the fueros; and they called him Justice of Aragon, before whom to bring their grievances; and they had many other fueros, concerning the good of the republic, as more fully appears in the said *fuero general.*[47]

Immediately after this, Beuter relates the accession of Iñigo Arista, reverting to the account of Charles of Viana. So, the sentence concerning the Justice of Aragon has been interpolated into the Charles of Viana narrative, although, as we have seen, Beuter's procedure overall is to interpolate Charles of Viana's account into traditional Aragonese historiography.

This is truly scissors-and-paste history. From Marineus, most likely, Beuter had the story of a single condition imposed at the time of Iñigo Arista's election;[48] from Charles

---

[47] Beuter, *Coronica general*, II, vi (*ed. cit.*, II, 27): *"Ordenaron tambien que huviesse un juez entremedias dellos con el Rey, para que juzgasse si el Rey mantenia los fueros, y llamaronle justicia de Aragon, ante quien pudiessen apelar de los agravios, y hizieron muchos otros fueros, a cerca el bien de la republica, como mas largamente parece por el dicho fuero general."* Danvila y Collado, *Poder Civil*, I, 290, notes that Beuter added a fifth Fuero to the basic four from the Navarre-Viana tradition, but he was not clear about its source.

[48] See above, n. 30. In 1524 Beuter had translated Marineus into Castilian as *Crónica Daragon*: see Felipe Mateu y Llopis, *Los his-*

of Viana he had a much more comprehensive story of fueros that were adopted. Charles of Viana evidently knew the most, but he did not know everything; so, after giving Charles of Viana's complete "Fuero," (i.e., False Fueros I-IV), Beuter supplements it with the Justice Fuero (i.e. False Fuero V) which he had encountered elsewhere. Beuter probably prided himself on being a much more thorough scholar than his predecessors by drawing together the fragmented remembrances of early Aragonese history.

We must still explain how Beuter can be excused the liberty of changing some crucial lines of Charles of Viana's text and making that narration appear as the Fueros of Aragon. This was certainly falsification; but the blame here must lie as much with Charles of Viana as with Beuter. Charles had not told his reader that what he offered as the *"fuero general"* was in fact a plagiarism of Book I, Title I, Chapter 1 of the Fuero of Navarre; and even more flagrantly he had announced that this Fuero was the work of "the Navarrese *and Aragonese* gathered together in Sobrarbe." Charles of Viana took the initial step in "Aragonizing" the Fuero of Navarre text.[49] Beuter's error was to conceive of "Sobrarbe" history as just another name for Aragonese history, and to subsume Navarrese history under it. Given these beliefs, it is understandable—if not excusable— that he should conclude that Charles of Viana's *"fuero general"* was in fact the earliest redaction of the Fueros of Aragon.

It is ironical that at the same time that Beuter wrote, the Aragonese authors of the prologue to the *Nueva Compilación* were also claiming that early laws used by the Navarrese should be thought of as the earliest laws of Aragon, but that the proper name for them was the Fueros of Sobrarbe. If we view this as a contradiction, contemporaries would have seen it as a chance oddity: the authors of the prologue had given the exact title, but not the substance; Beuter had given the substance under the wrong title.

---

toriadores de la corona de Aragón bajo los Austrias (Barcelona, 1944), p. 23.

[49] See above, pp. 55-57.

Zurita, Garibay, and Blancas

Gerónimo Zurita (1512-1580) was the greatest historian of Aragonese history during the 16th century, and perhaps of all ages. He is the first "official" royal historiographer (by act of the Cortes in 1548), the predecessor of his friend Blancas in that office. Zurita's massive *Anales de la Corona de Aragón,* organized, as its title implies, along chronological lines, has never been replaced as a narrative of Aragonese history.[50] This work, more than anything else, forced his successor, Blancas, to devote himself to antiquarian studies—in the good sense of the term—and write monographs on such subjects as the Justice and royal coronations.

It would be difficult to choose between Zurita and Blancas as scholars, since each was tremendously learned in narrative as well as archival sources of Aragonese history. The criticism usually leveled against Zurita is one rare in his age: that he was too cautious in his weighing of sources and shied away from resolving difficult problems.[51] Against Blancas the criticism is usually reversed: he was too anxious to resolve problems and thus saw more than the evidence offered. These criticisms are borne out in the treatment of the Sobrarbe legend: both Zurita and Blancas had almost all the evidence which we have today, but where Zurita treated it very cautiously, Blancas boldly melded it into the False Fueros of Sobrarbe.

Zurita's *Anales* is divided into two parts: the *Primera parte* (the part that concerns us) which was published first

[50] For a sympathetic discussion of the *Anales,* see G. Cirot, "Los 'Anales de la Corona de Aragón' de Jerónimo Zurita," *Bulletin hispanique,* XLI (1939), 126-41. Ample testimony to the monumental character of the *Anales* is given by the fact that the VII Congreso de Historia de la Corona de Aragon, held in Barcelona in 1962, was devoted to "Jerónimo Zurita y su obra" because it was the 400th anniversary of the first volume of the *Anales*; see *Hispania,* XXII (1962), 157-58 for a list of papers given at this Congress, and XXIII (1963), 153-59, for a review of the meeting itself.

[51] Cf. Sánchez Alonso, *Historiografía,* II, 32-36, for a brief critique of Zurita. The most extensive work on Zurita, it seems, remains Juan Uztarroz, *Progresos de la historia en el Reyno de Aragón, y elogios de Gerónimo Zurita* (Zaragoza, 1680; reprinted in part, Zaragoza, 1878).

in 1562, and the *Segunda parte* published in 1579. In the interim, in 1578, Zurita published in Latin a parallel work, *Indices rerum ab Aragoniae regibus gestarum ab initiis regni ad annum MCDX*, which must also engage our attention, since it presents the founding of the kingdom and the establishment of the Justice in a different fashion.[52]

The entire discussion, in four pages of the *Anales*, is entitled "*Dela election del rey Ynigo Arista.*" First of all, Zurita juxtaposes the opinion of the *Pinatense* (Garci Ximenez the first king) to that of Ximénez de Rada (Iñigo Arista the first) and then digresses with Charles of Viana's report of the concord which the Navarrese and Aragonese arrived at between themselves by adopting "*el fuero que dixeron de Sobrarbe.*" He gives a complete résumé of that fuero (Chapter VI of Charles of Viana), and then turns to the Justice of Aragon. "In this time, it is commonly accepted, the magistrature of the Justice of Aragon was introduced."[53] He cites first Cerdan and then alludes to "some authors" who speak of the origin of the Justice and the right of the people to depose a king and elect another, "*o fiel o pagano.*"[54] Zurita could not let this daring theory go by without comment: when the forces of the kingdom were not as strong as the authority of the laws, and the barons possessed the right to elect kings—as the Goths had done, in order to protect their liberty—the right to depose the king may have been possible; but when the kings became strong, the maintenance of peace brought an end to the

[52] The whole corpus of Zurita's writings is given in Latassa[2], III, 425-35, but the precise bibliographical information about the two works which concern us, the *Anales* and the *Indices*, is found in Sánchez, *Bibliografía*, II (see Index, *s.n.* Zurita). A history of the writing of the *Anales* is given in the very fine article by Ricardo del Arco, "Elaboración de los 'Anales' de Zurita. Un memorial inédito," *Hispania*, XVI (1956), 427-64.

[53] *Anales, Primera parte*, Lib. I, v (ed. 1562, I, fol. 7). Zurita also gives the Cerdan story when he comes to relate the legislation of the Cortes of 1348 which affirmed the Liberties of Aragon (cf. below, p. 187); *ibid.*, Lib. VIII, xxxii (ed. 1585, II, 229-30).

[54] *Ibid.*, Lib. I, v (ed. 1562, I, fol. 7ᵛ). It is a notable instance of the deceptiveness of Quinto, *Juramento*, p. 119, that he ends his long quotation from Zurita on the problem of the Justice just before Zurita speaks about the right to elect another king.

right of resistance theory. The proof of this lies in the Privilege of Union, says Zurita, which appears to be a latter-day expression of primitive right of resistance; it was abolished because it was repugnant to the general peace, and the protection of liberty was instead entrusted to the Justice of Aragon. Thus Zurita recounts the "Sagarra Story," which he probably had from Molino, with some gratuitous explanation of his own that makes the theory of resistance seem a primitive state of affairs.

In the last section of his chapter on Iñigo Arista's election, Zurita surveys quickly the argument about the armorial bearings of Navarre, Sobrarbe, and Aragon, which leads him to the prime question: "Which was the oldest kingdom, that of Sobrarbe (to whose domination the province of Aragon was subject) or Pamplona (which since has been called the kingdom of Navarre)?" When Zurita adduces "the introduction to the fuero and laws of Sobrarbe" as proof that the mountains of Sobrarbe were the locus of the election of the first king and that these same laws were also the first laws of Navarre, he reveals that he had in hand a copy of the Fuero of Navarre.[55]

From the foregoing résumé of Zurita's account of Iñigo Arista it is evident that all the important sources from both the Navarre-Viana and the Sagarra Story sides were known to him when he wrote the *Anales*. We have not done a great injustice to Zurita's account in recapitulating it so briefly, because the author himself relates the sources without trying to compromise differences. This bears out the criticism, mentioned earlier, that Zurita was not willing to be aggressively critical; but in this case his caution may have been a virtue, because the problem of early Navarre-Aragon history was far beyond the power of anyone in the 16th century to resolve. Zurita himself had not given his last word on the problem in 1562, however; in 1578 he told the story all over again in his *Indices*, composed in Latin; and the following year he reprinted the first part of his *Anales* with a few additional remarks. These additions to the *Anales* do not alter the substance of the earlier presentation; in fact

---

[55] *Anales, Primera parte*, Lib. i, v (ed. 1562, i, 7v-8).

they complicate the knowledge of it. Zurita himself, at the end of one of these additional remarks, concludes wearily: "*Tanta es la variedad en la confusion de los tiempos.*"[56]

The treatment of Iñigo Arista in the *Indices* is, however, worth some comment. The *Indices* are considerably shorter than the *Anales*, so that one should not expect the full rehearsal of conflicting sources; but one is not quite prepared for the ring of self-assuredness that prevails, and even less for the *volte-face* in respect to the touchy issue of the priority of Navarre or Aragon as the locus of the action. Zurita shows preference for Pamplona (i.e., Navarre) as the capital of Iñigo Arista's kingdom, although "our people think it was constituted in Sobrarbe." As for the Fueros of Sobrarbe, Zurita reports tersely that they were just the laws of rough and bellicose mountaineers and rustics which (an ancient writer claims) held sway also in Navarre.[57] But he gives no hint of their contents; so, the text of False Fueros I-IV is not given. Nor does he mention Iñigo Arista's offer to allow another king to be elected, "even a pagan"; so that the substance of False Fuero VI is also missing. On the other hand, Zurita devotes considerably more space to the creation of the Justice here than he had done in the *Anales*, relying chiefly upon the testimony of that most respected holder of the office, Cerdan. If Zurita was deluded about Cerdan's *Letra intimada* so as to think that it mentioned Iñigo Arista by name, he had the company of all the other historians of his age. He believed Cerdan's story about the Ephors of Sparta being the model upon which the founding fathers created the Justice, and he spends several sentences explaining how the avoidance of tyranny was a vital consideration even before there was a king.[58] Much later on in the *Indices*, when discussing

---

[56] *Ibid.* (ed. 1610, I, fol. 9).

[57] *Indices*, Lib. I, *sub an.* 845 (ed. Schott, III, 8): "*Nostri in Suprarbia terra Ainsae constitutum arbitrantur; ac leges tunc latas ferunt, quibus fori Suprarbii nomen inditum sit; quas rudibus hominum animis, & militaribus ingeniis, utpote bello vivere assuetis, montanis, atque agrestibus simplices, & militares fuisse apparet. His legibus & in Navarrae Regno, & Guipuscoae regione iura dici consuevisse vetustus scriptor refert.*"

[58] *Ibid.*

the Union, Zurita again eulogizes the Justice in very similar terms as quasi-Ephor (and also, now, quasi-Tribune). On this occasion he does not even bother to mention Cerdan; but neither does he show reliance upon the Sagarra Story as the prompter of his thoughts.[59]

All these things are most curious, considering the Zurita of the *Anales* who was so circumspect in his arguments. It is as if Zurita decided in the *Indices* to say what he really believed, and what he felt was quite reasonable for anyone to believe. The lavish praise he gives to the Justice thus does make an easy bridge to the great treatise on the Justice by Blancas just a decade later; on the other hand, Zurita appears in the *Indices* to be less enthusiastic about the myth of Sobrarbe than he had been earlier in the *Anales*.

It is but a short step from Zurita to Blancas, but between the former's *Anales* and the latter's *Commentarii* came the important work of Esteban de Garibay y Zamalloa, *Compendio historial de España*, published in 1571.[60] In terms of historical accuracy Garibay marks a step forward, for he is very skeptical about the whole story of Iñigo Arista's election. For this reason he could have operated as a check upon the growth of the legend of Sobrarbe. Marineus,

[59] *Ibid.*, Lib. III, *sub an.* 1348 (ed. Schott, III, 199). In effect, Zurita repeats in this 1348 entry what he had said in the equivalent place in the *Anales* (*Primera parte*, Lib. VIII, xxxii [ed. 1585, II, fol. 229v]); but he does not give the contents of the Privileges of Union in the *Indices* (cf. Lib. II, *sub an.* 1288 [ed. Schott, III, 136]) as he had in the *Anales* under the year 1287 (see above, Ch. IV, n. 36). It should be stressed that discussing the Justice in the context of the abrogation of the Union does not imply that the power of the Justice was limited as a result of Peter IV's action; on the contrary, the Justice emerges as the alternative to the baronial Union as the defender of individual rights. That is to say, the "liberal" view of later days, that the abrogation of the Privileges of Union was an attack upon the office of the Justice (which had supposedly existed from time immemorial as the bulwark of freedom), is not Zurita's viewpoint. Zurita does not seem to have regarded the Privileges of Union as a later-day recording of the primordial power of the Justice, a view, held by Blancas, e.g., which was the major illusion behind the creation of False Fueros V-VI. See above, p. 115, for Molino's propagation of the "liberal" argument in the early 1500's.

[60] Sánchez Alonso, *Historiografía*, II, 23, considered this work the first complete history of Spain, but not a distinguished work.

Vasaeus, Beuter, and Zurita seem to have been Garibay's chief modern sources, and among them he found enough contradictions about the early dynasties of Navarre-Aragon to wonder whether there ever did occur an interregnum between the successors of Garci Ximenez and the accession of Iñigo Arista. In a brief chapter entitled "Concerning the first interregnum which authors say occurred in Navarre in this time, and the difficulties there are about it," Garibay gives a rapid summary of events: the embassy to the Franks, Lombards, and the Pope; the adoption of a fuero (he gives the gist of False Fueros I-IV); the decision to "have a judge, to whom the people could have recourse in order to preserve their fueros"; and the offer of Iñigo Arista, when elected, to allow the people to resist a law-breaking king and "freely to elect another king . . . not only a Christian prince, but even a pagan." The people felt revulsion at the notion of an infidel king because it was so inconsonant with religious principles; Garibay himself doubted the whole story.[61] He claims Zurita as an ally in skepticism, and apologizes to the reader for not being able to be more certain on this point. There is something commendable in Garibay's critical attitude, to be sure, but he had no devastating arguments to make and therefore had no appreciable effect in stemming the tide of the Sobrarbe legend.

The account of the origins of Aragon given by Gerónimo Blancas in his *Commentarii* is much more detailed than any previous known work. It is better documented not only within the narrative but also in separate quasi-bibliographical chapters which Blancas intersperses regularly. Blancas was a superior scholar in his time, and my accusation that he helped propagate the legend of Sobrarbe—especially by his Fueros of Sobrarbe, which we have been constrained

---

[61] *Compendio historial*, Lib. xxi, c. 14 (ed. 1628, iii, 27-28). The key passages quoted above read: " . . . *y que huviesse un juez, ante quien pudiessen hazer recurso, para la conservacion de sus fueros*" and ". . . *pudiessen libremente elegir otro Rey, sin caer por ello en ningun mal caso, y a tanto estienden este articulo, que les permitio, que la election pudiessen hazer, no solo de Principe Christiano, pero aun de infiel, pero que lo tocante a infiel no quisieron admitier, como cosa fea y mal sonante.*"

by utility to label always as "False"—is not intended to dismiss him as just a romancer; positivist historiography has done that often enough, and its effect is stultifying.

The title of Blancas' *magnum opus*, when finally published, was *Commentaries Upon Things Aragonese*; he had changed its name at least twice during the decade before its publication in 1588. There are indications that he hesitated to publish the work, and positive evidence that once during these ten years he had been stopped from publishing it. The manuscript of the *Commentarii*, which became known in the 19th century, contains many short pieces —letters, dedications, introductions—which were not published in the final work, and from these we can reconstruct the following story.[62]

[62] *Aragonensium rerum commentarii* (Zaragoza, 1588; reprinted in 1605 in Schott, III, 366-839) and *Comentarios de las cosas de Aragon* (trans. by P. Manuel Hernandez [Zaragoza, 1878]) are the titles of the original Latin and Spanish translations; but the first footnote in the latter edition (p. 14, n. 1) tells us that the autograph manuscript (fol. 13) has a different title and opening sentence. The title, according to Hernandez' translation (he does not give the original Latin phrasing), was "*Comentarios á los Fastos sobre los Justicias de Aragon, por el zaragozano Jerónimo Blancas*," and the opening sentence read: "*Antes de tocar el orígen de esta magistratura, principal objeto de nuestra obra, justo será que señalemos con la posible brevedad la forma, el principio, los incrementos del estado de Sobrarbe y del aragonés, y veamos cómo llegó este Reino á tan colosal grandeza. Delicioso es en sí mismo este conocimiento, y muy propio, además, para la explicacion de nuestro asunto.*" Blancas' autograph was known to Don Marcial Lorbés, a friend of Hernandez'; and the latter, by comparing it with the printed versions, was able to expose what notable omissions had taken place. Besides the suppressed Oath and Privileges of Union, the manuscript drafts of early dedications, brought to light by Hernandez, have been valuable to me in the present study. Still, one wishes that Hernandez had provided the original Latin of the suppressed parts along with his Spanish translations of them. The tradition that Blancas first composed the *Commentarii* in Spanish is based upon the considerable authority of Juan Francisco Andrés de Uztarroz, the early 17th-century editor of Blancas' works. In a memorial to Blancas, Uztarroz informs us that "*antes que le compusiera sus Comentarios en idioma latino, los escribió en lengua española, cuyo MS. original tiene el doctor D. Jaime Aznarez, catedrático de Cánones de la Universidad de Zaragoza*" (ed. Hernandez, pp. x-xi—the same text, I believe, that appears at the beginning of Uztarroz' edition of Blancas' *Coronaciones* [Zaragoza, 1641]). From the documents cited in the following pages, it is evident

By the year 1578 Blancas had drawn up a list, based on voluminous research, of the Justices of Aragon he could identify by name. He called this the "Registers [*Fasti*] of the Justices of Aragon," and informed his readers that he proposed to make some commentaries upon these registers.[63] If this original version of the *Fasti* was ever published separately, it was brief indeed, no more than one folio page, recto-verso.[64] Some time between 1578 and 1581 he wrote to Marcos Guillen del Sesmero, Archpriest of the Cathedral of Zaragoza, seeking authorization to publish the *Fasti*, "explained by some commentaries."[65] If permission was

that this early draft comprised only the very brief *Fasti*, with some *Comentarios* (see next two notes), hardly even comparable with the massive final work.

[63] In the brief letter to the reader preceding the original *Fasti*, he says ". . . *estos Fastos, que en breve plazo me propongo ilustrar con algunos Comentarios*" (*Comentarios*, ed. Hernandez, p. 486). I assume the date of this is 1578 because the *Fasti* itself (*ibid.*, p. 487) gives the dates 1554-1578 to the current Justice, Juan de Lanuza IV, although he held that office until 1591.

[64] *Comentarios*, ed. Hernandez, pp. 486-87. In the dedication to the *Commentarii* as finally published in 1588, Blancas asserts that he had earlier published the *Fasti*: "*In primis autem cum superioribus annis quosdam de Iustitiis Aragonum Fastos edidissem, singula tantum eorum nomina, nudamque annorum seriem complectentes; eos nunc decrevi plenioribus hisce Commentariis illustrandos, ut qui primum nudi, atque inornati propositi fuerant, . . . nunc quasi vestiti*" (ed. Schott, III, 569—cf. Hernandez, pp. 2-3); and some Aragonese bibliographies have listed a *Fastos de los Justicias de Aragón* by Blancas with the imprint Zaragoza, Simón de Portonariis, 1587. The prime authority on 16th-century Aragonese bibliography, Sánchez, *Bibliografía*, II, 368, No. 667, records this old bibliographical tradition, but displays no knowledge of an actual copy which would confirm it. It is possible that a mistake was made at some time involving the imprint of another of Blancas' works, his *Effigies* [*et*] *Inscriptiones*, which does have the city, publisher, and date given above; in any event, it is very unlikely that Blancas would have published in 1587 this trivial little piece, already finished in 1578 (see previous note), when we know that by 1584 he had expanded it into a great work (see next note).

[65] The *terminus ad quem* 1581 seems plausible because Blancas employs the simple title "*Jerónimo de Blancas, Zaragozano*" in this letter (cf. *Comentarios*, ed. Hernandez, p. 485) instead of "*Regni Historicus*" as he always did after succeeding Zurita as Royal Historiographer in 1581. The passage in question, in the Spanish translation of Hernandez, *ibid.*, reads: ". . . *te remito ahora, aclarados con*

given, Blancas did not carry out his design. By 1583 the manuscript had grown considerably—it was now called "Commentaries Upon the *Fasti* of the Justices of Aragon"— and Blancas gave it to the famous humanist scholar, Antonio Augustin, Archbishop of Tarragona, to read. Augustin was extremely enthusiastic and early in 1584 wrote Blancas a letter urging publication.[66] It was probably then that Blancas submitted his work to the Council of Aragon for approval and was turned down. The king himself, Philip II, overruled the Council's decision, granting permission to his royal historiographer (Blancas had received that office the year after the death of Zurita in 1580), provided certain changes were made.[67] When the work finally appeared in 1588, it was dedicated to the eight deputies of the kingdom of Aragon (earlier it had been dedicated to the current Justice of Aragon, Juan Lanuza IV, and at another time to Antonio Augustin).[68] In the preface Blancas

---

algunos Comentarios, los Fastos *sobre los Justicias de Aragon, que antés publiqué movido principalmente por tu autorizado testimonio.*" It seems that at this point the work was dedicated to the Justice of Aragon, Juan de Lanuza IV; for immediately following the list of the *Fasti*, there is a dedicatory letter to that dignitary.

[66] *Comentarios*, ed. Hernandez, pp. 471-75, dated Tarragona, February 1, 1584. The letter consists mostly of "Notices" which the learned Archbishop added to Blancas' treatise, and also some corrections of Blancas. I judge that the work was by then nearly its final size because of the reference to "*el gruesco volúmen de tus Comentarios*"; and that some hint of publication troubles is given by these words: "*De suerte, que yo pasaria plaza de ingrato para con ella* [*i.e., le dignidad y honra de la patria*], *si te retrajera de su publicacion.*" At this point, or perhaps just afterwards, Blancas dedicated the work to Augustin, for Hernandez gives a fragment of such a dedication (p. 491; cf. p. 7, n. 1). Augustin died in 1586, which would account for the ultimate dedication to the eight deputies of Aragon (see below, n. 68).

[67] See below, n. 70.

[68] A fragment of an early dedication to the deputies, dated simply "1 May," is given by Hernandez, pp. 492-96. The printed Dedication (ed. Schott, III, 568-71; ed. Hernandez, pp. 1-6) is dated September 1, 1588, and the "*Approbatio*" and "*Auctoritas Editionis*," given respectively by Diego de Monreal, Canon of Zaragoza, and Andrés de Bobadilla, Archbishop of Zaragoza, are dated May 13 and April 1 (ed. Schott, III, 567). The quondam dedications to Juan de Lanuza IV and Antonio Augustin are mentioned above, nn. 65-66.

tells the reader that he changed the title at the last minute from "Commentaries Upon the *Fasti* . . ." to "Commentaries Upon Things Aragonese" because the scope of the final work far exceeded the original composition.[69]

In this sequence of events, the episode that bears the most interest from a political point of view is the prohibition by the Council of Aragon, which was overridden by the king. The former found that Blancas' work was inclined to glorify too highly the office of the Justice, and the king's approval correspondingly called for the removal or emendation of things bearing upon the Justice.[70] As we have seen, Blancas did withdraw the two items which were most inflammatory, the Oath (which had not yet even been alluded to in any Spanish writing) and the Privileges of Union (which had never been published anywhere *in extenso*). Withal, and even adding the last-minute title change which disguised the concentration of the work upon the history of the Justice, the *Commentarii* was a very vigorous, and in some places even passionate, testimonial to the greatness of the Justice. What the book may have contributed to the 1591-1592 uprising in Aragon, which grew out of a test between the Justice's power of *manifestación* and the processes of royal justice against an escaped prisoner, we cannot be sure; but no document bore so many proofs of the quondam authority of the Justice as did Blancas' *Commentarii*.[71]

Aside from the book's immediate repercussions, the prob-

[69] "*Non possum non vehementer eorum consilium, ac factum approbare, qui censuerunt Opus hoc, minime,* Commentarios in Fastos de Iustitiis Aragonum, *quemadmodum initio constitueram, sed potius,* Aragonensium rerum Commentarios, *inscribendum; quod plura in se contineat, quam quae priori illi aeque subiici posse viderentur inscriptioni*" (ed. Schott, III, 569); cf. ed. Hernandez, p. 3.

[70] Lacarra, "Aragón en el Pasado," pp. 341-42; "*Cuando éste solicitó licencia del Consejo de Aragón para imprimir sus* Comentarios de las cosas de Aragón, *se le denegó 'por ir encaminado a levantar el magistrado del Justicia de Aragón.' Pero Felipe II, más conciliador y tolerante que sus consejeros, respondió que 'se vea si se puede quitar o enmendar lo que trataba del Justicia.'*"

[71] Cf. *ibid.*, p. 342, in which Lacarra observes that "*la obra de Blancas ofrecía un arsenal de doctrina*" on legalistic grounds for the resistance to Philip II. See further below, Ch. VII, n. 9.

lem of its long gestation as an intellectual creation deserves attention. The *Commentarii* should be viewed as two distinct treatises, almost equal in length. Each covers the whole span of Aragonese history, from its founding in the 8th century as the kingdom of Sobrarbe to Blancas' own day. The first treatise is organized in terms of the rulers of the kingdom, one chapter per king (with odd digressive chapters here and there), but in fact stresses justice and the Justice of Aragon wherever possible. The second treatise is devoted explicitly to the "Dignity of the Justice of Aragon," and the last portion of it—the original *Fasti*, plus a paragraph or more of text for each name—is organized in terms of one chapter per Justice. The transition from the first to the second treatise is marked by the abrupt remark: "Now, however, to deal with the principal matter" (*Nunc autem ad rem*)—as if everything that had gone before was prefatory.[72] Indeed, in the original draft of the opening sentence of the first treatise Blancas announces that his main object is to record the history of the Justice, but that he is starting out by giving an historical background:

Before touching upon the origin of this magistrature, the principal object of our work, it will be fitting for us to point out with all possible brevity the form, the beginning and the growth of the state of Sobrarbe and of the Aragonese, so that we may see how this kingdom arrived at such grand size. This knowledge is delightful in its own right, and moreover it is very appropriate for the explanation of our subject.

In the printed version, the "prefatory" tone was altered, and rightly so because the introductory treatise turned out to be lengthier than the essay on the Justice that followed.[73]

[72] The first treatise is found in Schott, III, 577-716, the second on pp. 716-833; ed. Hernandez, pp. 14-261 and 262-470 respectively. For the *Nunc autem ad rem*, see Schott, III, 716.

[73] Cf. the manuscript text quoted above (from the Spanish version by Hernandez, p. 14, n. 1) with the printed version: "*Aragonensem Historiam scripturus, copiose satis enim, cum vulgaribus, tum Latinis literis ab aliis illustratam, id mihi tantum proposui, praecipua ut illius Capita summatim perstringam, ea praesertim, quae ad explicandam Iustitiae Aragonum Magistratus vim, & dignitatem*

Some parts of the *Commentarii's* second treatise seem surely to have been written before any part of its first treatise: the chapter-per-Justice section with which it concludes, for example, is an expanded version of the original *Fasti*. A convenient thesis that would account for the most troublesome question of the relationship of the two treatises—that is, the exact duplication of arguments on some occasions, yet on other occasions the offering of disparate proofs for the same argument—would be that the second treatise as a whole was composed first. Without having the autograph of Blancas to work with, however, this would be difficult to establish.

The section of the *Commentarii* which commands most attention, of course, is the chapter on the Fuero of Sobrarbe, where the False Fueros are presented in the form reproduced in our frontispiece. It occurs early in the first treatise, along with a shorter chapter on the interregnum, between the expiration of the dynasty of four kings begun by Garci Ximenez and the inauguration of the new dynasty under Iñigo Arista. We have shown how Blancas derived False Fueros I-IV from Charles of Viana, to whom he refers as a source:

Only fragments [of the Fuero of Sobrarbe] are extant, having been preserved by Prince Charles and a few other writers, which have been gathered together by us in this place.[74]

This reference to "other writers" is all that Blancas chose to give at this time. He certainly knew the sources of the Sagarra Story, for elsewhere in the *Commentarii* he gives long quotations from Cerdan and from Bages' and Molino's

---

spectent. Cuius institutio cum ex ipsis Regni primordiis pendeat, Regnum vero, prius fuerit Suprarbiense dictum: ab Hispaniae clade scribendi initium ducere oportet, unde haec omnia fuerunt, tanquam a quibusdam seminibus, orta, & concreta" (ed. Schott, III, 577). In effect, what was intended to be a brief historical background to the treatise on the Justice ended up as a full treatise in its own right which happened to stress matters of law and justice, and particularly the office of Justice.

[74] The Latin original of this will be found in the long quotation above, Ch. III, n. 45.

versions of the Sagarra Story. (These occur in the opening section of the second treatise.[75]) If, as may be the case, he had written this treatise first, then we can understand his not repeating the full texts again. But some cross reference to the later quotations we have a right to expect.

It is possible, of course, but hardly probable, that Blancas composed False Fueros v and vi (as we find them in the chapter on the Fuero of Sobrarbe) out of secondary sources such as Beuter, and that he regarded Cerdan, Sagarra, Bages, and Molino as only corroborative, which would justify relegating them to another section of his work. In this case, Blancas would have been deceiving himself, and cannot be accused of concealing the evidence which moulded his ideas.

Another text which Blancas regarded as vital for False Fueros v and vi was the Privileges of Union. Yet he suppressed publication of the text, and also dropped from the published work the following observation made in the earlier text:

The principal impulse that has moved us to give them [the Privileges of Union] space in our work has been that we see in them the outline of the Fuero of Sobrarbe, which we have already dealt with. Even if the authority of our Justice had not yet reached its apogee [in 1287]—but, since the supreme power of the *ricoshombres* was in its vigor, the Aragonese believed that the Union was the best means to preserve liberty—we, however, can clearly see the primitive dignity of this magistrate in the Privileges of Union, since they sanction again the supreme power of his veto established by the Fuero of Sobrarbe. It says, expressly, that the

[75] Ed. Schott, iii, 720-22; cf. ed. Hernandez, pp. 268-71. That Blancas considered these to be primary sources for the original Fuero of Sobrarbe can be inferred from a remark which he makes in the preface to the *Commentarii*. He comments upon the injury which can be wrought upon historical knowledge by such compilations as Daux's *Observantiae*, citing Antich's lament (cf. the place cited above in Ch. iv, n. 17) about the loss of knowledge of venerable practices this had entailed; cf. ed. Schott, iii, 572; ed. Hernandez, p. 8. No specific examples are given by Blancas in this connection, but surely he had in mind, above all, the Sagarra Story, saved for us by Antich.

king cannot punish against the *firmas de derecho* and verdict of the Justice of Aragon, and in this rests the sum of our liberties. Certainly, we cannot understand why they are called by the name "Privileges of Union," seeing that they have little to do with it and very much—almost totally—with the ancient Fuero of Sobrarbe.[76]

Although the gist of the Privileges and the gist of the above quotation were inserted in the printed work,[77] the reader still could not easily see the relationship between False Fueros v and vi and the Privileges. Again, we have a right to expect that in the chapter on the Fuero of Sobrarbe at least a cross reference would be made to the Privileges of Union; but there is none. In sum, therefore, two of Blancas' most important testimonials to Fueros v and vi were not recorded in his grandiose presentation of those Fueros. The chapter on the Fuero of Sobrarbe became a *locus classicus* in the following centuries for the arguments among Spanish historians about the origins of Aragon; but basic evidence that helped shape this chapter is almost concealed in distant parts of the *Commentarii*—if, indeed, not suppressed before the printing of the volume.

If we disallow the hypothesis that Blancas was trying to obfuscate his arguments deliberately because he felt that they were too tenuous, we may with confidence advance this counter-hypothesis—namely, that he was so unthinkingly convinced of the efficacy of an original constitution for Sobrarbe-Aragon that he saw no reason to argue the matter *per se*, but rather treated it separately under different headings. So, in the chapter-per-king treatise, he

[76] From the Spanish rendition by Hernandez, p. 167n.

[77] Ed. Schott, iii, 662 (cf. ed. Hernandez, p. 168): "[*Illa duo memorabilia Unionis Privilegia*] *Continent enim, quam initio expressimus, Fori illius Suprarbiensis seriem, ac de Iustitiae Aragonum potestate non pauca. Expresse enim cavebatur: Ne contra Iustitiae Aragonum interdictionem, quam nos Iurisfirmam vocamus, Regem in quosvis animadvertere liceret. Quod si fieret, dabatur nostris libera illa, quae fuerat in Suprarbiensi Foro, optio delata.*" Blancas then gives his reason for not presenting the document in full, as discussed above, Ch. iv, n. 38. Blancas also links the Privileges of Union to the Fueros of Sobrarbe when discussing the office of the Justice of Aragon; cf. ed. Schott, iii, 724.

tries to give a full narrative rendition of the facts of Iñigo Arista's election, with a minimum of analysis; a good reason to do this lay in the indecisive—even skeptical—fashion in which his two immediate predecessors, Zurita and Garibay, had handled this episode.[78] Then later on, when concentrating upon the office of the Justice exclusively, he again treats the matter in (we might say) a fuller bibliographical fashion.

The temptation is great to assume that Blancas was convinced of the authenticity of an ancient Fuero of Sobrarbe because he had seen manuscripts bearing that title. While it is true that he had seen such manuscripts he was very skeptical about them. He found in them many laws which obviously were of later origin, and he found lacking in them certain laws which he was convinced belonged to the original compilation. "If you ask my opinion," he addressed the reader rhetorically, "it was not long ago that fragments of these laws fell into the hands of someone who thought himself expert in historical matters, who, trying to elucidate them, obscured them."[79] We do not know whether he is referring here to the Fueros of Tudela-Sobrarbe, to the Fuero of Navarre, or to some other collection containing the famous apparatus that give birth to False Fueros I-IV; but in any event we must allow his perspicacity in warning the reader about the contents of manuscripts which bear the label "Fuero of Sobrarbe." Contrariwise, of course, we must note the irony of Blancas' committing the selfsame error by his reconstruction of the ancient Fuero of Sobrarbe. Still, it is useful to know that Blancas' conception was quite independent of the "Sobrarbe" manuscripts which have received so much attention in recent times.

After bringing together Blancas' sources from their scattered locations throughout the *Commentarii*, we will not

[78] See above, pp. 133-36.
[79] Ed. Schott, III, 719; ed. Hernandez, p. 266. In the first edition of the *Commentarii* (1588) this passage occurs on p. 289, and in the copy of this edition in the Houghton Library of Harvard University, we find this marginal note in the hand of Prescott: "Whatever be the genuine antiquity of the Forum Sobrarbiense, it shows that ideas of national liberty were very ancient with the Aragonese."

be far amiss in assuming that the author was convinced of
the existence of the primitive Fuero of Sobrarbe by a chain
of reasoning something like this:

1. Cerdan tells us that the Justice was created at the time
   that the first king was elected, and Sagarra reports that
   this occurred at the election of Iñigo Arista; these two
   jurists preserved this precious story, which was transmitted through the centuries just as many customs and
   usages of the laws have been preserved for centuries before being recorded.
2. Charles of Viana reports that a "general fuero" was
   adopted at the time of the election of Iñigo Arista as king
   of Navarre, and he gives some provisions of it.
3. The chronicle tradition of our nation teaches us that the
   kingdom now called Aragon was originally called Sobrarbe, and that Iñigo Arista was one of its early kings.
4. The recent edition of the laws of our land reports in its
   prologue that the earliest code of our land was called the
   Fuero of Sobrarbe, which was also used by the Navarrese.
5. It is manifest, therefore, that the *fuero general* mentioned
   by Charles of Viana (and applied by him to Navarre),
   along with the laws reported by Cerdan and Sagarra, are
   vestiges of the same Fuero of Sobrarbe drawn up during
   the interregnum between the fourth and fifth kings of
   that nation.

A major enigma Blancas had to deal with was the great
gap—two and one-half centuries according to his calcula-
tions—between the establishment of the Justice under the
grand auspices of the Fuero of Sobrarbe (868, by Blancas'
reckoning) and the earliest record of an incumbent of the
office of Justice. It was easy enough to adopt a Ciceronian
metaphor and say that the Justice had lived on in the Fuero
of Sobrarbe, as if sheathed in a scabbard[80]; but how were

[80] *"Magistratum ipsum in antiquis illis Suprarbiensis Fori tabulis
inclusum, tamquam in vagina reconditum exstitisse,"* adapting verbatim *Orat. in Cat.* 1,2,4, where Cicero's subject was the *senatus
consultum*; ed. Schott, III, 787 (cf. ed. Hernandez, p. 390), at the
head of the *Fasti*, and again in the section referred to in the next
note (ed. Schott, III, 725; ed. Hernandez, p. 276).

the primordial liberties preserved during these "dark ages"? Blancas offered the following explanation. In the earliest times the elders of the nation circumvallated their liberties with three strong walls: the prefecture of the Justice, the immense power of the *ricoshombres*, and the energetic force of the Union. The first of these was civil and forensic, the second domestic, and the third warlike and popular. The inventors of these three walls, and those that followed them, bestowed more strength and efficaciousness upon the latter two than upon the Justice. Starting with the reconquest of Zaragoza in 1118, however, the Justice became steadily more important. By the time of the Privileges of Union (1287) the Justice had achieved a power roughly equal to the barons, and after the quashing of the Union (1348) the Justice entered the golden age of his power. We know little about the 10th and 11th centuries because few documents of those rough times survive; but the fragments of the Fuero of Sobrarbe and the allusions in the Privileges of Union bear witness to the continual tradition of the Justice of Aragon.[81]

Two problems that had vexed Blancas' predecessors—what was the name of the first kingdom? and who was the first king?—are solved by Blancas in a decisive and well-argued fashion. We need record only the essentials. First of all, Blancas adopts Vagad's device of calling the nation the kingdom of Sobrarbe, and he includes within it the histories of Navarre and Aragon; but, whereas Vagad had kept the title of Sobrarbe in the official style of the kings of Aragon throughout the ages, Blancas drops it with the advent of Sanchez Abarca in the early 10th century. Sobrarbe,

---

[81] Most of the foregoing comes from the end of the first chapter of the second treatise, just before Blancas begins a long digression upon the nobility of Aragon; cf. ed. Schott, III, 724-25; ed. Hernandez, pp. 275-77. If the hypothesis I have advanced is true (that the second treatise was written first), then the section on the nobles represents Blancas' first effort to bridge the gap between the establishment of the Fuero of Sobrarbe and the beginning of recorded history of the Justices in the 12th century; if he could not tell the story of the Justice during that interval, he could show how the other two "walls" of liberty operated. For thoughts somewhat along these lines in Blancas, see ed. Schott, III, 638; ed. Hernandez, p. 125.

therefore, is proto-Aragon in the larger sense, so that its laws are quite rightly the heritage of Aragon. The *county* of Aragon, on the other hand, existed very early within the realm of Sobrarbe, and finally its name was applied to the whole kingdom.[82]

The dynastic order adopted by Blancas was basically the same as Beuter's: the dynasty of Garci Ximenez (who, as in Beuter, was contemporaneous with Don Pelayo) and his three successors; an interregnum and law-making assembly; the election of a new dynast, Iñigo Arista. The interregnum and the assembly are separate chapters in Blancas, and he makes the transition from one chapter to the other at the same point in his narrative as Charles of Viana had done in his chronicle. Earlier we compared the texts of the two authors and noticed how Blancas by his terminology completed the process begun by Viana of "Sobrarbizing" the famous law-making incident.[83]

Blancas tells us that he would have liked to give the Fueros in their genuine native idiom, but that the injury of time upon the original form has been too great. By the "genuine native idiom" he probably meant the quaint Spanish of the Oath, as we shall observe shortly—and to be sure not even the 13th-century versions of False Fueros I-IV (as, e.g., in the manuscripts of the Fuero of Navarre or Tudela-Sobrarbe) had language quaint enough to match the Oath. In any event, Blancas chose to render the False Fueros in Latin. This gave him considerable latitude of expression

---

[82] For Vagad, see above, p. 106. For Blancas on Sanchez Abarca, see *Commentarii*, ed. Schott, III, 616ff (ed. Hernandez, pp. 87ff); on the County and Counts of Aragon, *ibid.*, ed. Schott, III, 585 and 592ff (ed. Hernandez, pp. 31-32, 46ff). One of the best of the essays which digress to consider controversial problems is on "Various Opinions of Authors Concerning the Origins of the Kingdom of Sobrarbe" (ed. Schott, III, 598-609; ed. Hernandez, pp. 56-73). The relationship of the Aragonese and the Sobrarbeans, of the county and the kingdom, is summed up in these two sentences: "*Atqui nostros quotiescunque dico, & Aragonenses, & Suprarbienses intelligo. Nam etsi minima illa Aragonensium Resp. Comitum adhuc continebatur imperio, ex quo tamen Comites ipsi semper fuerunt Regibus nostris addicti, communis eorum esse una, & eadem cum Suprarbiensi Rep. censebatur*" (ed. Schott, III, 586; ed. Hernandez, p. 34).

[83] See above, Ch. III, n. 44.

in respect to Fueros I-IV because (to my knowledge) they had always been rendered before in Spanish. With False Fueros V and VI, on the other hand, he did not have as much license, since they were already in Latin in the Sagarra Story (i.e., Antich and Molino). None of these considerations, however, seems to have affected Blancas. All the False Fueros, as we observed earlier, were rendered in the style of the *XII Tabulae*.[84]

An additional "Romanizing," and at the same time "legalizing," that has escaped notice is the manner in which Blancas rendered False Fuero V. This "Justice Fuero" was the most important of all the enactments of the interregnal assembly in Blancas' eyes, and he selected an appropriate classical garb for it: the *senatus consultum ultimum*, the "Last Decree" of the Roman Republic.[85] "*Ne quid respublica detrimenti caparet*" (Lest harm befall the republic) becomes "Ne quid *autem damni* detrimentive *leges aut libertates nostrae patiantur*" as the precautional sanction for the creation of the Justice:

But lest damage and harm befall our laws and liberties, there shall be a certain *judex medius* to whom it shall be right and proper to make appeal from the king if he will have injured anyone, and [to whom it shall be right and proper] to check injustices if perchance they will have arisen in the republic.[86]

Blancas' skill in utilizing classical locutions can be found

---

[84] Blancas' remarks about the native idiom of the Fueros are contained in the passage quoted above, Ch. III, n. 45. Some remarks about his Latin translation and the style of the *XII Tabulae* will be found above, Ch. III, n. 46.

[85] S. C. Ultimum (technically, S. C. de Re Publica Defendenda) is found in many places in classical literature: e.g., Caesar, *Bell. Civ.*, I, 5, 3; Cicero, *Epist. ad Fam.*, XVI, xi, 2-3; and Sallust, *Cat.*, XXIX, 2. A good summary of the decree, with references to much modern literature on it, is given by Chaim Wirszubski, *Libertas as a Political Idea at Rome during the Late Republic and Early Principate* (Cambridge, 1950), pp. 55-61. It is perhaps worth noting that Blancas, when summarizing the debate of the assembly which led to the adoption of the Fueros of Sobrarbe, also uses the locution *ne . . . quid caperet Resp. detrimenti*; see above, Ch. III, n. 44.

[86] The full Latin text is given below, Appendix III.

throughout his writings; but the present example, aside from its syntactical elegance, stands out because of the direct analogy it suggests between the basic constitutional principles of Rome and Aragon. The "Last Decree" of the Roman Republic suspended normal government and gave arbitrary powers to the consuls in the case of a great emergency; the "Justice Fuero" of the Sobrarbe-Aragon assembly aimed at assuring regular justice against the arbitrary power of the king. Upon reflection, the analogy is not quite appropriate. Indeed, it could be called maladroit unless one is sufficiently persuaded by the similitude of Consul and Justice, *qua magistratus*, to disregard the contrariety between permitting arbitrary rule in order to save the republic in one case and placing checks upon the legitimate ruler in order to save the laws in the other.

For the substance of False Fuero v Blancas seems to have paid more heed to the Spanish rendition by Beuter than to the Latin renditions which he knew from Bages and Molino: the latter two had not used the term "appeal" nor referred to the "good of the republic" as had Beuter.[87] But none of these sources provided Blancas with the phrase which was most radical: "*si aliquem laeserit*" (if [the king] will have injured anyone). This has been especially noxious to monarchists, who have taken it to insinuate that every *rex* is potentially an ogre and, perhaps worse, to imply that the *judex medius* is poised in some way as a superior authority ever ready to chastise the monarch.[88] False

[87] See the texts of Antich and Molino, above, pp. 82-83 and 112; also Beuter, above, n. 47.

[88] Fuente, *Estudios*, II, 148-51, and Danvila y Collado, *Libertades*, pp. 349ff (esp. p. 353), and *Poder Civil*, I, 334, are examples respectively of passionate scornfulness and controlled censure of the *si aliquem laeserit* phrase. Quinto, for whom Blancas was essentially a hero (see above, Ch. II, n. 18), gives the text of False Fuero v in one note, and talks around it with technical arguments in another (*Juramento*, pp. 124, n. 1, 125, n. 2). See also Marichalar and Manrique, *Historia del derecho*, VI, 268. In Roman Law there is a close verbal antecedent to the idea of not injuring another person (using the same verb, *laedo*) in the famous dictum of Ulpian (*Dig.* 1,1,10): "*Iustitia est constans . . . §1. Iuris praecepta sunt haec: honeste vivere*, alterum non laedere, *suum cuique tribuere.*" Henry of Bracton

Fuero v certainly goes further than False Fueros i-iv toward conceiving the origin of the nation upon the basis of a contract. Right of resistance is given explicit institution. In Blancas' presentation, this does not antedate monarchy itself in Sobrarbe, for there had already been a dynasty of four kings. Thus he avoids the dilemma of imagining some other authority as existing before kingly authority, which was the fount of all authority. Interregnal authority was not pre-regnal or anti-regnal, Blancas would probably have argued if pressed upon this point. Thus the avowed purpose of the interregnal assembly, namely, to place checks upon the kingly office before allowing a new incumbency, was not extra-legal.[89]

It is a far cry from the powers of *manifestación* and *firmas de derecho*, which everyone knew had been exercised by the Justice for centuries, to the militant tone of *Widerstandsrecht* of False Fuero v. But Blancas was not through: he immediately brings forth False Fuero vi as proof that the monarchs themselves, willingly and avowedly, accepted the popular right of resistance.

After the capital-letter rendering of False Fueros i-v, Blancas digresses to tell the reader once more that the Justice was the *praesidium libertatis*, and that the new king was certainly bound to recognize this fact and swear to it. "Having decided upon these fundamental elements of the liberty of the country," the people then sought a new king. The choice fell upon Iñigo Arista, already King of Pamplona, and the terror of the Moors. He was called to an assembly, and apprised of the laws to which he had to agree. He found them quite harsh, especially the one concerning the Justice of Aragon; but, upon reflecting that he was being given a kingdom already freed from its enemies, he

---

applied it in 13th-century England: *"et quod nullus alium laedat"*; ii, 304 (ed. Woodbine).

[89] In the chapter on the interregnum, Blancas does not discuss the authority of the assembly in these legal-philosophical terms, but elsewhere he comes close to it: viz., in the chapter on the first king, Garci Ximenez, and in the second treatise of the *Commentarii* where he gives the texts of Cerdan, Antich, and Molino; see ed. Schott, iii, 582, 720-22; ed. Hernandez, pp. 30, 268-71.

ratified all the laws already decreed (False Fueros i-v),
and then went further and proposed "another new law or
privilege":

If it should happen in the future that the kingdom be op-
pressed by him contrary to the fueros and liberties, he
would allow free access into the kingdom to another king,
Christian or infidel, whom they would approve.

Immediately Blancas adds this remark, however: "Because
our people deemed that which he conceded concerning
the infidel king to be shameful and improper, in no wise
did they suffer themselves to go along with it." Then Iñigo
Arista swore to uphold the laws, and thereupon he became
the new king of Sobrarbe.[90]

Blancas' presentation of False Fuero vi and his comments
about it both have features designed to persuade the reader
in a subtle fashion. First of all, the capital-letter rendering
of the entire Fuero makes it seem to be one with False
Fueros i-v, even though it is separated from them in his
text. Just as important is the question raised by the popular rejection of Iñigo Arista's offer: does this apply to the
whole Fuero, or only to the *etiam paganum* provision of
it? An exact reading implies that the latter is the case; for,
had Blancas meant that this whole new "law or privilege"
was rejected, he would have no right to capitalize it in his
text. Conclusive evidence comes from another passage in
the *Commentarii*, namely, from the discussion of the Privileges of Union, where he links the right to depose the king

[90] The text of False Fuero vi is given below, Appendix iii. The
vital sentences just before and just after it (ed. Schott, iii, 589-90;
ed. Hernandez, pp. 39-40) are as follows: "*Innico itaque Rege ad se
evocato, ac legibus, quas praestatuerant, eidem ostensis, durissimum
sibi visum tradunt, quod de Iudice Medio praecautum apparebat.
Attamen re ipsa attentius considerata, & perpensa, cum sibi ultro
Regnum ab hostibus ereptum deferretur: nedum ipsas leges sanxisse
ferunt, verum nostris novam aliam, sive legem, sive Privilegium
irrogasse huiusmodi: Quod . . .* [then the text of False Fuero vi].
*Nostros vero id, quod de Rege infideli concedebatur, quia turpe, ac
indecorum iudicarunt, nequaquam sibi impertiri fuisse passos. Iurisiurandi ergo religione praestita, Pompelonensis Rex Innicus, in eodem
Arahueste oppido, in Suprarbiensem Regem evectus fuit.*"

in that document to the Fuero of Sobrarbe.[91] So, Blancas follows the trend of historians since Vagad as far as the discounting of the *etiam paganum* phrase is concerned, but otherwise he allows the essential legality of the Fuero to stand as it was presented in the Sagarra Story. Perhaps he was swayed by the fact that False Fueros v and vi are virtually united in the Sagarra Story, so that he could not reject one without casting some doubt on the other; and he could suffer no incredulity to affect the "Justice Fuero," which was the pivotal evidence for his whole design of early Aragonese history. In any event, everyone since Blancas' time has taken the "royal disclaimer" to be one of the Fueros of Sobrarbe, and we are fully justified in calling it False Fuero vi.

After "elevating" Iñigo Arista to the throne, the printed versions of the *Commentarii* round out the chapter on the Fuero of Sobrarbe by giving oblique evidence of the wisdom of the Pope who had advised "our people" to draw up a code of laws, and as a finale gives this quotation which everyone would recognize: "Among us laws were established before kings were created" (*Apud nos prius leges conditas, quam Reges creatos fuisse*). "I believe," says Blancas, "that these words which are found in the prologue to our code of laws today allude to the very laws which we have just shown were adopted during the first interregnum in our nation's history."[92] When he said this, Blancas no doubt considered that he, the royal historiographer, had done a great service to the nation by giving the substance of the laws which had been called the "Fueros of Sobrarbe" by the jurists who drew up the *Nueva Compilación* in 1551. The legend of the kingdom of Sobrarbe and its "Fueros" thus became sealed for centuries to come.

What readers of Blancas' *Commentarii* did not know, however, was that the author had yet more evidence regarding the election of Iñigo Arista that he could have published, but did not. He had found another fragment of ancient Sobrarbe lore, one which preserved the primitive

---

[91] See above, n. 77, and the text to which it pertains.

[92] Ed. Schott, iii, 590; ed. Hernandez, pp. 40-41.

vernacular language; and he had recorded it in his own manuscript immediately after the passage reporting how Iñigo Arista had been made king:

At the time of this election of Arista, moreover, we can with some good reason declare that there began to be used that memorable old form of creating kings among our people in former times, the form made so well-known by François Hotman, a French author of great eminence in our time; notwithstanding that at the same time it has not been hallowed at all by venerable writings of our people that I know of, yet in this form it was transmitted among our people not by any divination or conjecture but by the unchanging opinion of everyone from the earliest times; and both in the times of our ancestors and in our times it is spoken of among us in daily conversations, so that it should not in the least be fitting for anyone to be undecided concerning its fidelity and truth. On this occasion I have decided to write it down in the same vulgar tongue, that is, in our vernacular way of speaking, by which here and there it is published, whereby the joining together of our ancient words may show the great gravity of the sentiments more sharply than if they were read in Latin. For among our people, as far as what they call customs and antiquities are concerned, it has been accepted as a tradition of our forbears that our ancestors when they decided upon a king, for the purpose of diminishing his majesty lest he should show himself excessively exalted to them, were wont to address their king: "WE WHO ARE AS GOOD AS YOU, AND CAN DO AS MUCH AS YOU, TAKE YOU AS KING PROVIDED THAT THERE IS ALWAYS BETWEEN YOU AND US ONE WHO COMMANDS MORE THAN YOU." [¶] Quite correctly, then, Hotman, when he strives to show the nature of the form of governing of the Gauls in bygone times, after he had enumerated the ancient forms established by the philosophers themselves as well as later by others—by the Spartans as well as the Romans, and then by the Germans, by the English, and by the Gauls and others, indeed by almost all the other nations of the world—judged that our form of governance often excelled the others.[93]

The capital-letter rendering of the Oath was done by the modern editor who resuscitated this long-lost passage from

[93] "*Tunc autem in hac scilicet Aristae nostri regis cooptatione, priscam illam memorabilem regum apud nos olim creandorum formam a Francisco Hotomano perquam gravi saeculi nostri gallo scriptore tantopere celebratam, usitari coepisse merito quidam possumus affirmare; cum tametsi a eadem sollemnibus, quod sciam scripturis minime nobis esset consecrata verum ita apud nos non divinatione quaedam aut conjectura, sed constanti omnium fama a priscis nostris saeculis ducta, et majorum aetate et nostra quotidianis apud nos hodiernis etiam sermonibus celebratur ut de illius fide ac veritate minime quemque deceat haesitare. Eam statui vulgari ipsa lingua, hoc est vernaculo nostro loquendi genere quo passim affertur hoc loco annotandam, quo acriorem prae se ferat sententiae gravitatem ipsamet priscorum nostrorum vocabulorum conglutinatio, quam si latine legeretur. Apud nos enim hactenus antiqua et vetera quam vocant majorum traditione receptum est majores illos nostros dum regem sibi statuebant, ad ipsius majestatem extenuandam, ne nimisse suis elatum se praeberet, ita regem ipsum afferi solitos: 'Nos tan buenos como vos, é que podemos más que vos, tomamos á vos por Rey, con que haya sienpre entre vos, y nos un que mande más que vos.' Unde merito Hotomanus ille, dum ostendere nititur qualis fuerat antiqua galli constituendi regni forma, postquam veteres enumeravit, tan ab ipsis philosophis tan etiam post ab illis, Lacedemoniis quam a Romanis deindeque a germanis, anglicis, galliis, aliisque fere omnibus mundi nationibus constitutas, nostram caeteris multum praestisse demontrans ita de eadem judicavit.*" For the most part I have given this text as it is found in Lasala, *Constitución Aragonesa*, pp. 158-59, which is the only complete Latin rendition of it that I know; but it is so filled with typographical errors and bad constructions that I have freely changed it where necessary. Ximénez de Embún, *Orígenes*, p. 123, n. 3, gives a few sentences of the Latin, and provides a better text as far as he goes. (We should note, however, that Ximénez de Embún does not quote the lines in which Blancas refers to the traditional adherence to the Oath and the daily utterance of it; the existence of this kind of oral transmission would have been inimical to Ximénez de Embún's attack upon the Fueros of Sobrarbe as venerated old law. There is, therefore, a kind of dishonesty in Ximénez de Embún's not meeting the challenge of this passage.) These two authors are the only persons, besides Hernandez, who I am aware saw Blancas' autograph. Hernandez' Spanish rendition of the passage (p. 40, n. 2) must be heeded because of that author's obvious competence as a Latinist and his familiarity with Blancas' language and thought, as a result of translating the entire *Commentarii* into Spanish.

the autograph of Blancas, and so we may assume that Blancas put it in the same class as False Fueros I-VI. If it had been put in legal style and in Latin, we would probably be justified in calling it False Fuero VII; but in this case Blancas would not have departed from the vernacular, for he was obviously convinced that it represented the language in which all the Fueros of Sobrarbe had originally been couched.

Coming just after the enunciation of False Fuero VI and the election of Iñigo Arista, the Oath had much more precise location in Aragonese history than it had had in Hotman and other French writers. In the context of Iñigo Arista's election the phrase "We who are as good as you, and can do more than you" clearly refers to the interregnal assembly which had imposed some laws on the new king, if not to the right that had been granted to the people to depose the king. The phrase "between you and us one who commands more than you" is clearly a reference to False Fuero V, where the *judex medius* was created to arbitrate between the king and his people. To anyone as convinced of the genuineness of False Fueros V and VI as was Blancas, there was no reason whatever to doubt the authenticity of the Oath. He probably suppressed it when he published the *Commentarii* because it was not yet printed in any Spanish work and thus was a gratuitous glorification of the Justice which he might withdraw in order to placate the king and the Council of Aragon.[94]

[94] The earliest printed reference to the Oath in Spain (without the text of it being given, however) was, it seems, in 1590 by Portolés, *Scholia*, Pt. 3, *s.v.* "Libertates Regni," cited by Quinto, *Juramento*, pp. 76-78 (see above, Ch. II, n. 11). It is clear from the page references that Portolés had at hand either the 1573 or the 1576 edition of Hotman, which do not have the historical references to the Justice found in the third edition of 1586; when, therefore, Portolés refers to the notable words which the Aragonese used, "eo tempore, quo primum Aragoniae Regem elegerunt," he is saying more than could be properly inferred from Hotman. He is, in fact, drawing Blancas' conclusions. The first full citation of the text of the Oath in Spain, it seems, was in 1591 by Morlanes, *Alegaciones*, pp. 93-94 (cited by Quinto, pp. 80ff—see above, Ch. II, n. 11). This was also drawn from a pre-1586 edition of the *Francogallia*, and yet assumes that Hotman was referring to the founding of the kingdom. The point is

The history of the False Fueros of Sobrarbe would certainly have been different had Blancas not suppressed the Oath. In this case the Oath, instead of always being associated with Huguenots or the traitor Pérez, would have had the sanction of a leading historian of Spain, no less than the royal historiographer. The Oath would have assumed very early in its bibliographical adventures an important place in the Sobrarbe legend, and could not have been so often ignored by Spanish historians in the following centuries. Whether more serious scholarly attention to the Oath over the centuries would have brought out the truth of its origin is, however, not at all certain. For, as I shall soon argue, to understand the Oath one has also to know the full history of the Privileges of Union. Blancas probably suppressed the Privileges of Union, as he had the Oath, to placate the political sensibilities of Philip II; but the result was that he propagated for yet another three centuries the mischief which Peter IV had wrought by his edict *De prohibita unione*. That edict in the 14th century had quickly given rise to the Sagarra Story, which in turn became a vital part of the False Fueros of Sobrarbe. The continued suppression of the Privileges of Union in the 16th century is the most likely reason for the rise of the Oath; and Blancas, when he censored his *Commentarii* and suppressed both the Oath and the Privileges of Union—albeit unwillingly—contributed to the cause of ignorance which as a scholar we know he deplored.

---

that the Spanish all seem to assume that the Oath applies to Iñigo Arista's election; this must be due to their keen awareness of the controversy over that event. It might be noted that Portolés, while he seems to give credence to the Oath, does not give the text; Morlanes gives the text, but then scoffs at it.

Chapter VI · Royal Oaths in Aragon
and the Oath of the Aragonese

$\mathcal{T}$he aim of the foregoing chapters has been to establish the intellectual atmosphere in which the Oath "We who are as good as you . . ." came into being. There is more to be said concerning the legend of Sobrarbe and its False Fueros, but first we must examine very closely the text of each of the four "primary" sources of the Oath—Soranzo, Hotman–Beza, Blancas, Pérez—in order to see what textual variations may suggest about the true nature of the Oath, and whether different claims about when and where the Oath is supposed to have been pronounced will yield any clues about historical events that may have inspired it. We should remind ourselves, first of all, that only one of our primary sources—Blancas—connects the Oath with the Sobrarbe legend and laws, and, further, that he suppressed this opinion. Therefore, we are arguing for the Oath-Sobrarbe relationship despite the silence of most of our primary sources on this subject. For this reason it is incumbent upon us to let primary sources try to speak for themselves, and only when they fail us to bring in corollary evidence. Besides, we shall find that the Sobrarbe legend, while paramount, is not the only influential factor in the appearance of the Oath, and that different arguments—old ones of others, and new ones of mine—must be called up and examined before a full and reasonable explanation of the Oath can be given.

Supposed Ceremonial Circumstances of the
Oath of the Aragonese

The Oath by its very nature appears to be a ceremonial act, and instinctively one assumes that it must be an oath of allegiance—in this case, very qualified allegiance—which the people took to the king at his coronation. But when we examine our primary sources we find that sometimes the setting in which the Oath is pronounced is ambiguously represented and, more troubling, that no two authors give identical accounts.

Soranzo's *Relazione* does not mention a coronation at all. The Venetian ambassador is describing the difficulty which the king had with the Cortes of Aragon, and the Oath is offered as an example of the independent attitude which the Aragonese adopted in respect to the king. "When they accept [*accettano*] the king, they use these peculiar and very lofty words," are the words used to introduce the Oath.[1] The verb *accettare* could mean a coronation "acceptance" of the king by the people; but more likely it refers to the oath-taking which was performed at every meeting of the Cortes. Matters are somewhat complicated by the fact that the coronation in Aragon took place at the first meeting of the new king's Cortes, so that the coronation and normal oath-takings could be fused. Still, Soranzo seems to be referring to regular Cortes procedure, for this is the general context of his discussion when he mentions the Oath.

With Theodore Beza, the Oath is said to belong to both the coronation and the meeting of the Cortes: "*non solum in Regum . . . inauguratione . . . sed etiam in conventibus illis triennalibus.*"[2] Soranzo, it should be noted, had men-

---

[1] "*Quando accettano il re, usano queste proprie e altissime parole:* 'Noi, che valemo tanto come voi, giuriamo a voi, che non valete piu di noi, per principe ed erede del nostro regno, con condizione che conserviate le nostre leggi e la nostra libertà, e facendo voi altrimenti noi non vi giuriamo'; e gli presentano il libro sopra il quale sono notati i loro privilegi, che domandano *fueros,* e S.M. giura la confirmazione*" (*Relazione,* p. 85).

[2] "*Formula illa est insignis, quam Arragonii hodie etiam (nisi forte non ita pridem mutata est) non solum in Regum suorum inauguratione usurpant, sed etiam in conventibus illis triennalibus iterant, in quibus Rex sese apud suos ordines sistere solet, tum ut suis ius dicat, tum ab iis ius suum recipiat. Ibi enim post multas peractas caeremonias, inter eum quem Iustitiam Arragonensem vocant (qui supremae potestatis personam refert, cuique reges iureiurando se obstringere coguntur) & Regem ipsum, vel creandum, vel iam creatum Formula haec*

tioned in passing that three years was the minimal interval between Cortes. François Hotman, who we believe derived the Oath from Beza, says that the Oath was pronounced when *"in communi Aragoniae concilio Regem creant."*[3] Assuming that the phrase "common council of Aragon" means the Cortes, then Hotman would have us believe that the ceremonial was part of the coronation (i.e., at the first Cortes of the new ruler) when the king was "created." Also Blancas (who cites Hotman but gives a different version of the Oath) associates the Oath with the elevation of the king.[4] Therefore, Soranzo, Beza, and Hotman-Blancas give us three possibilities for the occasion of utterance of the Oath: only at the coronation (which coincided with the first meeting of the Cortes); only at meetings of the Cortes after the

---

totidem verbis pronuntiatur. NOS QUI VALEMOS TANTO COMME VOS, & PODEMOS MAS QUE VOS, ELEGIMOS REY: CON ESTAS & ESTAS CONDITIONES, INTRA VOS Y NOS, UN QUE MANDA MAS QUE VOS. Id est, Nos qui tanti sumus quanti vos, & plus quam vos possumus, Regem vos eligimus, his atque his conditionibus: Inter vos, et nos unus maiore est imperio, quam vos. En quo usque Hispani suos Reges in honore habuerint, prout debuerunt." (*De iure magistratuum* [ed. Lyon, 1580], pp. 71-72; the passage is translated below, p. 220). See above, Ch. II, nn. 3-4, for comments about the composition of Beza's tract and editions of it. As noted above (Ch. II, n. 7), the ceremonial circumstances of the Oath-taking as set forth in the *Vindiciae contra tyrannos* compare closely with those in Beza's work.

[3] *"Sed ex his gentium fere omnium institutis nullum aeque insigne memoratur, ut illud Hispanorum, qui cum in communi Arragoniae concilio Regem creant, rei memoriaeque consignandae caussa fabulam peragunt, hominemque inducunt, cui Iuris Arragonici nomen imponunt, quem Rege majorem ac potentiorem esse communi populi decreto sanciunt, tandemque Regem certis legibus et conditionibus creatum his affantur verbis, quae propter eximiam ac plane singularem gentis illius in frenando Rege fortitudinem proferemus: NOS QUI VALEMOS TANTO COME VOS, Y PODEMOS MAS QUE VOS, VOS ELEGIMOS REY, CON ESTAS Y ESTAS CONDITIONES, INTRA VOS Y NOS, UN QUE MANDA MA QUE VOS. Id est, Nos qui tanti sumus, quanti vos, & plusquam vos possumus, Regem vos eligimus, his atque his conditionibus. Inter vos & nos unus majore cum imperio est, quam vos"* (*Francogallia*, [ed. Geneva, 1573], pp. 85-86). See above, Ch. II, n. 3, for comments about other editions of the work. A translation of this passage is given below, in the text above n. 97.

[4] See above, Ch. V, *ad finem*.

coronation; at the coronation and at all subsequent meetings of the Cortes.

The *Relaciones* of Antonio Pérez presents a much more complicated setting for the Oath. Reading only the words which preface the Oath quotation, where Pérez says that the Oath is *"el modo antiguo de jurar à su Rey los Aragoneses,"*[5] we cannot tell whether he means Cortes, coronation, or some other occasion. But, reading on for several sentences after the quotation, it becomes clear that Pérez was referring to the election—i.e., coronation—of the king. He relates how the king (supposedly until very recent times) swore to uphold the Fueros, and the people then swore to obey him. Pérez implies, therefore, that the "people's" Oath related a few sentences earlier was the people's part of the reciprocal pledges to which he is now alluding. Still, a scrupulous reading of Pérez' text shows that he does not state precisely that the "old way of swearing" which he gives first is the same as the "oath by which the people swear obedience to the king" which he mentions later on.[6]

[5] *"Entre otros fueros ordenaron el fuero que se llamava de la Union, que contiene dos partes dignas de ser sabidas, y muy al proposito de la informaçion que voy dando. La una,* Que siempre que el Rey les quebrantasse sus fueros pudiessen eligir otro Rey, En cara que sea Pagano. *Palabras formales del fuero que trata desto. Y assy es de saber el modo antiguo de jurar à su Rey los Aragoneses, que es.* Nos, que valemos tanto como vos os hazemos nuestro Rey, y Señor, con tal que nos guardeys nuestros fueros, y libertades, y syno, No. *Y el modo del jurar de los fueros el Rey es con toda esta çerimonia, y reconosçimiento de la superioridad que tiene de derecho, y de la naturaleza de su instituçion el offiçio del Iustiçia de Aragon. Que assentado el Iustiçia en una silla, y cubierto su cabeça reçibe del Rey hincado de rodillas delante de sy, y descubierto, el juramento en un Crucifixo, y en los quatro Evangelios, de guardar, y observar los fueros, y libertades de aquel Reyno inviolablemente sò çensuras gravissimas de Summos Pontifiçes, En que se ha de advertir, que primero haze el Rey este acto, y juramento, que à el le juren la obediençia, continuando se en esto la orden del primer juramento. Que, como fue de election, y convençion, y de quien dava aquella parte de su Libertad, era, y es justo que reçiba primero el preçio convenido, que entregue la prenda. Y à la verdad el termino natural es, y acostumbrado entre las gentes en trueques, y mas de prenda de que se dize, que no ay oro porque se pueda vender"* (*Relaciones*, [ed. Geneva, 1654], pp. 143-44). See below, pp. 222-23 for an English translation of most of this passage.

[6] See previous note for the text.

Pérez was a master of innuendo, to be sure, but he was not often an outright fabricator, as his critics claim he was.

If our authors are very contradictory about the question of when the Oath was rendered habitually, they show a greater consensus about when it took place historically. Soranzo and Hotman imply that it enjoyed contemporary usage, by simple dint of using the present tense in their writings. Beza states positively that it is used "today," but immediately adds "unless by chance it has been changed not so very long ago." Pérez implies that it is a defunct custom, by saying that it is "the ancient manner of the Aragonese to swear to their king"; but the ambiguity of Pérez' which we just remarked upon allows us to believe that the Oath may have been the people's part of reciprocal oath-taking at coronations up to recent times.[7] Blancas, however, knew better than to assign the Oath to any Aragonese coronations of the past three centuries. He had made a comprehensive study of Aragonese coronations from the earliest records of them in the 13th century up to his own time. If, from the fact that this work contains no mention of the Oath, we conclude that Blancas had found no evidence of it, then it follows that Blancas had deprived himself of the right to believe in the recent existence of it.[8] As we have

---

[7] *Ibid.* Jerónimo Portolés, another Spaniard writing in 1590, when citing the Oath from Hotman (without quoting it), said (what Hotman does not say) that the Aragonese used the Oath when they elected the first king of Aragon; for this passage, see above, Ch. ii, n. 11.

[8] *Coronaciones de los serenissimos reyes de Aragon*, Zaragoza, 1641. The work, composed in 1584, was published by Juan Fr. Andrés de Uztarroz from Blancas' manuscript (Bibl. del Escorial, &-iii-4, which Arco, *Repertorio*, p. 95, No. 159, has compared with Uztarroz' publication and observed "*variantes en las palabras*"). It is frequently bound with two works on the Cortes of Aragon, one by Gerónimo Martel, *Forma de celebrar cortes en Aragon* (written in 1601) and the other by Blancas, *Modo de proceder en cortes de Aragon* (composed in 1585; notes by Uztarroz); see Arco, *Uztarroz*, i, 178, 182-87, for the editor's travails in getting this work published. I know of no evidence to support the statement of Percy Schramm, "Krönung," p. 577, n. 1, that Blancas' *Coronaciones* was first published in 1585; certainly the Uztarroz edition dates from 1641, and not 1651 as Schramm states. I have not been able to locate—nor, in fact, to verify the existence of—the work of Diego de Morlanes

seen, Blancas imagined that the Oath belonged to Iñigo Arista's election; further, the manner in which the Oath was recorded in his manuscript implies that it was a seventh Fuero of Sobrarbe. Blancas would probably have answered a query about the authenticity of the Oath by saying that it was plausible if, and only if, it had had application in the very early days of the kingdom, and that he himself believed this to be true because of the harmoniousness of the Oath with the Fueros of Sobrarbe which he himself had reconstructed. It must be significant that the one person of these times who was the most learned in the history of Aragonese institutions does not consider for a moment the possibility that the Oath was valid in modern times. This is strong testimony against the modernity of the Oath, overweighing the statements or implications of the other sources about its contemporary use.

Spanish Analogues to the Oath of the Aragonese

Many have sought, but always in vain, to discover a precedent or analogue to the Oath of the Aragonese in the ceremonial practices of the kingdom of Aragon.[9] Later in this

---

(ca. 1550-1610), *Tractatus de Jure Coronationis in Aragonensi Regno*, which Latassa[2], II, 368, says *"es muy citada."*

[9] Blancas' work on the Aragonese coronations (see previous note) could well have been undertaken to verify the historical existence of the Oath of the Aragonese; when it did not show up in the documents, it had to be consigned to oral tradition of great antiquity. Schramm, "Krönung," is not concerned with oaths as such (he accepted Quinto's verdict that Hotman invented the Oath of the Aragonese—see below, Ch. VII, n. 6), but rather deals only with the actual crowning of the king. He stresses the unusual practice of the Aragonese kings from 1276 onwards to crown themselves with their own hands, a practice which contradicts the spirit of the Oath. Testimony that the Oath of the Aragonese did not live on in oral tradition is found in the asseveration of several 13th-century writers that the oath of the subjects to James I of Aragon in 1214 was the first instance of its kind in Spain; see Pérez, *Orígenes*, pp. 209-10. The same author, in his *Textos políticos*, pp. 170-75, Nos. 315-22, cites several interesting examples of mediaeval Spanish oaths which are properly feudal—that is, openly stating or implying reciprocal relations between lord and vassal—but could be viewed by anyone untutored in feudal relations as exaggerating the power of the lord or the vassal.

chapter I shall advance a new nominee to be foster parent
of the Oath: the "royal jurisdictional oath" which originated
in the late 14th century. This oath did not apply in all the
lands of the mediaeval Crown of Aragon—i.e., Aragon,
Catalonia, Valencia, Sicily, and Majorca—but held force
only in the kingdom of Aragon proper. This oath, therefore,
has unqualified credentials. We should still allow, however, that the ideas and practices and momentous happenings in the other principalities of the Crown of Aragon could
have influenced the legend of primitive Aragon. Navarre's
historiography greatly affected Aragon's, as we have often
seen already, and so we should assume that the same
could be true of other regions contiguous to Aragon, and
especially of her two venerable neighbors, Barcelona and
Valencia.

One could, of course, range over all of Europe, and catalogue the limitations upon royal power in the institutions of
other mediaeval kingdoms such as Castile, France, and
England, and even more tellingly, recite the ideas of right
of resistance found in the writers of those countries as well
as of Italy and Germany. This has been done by Fritz Kern
and Kurt Wolzendorff, and the *Si no, no* Oath has its place
in the corpus of passages which they collected to prove the
doctrine of resistance in the Middle Ages and early modern
Europe.[10] Gathering analogous instances does help to make
the Oath of the Aragonese seem less novel than it appears
to be at first sight, but it does not advance significantly our
understanding of its historical apparition. The ideological
antecedents of the Oath which we have already brought
forth from Aragonese history and legal historiography allow us to deem superfluous any non-Aragonese evidence
which is not manifestly relevant upon documentary or
philological grounds.

This dictum against non-Aragonese sources will perhaps
make tenuous the three pieces of evidence about to be pre-

[10] Kern, *Gottesgnadentum*, Anm. 452 and Anh. xxxvii (numbered
the same in later editions); Wolzendorff, *Widerstandsrecht*, pp. 24-
25, who implies that the Oath belonged to the period 1461ff. Kern
and Wolzendorff between them overlook few writers on resistance
right since antiquity, but I would call attention to one, Eximeniç,
who will be discussed shortly.

sented. Still, if any examples which are not strictly Aragonese merit consideration, these do. They come from Aragon's three close neighbors, Valencia, Barcelona, and
Navarre; they belong to the crucial period, the late 14th
and the 15th centuries; and they represent the kinds of
things that would be influential: a significant political treatise, a spectacular defiance of the king of Aragon, and a
coronation oath.

In the kingdom of Valencia, which was incorporated with
the Crown of Aragon in the 13th century, the idea of reciprocal obligations between king and subjects underlay
the constitutional relationship with the king of Aragon. The
king, immediately upon his accession, was supposed to
swear before the Cortes to uphold the laws of the land, and,
at least according to 16th-century scholarly interpretation,
the Valencians were not bound to obey the king until this
was done.[11] In Valencia, as in Aragon, Renaissance legend-
making may have tended to transform the operation of traditional feudal relations and municipal charters into the-
ories of popular resistance. But in Valencia we also find an
authentic bit of evidence not matched in Aragon: the existence, already in the late 14th century, of a theoretical presentation of the right of resistance in a very comprehensive
treatise by a famous personage. This treatise does not pre-
tend to describe any contemporary principality, but its
premises betray that Valencia was very much the model.
Fundamentally, moreover, the doctrine of resistance set
forth corresponds to the legend of Aragonese resistance
embodied in the False Fueros of Sobrarbe and even to the
Oath of the Aragonese.

The author of this treatise was Francesch Eximeniç

[11] Hinojosa, *Influencia*, p. 71, citing, among other things, a privilege granted by Alfonso IV in 1329 to the effect that if the king
did not swear to uphold the fueros, "*et juramentum pro ipsis servandis
prestiterit non teneamini eum in regem vestrum aut dominum recipere
nec sibi in aliquo respondere*" (*Aureum opus regalium privilegiorum
civitatis et regni Valentiae* [Valencia, 1515], fol. 86ᵛ; also in Probst
[cited in next note], pp. 15-16). The same example, and others,
are given by López-Amo y Marín, "Eximeniç," pp. 30-32, who cites
chiefly Pedro Jerónimo Tarazona, *Instituciones dels Furs y Privilegis
del Regne de Valencia* (Valencia, 1580).

(1340-1409), and of the two titles by which it is usually called, the *Regiment de Princeps* and the *Dotzé*, the former should be preferred because it denotes the subject, although the latter describes it best bibliographically as the Twelfth Book (*Libre Dotzé*) of Eximeniç's encyclopedic work, the *Crestia*.[12]

Modern Catalan writers have pointed with pride to Eximeniç as one of the first encyclopedists in a vernacular language. His work, however, might equally well be called one of the last *Summae* of mediaeval times, for its learning reflects Eximeniç's scholastic education in France. The novelty of Eximeniç's writing comes less from its learning, however, than from its use of experience as a guide to knowledge.

Eximeniç lived an active life in the royal court as confessor to the Infante and in Valencia as an advisor to the city government. Cities held an exalted position in his political thought as one of the two natural forms of political life, the other being the Universal Empire. Ideally, says Eximeniç, cities should be bound together by the direct lordship of the Empire, but in fact kingdoms have developed as substitutes for the Empire. This occurs because the cities willfully submit to a prince. At its base, therefore, royal rulership is a practical matter, constituted by the peo-

[12] The definitive bibliography of Eximeniç's writings, including manuscripts as well as printings, is by J. Masso y Torrents, "Les Obres de Fra Franchesch Eximenis," *Anuari de l'Institut d'Estudis Catalans*, III (1909-1910), 588-692. A good general review of Eximeniç's political thought is by J. H. Probst, "Francesch Eximeniç: ses idées politiques et sociales," *Revue Hispanique*, XXXIX (1917), 1-82; but the most important work to consult now is Angel López-Amo y Marín, "El Pensamiento Politico de Eximeniç en su Tratado de 'Regiment de Princeps'," *AHDE*, XVII (1946), 5-139, who gives a full bibliography of earlier works and a fuller analysis of the *Dotzé* than any of them. Of the eight parts into which the *Dotzé* is divided, the first four (Chapters 1-473) were published in 1484 and reprinted around 1900 in a limited edition; Pts. V through VIII (Chapters 474-907) exist only in a single manuscript in Valencia. Pt. III (Chapters 357-395) was written first, in 1383, as a separate treatise entitled *Regiment de la cosa pública*, dedicated to the jurors of the city of Valencia. It has been published several times in our era, but no serious scholar should delude himself that it represents fairly the entire *Regiment de Princeps*; in terms of resistance theory, it is one of the more anemic sections.

ple for secular reasons. The key to the relationship between the communities and the people is the original compact.[13]

Men, according to Eximeniç, are naturally free, and the constitution of the community—the *cosa publica*—is freely arrived at by the exercise of this natural liberty. Political liberty, on the other hand, involves acceptance of the jurisdictional authority of the prince, who agrees to enforce the laws. The prince who fails to uphold the laws undermines the foundation of his very being. He may be resisted, and even overthrown, although power should then be given immediately to another prince.[14]

Every ruler is elected in Eximeniç's scheme. This is obviously the case with the first king, but it is not less true even when his descendants come to royal power by the agency of dynastic succession. Eximeniç reasons thusly: every king must swear to uphold the laws; the oath of later kings reaffirms the compact made with the first king and also binds them to the actions of all their predecessors; thereby the originally free action of the people in making the compact is perpetually reasserted. A fixed line of succession is indeed best, but the people are not bound to follow it by accepting the heir apparent, any more than they have to endure the rule of a legitimately installed prince who becomes a tyrant. In effect, Eximeniç has an abiding belief in the necessity of royal power, but—by traditional mediaeval standards—has a very meagre regard for the right of any given individual to exercise that power.[15]

---

[13] For the role of the city, see López-Amo y Marín, "Eximeniç," pp. 51-74; for the Empire, pp. 77-81; for the compact, pp. 83-123 and *passim*, esp. p. 87, where this passage from *Dotzé*, Pt. II, Ch. 156 is paraphrased: *"jamés les comunitats no donaren la potestat absolutament a negún sobre si mateixes, sinó ab certs pactes e leys . . ."* (quoted by Norbert d'Ordal, "El Princep segons Eximenis," *Miscellania Patxot* [Barcelona, 1931], p. 319). Eximeniç prophesied the imminent disappearance of all kingdoms and the rule of a single universal secular power (the Crown of France!—cf. Pérez, *Orígenes*, pp. 106-08, 198); *"Según esto,"* López-Amo y Marín concludes (p. 79), *"es claro que la nación o reino no supondría tampoco una realidad política, sino un vínculo ideal que uniera a las ciudades y que podría sustituirse por el universal del imperio."*

[14] López-Amo y Marín, "Eximeniç," pp. 87-88, 94.

[15] *Ibid.*, pp. 95-97, 111-12; cf. *Dotzé*, Pt. 5, Ch. 670 (quoted in *ibid.*, p. 95, n. 44): *"que vos donchs, senyor, siats Rey e en tan gran*

Like most mediaeval writers, Eximeniç is not very clear on the procedure of resistance, except insofar as he allows that the Church should have an important rôle. The nobles, who should always have a crucial position in the administration of royal power, keep the king within bounds; and the Cortes, which must always approve royal legislation, acts as the guardian of the people's interest in the compactual relationship with the king. The barons and the burghers, therefore, have the rôle of vigilantes with respect to the king, and presumably will be involved in vigorous action against a would-be tyrant.[16] But as for concrete instances of resistance, the reader is offered only a few scanty examples from history and left for the rest to his imagination. Nevertheless, the case for limiting royal authority is stated by Eximeniç in so many different ways, and at such length, that he provides a veritable glossary of resistance theory, one which was drawn up in a time and place that would allow it to influence the growth of the legend of Aragon.[17]

Using just the passages from Eximeniç quoted by modern

---

estament per sola ordinacio e gracios estatut del poble . . . , que ells han dat graciosament a vostres predecessors e apres a vos. . . ."

[16] On the Church, see *ibid.*, pp. 124ff; on the nobles, Cortes, and other checks on the king, pp. 111-23.

[17] Before giving his analysis of Eximeniç's thought, López-Amo y Marín provides the reader with a summary of Catalonian relations with Aragon up to the time of Eximeniç. He stresses indigenous reasons why Barcelona and Valencia each maintained a spirit of independence vis-à-vis the king; but also opines that these two principalities could have been influenced by knowledge of the Aragonese spirit of resistance, which he says was already the subject of legend in the 13th century. In short, López-Amo y Marín adopts the thesis of Oliver y Estellar, *Nacion y Realeza* (discussed above, Ch. I, n. 20), whom he cites several times, and he puts the Sobrarbe myth into Aragon in the high Middle Ages. Eximeniç's theory of resistance, accordingly, could well reflect Aragonese history and legend. For key passages illustrating this matter, see *ibid.*, pp. 13-14, 30-31, 33, 98, 114. The chief fault of this line of reasoning lies in the belief that the Sobrarbe legend was affixed to Aragonese history in the 13th and 14th centuries. This idea is very widespread, and I have tried in the present work to show its fallaciousness. So, if López-Amo y Marín's speculations about relations between the legend of Sobrarbe and the political thought of Francesch Eximeniç are to have any validity, his notion of which was the subject and which the object of influence must be reversed.

writers, one can document the "spirit" of the Oath of the Aragonese at considerable length. The two passages that I will adduce have more than the spirit of the Oath, however; they also suggest its wording. The first is an anecdote about a king of León, drawn from "Gondiçalvus." The king, confronting a man who he thought was a traitor, ordered his execution, but a high personage of the king's court intervened saying that he could not do this "because the law opposes it, and the fuero of the land, which are things stronger than you (*coses pus forts que vos*) and which command more than you (*qui manen mes que vos*) and which command you."[18] By law, the accused must receive a judicial sentence.

With a very slight verbal alteration, changing *coses* (i.e., the law and the fuero) into *nos* (i.e., the persons addressing the king), a near-equivalent to the opening words of the Oath of the Aragonese can be extracted from this passage (*Nos qui valemos tanto come vos, e podemos mas que vos*), or, just as well, the last phrase of the Oath referring to the Justice (*un que manda mas que vos*). In any event, it is an instance of a public admonition to the king that there is a power greater than his own which orders more than he does.[19]

[18] "*car la ley hi contrasta, e lo fur de la terra, qui son coses pus forts que vos, e qui manen mes que vos, e qui manen a vos . . .*" (*Dotzé*, Pt. II, Ch. 161, quoted by D'Ordal [above, n. 13], p. 326, and by Andrés Ivars, "El Escritor Fr. Francisco Eximénez en Valencia," *Archivo Ibero-Americano*, xxIV [1925], 340). The latter article, plus two others (xIX [1923], 359-98; xX [1923], 21-248), are the three most important, for our problem, of the seven-part series published in this journal by Ivars during 1920-1926.

[19] The well-known Spanish maxim, "*Allá van leyes o quieren reyes*" (Thither go laws where kings desire) carries a different lesson than the story reported from "Gondiçalvus." If this writer is Gonzalvo de Hinojosa, Bishop of Burgos (d. 1327), and the work in question is such a one as his still unprinted but widely copied *Chronica ab origine mundi* (cf. Fernández Duro, "La crónica general de Gonzalo de la Finojosa," *BRAH*, x [1887], 438-43; M. C. Diaz y Diaz, *Index Scriptorum Latinorum Medii Aevi Hispanorum*, II [=Acta Salmanticensia. Filosofia y Letras, xIII:2; Salamanca, 1959], 399, No. 2064), then we can make some interesting speculations. The oldest known record of the maxim is found in the mid-13th century, in Ximenez de Rada's *Chronicon*, vI, 26: "*Quo volunt reges vadunt leges*"

The second passage is even more tantalizing. The people dialogue with the king, on equal terms, and impose the condition of accepting him:

If you will do these things, we will have you from that moment on always as king; if not, from that moment you are considered deprived of the realm and separated from it forever.[20]

All the militancy, and almost the exact wording of "If not, not" is found here. Even more significant, perhaps, is the fact of the people's uttering a declaration of conditional acceptance of the king, presumably at his inauguration. This kind of ceremonial circumstance has seemed the most

---

(ed. Schott, II, 107). Gonzalvo de Hinojosa translated Ximenez de Rada's work into Spanish in the early 14th century, rendering the maxim as *"Van leyes do quieren reyes"* (see *CDIHE*, cv [Madrid, 1893], 407), but he could well have known a variant form of the maxim already widespread in the 13th century in which the verb *querer* is replaced by *mandar*, yielding *"Allá van leys o mandan Reys."* We know about this from a writer who glossed the maxim and criticized the authoritarian implication of *mandar* (cf. A. G. Sola-linde, *"Allá van leys o mandan Reys," Revista de Filología Española,* III [1916], 298-300). Now, Gondiçalvus' story (as reported by Eximeniç) employs the authoritarian verb *mandar* (*maner* in Catalan) but turns the point around so that the king is the object and not the subject of it. Would anyone referring to the king and the law, and using the verb "to command," be likely *not* to have the maxim in mind? Gondiçalvus' story has the mark of a rhetorical invention—and, fittingly, Gonzalvo de Hinojosa was much given to inventing dialogues, as can be seen from his original continuation of Ximenez de Rada's chronicle (i.e., *CDIHE*, cvi—see the remarks in the preface to vol. cv)—so that we may have here an instance in which a constitutional maxim provided an author with the basis for a fabulous dialogue between the king and a royal official. This is the kind of process which may have brought the Oath of the Aragonese into existence.

[20] *Dotzé,* Pt. v, Ch. 673: *". . . si acquestes coses farás [las estipuladas en el pacto] . . . tostemps te tendrem axi com a rey a tu e als teus; si no, ara per lavors te reputa per privat del regne e per exellat daquell pera tostemps."* This is all that is quoted in my source, López-Amo y Marín, "Eximeniç," p. 103, n. 70, except for a short phrase preceding it, apparently from the previous page of the *Dotzé* but still connected with the people's declaration: *"car nos no y fariem pus."* In his text López-Amo y Marín reports the dialogue form: *"El pueblo dialoga con el rey de igual a igual y le impone sus condiciones; si las guardas, etc."*

implausible part of the Oath, and certainly has been the most difficult to illustrate from mediaeval history or literature.

What significance should be attributed to these passages with regard to the Oath of the Aragonese? If one operates upon the assumption that the Oath was contrived as a learned forgery during the Renaissance, then one must allow that any literary source known at that time could have been an inspiration for it. The most likely stimulant would be a political circumstance approximating the one given in the Oath, and so much the better if the locale were Spain. By these criteria, Francesch Eximeniç could be seriously considered as a progenitor of the Oath. He was a servant of the kings of Aragon; his political thought had to be taken by the reader as relevant for the kingdom of Aragon; and his works were well known at least in parts of the realm. That he wrote in Catalan and not in Castilian would make little difference to an educated Aragonese; besides, the orthography of the Oath is unusual.[21] Working on the principle of literary analogues, therefore, a better case can be made that the writings of Eximeniç influenced the Oath than that those of any other single writer or combination of writers did so. But the case is only as strong as one's faith in the premise that literary antecedents are crucial.

The county of Barcelona was the first of the great annexations that went to make up the powerful Crown of Aragon in the high Middle Ages, and at least in economic terms it was probably the most powerful constituent of that kingdom. The Catalan Cortes was fully developed by the end

---

[21] Quinto, *Juramento*, pp. 23-30, scrutinized every word of the Oath (Hotman's version) in order to show that it was the product of someone ignorant of Spanish. Quinto did not know the manuscript in which Blancas, in the 16th century, had accepted the language of the Oath as the genuine old vernacular; see above, Ch. v, n. 93. Blancas knew Hotman's version, but did not follow it slavishly; did he perhaps report the oral version current in his time? Antonio Pérez, in the 1590's, may have set down the "purest" version of all; see below, p. 225. In sum, it seems to me that the problems surrounding the authentic text of the Oath are too great to make extensive speculation about its orthographical and grammatical peculiarities worthwhile.

of the 13th century. Through it and along with it the powerful class of feudal barons maintained the separate identity of the county. Even more than Valencia, its sister in language and culture, Barcelona was quick to take offense when its liberties or privileges seemed threatened. One of those occasions was the dispute over the succession to the throne in 1460-1461, which led to a civil war. On the eve of the outbreak of hostilities, the king, John II, was defied in public by a nobleman speaking on behalf of the Catalonian people; the things he said and the way he said them are worth recounting.

The speaker was Guerau Alemany de Cervelló, a partisan of John II's eldest son, Charles of Viana, whose primogenitary right John was trying to transfer to a younger son, Ferdinand, who was Charles' half-brother. The Barcelonians held that Charles' hereditary claims were vouchsafed by the laws of the principality of Catalonia; and as John II's efforts at persuasion became more and more feeble, the defiance of his Catalan subjects became more eloquent. In Barcelona, in February of 1461, Alemany de Cervelló confronted the king and declared:

We ask chiefly of your royal majesty that you observe our liberties, as you have sworn to them. . . . Therefore, in the name of all the principality of Catalonia I beseech you to restore these things to their pristine state.

When the king failed to respond, Alemany de Cervelló put his hand on the hilt of his sword, in sign of rebellion, and repeated the demand. Finally he unsheathed the sword completely and uttered this threat:

All Catalonia reminds you of the oath which you took, and will obey you not at all now that you do not uphold all that you swore.

The king finally responded: he called the Catalans traitors. He stormed out of the room, and the next day the Catalan uprising began.[22]

[22] I have taken the entire account from Jaime Vicens Vives, *Juan II*, pp. 226-27, who found the narrative in a document in the

The aspect of this incident which makes it worthy of consideration is not its verbal similarity to the Oath of the Aragonese: the written narrative shows rhetorical embellishment[23] and, besides, the documentary source is not likely to have been widely known. There is no reason, however, to doubt that the incident itself occurred in a like manner. This is precisely the kind of momentous event which would become the subject of legendary recital. It is not less likely to have stimulated the growth of something like the Oath than purely literary texts such as those of Eximeniç. I do not say that either one of them is actually related to the Oath, but if the Oath existed for a while as a spoken "tradition" before it was set down in print, I think it is more likely that it developed as a fictional narrative about some actual historical event, put in a form which corresponded to some prevailing notions of public law, than as a spontaneous contrivance by a person learned in mediaeval literature. A nobleman, speaking on behalf of the whole principality, defies the king of Aragon and disavows him because he has broken his oath. The "pristine state" of things must be maintained. The people stand for the cause of the ancient law. With the addition of portions of those common elements of legend whereby a signal remonstrance betokens an ordinary right and the side of the right expresses hoary custom, this incident in Catalonia could become proof of an ancient right of the people to accept the king of Aragon on condition that he swear to uphold the laws, and if not, not.[24]

The third of our "analogues" to the Oath of the Aragonese

Archivio de Stato in Milan. Alemany de Cervelló's two declarations are as follows: *"Rogamos sumamente a tu real majestad que observes nuestras libertades, como las juraste. . . . Por tanto, en nombre de todo el Principado de Cataluña te requiero para que devuelvas estas cosas a su prístino estado."* And *"Cataluña entera te recuerda el juramento que le prestaste, y no te obedecerá en nada, ya que cuanto juraste no mantienes."*

[23] Vicens Vives, *loc. cit.*, makes this observation, but adds that he thinks that the report is basically valid.

[24] See below, p. 241, for further reflections on methodology which continue the thoughts just expressed.

is a coronation ceremony of the kingdom of Navarre. But it is not, as one might guess, the famous mediaeval Navarrese *alzar el rey*, the "Germanic" elevation of the king upon a buckler, to the accompaniment of the "thrice-royal" cry: *REAL, REAL, REAL*.[25] This is found in Fuero of Navarre 1,1,1, coming directly after those parts of that law which were the source of False Fueros I-IV. But *alzar el rey* itself plays no role in the final elaboration of the legend of Sobrarbe. Succinctly put, a section (about the first half) of *FN* 1,1,1 was naturalized in the historiography of Aragon as part of that country's supposed first code of laws, the Fueros of Sobrarbe; but not so *alzar el rey*, which is the second half of *FN* 1,1,1. Gerónimo Blancas was probably responsible for this, for, when he came to formulate the primitive constitution of Sobrarbe, he knew of another old inaugural ceremony which was said to belong to early Aragonese history.[26] This other ceremonial was contradictory in spirit to *alzar el rey*, and more consonant with the False Fueros of Sobrarbe. At least this ceremonial—I refer, of course, to the Oath of the Aragonese—was harmonious with False Fueros V-VI. In brief, *alzar el rey* went well enough with False Fueros I-IV, but the Oath of the Aragonese fit perfectly False Fueros V-VI which spoke of the Justice of Aragon and the right to disclaim the ruler. Such, we may guess, was Blancas' reasoning, for he says nothing at all about *alzar el rey*, but makes the Oath of the Aragonese into a virtual seventh False Fuero of Sobrarbe. When printing his work he also suppressed the Oath, leaving his version

[25] The *alzar el rey* ceremonial is given below, Appendix III, at the bottom of the columns where *FN* I, 1, 1 is transcribed from the Fuero of Navarre and Charles of Viana. Sánchez-Albornoz, *"Ordinatio Principis,"* p. 5, states that there is no evidence of raising the king on a shield in Gothic Spain.

[26] Blancas, as we have seen, cites Charles of Viana as his source for False Fueros I-IV; very likely he also knew Pedro Antonio Beuter's *Coronica general* (1551), in which Charles' narrative is even further "Aragonized." Yet both Charles and Beuter include *alzar el rey* as part of what is (to them, at least) an Aragonese practice; see below, Appendix III, for Charles; above, Ch. V, nn. 42, 46, for Beuter. We have to conclude, therefore, that Blancas did not exclude *alzar el rey* out of ignorance.

of the legend of Sobrarbe without any royal inauguration ceremonial. His action of excising *alzar el rey* was decisive, for that ceremonial has not been associated with Aragonese history.[27] His suppression of the Oath, on the other hand, was counteracted by the writings of Hotman, Pérez, *et al.*, which have propagated the myth of the Oath as a fundament of the kingdom of Aragon.

There is a coronation ceremony in Navarre which does merit consideration, albeit brief, for its analogousness in spirit to the Oath of the Aragonese. I refer to the coronation of Jean d'Albret in 1490, in which the new monarch was required to add this sanction to his coronation oath:

And we wish, and it pleases us, that if we should contravene that which we have just sworn, or any part of it, the estates and the people of our kingdom of Navarre are not held to obey us in any manner in whatever we will have contravened.[28]

True, this is the king's oath, not the people's, and allows only partial disobedience to, not total rejection of, the

[27] José María Antequera, in his influential textbook, *Historia de la legislación española* (4th ed., Madrid, 1895), p. 312, does contrast the Oath to *alzar el rey*, but few have faced up to the problem at all. It seems significant to me that Blancas omits *alzar el rey* from his work on Aragonese coronations as well as from his *Commentarii*. Uztarroz, in his notes to Blancas' *Coronaciones*, pp. 12-13, comments that *alzar el rey* is found in Title ɪ of the "Fueros of Sobrarbe" (i.e., either Tudela or Navarre), but he does not try to connect this with what Blancas says about Aragonese oaths in the *Coronaciones*, nor with what he says about the Fuero of Sobrarbe in the *Commentarii*. Quinto, *Juramento*, pp. 441ff, does insist that *alzar el rey* is the proper old coronation ceremonial, citing Uztarroz and others. Since *FN* ɪ,1,1 refers to Spain generally, *alzar el rey* could be believed to have been practiced in any part of the country. Most, however, associate it with Navarre; viz., Schramm, who discusses it in his article on Navarre ("König von Navarra"), but not in his article on Aragon ("Krönung").

[28] "Y queremos, y nos plaze, que si en lo sobredicho que iurando havernos, o en partida de aquello viniessemos econtra, que los dichos estados y pueblos de nuestro dicho Reyno de Navarra no sean tenidos de obedescernos en aquello que seriamos venidos encontra en alguna manera" (Pierre Olhagaray, *Histoire de Foix, Béarn et Navarre* [Paris, 1609], p. 439). A French translation is found in G.–B. Lagrèze, *La Navarre française* (Paris, 1881-1882), ɪɪ, 29.

ruler. Nevertheless, it is a concrete instance of right of resistance in the coronation oath of a neighboring kingdom
(whose history was sometimes inseparable from Aragon's)
less than a century before our first recorded example of the
Aragonese "Oath." Other than the fact that both oaths
share a certain spirit of the right of resistance, nothing can
be said about the relationship of their contents. The Aragonese Oath was certainly inspired by facts (and myths)
of its own history. The fact, however, that some of its early
protagonists claim it was a contemporary or near-contem-
porary usage makes it worthwhile to keep the Navarrese
coronation in mind as a nearby and near-past incident, akin
in spirit to the Aragonese Oath.

Xavier de Quinto's Explanation of the Oath

As we have said several times, Xavier de Quinto, who wrote
in 1848, has become the champion debunker of the Aragonese Oath. He even put forth an elaborate explanation of
how a Renaissance fabricator of myths could have worked
this mischief by culling phrases and incidents from the
broad sweep of Spanish history. Unfortunately for Quinto,
he selected François Hotman as the myth-maker. But
Quinto's arguments are easily transferable to any other person of those times who was a scholar of sorts; and, since
we have no better idea than Quinto did who actually first
coined the Oath, we should review his assemblage of historical and philological antecedents and criticise them
before presenting our own. Since most modern "explana-
tions" of the Oath derive from Quinto, we shall cover the
work of a century of scholars in the process.

Curiously, Quinto believed in the authenticity of the
Fueros of Sobrarbe, not only in the form of Blancas' False
Fueros, but also as they were paraded on the bindings of
the Fuero of Navarre (i.e., Quinto accepted the epigraph,
prologue, and Book I, Title 1, Chapter 1 as *urnavarrischen*,
therefore Sobrarbean). He believed in the early kingdom
of Sobrarbe, and presumed that it must have borrowed
heavily from the Visigothic kingdoms that had expired not
long before. The Fueros of Sobrarbe, therefore, found ante-

cedents in the famous Visigothic law code, the *Fori Judi-cum* (*Fuero Juzgo* in its mediaeval Spanish form), and also in the legal and political canons of the Councils of Toledo. These sources, together with the Fueros them-selves and supplementary incidents drawn from chronicles of Aragonese history, had provided Hotman with the raw materials for his concoction of the Oath.[29]

To Quinto's way of thinking, the most telling phrase in the Oath was *"elegimos rey con estas y estas conditiones"* (we [the people] elect you king on such and such condi-tions). In Aragonese history this could only refer to the very first king—i.e., the first king of Sobrarbe—or to the mo-ment when, at the lapsing of a dynasty, a new one was chosen; otherwise, Sobrarbe-Aragon observed the rule of hereditary succession. The Visigothic kingship was elec-tive, of course, and it probably provided the model for the first "Aragonese" election. In short, the key to understand-ing the Oath lies in the Fuero of Sobrarbe (i.e., Fuero of Navarre) prologue and first chapter (*alzar el rey*), which echo the title on election of princes in the *Fori Judicum* and also the canon of Toledo IV. Upon this basis, Quinto argues, Hotman contrived the peculiar conditions of his Oath by drawing on a variety of phrases of, or thoughts about, Aragonese history.[30]

[29] Quinto, *Juramento*, pp. 176-209, 439-84. Quinto could not have related the Oath to the Fueros of Sobrarbe on the basis of what Blancas had said, because Blancas' autograph was still not public knowledge in 1848 when Quinto wrote. Quinto was led into the Sobrarbe maze chiefly because of Hotman, for by chance Quinto used the last edition of the *Francogallia* (1586 [see above, Ch. II, n. 10]—in fact, Quinto uses the 1600 reprint of it), where Hotman had added information on the Justice drawn from Marineus, Vasaeus, and Zurita. Thus the Sagarra Story, connecting the Justice with the election of the first king, appeared in Hotman as an afterthought of his first presentation of the Oath in 1573. Quinto took this as evidence that Hotman was learned in Aragonese history, and con-cluded that this historical apparatus would show us how Hotman contrived the Oath. The reverse is true: Hotman knew no Aragonese history to begin with, but got the Oath as a rumor; later, he tried to substantiate the Oath, and coincidentally stumbled upon information about the Justice which (as we now know) was relative to the Oath.

[30] Quinto, *Juramento*, pp. 441-73, esp. 454-57. Concerning the *Fori Judicum* and the Councils of Toledo, see below, Ch. VII, nn. 1-3.

We can summarize Quinto's explanation of Hotman's version of the Oath briefly:

NOS QUE SOMOS TANTOS COMO VOS refers to Alfonso III's remark about the Union: *"lo antiguo, cuando habia en el Reyno* tantos *Reyes* como *Ricos hombres,"* which is recorded in Zurita's *Anales.*[31]

Y PODEMOS MAS QUE VOS refers more generally to the Union's dominance over the kings for different, brief spells.[32]

ELEGIMOS REY CON ESTAS Y ESTAS CONDITIONES (see previous paragraph).[33]

INTRA VOS Y NOS refers to the "intermediary" function

[31] Roman mine. For the place in Zurita, see above, Ch. v, n. 59. Note how Quinto corrupts the text of the Oath, saying "We who *are as many* as you" (*somos tantos*) instead of, as do all the primary texts "We who *are worth as much* as you" (*valemos tantos* or *tan buenos*—see Appendix I). The Alfonso III statement, from Zurita, has also been used by Michavila y Villa, *"Apuntes para el estudio de la vida social del Reino de Valencia en la época de los Reyes de Aragón," III Congrés d'Historia de la Corona d'Aragó* (Barcelona, 1908), II, 135, as a way of illustrating the power of the barons during the Union; but he does not relate it to the Oath. In an earlier passage in the same article (p. 118), however, this author alleges in a vague fashion the laws of Alfonso's time which could have allowed the barons to say to the king, *"Cada uno de nosotros vale tanto como vos, e todos juntos mas que vos"* (which is one of the score of garbled forms of the Oath propagated by modern scholarship—see above, Ch. II, nn. 16-17), and he implies that this "oath" came into being in the time of Alfonso III by stating that its terms were not appropriate to the age of James I. This argument is carried forth by Shneidman, "Thirteenth Century Aragon," p. 172, who draws the conclusion that this "oath" (as just cited from Michavila) could well have been invented by the Barons during Alfonso's time; further, Shneidman says that the phrase "may be an old Visigothic expression," and cites Michavila y Villa not quite accurately as a source of this idea.

[32] Quinto, *Juramento,* p. 474.

[33] Quinto, *Juramento,* p. 475. In addition to the word *elegimos,* upon which Quinto placed so much stress, we should take note of the word *condiciones,* which is used by Cerdan in relation to the election of the Justice (above, Ch. IV, n. 9) and by Molino in relation to the right to depose a law-breaking king (above, Ch. v, n. 26); also, both these sources refer to the "election" of the king.

of the Justice of Aragon which is contained in the common eponymic form *judex medius (juez medio)*.[34]

UN QUE MANDA MAS QUE VOS refers to those powers of the Justice which have allowed him from time to time to make decisions "against the exigencies of the monarchy."[35]

Quinto also accounts for the differences between Hotman's version of the Oath and Pérez'. He believed that Pérez took the Oath from Hotman, making no substantial alterations except for the addition of the three words which were to become the epitome for the Oath: *Si no, no.* Quinto found these exact words in the *Fori Judicum:* "*Rex eius eris si recta facis,* si *autem* non *facis,* non *eris,*" and the context in this Visigothic source is perfectly harmonious with the spirit of the Oath.[36]

With respect to the *Si no, no* phrase, there is good reason to believe that Quinto was correct. Also, calling the Justice an intermediary had been common even during the late Middle Ages, and there is no reason to doubt that this is meant in the Oath. But for the rest of the phrases, Quinto's derivations are either flimsy on philological grounds, or else are without philological grounding and therefore completely heuristic. He entered the right domain when he took the Fuero of Sobrarbe into consideration, and he was on the right track, obviously, when he pondered the role of the Justice in Aragonese history. But he had no chance of plotting the true location of the Oath within the Sobrarbe complex unless he had treated the Sobrarbe legend and laws with the same skepticism that he had the Oath. Quinto was right in assuming that the Oath was derived in part from the Sobrarbe legend and laws, but he was right for the wrong reason. He believed that the Sobrarbe apparatus embodied 9th-century truths, and the Oath was a 16th-

[34] Quinto, *Juramento,* p. 475. The "intermediary" notion is prominent in the Sagarra Story (see below, Appendix IV; also above, Ch. IV, n. 23), in Cerdan (above, Ch. IV, n. 9), and in the "historical" versions in Vagad and Zurita (above, Ch. V, nn. 12, 53).

[35] Quinto, *Juramento,* p. 475.

[36] See below, pp. 227ff.

century lie based upon it. In fact, everything under consideration is a myth. The Oath is simply the last phase of the process of myth-making, and for that reason naturally depended upon the earlier development.

The Oath has a peculiar kinship with False Fuero vi. They make a perfect pair: the Oath warns the king at the time of his accession that he is being accepted on condition that he uphold the laws, and False Fuero vi allows the deposition of a king who has broken the law. If Quinto was convinced that the Fueros of Sobrarbe had done much to mold the Oath, we would expect that he would stress the relationship with False Fuero vi more than anything else. To be sure, Quinto, the staunch monarchist, could not really believe in the authenticity of False Fuero vi, and he found solace in the many arguments that had been devised to explain it away; at best it was a rhetorical gesture made by Iñigo Arista that had never had force as a law.[37] Still, it was in the chronicles, in sometimes treacherously deceiving fashion, and it is just the kind of evidence that a regicide-minded heretic (Hotman, in Quinto's eyes) would turn to account. But Hotman never mentions this famous segment of the Sagarra Story, with its controversial phrase *alium regem, etiam paganum*. Quinto must have been puzzled by this omission, although it is now very easy to explain: Hotman had simply never happened upon a source which mentioned it.[38] Had Quinto not been so obsessed with his belief that Hotman was the inventor of the Oath, and therefore been freer to consider the connection between the

[37] Quinto, *Juramento*, pp. 459-61, where he links this "Sobrarbe" law, as he had others, to the Fourth Council of Toledo: *"verum etiam et sui ordinis dignitate privetur"*; see below, Ch. vii, n. 3.

[38] We have remarked that Hotman's effort to substantiate the Oath from historical sources was handicapped by his use of strictly Latin sources (Vasaeus, Marineus, Zurita's *Indices*), presumably because he did not know Spanish. Unless I am mistaken, the only Latin printed source of False Fuero vi that Hotman could have known (but did not) was Molino's *Repertorium*. Thus, by a sheer quirk, Hotman never came across either of the two things which would have served best his argument about resistance right in Aragon: False Fuero vi and the Privileges of Union. Both of them are fully spelled out in Zurita's *Anales* of 1562, which Hotman either did not have, or could have had but could not have read.

Oath and False Fuero VI, he would at least have had at hand—no matter what he did with it—the vital ideological source of the Oath of the Aragonese people.

Although Xavier de Quinto made a score of errors in his treatise on the Oath of the Aragonese, he did perform one great service: by his exhaustive survey of the relevant documents he made it clear that the Oath belonged to the 16th century, and not to earlier Aragonese history. He was foolish to insist that he had found the exact year (1573) and author (Hotman); but even the uncovering of Giovanni Soranzo's *Relazione* of the year 1565, though it pushes back the *terminus a quo* by eight years, does not by itself disturb the argument of a Renaissance origin of the Oath. What should be ended is the search for a villain, because Soranzo had none of the treacherous motives that a Quinto could discover so quickly in a Hotman. Soranzo reported a rumor, and beyond doubt the Frenchmen Beza, Hotman, and Bodin were doing the same.

Dating the Oath of the Aragonese

The Oath was a rumor that suddenly began to appear in several places in 1565. We have no idea who started it, but we have a good idea of the sets of related ideas to which it belongs. In a sense, Blancas had already seen this connection in the 1580's, when he linked the Oath to the Fueros of Sobrarbe in his manuscript writings; and Quinto, and many others after him, have stressed it time and again. Now, in our turn, we have reviewed the Sobrarbe legend and laws at great length—but with a different spirit; and therefore at the end we see the relationship of the Oath to the Sobrarbe legend quite differently. We have looked at the Sobrarbe legend as an example of a Renaissance myth about mediaeval history, which in itself is not unusual, although its period of incubation is quite long (200 years) and some stages of its complex development are still not too clear. The cycle of growth of that legend shows that the most rapid change took place near the end. Indeed, not until 1550 did the two long-separated parts of the legend finally come together, after which it took just one generation for the final form to be achieved by the lucubration of Gerónimo Blancas. In this same period of the final formulation of the Sobrarbe legend, the Oath appeared for the first time, bearing many familiar traits.

A simple finale might be written at this point, saying that we should not be too surprised to find such a thing as the Oath appearing in 16th-century Aragon once we have properly understood the making of the legend of Sobrarbe. The Oath was just a variant form of False Fueros v and vi before Blancas actually made them into Fueros of Sobrarbe. If we left it at that, we would be spared having to date the origin of the Oath with exactitude, for it would be technically possible for the Oath to have been concocted at almost any stage along the road traversed by the Sagarra Story; and, if all reasonableness would insist that it belonged to the later stages of growth of the Sobrarbe legend, it would seem to make no difference whether that was the 1530's, the 1540's, or the 1550's. Clio's graveyard is filled with scholarly labors (*viz.*, Quinto's) which have insisted that "this is the first instance of such-and-such." On the other hand, to leave the origin of the Oath in this still-parlous state would be a faint-hearted action if, in fact, I did have strong beliefs as to its special circumstances. I do. For what it is worth, therefore, I shall proceed to argue that the Oath came into being not more than fifteen years, and perhaps less than two years, before Giovanni Soranzo wrote home to Venice about it in 1565.

The year 1562 is a good *terminus a quo* for the origin of the Oath because it was then that the first volume of Zurita's *Anales* appeared. In terms of "firsts," it seems safe to say that no earlier work in the vernacular had offered the gist of both False Fueros v and vi[39] (at least no earlier vernacular work that deserves to be mentioned in the same breath with Zurita's); so that if the Oath is adequately explainable as a variant of those famous "laws" about the origin of the Justice

---

[39] Beuter is discounted because he had only False Fuero v when he wrote in 1551, while Vagad, in the 1490's, had split False Fueros v and vi between Garci Ximenez and Iñigo Arista, and had greatly devalued their revolutionary impact.

and the right to depose a law-breaking king, then at least the opportunity to make this twist was much greater after 1562 than it had been before. But there was something else contained in this first volume of the *Anales* which we have very sound reason to believe had not been recorded by anyone, in Latin or in the vernacular, for two centuries—a notorious document relative to "Aragonese Liberties" which could have served just as well as Fueros v and vi as an inspiration for the Oath. I refer, of course, to the Privileges of Union. Zurita did not give a transcript of them, to be sure, but he gave a very accurate résumé of them in some 300 words. This was the "first time" [*absit omen*] since Peter IV's edict *De prohibita unione* in 1348 that we find a full explanation of the condemned articles of 1287.[40] On the other hand, we can be quite confident that little more than a decade before Zurita published the first volume of the *Anales* the question of the contents of the Privileges of Union, if not their exact articles, must have been debated by an august body of Aragonese jurists, that is, by the panel which was commissioned to reform the Fueros of Aragon, and which published the *Nueva Compilación* in 1551.

The commission's task, it will be recalled, consisted of two main problems: to trim down the unwieldy mass of laws that had accumulated since 1247; and to organize the remainder into topical divisions.[41] It might be very revealing to have the minutes of the meetings where *De prohibita unione* was discussed. If anything would seem to be archaic, and ripe for the wastebasket, it would be this two-hundred-year-old royal fit of pique against a baronial organization that had already been quashed on the battlefield once and for all. Did the commissioners really feel that it might still be dangerous to let Aragonese nobility know about the rights which their forebears had wrung from kings two centuries earlier? Did the commissioners perhaps feel that Peter's solemn injunction against knowledge of the Privileges of Union for all time to come obliged them to keep *De prohibita unione* perpetually in force? The an-

---

[40] See above, Ch. iv, n. 36.
[41] See above, pp. 119-21.

swers to these questions hinge on a third one: did the commissioners themselves know the provisions of the Privileges of Union?

On an earlier occasion, I built an important part of my explanation of the origin of False Fueros v and vi upon the state of ignorance which was solemnly decreed by the edict *De prohibita unione*. I guessed that some officials who had to enforce this edict must have been frustrated by the disappearance of the document: how could they search it out and destroy it if they had never been trained to recognize it?[42] This circumstance had to have been realized in the years 1549-1551, when the commission deliberated over *De prohibita unione*. Whether they got hold of a copy of the Privileges of Union (and one would assume that the copy Zurita is known to have possessed a decade later would have been available to them) and decided that it was still dangerous enough to warrant the reaffirmation of *De prohibita unione*, or whether they remained in ignorance of the Privileges of Union and renewed *De prohibita unione* just to be on the safe side—in either case there must have been a lively discussion of the famous old Union compact. We only have to imagine the spreading of a rumor about the commissioners' deliberations in order to have the conditions which would foster a myth such as the Oath. If this were true, we would have the delightful symmetry of *De prohibita unione* on two different occasions giving rise to antiroyalist fables: the first time, after 1348, to the Sagarra Story; the second time, after 1551, to the Oath. In this case, False Fueros v and vi and the Oath would be siblings, two

---

[42] See above, p. 96, to which may be added these remarks by Blancas (from the suppressed parts of the *Commentarii*): "These, then, are those two ancient privileges that once caused such clamor among us. Frequently we have seen them praised in the writings of our ancestors; but not a single copy is readily found. For on being abolished by a law of Peter IV with unanimous consent of the kingdom, not only did the originals perish, but as many copies as were at hand, together with almost all the documents of our early history. Hence, in great part, arose the confusion and obscurity introduced therein" (ed. Hernandez, p. 167, n. 1, coming immediately after Blancas' rendition of the Privileges and before the quotation given above, Ch. v, n. 76).

hundred years different in age—a circumstance which, to my way of thinking, is just as plausible as the former's being the latter's parent.

It is perhaps academic to ponder—assuming that the Oath is related somehow to the renewed official commitment to suppress the Privileges of Union—whether the Oath arose when there existed no published version of the Privileges, or after 1562 when Zurita gave his excellent summary of them. One clue, involving one word, might incline us toward the latter alternative. Although Zurita's synopsis of the Privileges of Union is complete, and often follows the original phraseology very closely, he made one great slip. In the most sensitive part of the document, where the right to reject the law-breaking king is declared, the Privileges of Union had said:

Ante sines algun blasmo de fe é de layaltad podades facer, et fagades *otro rey et seynnor qual queredes é d'on queredes. . . .*[43]

But Zurita renders this passage thus:

Antes sin algune note de infamia y de la fidelidad que le devian, pudiessen eligir *otro rey y senor, qual quisiessen. . . .*[44]

The notion of "election" is fully contained in both passages, but Zurita actually uses the word itself. In the Huguenot versions of the Oath, the pivotal word is *"elegimos."*

It will be well to terminate these speculations about the relationship of the Oath to the Privileges of Union by recalling where the case is weak: the Privileges of Union do not involve a ceremonial interchange of pledges between king and barons, whereas the supposed Oath demands that one think in terms of ceremonial. We have seen that the Oath seems to be alien to Aragonese coronations and Cortes oath-takings. But there is one ritual oath-taking in Aragon which involves the King and the Justice as its main characters, yet is quite separate from the coronation and the Cortes. Moreover, this ceremonial was performed just two

---

[43] See above, Ch. IV, n. 31.
[44] See the place cited above, Ch. V, n. 54.

years before Soranzo recorded the Oath in his *Relazione*. Thus, no matter how wildly inaccurate the Oath is, it may well have roots in an actual historical event.

The Royal Jurisdictional Oath

Each of the four primary versions of the Oath differs from the others in some respect, but the Oath as presented by Soranzo separates itself from the others in a drastic fashion. This singularity does not leap out at the reader. In fact, the more knowledgeable one is about the history of the Oath, the less likely one is to notice it. The fact is this: Soranzo's Oath does not involve the king.

Soranzo himself seems to have been deceived, for he introduces the Oath by saying, "When they accept their king (*quando accetano il re*) they are used to employing these exact and lofty words." But in the "exact words" the king does not appear:

We, who are as good as you, swear to you who are no better than we, as prince and heir of our realm (*per principe ed erede del nostro regno*), on condition that you preserve our liberty and laws, and if you do otherwise we do not swear to you.[45]

If Soranzo had said simply "prince" there would be no reason to assume that he meant anyone other than the king; but by the same token if the Oath (as he heard it) included the word "heir" it cannot refer to the king at all. The king cannot be accepted as the heir of the realm—he gives up that status when he becomes king. So, we have our choice whether to believe that Soranzo was correct in reporting the Oath but was mistaken in assuming that it applied to the king, or that he recorded the Oath incorrectly, or that he recorded it correctly but that his informant was muddleheaded.

The second of these possibilities hardly warrants serious consideration, for while an Italian might easily substitute "prince" for "king," he would have no reason to invent the absurd appelation "prince and heir" in place of "king." The

---

[45] See above, n. 1, for the complete text of Soranzo.

first and third possibilities, on the other hand, are not mutually exclusive. As we shall see, each of them may bear some truth and some error. To put it succinctly, Soranzo was reporting an Oath that did apply to the king on some occasions, but his informant happened to give him the form in which the same Oath was used on another occasion, applied to someone else—i.e., to the "prince and heir." This would-be error comes almost as a revelation, for it points the way directly to an unusual aspect of late mediaeval Aragonese constitutional history that dramatizes the actual power of the Justice and at the same time blends perfectly with the legend about the Justice which grew up so rapidly in the 16th century.

We must begin back in the year 1348, at the Cortes where Peter IV enunciated *De prohibita unione*. We have seen the negative characteristics of that particular "constitution," which became the first item in Book x of the Fueros of Aragon, but we have also noted in passing that otherwise this Cortes saw much legislation which affirmed many liberties of the people. In effect, Peter IV sifted out the execrable claims of the Union, but immediately placated his subjects by affirming the fundamental rightness of many laws and privileges which should not be confused with the selfish ends of the baronial insurrection.[46] One of these edicts declared the "things"—that is, laws, privileges, liberties, and usages—which the king and all royal officers were obliged henceforth to swear to uphold. In this edict, known by its incipit *De his quae dominus rex*, Peter IV calls upon himself to swear upon the cross and Evangels to guard the valid laws of the land. Moreover, Peter decreed,

We wish and also we command in perpetuity that our successors should be held to take a similar oath before they will be sworn to and crowned as king.

Likewise, all royal officers are ordered to take this oath: the governor of Aragon, the regent (if there be one), the Justice of Aragon, and all other judges and officials of the

---

[46] See above, Ch. iv, n. 35, for remarks and bibliography on the Cortes of 1348.

realm. *De his quae dominus rex* entered the Fueros of Aragon directly following *De prohibita unione,* and it was in effect a counteraction to it: the Privileges of Union were to be obliterated from memory, but the true liberties of the land were to be vouchsafed forevermore by every king and every royal official.[47]

Still during the reign of Peter IV, at the Cortes of Calatayud in 1366, the edict entitled *Quod primogenitus* expanded the scope of the oath provided for in *De his quae dominus rex.* The main purpose of *Quod primogenitus* was to unite two important aspects of royal succession which had hitherto been separate. One was the declaration of the

[47] *De his quae dominus rex* is found on fol. LVIr-v of all the pre-1551 editions of the *Fori Aragonum,* and as Fuero N⁰. 29 of the editions of the *Nueva Compilación.* These excerpts are the most important clauses: "*Promitimus in bona fide regali, et iuramus super Crucem Domini nostri Ihesu Christi, et eius Sancta Quattuor Evangelia coram nobis prosita . . . quod nos in nostra propria persona custodiemus, observabimus . . . et faciemus inviolabiliter observari et custodiri foros infrascriptos, specialiter sub rubrica praemissa contentos, necnon, et alios foros, privilegia, libertates, usus, et consuetudines dicti regni Aragonum. . . . Volumus et etiam ordinamus in perpetuum, quod simile iuramentum teneantur successores nostris facere antequam iurentur, et coronentur. Et etiam quod gubernator Aragonum qui est . . . et Iusticia Aragonum, et omnes alii iudices et officiales dicti Regni . . . iurare teneantur.*" Although non-royal personages are included in this edict, another oath exclusively for royal officers to uphold the Fueros, etc., was provided in the same Cortes: *De Iuramento Praestando per officiales* (pre-1551 eds., fol. LVIIvff; N⁰. 159 of the *Nueva Compilación*). It should be noted, lest a misconception arise, that an oath of kings to uphold the laws was common coin in mediaeval monarchies: for Spain, see Sánchez-Albornoz, "*Ordinatio Principis,*" and Mayer, *Historia,* I, 95-97, 312; for England, see H. G. Richardson, "The Coronation in Medieval England: the Evolution of the Office and the Oath," *Traditio,* XVI (1960), 161-74; for France, see Marcel David, "Le serment du sacre du IXe au XVe siècle," *Revue du moyen âge latin,* VI (1950) 5-272. To illustrate the universality of the idea, we have the sweeping statement by Baldus in the mid-14th century, "*Nota quod omnes reges mundi in sua coronatione debent iurare iura regni sua conservare et honorem coronae,*" when glossing the decretal *De Iureiurando* of Pope Honorius III (=c. 33, X, 2, 24; ed. Friedberg, *Corpus iuris canonici* [Leipzig, 1881], II, 373) in his *In Decretales* (Venice, 1580), fol. 261v. This place is cited by Ernst H. Kantorowicz, "Inalienability," *Speculum,* XXIX (1954), 500f, esp. 501, n. 66, reprinted in his *Selected Studies* (Locust Valley, N.Y., 1965), pp. 149f, esp. p. 150, n. 66.

right of the first-born in the Cortes, a custom which went back to the 13th century, and which Peter IV had observed in 1352 when he had had the primogenitary right of his son John decreed immediately after he was born.[48] The other question was the administrative power of the Procurator General. A primogenit (as I shall call him henceforth[49])

[48] Peter IV is apparently the only king who had the parliamentary decree regarding his son's primogenitary right made part of the *Fori Aragonum*; see the pre-1551 eds., fol. LXVIII. For a recent discussion of the problem of the title *primogenito e heredero*, see Percy E. Schramm, "König von Aragon," pp. 110f.

[49] The word "primogenit" was used in English and Spanish at least until the 16th century. An acceptable synonym for it, in the old usage, would be "successor," but that has acquired the connotation in English of one who has already succeeded instead of one who is going to succeed. In Spanish law of the 14th and 15th centuries the word *heredero* (or Latin, *heres*) was not used often, but in the centuries before and after then it was common. In 16th-century France the word was avoided more scrupulously than ever before, because crown succession should never be thought of as comparable to private law inheritance; see my *Juristic Basis*, pp. 12ff. French writers of the 15th and 16th centuries were of the opinion that the royal succession in Aragon was susceptible to testamentary dispositions; e.g., Jean de Terre Rouge, in his tractate on the French succession written in 1418/1419 (Tract. I. Art. 1, concl. vii; ed. as appendix to Hotman, *Disputatio de Controversia Successionis* [Basel, 1585], p. 78), said that he had seen *publica instrumenta* to this effect, and Charles Du Moulin in the mid-16th century refers to the right of the king of Aragon to manipulate the succession and even to deny the right of the primogenit (see *Juristic Basis*, p. 27). The truth of the matter seems to be the following. In the 12th and 13th centuries the royal testament was an important factor in the succession, but ceased to be so in the 14th century; see Schramm, "König von Aragon," pp. 112ff. In the 14th and 15th centuries, the legislation concerning the primogenit seems to have overridden all testamentary considerations. But in the 16th century we again find the king of Aragon, Ferdinand the Catholic, making important testamentary dispositions. The opinion of Du Moulin just referred to may have been based upon this instance in recent history; but the reference to "public instruments" a century before by Terre Rouge remains a mystery to me. I have not pursued the Spanish scholarly literature on the problem, but a good place to begin would probably be the book by Xavier de Quinto in 1840, *Del derecho de suceder les hembras á la corona de Aragon* (see above, Ch. I, n. 4), which was criticized by José Morales Santisteban, *Estudios historicos sobre el reino de Aragon* (Madrid, 1851), pp. 37-72, and then immediately defended by Quinto in his *Respuesta que á don José Morales Santisteban* (Madrid, 1851).

had been given this power just after 1300, but it was only with Peter's edict *Quod primogenitus* in 1366 that this practice was made the rule. Fourteen years was declared the age at which the primogenit should enter the office of Governor General (thenceforth the title of the office).[50] Before assuming these jurisdictional powers, the primogenit was obliged to swear the same oath which the king and others were bound to swear according to *De his quae dominus rex*. Along with the primogenit, his officers (i.e., Chancellor, Vice-Chancellor, and Lieutenants) also had to take the oath. As Peter IV says in the text of the edict, the primogenit should not have any greater prerogative than the king himself. That is to say, the primogenit should not be exempt from the oath, wherewith Peter acknowledges that the oath does constitute a limitation upon the royal prerogative.[51]

[50] For the development of the office of Governor General, see Lalinde Abadía, *Gobernación general*, esp. pp. 50, 160 for the facts which I have cited. In the early 14th century, Martin I of Aragon decreed that the primogenit should have the title of Duke of Gerona (in Catalonia), which we may compare to the adoption of the titles Dauphin and Prince of Wales for the heirs-apparent to the French and English thrones in roughly the same epoch. Peter IV's son, John, was the first to whom this could be applied, and it was in 1352. Also in 1414 it played a role in the establishment of the Trastámara dynasty in Aragon, but the title never really acquired much meaning. See Blancas, *Coronaciones*, pp. 85, 220ff, 237; Baron de Rio Tovía, "El Ducado y Principadado de Gerona," *RABM*, XLVII (1927), 296-99.

[51] The important parts of *Quod primogenitus* are as follows: "*Statuimus quod filius primogenitus noster vel alterius regis successoris nostri qui pro tempore fuerit Aragonum, qui in eodem regno debeat succedere, regat officium gubernatoris, seu procuratoris generalis dicti Regni, ac regere possit, et eodem officio uti, et exercere iurisdictionem civilem et criminalem eiusdem in dicto regno postquam habuerit xiiii annos. . . . Ita tamen quod antequam utatur, aut uti possit dicta iurisdictione, teneatur in dicta civitate Caesaraugustae, ne subditi nostri eiusdem regni ignorantiam valeant allegare, publice, praesente iustitia Aragonum praestare iuramentum secundum forum [scil., De His Quae Dominus Rex], et iurare servare foros, privilegia, libertates, usus, et consuetudines dicti regni, prout nos, et antecessores nostri fecimus . . . cum primogenitus noster vel alterius Regis successoris nostri qui pro tempore fuerit, non debeat habere maiorem praerogativam quam nos . . .*" (pre-1551 ed., fol. LXX[v]; *Nueva Compilación* N⁰. 28). The edict then goes on to refer to a "new Fuero" on the same subject called *Quia secundum Forum in poenis corporalibus*. This turns out to be an edict which Peter IV had first

As significant as anything else in *Quod primogenitus* is the fixing of additional conditions as to where and how the oath shall be administered. *De his quae dominus rex* had called for the oath to be sworn upon the cross and Evangels, and this was retained. But *Quod primogenitus* adds that the oath should be taken in public, in the city of Zaragoza, in the presence of the Justice of Aragon. The reason for this, Peter asserts, is to avoid the possibility of his subjects' claiming ignorance of the deed; but the effect of it, in the long run, was to imply that the civil authorities of Zaragoza, and specifically the Justice of Aragon, were the ones who were receiving the oath. Not only before God, but also before the people: such was the formulary of *Quod primogenitus*.

The successor to the throne was now bound by an oath which was more carefully defined than the oath of the king. Furthermore, since *Quod primogenitus* did not say that the primogenit's oath as Governor General preempted the oath which the king was required to take according to *De his quae dominus rex*, it now appeared that a person who entered into primogenitary jurisdiction and then later succeeded to the throne would have to take twice the identical oath to uphold the laws, privileges, and so forth. But as king, according to *De his quae dominus rex*, he would not have to take that oath publicly in Zaragoza, in the presence of the Justice. As king, that is, he would have to swear an oath in less binding circumstances than he did as primogenit.

In the century that followed, according to the scanty records of royal ceremonial, the special features of the primogenitary oath of 1366 were applied to the royal oath called for by the edict of 1348. That is to say, the oath which the king had to take before his coronation—and quite separately from his coronation oath—came to be referred

---

promulgated two years earlier at the Cortes of the kingdom of Aragon, and is now reaffirming at a General Cortes of the Crown of Aragon. The contents of the earlier decree will be found in Martin Daux's *Observantiae*, Tit. IX, § Actus Curiarum (ed. 1542, fol. XLVI^v), where it is quoted by volume and page from the registers of the Cortes of Zaragoza for 1364, with the slightly different incipit, *Cum secundum Forum. . . .*

to as his oath of "exercising jurisdiction"; and it was usually taken in Zaragoza in the presence of the Justice of Aragon.[52] Finally, in 1461, this practice became the law of the land when King John II issued the edict *Coram quibus* at the Cortes of Calatayud:

We decree that before our successors and Lieutenant Generals (if there should be any) and primogenits can exercise any jurisdiction they are bound to swear publicly, in the city of Zaragoza in the Cathedral Church of San Salvador, before the high altar, in the presence of the Justice of Aragon, and in his power, and also in the presence of the four Deputies of the Realm, one from each of the "arms," and the three Jurors of the city of Zaragoza, those things which we and our successors on our part, and the Lieutenant Generals and primogenits on their parts, are held to swear by the law and custom of the realm.[53]

The edict then specifies who shall receive the oath if by chance the office of Justice of Aragon is momentarily vacant, thus leaving no doubt that the primary intent of

---

[52] Cf. Blancas, *Coronaciones*, pp. 202 *et sqq.*, and Quinto, *Juramento*, pp. 312ff.

[53] Despite its Latin title, the text of *Coram quibus* is Spanish: "*Por quanto por algunos es puesto en dubdo, como nos y nostros successores somos tenidos jurar antes que podamos de alguna iurisdiction usar. Por tanto de voluntat de la cort statuimos: que nostros successores, e los Lugartenientes generales, en caso que lugartenient se pueda fazer, e primogenitos, antes que puedan usar de alguna iurisdiction, sian tenidos jurar en la ciutad de Zaragoza en la seu de sant Salvador davant laltar mayor publicament present el iustitia de Aragon y en poder suyo, e presentes quatro diputados del regno, uno de cada brazo, y tres iurados de la ciudat de Zaragoza, aquellas cosas, que nos, y nostros successores, e Lugartenientes generales, e primogenitos in sus casos, de fuero e costumbre del regno, somos, e son tenidos jurar*" (pre-1551 ed., fol. cLv^v; *Nueva Compilación*, N⁰. 28). The remaining one-third of the edict (not given here) concerns principally the contingency of having an alternate for the Justice. The inclusion of the Lieutenant General in these provisions reflects the important station he had achieved during the long years that John II held that office in Aragon while his brother, King Alfonso the Magnanimous, chose to reside in Italy. By another decree of 1461, John II made the Lieutenant General the peer of the primogenit in his powers (viz., *De officio locumtenentis*, pre-1551 ed., fol. cLvii; *Nueva Compilación*, N⁰. 39).

Coram quibus is to invest the office of Justice with the major role in validating the exercise of power by the three main bearers of sovereign power.

According to *Coram quibus*, every person who becomes king of Aragon must twice in his life take a civil oath upon "entrance into power": first when he begins to exercise king-like jurisdiction as heir to the throne, and again when he begins to exercise jurisdiction as king in his own right. We may name this oath, without any ambiguity, the royal juris-dictional oath. On grounds of theory of rulership, the oath solves some important problems of dynastic right to the throne. In the monarchies of Europe which were not elec-tive, it had become the practice to allow the heir to the throne to assume virtually royal powers during his prede-cessor's lifetime. This was well supported by legists using arguments from Roman Law, among other things;[54] but the practical purpose, of course, was to train the successor in the art of governance. In Aragon, as nowhere else to my knowledge, a ceremonial investiture of the heir with these powers was accomplished by the decrees *Quod primogeni-tus* and *Coram quibus*; and thus the propriety of this cus-tom and the punctilio of its execution were made part of the constitution of the land.

A more difficult problem concerned the king himself: under what authority did he exercise power in the interval between his predecessor's death and his own coronation? In France and England, since the 1270's, it had become customary, without ever being legislated upon, to allow the king-elect to exercise full legal jurisdiction immediately upon the death of his predecessor, withholding from him only the robes of office and certain magical powers of king-ship until he was crowned.[55] In Aragon, the prescription of

[54] See my *Juristic Basis*, pp. 22-25; also Ernst H. Kantorowicz, "Zu den Rechtsgrundlagen der Kaisersage," *Deutsches Archiv*, XIII (1957), 126-50, reprinted in his *Selected Studies* (Locust Valley, N.Y., 1965), pp. 291-307.

[55] See my *Royal Funeral Ceremony in Renaissance France* (= Tra-vaux d'Humanisme et Renaissance, XXXVII; Geneva, 1960), 183f; the main subject of this book is the unusual funeral ritual which the French developed in part as a solution to the problem of the in-terregnum between the death of one king and the coronation of

De his quae dominus rex provided for a civil ceremonial to invest the king with legal powers before his coronation. This solved a delicate problem concerning the royal coronation, because Aragon observed the practice of combining the coronation with the first meeting of the Cortes of the new king.[56] How could he call a Cortes if he were not yet crowned? (Other European monarchs held their coronations separately, before summoning Parliament.) The jurisdictional oath at least answered this question, by giving the king legal rights, such as that of summoning a Cortes, before he was crowned.

As it happened, the actual coronation of the king of Aragon fell into disuse after the early 15th century, although the coronation oath—which should probably be

---

the next. It is worth noting that when Alfonso III used the name "king" immediately after the death of his father in 1285, there was much grumbling about it until he held a Cortes in 1286 (Blancas, *Coronaciones*, p. 231). This shows that the king of Aragon tried to assume the practice of immediate legal succession in just the same years that this was done in England and France; but whereas in the latter countries it remained the custom ever afterwards, in Aragon it was defeated in the next century and the royal jurisdictional oath established in its place.

[56] That the first royal coronation in Aragon took place in 1204 (Peter I) is now universally agreed; see Schramm, "Krönung," pp. 579ff. There is, however, a legend to the effect that Ramiro I (1035-1063) was the first crowned king of Aragon. Paul Kehr, *Das Papsttum und die Königreiche Navarra und Aragon bis zur Mitte des 12. Jahrhunderts* (= Abh. der Preuss. Akad., phil.-hist. Kl., 4; 1928), 10, n. 1, had found the legend in Garibay's *Compendio historial*, xxxi, 16 (ed. 1628, iv, 9), but confessed ignorance of its origins. Schramm, "Krönung," p. 579, n. 2, provided this answer: Garibay got it from Jacobus Valdes, *De dignitate regum regnorumque Hispaniae* (ed. prin., 1602), who in turn took it from "Beuter, Lib. 2, cap. 8"—i.e., says Schramm, from "Michael Beuther, 1522-1587, *Prof. der Geschichte in Greifswald und in Strassburg.*" My comment is this: Garibay could hardly have derived the legend from Valdes, since the first edition of the former's work was in 1571, thirty years *before* the appearance of the latter's. Secondly, while it would be fascinating to have the legends of Aragon be part of the intellectual milieu of Strassburg, where François Hotman was a professor in the late 1550's, it would be best for the scholar who sets out to find "Beuter, Lib. 2, cap. 8" to examine first the Valencian Pedro Antonio Beuter's *Coronica general* (ed. prin., 1546-1551; see above, Ch. v, n. 41), before perusing any of the works of the German Michael Beuther in an effort to discover which one of them Schramm thought spoke about Aragonese coronations.

called the inauguration oath—survived as part of the meeting of the Cortes. This was a reciprocal oath: by the king to uphold the Fueros and by the Estates to obey the king. It seems to have become a standard feature of every meeting of the Cortes. With the disappearance of the coronation, we can imagine that the jurisdictional oath acquired more and more importance. Still, it did not supersede the Cortes oath, and we shall see why this was so.[57]

Aside from these constitutional niceties, there were always issues of power at stake in the evolution of the royal jurisdictional oath. From a long-range point of view we are struck by the steady hedging in of royal power which the three edicts reflect. The first of them, *De his quae dominus rex*, shows nothing of contentiousness: it is impersonal, involving the whole corporation of royal officers, under God, in the duty of upholding the laws. The second and third edicts, however, focus upon certain individuals and give their oath a special—almost contractual—character with respect to the people. The Justice of Aragon emerges as the protagonist of the ceremonial who symbolizes the popular cause; but we should not overlook the presence, in the final formulary, of the deputies of the kingdom and the jurors of Zaragoza.[58] Since the evidence shows that during the late 14th and early 15th centuries the jurisdictional oath was usually taken *de facto* in the hands of the Justice, the *de iure*

[57] The last royal coronation in Aragon was that of Ferdinand I in 1414; see Schramm, "Krönung," pp. 593ff. However, a law was passed in the Cortes of 1461 entitled *De Iure Coronationis* (*Fori Aragonum*, pre-1551 eds., fol. ccx; *Nueva Compilación*, No. 578) which concerns the tax (*dreyto de Coronacion*) which could be levied upon various corporative bodies by the ruler, or his queen, to pay for the ceremonial. It was specified that one year's *caucion* must be given; that the ceremonial must actually be held in the city of Zaragoza; and that the payment of the *dreyto* should be in two installments, half six months after the *caucion*, and half one month before the celebration itself. The coronation ceremonial appears to be optional, and the tenor of the law implies that monarchs may have been trying to levy the *dreyto de Coronacion* and then not go through with the ceremony.

[58] In fact, the presence of the jurors is called for in the 1366 edict regarding the primogenitary oath in the kingdom of Aragon (see above, n. 47), although they are not mentioned two years later in *Coram quibus*, which applied to all the realms of the Crown of Aragon.

statement of his rôle in the 1461 edict should be regarded as less significant than the addition to the ceremonial of representatives of the kingdom and of the capital city.

Thus far we have considered the jurisdictional oath from the point of view of limiting royal power. There is usually some *quid pro quo* for royal acquiescence to such pressure, and in 1461 the king had in mind the furtherance of his immediate political purposes in a fashion which relates directly to the decree *Coram quibus*. Early in 1460, the Catalonians began a revolt, and the breach with their sovereign was marked by acclaiming his eldest son as primogenit and heir to the throne. John II had long been estranged from his son, Prince Charles of Viana, and had striven, usually with success, to thwart Charles' political ambitions. In 1451 another son, Ferdinand, was born to John, and thenceforth he bent all his efforts upon providing him with a great inheritance. Fortunately for John and Ferdinand, Charles of Viana died at the end of the summer of 1461. While this did not abate the Catalonian revolt, it did give John an opportunity to steal a march on the legal front by dramatizing the fact that Ferdinand was now first in the line of royal succession. Ferdinand was only ten years old, to be sure, and therefore could not exercise the traditional primogenitary jurisdiction, but the important matter was to have the Cortes recognize his dynastic right. The following arrangement was made. John, as legal tutor for Ferdinand, swore the "Oath of Primogeniture" on his behalf, in the hands of the Justice of Aragon, and the assembled Cortes at Calatayud then swore allegiance to Ferdinand as primogenit. John had to vow that no primogenitary jurisdiction would be exercised until Ferdinand reached his majority and took the jurisdictional oath in Zaragoza in the hands of the Justice. It is against this concession by the Cortes that we should understand the more stringent rules about "entrance into power" which the king conceded by the decree *Coram quibus*.[59]

[59] Vicens Vives, *Juan II*, pp. 215-35, sets forth fully Charles of Viana's claims as primogenit and summarizes the turbulent affairs of 1458-1461. See above, n. 22, for the defiant actions of the Cata-

With the enunciation of *Coram quibus* in 1461 the legislation regarding royal oath-taking was completed. There were now four distinct ceremonials involved, and they may be divided into pairs. One set may be called the dynastic, the other the jurisdictional. The dynastic oaths were performed at a meeting of the Cortes, the jurisdictional ones at Zaragoza in the power of the Justice of Aragon.[60] The dynastic oaths occurred first and last in the series of four: for the underage primogenit and for the new king; and they were accompanied by a reciprocal oath on behalf of the people to obey the royal personage. The jurisdictional oath was given twice in the interval, first upon the primogenit's assuming jurisdiction at the age of fourteen, and then again when the predecessor died; this oath was unilateral. To round out this prospectus we can see that the dynastic oath served principally the purposes of the rulers, while the jurisdictional oath served the purposes of the people.

There is evidence that persons directly concerned with these oaths were often unaware of the distinctions between them, but in juristic circles in Zaragoza the distinctions between the oaths were scrupulously adhered to. One important reason for confusion lay in the distinction, easily forgotten, between the Crown of Aragon and the kingdom of Aragon. The Crown of Aragon included several principalities, chiefly Aragon, Catalonia, Valencia, and Sicily. The first three of these had separate Cortes, although as often as not all three might meet together in a General Cortes. Since the dynastic oaths applied to the Crown of Aragon, they were taken at the meeting of a General Cortes. The jurisdictional oaths, however, since they were given in the

lonians, full of the spirit of the Oath of the Aragonese. For the "Oath of Primogeniture" sworn on Ferdinand's behalf in 1461, see Blancas, *Coronaciones*, pp. 246f, and Quinto, *Juramento*, pp. 318-19.

[60] The king's oath before the Cortes was also taken in the hands of the Justice, but then the Justice in turn (along with the deputies, etc.) took his oath in the hands of the king; see Blancas, *Cortes*, pp. 108-10. This kind of reciprocal oath-taking by all officials stressed the subservience of the corporation of rulers to the law, in contrast to the singular oath of the king at the special ceremonial for his entrance into jurisdictional power, when it had to appear that he was being subjected to a special test.

presence of officers who had power only in the kingdom of Aragon, could almost be regarded as local. Especially when we reflect upon the historical circumstances which brought about the unification of Spain, and reduced the kingdom of Aragon almost overnight to the status of a third-rate power, we can understand the jealousy with which the Aragonese guarded the observance of the jurisdictional oaths. The dynastic issue had been a major concern of the Aragonese as long as they constituted the principal element of the independent Crown of Aragon; but after the times of Ferdinand the Catholic control of the dynastic issue simply passed out of the hands of the Aragonese. The Fueros of Aragon remained, however, as the law of that land, and the jurisdictional oaths embodied in those Fueros could always be demanded of the rulers. We can say that to all intents and purposes, the Aragonese lost the power to choose their own king with the advent of the Habsburgs, but that they still held the right to authorize the exercise of royal jurisdiction within their borders. To this extent some degree of native control over the king was maintained. Thus the accident of dynastic developments brought about a situation quite unforeseeable in 1461. In that year, the jurisdictional oaths were of capital importance because the land where they applied was the major segment of the independent and powerful Crown of Aragon. Two generations later, when Aragonese independence had become just a fiction, the jurisdictional oaths became just an oddity of local practice—or at least so it seemed to the Habsburg monarchs.

Everyone knows the final outcome of the labors of Ferdinand and Isabella to unite Spain under a single dynasty. By an incredible series of accidents a teen-age Flemish boy, the son of their third eldest offspring (Joanna) finally acquired the Spanish crown in 1516. In the thirty-five years before this Ferdinand had had several of his descendants sworn as primogenits before the Cortes, and some had even entered jurisdiction in the power of the Justice of Aragon; but the one who finally succeeded had never even been in Spain before, let alone conformed to any of the primogenitary ceremonials in Aragon. Only against the background of Ferdinand's earlier problems of succession in Aragon can one fully appreciate the difficulty which Charles faced when he acquired the throne in 1516.

First, Ferdinand himself. We saw that he was recognized as primogenit by the Cortes of Calatayud in 1461. When he came of age he entered into jurisdiction according to *Coram quibus.* When his father died in 1479, he immediately entered into royal jurisdiction by the same prescription. Not until two years later, however, did he hold a Cortes, and receive his subjects' oath to him as king; during the interim (as Blancas later guessed, correctly) Ferdinand seems to have been content with the oath of allegiance which had been sworn to him as primogenit when he was only two years old. In other words, he needed to be scrupulous only with regard to the jurisdictional oaths.[61]

Ferdinand and Isabella's only son, John, was recognized as primogenit by the Cortes in 1481 while still an infant, and he entered into jurisdiction when he came of age in 1493.[62] He died in 1497, however, and since he had no children and none of his sisters had had any male offspring, nor could it be hoped that his mother would have any more children, the right of succession had to be invested in the first-born child of Ferdinand and Isabella, herself named Isabella, who was already Queen of Portugal. There was no problem in having Isabella as primogenita in Castile, for her mother proved sufficiently the propriety of females' ruling in their own right in that nation; but Aragon's sole example of independent female rule, Petronilla (1162-1164), was far in the past, and, in fact, she had been forced to abdicate. Trouble brewed when the younger Isabella was brought to a Cortes at Zaragoza in 1498. Her sojourn in Zaragoza, however, turned out to be a moment of *accouchement*, and Isabella died in childbirth. Her baby, a boy, survived, and the urgency of the dynastic situation

[61] For Ferdinand's primogenitary exercise of jurisdiction see Zurita, *Anales, Secunda Parte,* Cinco Lib. Post., Lib. xvii, liii (ed., 1579, ii, fols. 127-28); on his royal jurisdictional oath, see Blancas, *Coronaciones,* p. 246, and Quinto, *Juramento,* pp. 319-20.

[62] Blancas, *Coronaciones,* pp. 247-48.

demanded that he be recognized as primogenit while still in swaddling clothes, no matter the indecorous haste of acting so soon after his mother's death.[63] But this boy also died within two years, and the right of succession now passed to the third child of Ferdinand and Isabella, Joanna. At the Cortes of 1502 in Zaragoza, the Aragonese accepted Joanna as primogenita, and allowed her and her husband Philip (Duke of Burgundy) to enter into jurisdiction as Governors General of the land.[64] No provision was made for their two-year-old son Charles, who had been born and raised in the Lowlands. This was the last public action concerning succession and the exercise of jurisdiction in Aragon taken during Ferdinand's lifetime, and it turned out to be woefully inadequate. Ferdinand was preceded to the grave by his son-in-law, Philip, and witnessed the lapse of his daughter Joanna into insanity. Thus when Ferdinand died in 1516 Aragon found itself without a king and without any mentally competent person who had legally entered into royal jurisdictional status. An interim was deemed to exist, and regent powers, at least in part, were vested in the Justice of Aragon.

Charles I of Spain had considerable difficulties in securing recognition in both Castile and Aragon, not to mention in Catalonia. Ferdinand himself had complicated matters by changing his mind about the regency in his later years.

[63] Ricardo del Arco, "Cortes Aragonesas del los Reyes Católicos," *RABM*, LX (1954), 89-90, presents new documentary material regarding the recognition of Isabella as primogenita in 1498, but the fullest account of all the events of 1498 is found in Blancas, *Coronaciones*, pp. 210-20, 248-49. When the babe Miguel was declared primogenit, the oath taken on his behalf mentions the jurisdictional oath which must be taken at the age of fourteen; following this oath, the Archbishop, King Ferdinand, and the Justice of Aragon all made short statements and the event was cried in the streets.

[64] Blancas, *Coronaciones*, pp. 250-58, including the full text of the oath; abbreviated in Quinto, *Juramento*, pp. 320-21. On this occasion it seems that the dynastic oath in the Cortes was fused with the jurisdictional oath which should be taken in the Cathedral Church. The Justice of Aragon received the oath, however, which meant that the most important condition of *Coram quibus* was observed. This was a Cortes of just the kingdom of Aragon, held in Zaragoza; I do not know whether the dynastic oath was repeated in the next year in the Cortes of Catalonia.

By a testament he drew up in 1512, Joanna was recognized as successor, with Charles as regent due to her infirmity; but Charles' younger brother, Ferdinand, who had been raised in Spain, was designated to take Charles' place until the latter could come to Spain. Early in January of 1516 it was proposed that Charles should come to Spain and be recognized as heir in all the Spanish kingdoms, and his brother Ferdinand sent to be governor in the Lowlands. Just a few days later, and on the eve of his demise, King Ferdinand drew up another will in which the right of succession was vested in Joanna, with Charles as legal heir; until Charles' arrival in Spain, Cardinal Ximenes should be regent in Castile and the Archbishop of Zaragoza regent in the realms of the Crown of Aragon. Thus Charles had operating for him the wishes of his grandfather and the fact that he was the elder of the direct male heirs of Ferdinand and Isabella. Against him was the fact that he was a foreigner in a land famous for its xenophobia.[65]

In Brussels, not long after the news of Ferdinand's death arrived, Charles was proclaimed King Catholic jointly with his mother. It was over a year before Charles embarked for Spain, however, and only in the early months of 1518 that he began the rounds of Spanish realms to secure recognition from the various Cortes. That he was welcome at all in Castile was due chiefly to the forceful rule of Cardinal Ximenes during the two years after Ferdinand's death. The famous prelate put down all rebellions and foiled all plots to secure a succession different from what Ferdinand had ordered. The Castilians were particularly fearful of the influx of Netherlanders and spiteful of the precedence they were granted in ceremonial; that Charles did not speak Spanish was particularly insulting. But they did swear allegiance to him as co-ruler with his mother in the Cortes of Valladolid in January 1518. Near the end of March, then, Charles made his way toward Aragon.[66]

It has appeared to many historians that the quarrel be-

[65] The foregoing is drawn chiefly from Merriman, *Spanish empire*, Book v, Chapter xxi (ed. 1925: iii, 3-14).
[66] *Ibid.* (*ed. cit.*: iii, 14-36).

tween Charles and his Aragonese subjects stemmed from a genuine reluctance on their part to accept him as legitimate ruler. The Aragonese did share with the Castilians the fear of foreign influence, and like them they insisted that Charles share his royal title with his mother; save for that, however, the peculiarities of the Aragonese obstreperousness should not be laid to the count of dynastic issues, but to the legal technicalities of the jurisdictional oath. This is what is at stake in the oft-quoted letters of Peter Martyr (Anghiera) written late in the year 1517. On November 23, just a few days after Charles had set foot on Spanish soil, Peter Martyr reported that the Aragonese were remonstrating that they would greet Charles as prince but not as king, for it was forbidden to call him king until he had sworn inside the kingdom that he was going to preserve their laws.[67] On December 30 an even more revealing report was given by Peter Martyr:

The Aragonese, having been ordered by the king that they convene the Cortes [*conventus*] of their realm, answered that nothing was owed to his authority because he was not king, but only prince and heir. He must first come and swear the observance of the laws of the kingdom, then he may be elevated as king—if it is permitted to call him king in his own right while his mother is alive; meanwhile, they thought it proper for the Justice of Aragon to convoke the Cortes of the people [*curiae regnicolarum*].[68]

[67] Peter Martyr, *Opus Epistolarum* (Alcala, 1530), fol. cxxxvii[v] [Ep. 604]: "*Particularius alias habebitis de hac turbula tonante ab Aragonicis oratores adsunt. Carolum tanquam principem non autem Regem salutarunt. Eat ad se hortantur & orant. Non licere illum appellare Regem, nisi prius in regno se illorum privilegia servaturum iuraverit. Sic vivitur*" [23 November 1517].

[68] *Ibid.*, fol. cxxxviii [Ep. 606]: "*Aragones a rege requisiti ut conventus regni cogant, responderunt nil debere illius imperio agere, quia non sit rex, sed princeps tantum haeres. Eat iuretque legum regni observantiam prius dehinc in regem erigetur si matre vivente fas est regem dici, per suum interea iustitiae praefectum convocari oportere aiunt regnicolarum curias*" [30 December 1517]. There were historical precedents from the 13th century (the reigns of James I and Alfonso III) of Cortes' assembling in Aragon without being summoned by the king.

Without having to credit Peter Martyr with a good knowledge of Aragonese law, we can still see the protocol that the Aragonese were going to demand. They already recognized Charles as "prince and heir," which seems to indicate that they respected the testamentary wishes of Ferdinand as much as if they had been registered by a parliamentary recognition of primogenitary rights. It was not certain what title Charles should have in the future, but it was unequivocally clear that his first act must be to come to Zaragoza and swear the jurisdictional oath in the hands of the Justice of Aragon. The regency council which was in correspondence with Charles did heed his wish that a Cortes be assembled, but this was done almost as a personal favor to him. There was no authority conceded to him; instead the Justice of Aragon assumed the powers of regent.

In the last days of January 1518, Charles (still in Valladolid) issued summonses for a meeting of the Cortes of Aragon to be held the following March 20; but, far from being obeyed, this action only caused the Aragonese to assemble immediately upon their own initiative in order to debate the legality of Charles' action and decide how they should respond to it. For almost two months this assembly, which consisted of deputies to the Cortes, judges, jurisconsults and learned men, pitted its wits against those of the new king—or "prince" as they preferred to address him —in a series of letters and visits of envoys back and forth.[69] Charles always allowed that he intended to swear to uphold the Fueros and Liberties of Aragon, as his predecessors had done, but it took some time to convince him that it was not sufficient that he do this as he had in Castile, at a meeting of the Cortes and in conjunction with the oath of allegiance sworn to him by his subjects, but that he must

---

[69] The most complete record by far of these negotiations is given in Argensola, *Anales de Aragon* [*desde 1516 hasta 1520*]. Another continuator of Zurita, Dormer, *Anales de Aragon desde . . . 1525 . . . hasta . . . 1540*, also reviewed the early events of Charles' reign; and, while he relies very heavily upon Argensola, he mentions some incidents and documents of the year 1518 not found in Argensola (see below, n. 74). Another avowed continuation of Zurita, Blasco de Lanuza, *Historias ecclesiásticas y seculares de Aragon*, antedates the works of Argensola and Dormer but offers less for our problem.

also take this oath, alone, before he could even preside at
a Cortes.[70]

The Aragonese seem to have enjoyed the opportunity
provided by these negotiations to display their virtuosity
in legal disputation. In a mood of mock piety, they pleaded
with Charles that he not force them to be law-breakers by
attending an illegal Cortes. For, they said, they had sworn
allegiance to his mother as successor to the throne, and
she had entered into jurisdictional power as Governor General; she alone, therefore, had the power to convoke a
Cortes. "To call a Cortes," they said, "belongs only to a
sworn king."[71] If, on the other hand (said the deputies and
other officials), they should obey Charles as if he were a
sworn king, they would be violating their oath of allegiance
to his mother and would open themselves to criminal
charges in the court of the Justice of Aragon, "and be condemned to death as officers delinquent in their offices."[72]

[70] Argensola, pp. 463-76, documents the first few rounds of correspondence between the Aragonese and Charles, up to March 16;
see esp. pp. 470-71 for Charles' professions of good faith. Dormer,
pp. 76-77, 79, sums up these events but does not bring out at all
well the issues of protocol involved. Blasco de Lanuza, *Historias*, I,
152-53, refers to the controversy over Charles' oath only when describing the events that took place after Charles had arrived in, or
near, Zaragoza, thus giving the erroneous impression that the Aragonese invented this trouble at the last minute. Blasco de Lanuza
alleges a work not available to me: Prudencio de Sandoval, *Historia
de la vida y hechos del Emperador Carlos V* (Pamplona, 1614-1618),
2 vols.

[71] ". . . *de Fuero destos Reynos el llamar Cortes no pertenece sino
à Rey jurado*" (Argensola, p. 473, citing a letter to Charles dated
March 11).

[72] "*Y sino guardan lo sobredicho* [oath taken in General Cortes to
Joanna], *puedan ser acusados criminalmente por la Corte de el
Justicia de Aragon, y condenarlos à muerte, como Oficiales delin-
quentes en sus Oficios*" (*ibid.*, p. 488, citing instructions to the
Aragonese ambassadors, dated April 15). In fairness to the sincerity
of the Aragonese officials, we should recall that in 1518 the extent
of Joanna's disability was still much debated. Regency officials did
not help matters by their policy of keeping her secluded, for this
gave rise to dark rumors that she was more a prisoner than an in-
valid. But even those who were convinced that she was quite mad
could raise the possibility of her suddenly recovering her wits and
becoming again the legitimate ruler; the status accorded to Charles
had to take this into account.

Moreover, it was not only the laws of Aragon which dictated that Charles must first come and swear to the kingdom before the kingdom swore to him; it was also conformable to common law (*Drecho comun*). Consider this: if Charles could not be recognized as king until he took his oath, but he waited to do this until his subjects took their oath to him, then he would be taking his oath to them as king but they would be taking their oath to him only as prince.[73]

How much Charles was persuaded by arguments such as these we cannot tell, but he did finally yield the point that he should take the jurisdictional oath the day he entered Zaragoza, and he appointed some of his officers to negotiate the terms of the oath. Meanwhile, the date of the Cortes had to be advanced several times, and in the first week of May Charles finally approached the capital of Aragon.[74]

[73] "*Y esto, no solamente se prueba por Fuero de este Reyno, pero aun por Drecho comun. Segun el qual, assi mismo, seria inconveniente que se hallasse aver jurado su Alteza al Reyno, Fueros y Libertades, come Rey, y que el Reyno en Cortes no huviesse jurado à su Alteza sino como Principe*" (*ibid.*, p. 489, citing the same document).

[74] On the question of Charles' transit from Valladolid to Zaragoza, Dormer offers more details than Argensola. The latter simply reports that Charles left Valladolid in the early days of April (Argensola, p. 483); gives *in extenso* the text of the "Instruction" to the Aragonese ambassadors (pp. 485-91—excerpts are quoted in the two previous notes); and then speaks about Charles' arrival in Zaragoza and the oath-taking ceremonial (pp. 495ff—see below, nn. 80-81). Dormer supplements Argensola in the following ways. (1) On pp. 76-77 he gives the documents, with the names of witnesses, whereby the Justice of Aragon prorogued the meeting of the Cortes three times because Charles could not keep to his original plan of coming on March 20 (Argensola, p. 484, mentions these prorogations in a few words). (2) On p. 78, Dormer recounts Charles' first stop in Aragon, in Calatayud, on April 26, and the ritual of the swearing of the privileges which took place in the Cathedral; see below, n. 84, for the text of this document. (3) On pp. 80-82, Dormer gives letters written by Charles on April 30 and May 3, from Calatayud, which show that the debate over the oath was still unsettled at that late date. (4) On p. 84 he describes the arrival of Charles in Zaragoza (see next note); on pp. 84-85, a last-minute discussion of the oath by the Aragonese Assembly while Charles was already in the suburbs and prepared to make his entry; and on pp. 85-86, several details of the actual oath-taking which complement the account

As Charles neared the city, on May 6, he was greeted by the jurors and citizens of Zaragoza, who sallied forth to meet him. This may have been the occasion which gave rise to the story that Charles was hailed as king before the official oath-taking, much to the annoyance of those who had prepared the constitutional aspects of the festivities exactly in order to avoid any such acclamation until he had formally entered into jurisdiction. In any event, Charles installed himself just outside the city, in the royal palace of the Aljaferia, and three days later, on May 9, made his ceremonial entrée into *La Seo* (the Cathedral Church of San Salvador) where he took the oath of jurisdiction in an elaborate ceremonial, the details of which will be examined later. Afterwards all parties retired to the nearby Palace of the Deputation, where the dignitaries did homage to Charles by kissing his hand. This ended the May 9 formalities. But, although Charles now had royal powers—co-regnal powers, that is, with his mother—he still had not been officially acclaimed king by the Cortes.[75] And the

---

given by Argensola (cf. below, n. 81). My reconstruction of the dates given in Charles' itinerary conforms to the dates given in Manuel de Foronda y Aquilera, *Estancias y viajes del Emperador Carlos V* (Madrid, 1895), p. 20.

[75] Dormer, pp. 84-85, alone fixes the chronology of events clearly and correctly. Regarding the preemptory acclamation of Charles as king, there are three bits of evidence. (1) Dormer, p. 84, speaks of the extramural reception: *"y a buena distancia salieron a recibirle los Jurados, y Ciudadanos."* (2) Argensola, p. 495, records an incident he had found in the Chronicle of Gaspar Escolano (presumably *Decada primera de la . . . Ciudad y Reyno de Valencia* [Valencia, 1610-1611], 2 vols., a work not available to me): *"Este Micer Garces, estando el Rey en Zaragoza, hizo que el Pueblo le jurasse en la Aljaferia, y fue tan grande el alboroto que se movió por los tres Estamentos de aquel Reyno, pidiendolo por contrafuero, que huvo el Rey de renunciar al Juramento, y jurar de nuevo, segun la antigua costumbre de Reynante y Conreynante, con la Reyna su Madre, etc.";* but Argensola goes on to say that he himself has found no substantiation of this incident in the registers of the Cortes or other official documents. I can say this much: this event would not have taken place on May 9, as Argensola makes out, but rather on May 6 when Charles first arrived in Zaragoza and established himself in the Aljaferia (cf. Dormer, p. 84), or else on May 7 or 8, while he resided there. (3) Dormer, pp. 85-86, reports that as Charles passed through the streets on his way to *La Seo* to take the jurisdictional

Cortes was not to meet for another eleven days. The Aragonese, busy preparing their gravamina, had still not spelled out the details of Charles' sharing of power with his mother, nor regulated the succession. Some Castilians who had accompanied Charles from Valladolid to Zaragoza were incensed by what they felt was a lack of respect being shown to Charles; for them, the recognition accorded by the Cortes of Castile should have ended all debate about Charles' status. There was even some bloodshed between them and the Aragonese, and Charles had this early opportunity to act as peacemaker between factions of his temperamental new subjects.[76] The Cortes of Aragon finally opened its first session under the new king on May 20. Not for more than two months, however, did the "kingdom" finally swear to its new sovereign. In this ceremonial, performed on July 29, Charles repeated his entire May 9 oath and then the representatives of the Cortes took their oath of allegiance to him and his mother as co-rulers of Aragon.[77]

The only way to make sense out of these confused events is to appreciate the unique function of the jurisdictional oath in the Aragonese constitution. In taking that oath, Charles acknowledged co-rulership with his mother. Since we know that this oath was the subject of long negotiations, it must have been very carefully drawn up by the

---

oath on May 9, he was hailed by groups of artisans: *"Viva, Viva el Señor Rey."* One safe conclusion can be made from this evidence: there were many occasions when the populace, in a spontaneous fashion, could have violated the taboo which the jurists tried to place upon the show of regal pomp or the use of the royal title before the king swore the jurisdictional oath.

[76] Blasco de Lanuza, *Historias*, p. 153, reports the altercation, but his narrative is so compressed that it is difficult to place this incident in the sequence of events. Most likely the altercation occurred after Charles had sworn the jurisdictional oath (May 9), either in the interval of eleven days that followed before the Cortes finally assembled (Argensola, p. 505, mentions the difficulty of preparing this Cortes), or in the two months or more afterwards during which Charles was still not officially acclaimed as king by act of the Aragonese Cortes (see next note).

[77] Argensola, pp. 548-50, records the séance of July 29, where the king swore his oath again; and on p. 555 he gives the oath taken by the Cortes to Charles.

Aragonese. They had made their basic decision about Charles' status even before he arrived in Zaragoza, and partook in a ceremonial which revealed that decision long before they themselves finally took an oath to Charles. Once the jurisdictional oath had been taken, the continued discussion of Charles' position became a kind of game—a game with potentially serious consequences, to be sure. Concessions could still be wrung from the king. After all, Charles was expecting a subvention, which meant that he would have to hear the grievances and petitions of his subjects first. But even before that, during the two months until his subjects finally swore formal allegiance to him, he had to preside at sessions of the Cortes where they disputed the title and prerogatives which he should have as king.

All this was due to the faulty status which he had had, in strict terms of the law, during his primogenitary period. He had been prince in name, but had never held any power of jurisdiction. After May 9, 1518, he was able to exercise jurisdictional authority as a king, but still had not received an oath of allegiance from his subjects in Aragon. The Aragonese jurists and magistrates, as well as the delegates of the Cortes, were thus able to make a lavish show of their individuality as a nation. We cannot blame Charles, nor his Flemish counselors, nor the coterie of Castilians who had come to Aragon as part of his entourage, for being bewildered by the tune to which the Aragonese danced their legal fandango.

The resistance of the Aragonese in 1518 was essentially legalistic play without significant political consequences; yet, within the rules of the game, it did put the Justice of Aragon in an unusually elevated position vis-à-vis the king. The Justice of Aragon, by default, had been vested with virtually royal powers up to the moment when the aspirant to the throne took an oath in his hands and power.[78] Around

[78] There is some contradiction, which I cannot resolve, between the regency powers given to the Archbishop of Zaragoza by Ferdinand in 1516 (see above, p. 201) and the clear regency powers which Peter Martyr imputed to the Justice in December 1517, when Charles was still in Castile (above, n. 68). One answer would be that the Archbishop of Zaragoza was not in Aragon at the time,

this famous historical incident the mythical Oath could have arisen, for here was at least an instance of lively pretending that the king submitted to strict conditions before he was accepted by his subjects. This notion is reinforced not a little by the terms of the oath which Charles took, as well as by the formal procedures of the oath-taking.

First of all, the oath was so extraordinarily lengthy— over 2,000 words—that it must have taken a quarter of an hour to read; this alone was bound to appear demeaning to the king. The oath opens with a series of general asservations to uphold the fueros of the Cortes of 1348 and other specified Cortes since, where legislation had passed into the Fueros of Aragon. Even more generally, and more than once, the king swears to preserve the fueros, privileges, liberties, usages, and customs of the kingdom of Aragon. The main part of the oath, however, is devoted to specific issues which may be divided into two groups. One group consists of four fueros of the Cortes of Calatayud of 1461, in each of which it is specifically stated that the king and the primogenit shall swear to uphold a particular piece of legislation. Unless I am mistaken, this part of the jurisdictional oath of 1518, as well as the general opening sections of it, were derived from Molino's *Repertorium* (1513), which was the best source available for knowledge of Aragonese legal usages.[79] The other group of issues to which the king swore, however, seems to be matters of special concern to the Aragonese in 1518. Concisely put, they prohibit tampering with the coinage and levying of excises, and they bind Charles to preserve in one union the various principalities of the Crown of Aragon. The last-named of these conditions reflects the Aragonese hope, which time proved to be in vain, that they might retain some measure of control over half—albeit the lesser half—of Charles' new imperium.

---

and the Justice was acting in his stead. It is not unlikely that the Archbishop was in Castile observing the course of Charles' acceptance in that nation.

[79] See the entry in the *Repertorium* under *"Rex,"* § *"De iuramento domini regis,"* ed. 1533, fols. ccxcvi^v-ccxcvii. It is worth noting that Molino was a member of the assembly which gathered in Zaragoza in February to negotiate with Charles; see Argensola, p. 465.

By and large, the Habsburg rulers gave no preference to Aragon, but treated it as just another one of the several principalities which made up the Crown of Aragon.[80]

As I have said, the sheer length of the oath, and the binding of the king to details of Aragonese law, were in some manner demeaning; but the procedural arrangements should not be overlooked, because they insinuate notions of status of oath-giver and oath-receiver even more strongly than the contents of the oath itself. Fortunately, we are well informed. Immediately upon entering the Cathedral Church, Charles knelt on a cushion and adored the cross. He then proceeded up the aisle as the choir and musicians began a *Te Deum* and stationed himself before the high altar during the celebration of Mass. Immediately afterwards, he mounted a richly decorated platform located between the altar and the choir, and knelt on a cushion before the Justice and the Eight Deputies of the Kingdom, who were dressed in long-trained gowns of brocade. The first words were uttered by the Protonotary:

The Most Serene Lord Charles, by the grace of God King of Castile and Aragon, etc., in the presence of the Magnificent and Circumspect Baron the Lord Juan de Lanuza . . . Justice of Aragon, and the Venerable [Eight Deputies, given by name and rank, as well as the three Jurors of Zaragoza, the Archbishop and other dignitaries]. The said Lord King declared . . . he was prepared and ready for all

[80] The oath was in Latin (see the parenthetical remark in the passage quoted in the next note), except for the final paragraph; but the only version I have seen is the Spanish version given by Argensola, *Anales de Aragon*, pp. 498-504, (also quoted in Quinto, *Juramento*, pp. 398-408). The final paragraph in Spanish, where Charles acknowledges his mother's rights, is worth recording: "*Et que la sobredicha Jura sea con esta salvedad, y no sin ella: Que atendido que la Señora Reyna Doña Juana, mi Señora y Madre, ha sido por los Aragoneses Jurada condictionalmente, por Princesa, é Reyna: é padece tal accidente, que la Governacion destos Reynos, por su persona no se puede hazer, plaze à Nos: Que la presente Jura del presente Reyno, sea fecha en nombre de la dicha Reyna, y nuestro, Conregnantes: y que sea, sin perjuizio de la dicha Reyna mi Señora, y Madre*" (Argensola, p. 504).

which, according to the law, he was obligated to swear in the power and in the hands of the Justice of Aragon.[81]

The oath was then taken, in Latin.

To grasp the meaning of this ceremonial on the plane of politics, one must pay attention to its dramatic *mise en scène*. *La Seo* in the 16th century had a virtually square floor plan, and the altar was located in a rather small apse. The platform upon which Charles knelt while taking the oath was so placed that Charles must have had his back to the altar and faced the assembled throng.[82] The Justice, standing closest to the platform, would thus have found himself between the king and people, which may have some importance in respect to one of the accounts of how

[81] "*De alli passaron hasta la Iglesia de San Salvador, que es la Sede Metropolitana. Y antes de entrar en ella (aviendose apeado, á pocos passos) se arrodillò ante un Sitial de brocado (hasta el qual, con toda solenidad le saliò à recibir el Clero.) Adorò la Cruz en las manos del Prelado. Comenzando á entrar, comenzaron tambien los Cantores, y los instrumentos musicos el Hymno* Te Deum laudamus. *Hizo oracion al Santissimo Sacramento ante el Altar Mayor: y estuvo con devocion atento à las Oraciones, y à las Ceremonias de la Iglesia. Luego subiò al Tablado, que entre el mismo Altar, y el Coro le esperava, aderezado magnificamente. Adonde, puesto de rodillas en otro Sitial, ante el Justicia de Aragon, y los ocho Diputados de Reyno, vestidos de Ropones rozagantes de Brocado, jurò al Reyno sus Leyes, en la forma acostumbrada, cuyo tenor (que entonces fue en lengua Latina) es el mismo, que el Rey Principe, y otros Reyes han jurado en diversas Cortes. Y traducirèmosle en Español. Antes de este Acto dixo à los Brazos en alta voz el Protonotario: El Serenissimo Señor Carlos, por la gracia de Dios Rey de Castilla, de Aragon, etc., presentes el Magnifico, y Circunspecto Varon el Señor Juan de Lanuza . . . Justicia de Aragon [y Diputados, y Jurados, etc.]. El dicho Señor Rey dixo . . . : Que estava presto, y à punto para todo lo que segun Fuero, era obligado á jurar en poder, y manos del Justicia de Aragon*" (Argensola, pp. 496-98). Dormer, p. 87, is less circumstantial in his account of the oath-taking, but the following information corroborates Argensola: "*La jura fue en la forma acostumbrada (puesto en un sitial el Libro de los Evangelios, y la Cruz) en poder del Justicia de Aragon; y arrodillado el Rey, ofreciò guardar inviolablemente los Fueros, Actos de Corte, usos, costumbres, libertades, y privilegios concedidos a los Aragoneses, especificando, y leyendo algunos como mas singulares.*"

[82] See the plan of *La Seo* in Vicente Lampérez y Romea, *Historia de la arquitectura cristiana española en la edad media* (2nd ed., Madrid, 1930), III, 311, or in Georges Pillement, *Les cathédrales d'Espagne* (Paris, 1952), II, 39.

our mythical Oath is supposed to have taken place.[83] We may be certain, in any event, that Charles occupied the platform alone; also, we may assume confidently that the king, even when kneeling, remained on a higher plane than the Justice and the others standing near him. This much compensation—albeit only in physical terms—must have been made, out of respect for the royal dignity, to offset the suggestion that the kneeling king was subordinate to the standing magistrates. Was there a parallelism intended between the king's initial act of kneeling before the cross when he entered the church and his kneeling before the magistrates when he took the oath? The impresarios of the ceremonial may well have conceived this as a way of distinguishing between the religious and civil aspects of the oath-taking. In any event, they must have been sensitive to the implications of the king's kneeling before the Justice; the simple fact that they erected a platform for the king proves this. But what the spectators saw in 1518 may not be what was remembered later on. At least to anyone who wished to emphasize the aspect of submission by the king, the mental image of him kneeling before the Justice would be the most pleasing recollection. It reversed the practice of the oath-taking in the Cortes, where the Justice knelt while the king (having descended from a throne set higher up) stood.[84]

The difficulties which Charles experienced with his Aragonese subjects in 1518 seem to have been well remem-

---

[83] See below, n. 101.

[84] Cf. Blancas, *Cortes*, p. 108. The oath taken by Charles in *La Seo* on May 9 was not the only—nor even the first—oath which he took on Aragonese soil before convoking the Cortes. On April 26, en route to Zaragoza, he passed through Calatayud and there took an oath on the missal to uphold the privileges of that city. I do not know what constitutional significance this may have had, but I give the account of it (from Dormer, p. 78) for what it is worth: ". . . *avia un trono bien compuesto, y Garcia Forcen, Vicario general por el Obispo de Tarazona Don Guillen Ramon de Moncada, tenia un Missal abierto; puso su Alteza las manos, y lo adorò, jurando en su nombre, y de la Serenissima Reyna Doña Juana su madre, por Dios, y los Santos Quatro Evangelios, guardar inviolablement el Privilegio de la Poblacion, y las demàs gracias, concessiones, libertades . . . concedidas a sus Ciudadanos.*"

bered by him many years later, when the time came for his son Philip to enter into primogenitary jurisdiction as Governor General. Immediately after the Cortes in Monzon in 1542, where all the principalities of the Crown of Aragon recognized Philip's primogenitary right as Governor General, Charles sent Philip to Zaragoza to have him swear the jurisdictional oath before the Justice so that he could exercise power in Aragon itself. The contents of the oath were virtually the same as those of the oath of 1518, but the rendition of it was differently arranged. After a religious service similar to the one at Charles' own oath-taking, Philip knelt at the high altar, before the cross, and placed his hands upon a missal as he swore the oath "in the power" of the Justice and in the presence of the Deputies, Jurors, and other dignitaries.[85] By thus carrying out simultaneously the separate provisions of *De his quae dominus rex* (to swear upon the cross and Evangels) and of *Coram quibus* (to swear in the power of the Justice), the kneeling of the royal personage appeared strictly as an act of reverence

---

[85] Quinto, *Juramento*, pp. 410-11, quoting Juan Ibando de Bardaxi, *Tractatus de officio gubernationis procurationis generalis regni Aragonum* (Zaragoza, 1592): "E assi estando el dicho Señor don Phelipe *Primogenito, y Principe susodicho, ante el altar Mayor de dicha Iglesia, arrodillado ante la Cruz de nuestro Señor Iesu Christo, puestas las manos sobre un libro Missal, hizo, y presto el Iuramento solemne infrascrito, en poder del dicho Mossen Lorenzo Ferrandez de Heredia, Iusticia de Aragon, presentes y assistentes los susodichos Diputados, y Iurados, y los testigo infrascritos, y otras muchas personas en el dicho iuramento intervenientes.*" The oath then follows (in Spanish, on pp. 411-19 of Quinto) and after it (pp. 419-20, still quoting Bardaxi) an account of the events preceding the oath-taking. Whether or not Philip knelt before the cross in a separate ritual before coming to the altar I will leave for the reader to judge from this passage: "*. . . y fue á la plaza del Aseo* [read: *de la Seo*]*, donde en medio della estava puesto un sitial de Brocado, y en el la vera Cruz, y de alli le tomo el Arzobispo, y lo dentro en la Seo. Su Alteza se rodillo en un sitial, que estava puesto al lado del Evangelio, junto al altar Mayor, donde hizo Oracion al Santissimo Sacramento*" (Quinto, *Juramento*, p. 420). In any event, the oath-taking followed directly after the Mass, without Philip's changing his kneeling position at the altar. Panzano, *Anales*, pp. 81-83, gives details of the event, making it very clear "*que no pudiesse exercer Jurisdicion alguna, sin que primero jurasse en Zaragoça en el asseo* [read: *La Seo*]*, assistiendo quatro Diputados . . . etc.*" (*ibid.*, 82).

for the Almighty and not as a submission to temporal magistrates.

As Governor General, Philip presided at several Cortes in Aragon during the later years of his father's reign. One of the important accomplishments of these years was the recension of the Fueros of Aragon and the issuance of the *Nueva Compilación* in 1551. All the edicts regarding the jurisdictional oath were reaffirmed,[86] showing that the Aragonese would not allow the new conditions of the king's being almost constantly absent from their land to affect his obligation to come and make an oath personally to them. Philip, if he were to honor the Aragonese custom, should come to Aragon as soon as possible after his father's death and swear the jurisdictional oath as king in his own right. The proper sequence of events was made somewhat moot by the fact that Charles abdicated in 1556. At the Cortes in Valladolid in March of that year, banners were raised for "King Philip." But the Aragonese were reluctant to accept this; as far as they were concerned, while Charles lived, he alone could be hailed as king. Philip had for years exercised authority as sworn *"Primogenito Principe,"* but he could have no greater authority than that until his father had died and he had sworn an oath as king in his own right.[87] When Charles did die, two years later, Philip was certainly obliged to make an early trip to Zaragoza. He did not. This must have caused grumbling in Aragon, for it revealed a kind of contempt of the Aragonese on Philip's part in that he seemed content to continue to rule the land in his capacity as Governor General. That he had a hearty dislike

[86] The locations of the 1348, 1366, and 1461 edicts in the *Nueva Compilación* of 1551 are given above, nn. 47, 51, 53.

[87] Cf. Blasco de Lanuza, *Historias*, Book ii, Chapter i (ed. 1622, ii, 3): *"se levantaron Pendones por el Rey Philipo, obedienco las Cartas. . . . Los Aragoneses tardaron mucho en esto, porque conforme las leyes deste Reyno, viviendo el Rey, no se admite con este titulo otro alguno; aunque sea el primogenito Principe jurado por sucessor despues de su Padre: porque el juramento se haze de obedecer al hijo despues de la muerte, y no en la vida del Padre. . . . el Rey Philipo primero . . . como Principe sucessor en la Corona de Aragon, desde el ano 1542 . . . nos avia governado . . . en nombre del Emperador, y no en el suyo."* (Text also in Quinto, *Juramento*, p. 463, n. 1.)

of his Aragonese subjects was no secret, and we can even believe that he would never have set foot in their land, after he became king, had it not been for the fact that if he ever wanted a subvention from Aragon he would have to convoke its Cortes and preside over it.

This finally came to pass in 1563, when Philip called for a General Cortes of the Crown of Aragon to be held in Monzon. The histories tell us about this assembly, for it was the occasion of acrimonious quarrels about the rôle of the Inquisition in Aragon. Almost lost from sight, however, is the fact that Philip went first to Zaragoza, several weeks before convoking the estates, and in *La Seo* swore his jurisdictional oath as king in the hands of the Justice of Aragon. It was not a ceremonial of great pomp because Philip had few persons of high station in his train, and many Aragonese were said to have been offended by this. Still, the ceremonial was solemn and impressive.[88]

[88] By chance, the two records of this event that I have found come from the hands of Giovanni Soranzo and Gerónimo Blancas. The former reported Philip's visit to Monzon in a letter written on September 18, 1563, summarized by Louis Prosper Gachard in the second edition of his *Don Charles et Philippe II* (Paris, 1867), which was the edition used for the recent Spanish translation, *Don Carlos y Felipe II* (Barcelona, 1963), where it is cited on p. 149 (nn. 19, 20, which refer to the text on p. 133). The only phrase actually quoted by Gachard refers to the Aragonese reaction to the relative meanness of Philip's entourage: " . . . *cosa che a molto dispiaciuto a tutti quelli signori Aragonesi a sene dogliono publicamente.*" In Blancas' *Coronaciones*, the Cortes of 1563 was the last event to be mentioned, and these words appear in the final paragraph of the book (p. 260): ". . . *que postereras del Año Mil quinientos sesenta, y trea ya* V. *Magestad les tuvo en su propria persona, porque era muerto el Emperador nuestro Señor, y* V. *Magestad fue servido en su primer ingresso de jurar de Rey en la Seo de Caragoça conforme al Fuero el dia que entrò en esta Ciudad antes de ir a Monçon, y despues se concluieron alla las Cortes.*" Dormer, *Discurso Historico-Foral*, pp. 99-100 (as in Bib. Nac. MS 7588, p. 56) reports that Philip II ruled in Aragon solely according to primogenitary authority until he took the royal jurisdictional oath in 1563. This work by Dormer—or rather the manuscript copy of parts of it—came to my attention only after the foregoing section on the jurisdictional oath had been written. The manuscript extracts are ample to assure me that Dormer's convictions about the importance of the oath are at least as strong as mine. Indeed, at one point he says that if the oath for some reason cannot be quickly sworn by the new king, then royal jurisdiction should be deemed suspended and the realm governed by its ordinary judges

These few observations about the event were made in a letter written by Giovanni Soranzo just after the fact. Two years later, Soranzo composed his *Relazione di Spagna,* and from this source we get the first known recording of the "Oath of the Aragonese." We are now in a position to consider that famous fictitious Oath in the light of the less celebrated but actual oath practice of the rulers of Aragon.

The Royal Jurisdictional Oath and the Oath of the Aragonese

If any one of the primary versions of the Oath of the Aragonese were compatible in all respects with the jurisdictional oath taken by the ruler when he came into power, so that the Oath could be explained as a corrupt notion of an actual Renaissance practice, then obviously there would have been little reason for the foregoing elaborate discourses upon mediaeval legal and historical thought. This is not to say that many comparisons cannot be found between parts of the jurisdictional oath—its contents or the ritual of its performance—and details of one or another version of the fictitious Oath; on the contrary, there are many such likenesses to be found. But no single version of the Oath has clear distinction in this respect. We shall be forced, therefore, to examine the correspondences in kind— that is, in the wording and then in the ritual circumstances— and then make general conclusions about how actual oath

---

(*por sus jueces ordinarios*); *ibid.,* p. 106 (ms cited, p. 60). This goes too far, in my opinion. Certainly one has to be skeptical about Dormer's views of the Fueros of Sobrarbe; cf. Part One of the *Discurso,* which is entitled "Que el juramento de las Señores Reyes de Aragon tuvo su origen en los fueros de Sobrarbe" (*ibid.,* pp. 1-45— copied *in toto* in ms 7588, pp. 1-33, according to a note on p. 33), which views False Fueros i-vi as parts of an old royal oath which the modern jurisdictional oath perpetuates in spirit. This illustrates that Sobrarbe mythography was lively in the 17th century—in fact, I think it reached its apogee then—and perhaps allows me to excuse myself for not having added citations from Dormer in my footnotes. For the purposes of the present monograph, the way in which I have organized and interpreted the evidence of the jurisdictional oath is not contradicted by Dormer's essay, but a penetrating study of this problem—something much needed—would have to reexamine Dormer's thesis very carefully.

practices must have lent substance or color to the fictitious Oath no matter what its "original" version was like.

Many pages ago we launched an exploration of the actual Aragonese oaths in order to discover what might have prompted Giovanni Soranzo to refer to the "prince and heir" instead of to the king, even though he claimed to be relating the method by which the people accepted their king.[89] We discovered that the king and the "prince and heir" both took a jurisdictional oath, and that this oath very clearly imposed legal conditions upon the exercise of power. As far as the use of the term "prince and heir" is concerned, we find it applied in 1517 to Charles I when he was en route to Aragon to assume royal power; and in 1542 Philip II had taken the jurisdictional oath as "primogenit and prince."[90] It seems likely that Soranzo's version of the Oath had reference to Philip II. If, then, we assume that the jurisdictional oath lies behind the fictitious Oath, the temptation is great to believe that the latter arose in the years 1563-1565. This would be the chain of reasoning: when Soranzo came to relate the Oath in the *Relazione* of 1565, he was describing the obstreperousness of the Aragonese with special relation to the Cortes of 1563 (at Monzon); he thought that the Oath had been part of that Cortes. But he had been misinformed, for the Oath was actually the one taken by Philip in Zaragoza some weeks before going to Monzon; the fictitious Oath grossly distorts the actual jurisdictional oath, of course, but the notion of limiting royal power is present in both of them.

One trouble with this thesis is that Philip II took the jurisdictional oath as *king* in Zaragoza in 1563, so that the reference to "prince and heir" is incorrectly applied to that occasion. That is to say, we would not only have to have Soranzo mixing up the time and place but also have to have him confuse the two occasions when the jurisdictional oath could occur. It would be much more feasible, therefore, to suppose that the Oath grew up in the years 1542-1563, during all of which time Philip exercised power as prince

[89] Above, pp. 186-87.
[90] Above, n. 68 (for Charles) and n. 85 (for Philip).

and heir. During the 1550's especially, we have noted, there was a rapid acceleration of the Sobrarbe myth about the power of the Justice and resistance to the king.[91] The Privileges of Union were known to some people during this decade, and the centuries-old edict *De prohibita unione* was renewed by the commissioners who revised the Fueros of Aragon.[92] In taking the jurisdictional oath as prince and heir in 1542, Philip had sworn "in the power of the Justice" to uphold the laws. The fictitious Oath, therefore, could be a conflation of the exaggerated claims of the Sobrarbe myth with the actual jurisdictional oath of 1542. Furthermore, if we suppose that malice and spitefulness toward Philip II were the main inspirations for the contriving of the fictitious Oath, we could even estimate the origin of the Oath in the period 1556-1563, the period when Philip was *de facto* monarch but declined to come to Zaragoza and take the jurisdictional oath as king. He was both king and "prince and heir"; he had taken the jurisdictional oath once, but was obliged to take it again. In this situation the confusion in Soranzo's account is not difficult to understand. There is still no proof that the jurisdictional oath was the sole inspiration for the fictitious Oath, but Soranzo's account shows us that the two were at least confused with one another by the 1560's.

The most important correspondence between the fictitious and jurisdictional oaths lies in the role of the Justice. Referring to the chart where the four versions of the Oath are compared (Appendix i), we should note that neither Soranzo nor Pérez makes any allusion to the Justice in the text of the Oath (although Pérez does involve the Justice as a protagonist in the giving of the Oath), whereas in the French versions and in Blancas' the Justice ("between you and us, one who commands more than you") is the warrantor of popular demands.[93] At this point the question to be raised is whether the locution used to designate the Jus-

[91] See above, pp. 181ff.
[92] Above, p. 184.
[93] See above, p. 156, for the reasoning that makes it clear that Blancas was thinking of the Justice.

tice refers to his intermediary position in law (*judex medius* was one of his traditional titles[94]), or to the physical position he occupied at the moment when the people pronounced the Oath. The most intriguing instance of the latter is the unusual staging of the jurisdictional oath of Charles I in 1518, when the king knelt on a platform facing the Justice and took his oath "in the hands and power of the Justice."[95] The element of submission to the Justice is there, and the oath itself was rather demeaning. Anyone who viewed that scene would have long remembered it; and the fictitious Oath could be a kind of imaginary antiphon of the people to what the king actually said and did on that occasion. The authority of the Justice as mediator is duplicated ritually in this grave moment as he stands between the king and the people. Thus the whole force of False Fueros v and vi is dramatized. In the middle of the 16th century, as Aragonese autonomy was becoming more and more just a memory, the recollection of prouder days would have provided a powerful stimulus to mythico-historical inventions such as the Oath. Far from being an isolated phenomenon, it is more like an appendage to a broad and complex historical legend that we have seen growing over the previous century and more.

Since the Oath of the Aragonese was supposedly uttered by the people, we cannot hope to find close verbal likenesses with any oath actually taken by a king. At best we can say that the fictitious Oath represents what might have gone on in the minds of the people at some actual royal oath-taking; and the occasion in 1518 is the most suggestive. On the other hand, some versions of the fictitious Oath are provided with a supplementary apparatus which describes the attendant ritual circumstances, and we have a right to demand that they be at least compatible with ritual of some real oath-takings if we are to believe that the fictional Oath and actual oaths are closely related.

Giovanni Soranzo provides no details of the ritual of the

[94] As, e.g., in False Fuero v. See also the passage cited above, Ch. v, n. 12.

[95] Above, pp. 210f.

Oath, although he leads us to believe that it took place at the meeting of the Cortes. Hotman and the other French authors also believe that the Oath was current practice (or only recently defunct), and they make it clear that the interplay between the Justice and the king is the main feature of the ceremonial. Blancas believes that the Oath had been extinct for centuries, and he gives no details of the ritual performance. Pérez, finally, also places the Oath in the distant past, but he gives us the most detailed, and most startling, account of just how it was performed.

Textual variations are so very slight among the various French versions of the Oath that we have to assume a common derivation; at the same time, the ritual circumstances are sufficiently different to merit close attention even if they represent nothing more than different authors' fancies. According to Beza, first of all, the Oath was either still current or had just recently been dropped, and it belonged to every meeting of the Cortes. First the king takes his oath to the people, then they theirs to him:

On that occasion, indeed, after many ceremonies have been gone through between him whom they call the Justice of Aragon (who personifies the Sovereignty, and to whom the kings believe themselves bound by oath) and the King himself, whether he be about to be or already has been made such, this formulary is pronounced, in just these words: WE WHO ARE WORTH AS MUCH AS YOU. . . .[96]

Hotman is less precise. The circumstance is the creation of the king in the "common council" of the Aragonese:

For the sake of the occasion at hand as well as for the memorializing of the deed, they carry out a drama: they bring forward a man, to whom they give the name "the Aragonese Law" [*Juris Arragonici nomen*], whom they establish by general decree of the people to be greater and more powerful than the king, and at the end they address the

---

[96] The full Latin text is given above, n. 2. The ceremonial situation described by the *Vindiciae contra tyrannos* derives from Beza and is not worth independent consideration.

king, who is begot by fixed laws and conditions, with these words: WE WHO ARE WORTH AS MUCH AS YOU....[97]

Jean Bodin's version of the Oath clearly seems to have come from the French printing of Beza's account, as far as the text is concerned, but Bodin claims to have certain information from a Spanish gentleman regarding the history of the Oath:

Whatever may be written about the kingdom of Aragon, concerning the old formulary that was observed towards the kings of Aragon, it is no longer practiced if the king assembles the estates, as I have learned from a Spanish knight. The formulary was that the great magistrate, that they called the Justice of Aragon, said to the king these words: WE WHO ARE WORTH AS MUCH AS YOU....[98]

Each of these three French versions is preposterous in at least one respect, so that the only safe generalization is that each of their distinguished authors was either badly informed or was a poor recorder of what he was told. Bodin's blunder lies in making the Justice the speaker of the Oath: even if the number of the subject of the sentence could be understood as singular (that is, the royal *we*), the reference in the third person to the "one between us and you" (i.e., the Justice) disallows that the Justice himself was the speaker. Hotman's error is in some ways worse: he does not even have the name straight. Instead of the Justice of Aragon, an officer of the realm, he has someone acting the role of the "Aragonese Law" for the sake of the dramatic submission of the king to the law.[99] Beza's fault is more in the way of an

[97] The Latin text is given above, n. 3.

[98] The French and Latin texts are given above, Ch. II, nn. 8-9. As is noted in the body of my text related to those two notes, the mention of the Spanish Knight was dropped in the Latin translation made by Bodin himself in 1586.

[99] When Hotman composed the *Francogallia* in 1573, he may well have known nothing about the office of the Justice, and his use of the term *Ius Arragonicum* may have been a learned emendation in order to make the coronation skit enact the traditional theme of the king beneath the law. After he had expanded this section in later editions of the *Francogallia*, however (see above, n. 38, but more importantly Ch. II, n. 10), and learned what the Justice of Aragon really was, he should have corrected his error.

exaggeration, when he says that the Justice "personifies Sovereignty." We can at least see the connection with Hotman's mistake in allegorizing the law. In sum, the French sources are so tainted by error or exaggeration that we would not be wise to draw serious conclusions from them about the relation of the fictitious Oath to the jurisdictional oath. While they do not hurt that thesis, they cannot be used to help it.

Unlike the errors made by foreigners, which stem from ignorance, the errors of Blancas and Pérez come from knowledge: that is to say, they are artful constructions based upon considerable learning. This is true above all about Blancas. He knew so well the history of the Justice of Aragon and the history of coronation and Cortes ceremonials that he would not make the mistake of saying that the Oath was current practice. At the same time, he was so convinced of the pristine grandeur of the Justice and the existence of the right of resistance in the original compact that he had no reason to doubt the quondam efficacy of the Oath. Being more learned, his legends are more verisimilar. To a lesser extent this is also true of Antonio Pérez. He would not commit the manifest blunder, but he would turn to account any information that supported his prejudices in a probabilist fashion.

At the point in his *Relaciones* where Pérez quotes the Oath, he is involved in a long disquisition on the authority of the Justice of Aragon. Describing the compact drawn up before the election of the first king (drawn largely, of course, from the False Fueros), he says:

Among other laws they established the one called the Union, which contains two parts worthy of being known and much to the point of the report being given here. One is *that whenever the king breaks their laws they can elect another king, even if he be a Pagan.* These are the very words of the fuero. And also there is known the old way that the Aragonese swore to their king, which is: *We who are worth as much as you have you as our King and Seigneur, provided that you preserve our fueros and liberties, and if*

not, not. And the king's manner of swearing the fueros is
with all the following ceremonial, wherein recognition is
given to the superiority possessed by the law and to the
naturalness of the establishment of the office of the Justice
of Aragon. The Justice sits in a chair, his head covered,
while the king, bareheaded, kneels on a cushion in front of
him, and the Justice receives from the king the oath, taken
on the crucifix and the four Evangels, to preserve and observe the laws and liberties of the kingdom under the
gravest censorship of the Pope. In the accomplishment of
all this, it should be noted that the king acts first and takes
his oath, then the subjects swear obedience to him, following therein the form of the first oath.[100]

Pérez then goes on to relate the second part of the fuero of
the Union, which is the Privilege of the Union to band together against the king. Leaving aside for the moment the
question of Pérez' misconceptions about the Union, let us
concentrate upon the Oath and the ritual attending it.

The *mise en scène* set forth by Pérez is, of course, quite
fantastic. It is not conceivable that the king, kneeling and
bareheaded, ever faced the Justice seated and covered.
Nevertheless, the scene is strongly reminiscent of the jurisdictional oath-taking by Charles I in 1518. The king was
kneeling, though whether bareheaded we do not know,
while the Justice, though not seated, probably was covered
since he was attired in his robes of office.[101] Also, the king

[100] See above, n. 5, for the Spanish text. The dating of Pérez'
Relaciones has only recently become clearly known. A "first edition"
appeared in 1591 (in Pau, apparently) but this contains only the
second part of later editions (concerning the liberation of Pérez in
1591) and not the first part of later editions (the historical background of the affair, including the discussion of the Justice which
concerns us). The second edition (Leon, 1593) has the complete
text, and the four different printings done in Paris in 1598 copy the
1593 text. A Dutch translation appeared in The Hague in 1596, two
more Spanish editions in Paris, 1624; at last, in 1849, the first printing in Spain occurred (Madrid, 1849; 2 vols.). This information
comes from A. Palau y Dulcet, *Manual del librero hispano-americano*
(2nd ed., Barcelona, 1948-1962), xiii (1961), 3-4, who brings together all the recent bibliographical work on Pérez.

[101] See the text above, n. 81. Marichalar and Manrique, *Historia
del derecho*, iv, 483, report a legend to the effect that during the

was on a platform, so that even when kneeling he must have risen above the Justice and the other officials. Still, there was deference to the Justice because the oath was taken in his hands and power; and the whole setting comes closer to Pérez' fanciful ceremonial than one would expect any historical example to do.

Not much need be said about Pérez' evocation of the Privileges of Union. He probably got the text from the résumé given by Zurita, and moved the occasion back from the 13th to the 9th century on his own initiative or because he had noted the gist of the Privileges in Blancas' Fueros of Sobrarbe, established at the founding of the nation.[102] We might well wonder, however, whether it was a coincidence

---

reign of Peter I (1094-1104) the custom of having the king take an oath to uphold the fueros as he knelt bareheaded at the feet of the Justice, who held a sword pointed at his heart, was abolished. These authors do not give their source, but I assume that it is some early modern history which built upon Pérez' account of the Oath. Whether Pliny's account of Trajan's voluntarily swearing to uphold the laws, while standing before the seated consul (*"Imperator . . . stetit ante gremium consulis, seditque consul principe ante se stante"*; *Panegyricus*, 64), had any influence upon the Aragonese ceremonial —be it the real or the mythical version—or whether the immediately following section where Pliny speaks of the prince beneath the laws (*"non est 'princeps super leges' sed 'leges super principem'"*; *Panegyricus* 65), influenced the protagonists of the False Fueros of Sobrarbe, I cannot say. I do not recall seeing this anecdote mentioned in any work written in the formative period of the Oath of the Aragonese, but in the 18th century it was used to refute the Oath. Diego Franco de Villalba, in his edition of the Aragonese law, *Fororum atque Observantiarum Aragoniae Codex* (Zaragoza, 1727; 2nd ed., 1743), glossing the 1348 edict *De his quae dominus rex* (quoted above, n. 30), lauds the promulgation of the royal and magisterial oath by Peter IV, compares his action with Trajan's, and asserts that it puts the lie to Hotman's invention: *"Ecce Trajani vestri clarum, saeculis reparamus exemplum; JURAT VOBIS, PER QUEM JURATIS. . . . Recedant ergo fallaciae, nec non adinventiones Othomani et durus Bruti Celtae."* (Quoted by Quinto, *Juramento*, p. 96.)

[102] William H. Prescott, in Section II of his introduction to *Ferdinand and Isabella* (3rd ed., Chicago, 1841), ɪ, 81, n. 6, realized that Pérez confounded the Privileges of Union with the Laws of Sobrarbe in the passage just preceding his quotation of the Oath. This made Prescott doubt somewhat the authenticity of the Oath, "especially because he [Pérez] is the only authority for this ancient ceremony." Considering the time that he was writing, Prescott may be forgiven his error about the authorship; but no matter what, he should have said "the only *known* authority."

that the two parts of our legend which Pérez puts together, the Oath and the Privileges of Union, are just the two things which Blancas had excised from the printed version of his *Commentarii*. Evidently the ban against the Privileges of Union was understood in the 1580's and 1590's to apply to the Oath as well, which was certainly not less libelous. When Pérez got the chance, from exile, to speak about the forbidden things, he may have interlocked them in his narrative as much for the reason that they were twinned as taboos as because they were complemental in his whimsical recreation of the history of the Justice of Aragon. On the other hand, the real oddity is not the association of the Oath with the myth of Sobrarbe but the anachronism of putting the Privileges of Union back several centuries. Perhaps we would do better to view the two parts of the Union which Pérez mentions as the outer halves of the sandwich, with the Oath as the meat of the narrative, than to regard the Oath as an interpolation. Blancas had put the Oath in his section on the founding of the nation, and this may well have been the general practice of Spaniards at least in the 1580's.

To develop any chronological arguments on the basis of the publication dates of the versions of the Oath could, however, be very deceptive. Pérez' version, the last to be published, is perhaps the most authentic. Pérez was born in 1540, so that he could have heard about the Oath even before Soranzo. Pérez was an important government official by the later 1560's, so he must have heard about the Oath by the time that it came to the attention of Hotman and Beza in the early 1570's. This is more than academic speculation. The reader may already have noticed in the chart in Appendix I that the accounts of Soranzo and Pérez, thirty years removed from each other by publication dates, resemble each other very closely. Neither of them contains the "Justice clause" found in the other versions, but each of them does contain a final clause not found in the other versions. In Soranzo this final clause is given in a prolix fashion, "and if you do otherwise we are not going to swear to you," while in Pérez it has the famous elliptical form, "and if not,

not." Did Pérez (or someone through whom the Oath was transmitted to him) perfect this clause in the Oath, which started with some awkward expression such as in Soranzo; or did Soranzo perhaps alter the original *Si no, no* phrase and spell out its meaning for some reason not known to us? We shall try to answer this question forthwith, but in closing now our long disquisition on the jurisdictional oath vis-à-vis the fictional Oath we have to remind ourselves that the principal transmission of the Oath for several decades was by word of mouth, that some tracks of its dissemination (especially among foreigners) could become quickly distorted while other traditions could remain quite uncorrupted. The same could be true about the circumstances according to which, in historical thought, the Oath was supposed to have been taken. In just the years that the Oath was becoming known, not long after it had come into existence, a major legend about Aragon was coming to fruition. The Oath could have originated as part of the legend, and then acquired a life of its own, or it could have originated as a quasi-perverse recollection of an actual oath taken by the king and then joined the larger legend. These possibilities could be multiplied, but in the absence of more evidence from Spanish sources we shall never know the precise chain of events. Again, as in the 14th century, the reverse effect of censorship saw the rise of a myth more seditious than the historical fact.

Chapter VII · If Not, Not
Slogan and Legend

$\mathcal{M}$ost of those people who have speculated about the origin of the phrase *Si no, no* have concluded that it derives from the following proverb, first made famous by Isidore of Seville and then incorporated into late editions of the Visigothic lawbook, the *Fori Judicum*, and its mediaeval Spanish equivalent, the *Fuero Juzgo*:

> King you will be if you do what is right,
> if you do not do so, you will not be king.[1]

The sentiment of this proverb suits the spirit of the Oath of the Aragonese perfectly, and the three-word slogan of the Oath is found in the last line of the proverb (*si non facias, non* eris). The fact that one of the sources was St. Isidore, *lumen Hispaniae*, naturally makes this derivation very taking.[2] But even more important is its appearance in

---

[1] St. Isidore, *Etym.*, IX, 3 (Migne, *Pat. lat.*, LXXXII, 342B): "*Unde et apud veteres tale erat proverbium.* 'Rex eris si recte facies, si non facias, non eris.'" *Fori Judicum*, Primus Titulus, §1 (ed. Madrid, 1815, p. I): "*Unde et apud veteres tale erat proverbium:* 'Rex ejus eris si recta facis, si autem non facis, non eris.'" *Fuero Juzgo*, Prim. Tit., § 2 (ed. Madrid, 1815, p. I): "*Rey serás, si fecieres derecho, et si non fecieres derecho, non serás rey.*" See below, n. 3, for some curiosities of the *Fori Judicum*—*Fuero Juzgo* incorporation of the Isidorean phrase. Among those who have seen the *Si no, no* phrase derived from *Rex eris* . . . are Quinto, *Juramento*, pp. 482-83; Danvila y Collado, *Libertades*, pp. 36ff; Balaguer, *Instituciones y Reyes*, p. 48; López de Haro, *Justicia mayor*, p. 563; and Kern, *Gottesgnadentum*, n. 452 (2nd ed., p. 210), who also shows the probable derivation of *Rex eris* . . . from Horace, *Ep.* 1, 1, 59 (cf. *ibid.*, n. 399; 2nd ed., p. 334).

[2] *Ibid.* The *Rex eris* passage from Isidore is frequently found (e.g., see next note) paired with another famous dictum by him, *Reges a recte agendo vocati sunt*, etc. (*Sentt.* 3, 48, 7; Migne, *Pat. lat.* LXXXIII, 719A), which seems to come from St. Augustine, *De Civ.*

the opening sentences of the most venerated lawbook in mediaeval Spain, because this gave it constitutional affirmation.[3]

Less attractive on philological grounds are some possible sources of *Si no, no* in Aragonese legal texts, but they are

---

Dei, v, 12; see, in addition to Kern (previous note), R. W. and A. J. Carlyle, *A History of Mediaeval Political Thought in the West,* i (London, 1903), 172, and also the learned note by Charles Plummer in his edition of Fortescue's *The Governance of England* (Oxford, 1885), pp. 181-82.

[3] The "Royal dicta," *Rex eris* and *Reges a recte agendo* (see previous note), are found in the prefatory material, consisting of eighteen laws, which was added to the *Fori Judicum* sometime after its original redaction. The *Monumenta Germaniae Historica* edition of the original 7th-century compilation (then entitled *Liber Judicorum* or *Leges Visigothorum*) does not even include this prefatory material (ed. K. Zeumer, 1902: *MGH, Leges,* Sect. i, t. i), while the "official" Spanish version and another learned Spanish edition of the 19th century both note that this prefatory material is absent from the best texts, and so give it special pagination (cf. ed. of the Real Academia Española [Madrid, 1815] and in *Los Codigos Españoles,* i [Madrid, 1847]). We should not depreciate the authenticity of this prefatory material, however, since most of the eighteen laws it sets forth are labeled as outcomes of various 7th century Councils of Toledo, and therefore are virtually contemporaneous with the lawbook. But a special relationship has developed between the "Royal dicta" and the Councils of Toledo, where there is in fact no relationship at all. This seems to be due to a simple bibliographical anomaly. The *Fuero Juzgo* is a Castilian version of the *Fori Judicum,* and the texts correspond completely; but the prefatory material is somewhat differently divided. In the Latin, each of the eighteen laws has a title and a statement indicating from which Council of Toledo it is derived; in the Spanish, the eighteen laws are given only numbers, not titles, while the sentence identifying the Council of Toledo source appears as the last sentence of the preceding law. To the unknowing, this will mean that the preceding and not the succeeding law is being referred to. This is especially deceptive in regard to the "Royal dicta." In the *Fuero Juzgo* they occur in the first of the two paragraphs into which the second law is divided, and at the end of this paragraph it is said: *"Esta lee fo fecha enno octavo concello de Toledo."* In the *Fori Judicum,* however, the "Royal dicta" appear as two separate paragraphs at the end of the first law, and the reference to Toledo viii belongs to the title for the second law. Thus the *Fuero Juzgo* imparts the false impression that *Rex eris* and its companion slogan are part of Toledo viii, a fact which, when joined with the likely derivation of *Si no, no* in the Oath of the Aragonese from *Rex eris,* inevitably leads anyone who believes in the legendary kingdom of Sobrarbe to tie early Aragonese law in with the 7th-century legislation on rulership which has such a promi-

worth mentioning because they belong to the apparatus of legend-making which we have been examining. First of all, the very line of the Privileges of Union from which False Fuero vi derives could have contributed to the Oath: *non tengades ni ayades por Reyes.* Granted that the use of two negatives here is poor philological ground on which to argue comparison with the Oath's *Si no, no,* no apology need be offered to remind the reader that the main points of the Oath (the Justice above the king, the king's tenure conditional) are the same ideas which grew out of speculation about the Privileges of Union after they were suppressed.[4] In the second place, possible sources of *Si no, no* may even be found in the sphere of the royal jurisdictional oath: the oath taken by Charles I in 1518 has a final

---

nent part in the decrees of the Councils of Toledo. Those decrees do indeed include principles of election and deposition of kings (esp. the crucial phrases of Toledo iv, c. 75: *"seipsum regno privavit,"* and Toledo viii, c. 10: *"sui ordinis dignitate privetur"*; Joh. Dom. Mansi, *Sacr. Conciliorum Coll.* [Florence, 1764] x, 640, 1220), and they do constitute an important episode in the political development of early mediaeval Europe (see José Orlandis, "La Iglesia Visigoda y los Problemas de la sucesión al trono en el siglo VII," *Settimane di Studio del Centro italiano di studi sull' alto medioevo, VII . . .* [Spoleto, 1960], 333-51, republished in his *Estudios Visigoticos III* [Rome/Madrid, 1962], pp. 43-56), but I regard the False Fueros and the Oath as late mediaeval developments and therefore excluded from direct institutional relationship with the Councils of Toledo and Visigothic rulership. Those who promoted the False Fueros and the Oath may, of course, have known about the "Royal dicta" in the *Fori Judicum* or its vernacular equivalent. This knowledge, it is clear, would enhance the verisimilitude of constitutional curbs on royal power existing in the lawbook of Sobrarbe. This conjecture forms part of what is to me the most interesting problem about the *Fuero Juzgo*: the likeness of the prefatory material in the *Fori Judicum / Fuero Juzgo* to the equivalent in the *Fuero de Tudela / Fuero General de Navarra.* Both concern the election of the ruler; both are affixed to an authentic lawbook by a process which we may charitably call *pia fraus*; and, as I see it, the False Fueros of Sobrarbe came into being in large measure to provide corresponding prefatory material for the law code of Aragon.

[4] The full passage from the Privileges of Union is cited above, Ch. iv, n. 31. Victor Balaguer, *Las Cosas de Aragon* (see above, Ch. i, n. 17), pp. 51-52, argued for this derivation of *Si no, no,* although in his *Instituciones y Reyes,* p. 48, he held to the Isidorean derivation. It may also be significant that Pérez linked the Oath with the Privileges of Union—cf. pp. 223, 225.

clause (spoken in Spanish and not in Latin as was the rest of that long oath) concerning his co-regency with his mother Joanna: "that said oath should be with this reservation and not without it" (*y no sin ella*).[5]

The phrase *Si no, no,* therefore, has many possible antecedents, in legal thought generally as well as in legal texts and oaths which impose conditions upon the king. Unless it could be demonstrated that one of those texts was surely the primary source of the idea, if not the precise words, and, further, that this source contributed significantly to the contrivance of the Oath as a whole, then I think we must conclude that these famous words merely constitute a supportive clause that provides a stirring slogan for the Oath without being a necessary part of it. In fact, neither the words nor the idea "If not, not" are to be found in the French versions of the Oath;[6] yet these versions are not thereby less forceful. *Si no, no* has become the trademark of the aggregate of Aragonese liberties, yet each part is quite genuine without it.

Antonio Pérez has been singled out as the innovator who added *Si no, no* to the Oath simply because his is the first printed work to contain those words.[7] The fact is, however, that the idea is fully embodied in the oldest recorded version of the Oath known to us, Soranzo's, which ends with the following phrase: "and if you do otherwise we are not going to swear to you." In this prolix form the notion could have been derived, as well as not, from some restric-

---

[5] Above, Ch. vi, n. 80.

[6] Some modern German authors do state that Hotman uses the words *Si no, no,* testifying to the seductiveness of those words to sum up the Oath; E. Hölzle, *Die Idee der altgermanischen Freiheit vor Montesquieu* (= *Historische Zeitschrift,* Beiheft V; Munich-Berlin, 1925), p. 51, was perhaps the first to make this slip, and it is repeated by Schramm, "Krönung," p. 580, n. 2, and "König von Navarra," p. 156.

[7] Quinto, *Juramento,* pp. 482-83. This line of reasoning complements Quinto's major argument that the Oath as a whole must be Hotman's invention because he was the first to print it (see above, pp. 176f), although Quinto also believed that Hotman knew about the *Fori Judicum* passage and was inspired by it without extracting the elliptical expression (*ibid.,* pp. 468-70); Quinto had a gift for ruining his own best arguments.

tive clause such as we noted in Charles I's oath in 1518. It is almost redundant, as found in Soranzo, because it had already been said in an earlier part of the Oath that the people were swearing to the king only upon certain conditions. If the final clause was originally as weak as this, then we should not be surprised that it does not appear in the French versions—just as we would be bothered if we were sure that the striking formulation *Si no, no* was already in the Oath in the 1560's but not in the French versions of the 1570's. Perhaps, therefore, we should assume that the final formulation of the slogan *Si no, no* was a rather late development, very likely drawn from St. Isidore or from the *Fuero Juzgo* and, maybe, even done by Pérez himself. In any event, the three words of the Oath most famous in later times seem to have only marginal utility for our task of explaining the genesis of the Oath.[8]

[8] "If not, not" had a Polish manifestation closely following in time the appearance of the Oath of the Aragonese, and perhaps affected by it. At the coronation of Henry of Valois as king of Poland in 1574, a nobleman (probably a Huguenot) cried out that Henry could not rule unless he swore the oath which he had earlier agreed upon. By the early 17th century, historians were reporting that this utterance had had the lapidary formulation: "*Si non jurabis, non regnabis.*" One suspects the formative influence of Isidore's dictum, or else an adaptation from the *Si no, no* phrase which had been appended to the Oath by Pérez but had probably been current for some time before that. If, however, one makes two not implausible assumptions—first, that the Polish formula *Si non . . . , non* actually evolved as early as the mid-1570's; and second, that the Aragonese *Si no, no* did not keep company with the Oath until Pérez wedded them in 1594— then it is possible to imagine that Poland's "If not, not" may have been the source for, and not the result of, Aragon's. Nevertheless, no matter which way the current of influence flowed in the evolution of the particulars of the "If not, not" concept, any major influence between the legendary Aragonese Oath and the unusual Polish coronation of 1574 must have proceeded from the former to the latter, simply on the grounds of temporal priority. The fact that the writers in one instance and the actors in the other were both Huguenots assures us that some such influence is very likely, and would be well worth investigating. What I know of the Polish incident comes from the article by Wacław Sobieski, "Si non jurabis, non regnabis: Spór o przysięgę królewską," *Reformacja w Polsce*, II (1922), 54-70, which my friend Ihor Ševčenko kindly summarized for me. Sobieski seems not to have known about the Aragonese Oath, so that a scholar with the requisite linguistic talents should reexamine the evidence used by Sobieski and perhaps revise his conclusions.

Nearing the end of this study, rhetorical nicety bids us return to some momentous occasion in the history of Aragon which is similar to the Constitutional Convention of 1868 with which we began, in order to illustrate the operation of our national legends in political history. Even without considering stylistic matters, however, we would have to say something about the revolt of Aragon in the years 1591-1592. Antonio Pérez was one of the main personages in that revolt, but Blancas also played an important rôle behind the scenes. Two of the principal issues were the authority of the Justice of Aragon and the right of the Aragonese people to resist a king who broke the law; and it is hard to imagine that the legends concerning these things— the Oath and the False Fueros—did not enter into the debate.[9]

Antonio Pérez was arrested in Madrid early in 1586, and for more than four years remained a prisoner there in vary-

[9] While it has been taken for granted by a critic as conservative and knowledgeable as Ximénez de Embún (*Orígenes*, p. 33) that the fables about the kingdom and Fueros of Sobrarbe helped excite the Aragonese during the *alteraciones* (sometimes called simply the *sucesos*) of 1591-1592, due at least to the publication of Blancas' *Commentarii* in 1588, nevertheless the case for the relation of the myth to the political uprising would require a detailed investigation which I simply have not been able to make. Besides the considerable body of manuscript sources (cf. Arco, *Repertorio*, pp. 203-11, Nos. 601-41), there are fourteen printed tracts of the years 1591-1592, devoted exclusively to the *alteraciones* (cf. Sánchez, *Bibliografía*, II, 395-427, among Nos. 704-35), which I have not been able to consult; one of them, Morlanes, *Alegaciones*, actually quotes the Oath from Hotman (see above, Ch. II, n. 11), and others should reveal at least traces of the Sobrarbe myth. Two readily available source books concerning the uprising are the Conde de Luna's *Comentarios de los sucesos*, written at the time of the revolt but published only in 1888, and Argensola's *Informacion de los sucesos*, written for the *Diputados del Reino* in 1604 but not printed until 1808. The latter (p. 190) refers to the oath which Bodin and Hotman claim the people pronounced to the king; Argensola does not quote the formulary, but says that it is a deception, and offers the actual oath taken by Philip II at the Cortes of Tarazona in 1592 as a refutation. For my account of the *alteraciones* I have relied chiefly upon the old but still useful work of the Marqués de Pidal, *Historia de las Alteraciones de Aragón*, 3 vols. (Madrid, 1862-1863), trans. into French by J. G. Magnabal as *Philippe II, Antonio Perez et le royaume d'Aragon*, 2 vols. (Paris, 1867).

ing strictures of confinement.[10] The charge at first was disloyalty to the king; later it was enlarged to include complicity in the murder of a royal official. Philip II was cautious in pressing the case against his former favorite and confidant because Pérez was believed to have hidden away many coffers of important state papers. When Pérez finally felt that his cause was hopeless he managed to escape prison; he fled northwards and crossed the border into Aragon. A short while later, just as royal agents were about to re-arrest Pérez, a lieutenant of the Justice of Aragon appeared, invoked the power of the *manifestación*, took Pérez into his custody, and placed him in the prison of the *manifestación* in Zaragoza. There he remained for a year and a half. The first time that Philip II's agents tried to transfer Pérez to the royal prison in Zaragoza, a popular demonstration bordering on violence forced them to return him to the prison of the *manifestación*. In Madrid, a judgment was rendered against Pérez *in absentia*, imposing the death sentence; but in Zaragoza the new trial begun under the jurisdiction of the Justice of Aragon seemed headed toward an acquittal. Finally, in September 1591, a strong contingent of troops was mustered to support a second effort to remove Pérez from the control of the Justice. As Pérez was brought out of the prison of the *manifestación*, however, a band of armed Aragonese appeared on the scene. The cry of "Liberty!" went up, and after a short skirmish the rebels held the town. Pérez, freed, lingered a few months in Aragon and then crossed over into France. He remained in exile in England and France for the last twenty years of his life.

The armed revolt, which was chiefly the work of a few disgruntled Aragonese noblemen, did not spread to many places outside the capital city of Zaragoza. Within a year it was put down by the king. Philip exacted vengeance

[10] Besides the work of Pidal mentioned in the previous note, I have relied mostly upon Gregorio Marañón, *Antonio Pérez* (Buenos Aires, 1947)—trans. into English by C. D. Ley (New York, 1955), in a reduced form—for the following brief summary of Pérez' adventures in Aragon.

upon the ringleaders and stripped the Justice of Aragon of much of his power; but he was otherwise quite lenient.

Viewed in terms of the career of Antonio Pérez, the revolt in Aragon may seem to have focused upon the power of the Justice of Aragon to act, Ephor-like, to protect a subject from injustice. In fact, the causes of the revolt can be traced back to conflicts between Aragon and Philip II that had been going on for decades. The climax of these quarrels came shortly before Pérez' appearance in Aragon, when Philip II appointed a Castilian as Viceroy in Aragon.[11] Castile was a foreign country as far as the Aragonese were concerned, and so they deemed Philip guilty of a *contra-*

[11] The background for the appointment of the Viceroy is treated by Pidal-Magnabal, *Perez*, I, 147-54, in this fashion. In 1588, Philip II had endorsed the action of the "Twenty"—a kind of vigilante group of Zaragozans—to remove a prisoner from the *manifestación*, but was then repelled when the Twenty killed that prisoner, and had to have royal officials quash them. At the same time, Ribagorza was in a near-rebellious state. The great need was to find someone outside partisan politics who had the power to cut through the jungle of legalism that paralyzed royal administration in Aragon. Appointing a non-Aragonese viceroy seemed to be the answer, but it only compounded the troubles because it violated the laws against foreign officials (see next note).

A further word is in order concerning the Twenty. The Privilege of the Twenty is supposedly a mediaeval institution dating back to a charter of privileges given to the city of Zaragoza by Alfonso I in 1119, which allowed a kind of martial law to be exercised by a select group of nobles in cases of great emergency (cf. Muñoz, *Coleccion*, I, 451-53). Later mediaeval examples of it are not to be found, although modern historians are ready to believe that it may have existed as a custom before the charter of 1119 (Pidal-Magnabal, *loc. cit.*; López de Haro, *Justicia mayor*, pp. 372ff). It appears in 16th-century historiography as an ancient privilege (cf. Molino, *Repertorium*, ed. 1533, fol. 265, who records the text but attaches no particular importance to it); and at the Cortes of Monzon in 1564 and 1584 the possibility of its reinstatement was discussed. The Cortes opposed it on these occasions, as did the king, who in 1588, though, did allow it to operate. One writer (Francisco Sanz y Ramón, *Privilegio de los Veinte* [Zaragoza, 1891]) saw the spirit of the Twenty in Blancas' first and third Fueros of Sobrarbe—a theory we can dismiss without comment. The Privilege of the Twenty, in brief, compares roughly with the legends we have been dealing with, as an example of the independent spirit of the Aragonese, and it has a similar aura of hoariness; but, since I have not found any Renaissance writer linking the Twenty with the Oath or the Fueros of Sobrarbe, I conclude that such a connection is only fancy.

fuero by having violated the law requiring that all officials of Aragon be Aragonese.[12] Pérez arrived on Aragonese soil when the resentment against the *Virey extranjero* was at a fever pitch, and he provided a golden opportunity for the Aragonese to retaliate against Philip II. Philip's legal process against Pérez had attracted worldwide attention, and everyone knew what embarrassment the king would be caused if his ex-minister should escape. Any way that the Aragonese could harbor Pérez would have been worth the trouble, considering how effectively that act would demonstrate their hostility toward the king—if not gain some advantage in negotiating with him. But the unbelievably good luck of the Aragonese (it seemed) was that they could harbor Pérez against royal justice by perfectly legal means—by a device, moreover, that was celebrated in the annals of their history and unique among the constitutions of the nations of Europe. In a single stroke of the pen, invoking the right of *manifestación*, the Aragonese could imagine themselves living again in the great past when kings who broke laws were brought to heel.

Fortunate as the situation turned out to be for Pérez, it was a disaster for the Aragonese. To begin with, the principle of the *manifestación* was degraded by being used for the sake of politics rather than justice. The will of the king

[12] "Quod officiales aragonum sint de aragonia," an edict of James II promulgated at the Cortes of Zaragoza in 1300 (*Fori Aragonum*, Book IX [pre-1551 eds., fol. XLIII]; *Nueva Compilación*, Book I, fol. XXXVI^v). Under the word *Extraneus* Molino summarizes several xenophobic laws and customs of Aragon (cf. *Repertorium*, fol. CXXXVI^v); Blancas, in his *Commentarii* (ed. Hernandez, p. 432), also takes notice of some of them. During the course of 1591, while resisting the efforts of the royal troops to take Pérez into custody, the Aragonese also invoked an edict against the presence of foreign troops in their land (cf. second article of the 1461 *De Generalibus Privilegiis Regni Aragonum*—pre-1551 eds., fol. CLXXXI). See also Argensola, *Informacion de los sucesos*, pp. 109-16; further, Pidal-Magnabal, *Perez*, II, 68-69, which summarizes the incident and shows how Pérez twisted the 1461 edict to apply against Philip II (cf. *Relaciones* [ed. Paris, 1598], p. 126). Obviously fundamental for this question, but unavailable to me, is Pedro Luis Martinez, *Discurso y alegaciones de derecho, en que se trata . . . el origen . . . de Aragon y . . . en que defiende . . . que la Magestad . . . no puede nombrar Virey extrangero* (Zaragoza, 1591), cited in "Latassa²," II, 266.

had to prevail in this instance, considering the gravity of the matter. The right of resistance might be dramatized for a while by using the *manifestación*, but if the king chose to use force the issue would quickly be decided in his favor. As it happened, however, the king turned the tables and got the law on his side by finding a way to circumvent the *manifestación*; the Aragonese, in the end, were the ones who had to resort to force.

The legal maneuvering of Philip II to get around the *manifestación* provided the occasion for Gerónimo Blancas to play his role in the Pérez affair. Philip II could have found no greater authority than Blancas to explain to him the history of the *manifestación*. Blancas' greatest work as an historian, begun before he had become royal historiographer but published only in 1588, was essentially a worshipful history of the office of the Justice of Aragon.[13] How much his fellow-countrymen were inspired by the *Commentarii* when they rallied behind the power of the Justice in 1590 we cannot be sure, but Blancas at that moment found himself being consulted by the king. He advised that there was one agency of the law against which the Justice of Aragon had never had the right to interpose his authority: the Inquisition. It took little doing by Philip to have a new case instituted against Pérez by the Inquisition, charging heresy, and it was on behalf of the Holy Office that the royal officials made their two abortive efforts to remove Pérez from the prison of the *manifestación* in 1591. This occurred only after Pérez had had a year's comfortable imprisonment in that building, however, and his personal safety had become synonymous with the Liberties of Aragon. The Aragonese contested the authority of the Inquisition, to be sure, and recalled Philip's past promises not to support its activities within their boundaries.[14] Still, Philip

---

[13] This is true despite the ways that he amended the work to suit the king—see above, Ch. v, n. 70.

[14] On Blancas' advising Philip II, see Marañon, *Pérez* (Eng. ed.), p. 268. Pidal-Magnabal, *Perez*, I, 411ff gives the text of a "Pasquin del Infierno," a contemporary tract attributed by some to Pérez, which places Blancas in Hell confessing to having forged the Enquiry of the Inquisition. A summary of the Inquisition in Aragon can be drawn

stood on as firm ground as the Aragonese in respect to the technicalities of the law. The basis of resistance had been rendered moot, and the rebellion of 1591-1592 lost much of its moral force.

The rôle of Gerónimo Blancas in these affairs was not an enviable one. As a scholar he had contributed to his country's pride in the past glory of the Justice of Aragon and had "recovered" the primitive code of laws which had established the right of resistance to tyranny at the beginnings of the nation. Then, as a royal advisor, he had helped to undermine the power of the Justice and pave the way to an inglorious revolt. Blancas died before the revolt broke out—Pérez interpreted this as a chastisement from heaven[15]—and it is well that he did not live to see the calamity that befell his native land.

The uprising of the Aragonese against Philip II in 1591-1592 was focused upon the claim of the Justice of Aragon, placing himself between the king and one of his subjects, to overrule royal jurisdiction. The uprising seemed to act out the Oath of the Aragonese. Antonio Pérez' *Relaciones*, which appeared shortly afterwards, established some kind of proof of the relationship between the uprising and the Oath. In every generation since then the Oath has found many believers. We have dealt only with those of the last century or so—the age, so to speak, of scientific historiography. During this period, in actuality, scholarly *dis*belief in the Oath has been more fashionable; Xavier de Quinto's *Juramento*, published in 1848, has been the chief authority

---

from Lea, *Inquisition of Spain*, I, 244ff, 439ff, esp. 451-52, where Lea relates the contest between the *firmas de derecho* of the Justice and the activities of the Inquisition in the period leading up to the Cortes of Monzon in 1563-1564. Giovanni Soranzo, in the same *Relazione* of 1565 in which he related the Oath (and on the page following it), recounts the quarrel at Monzon over the Inquisition. The Aragonese at one point threatened to walk out of the Cortes, but Philip gave in and promised to hear their grievances when he returned to Castile; Soranzo remarks wryly that Philip was just temporizing, and that in the future he would probably use the Inquisition more and more against the obstreperous Aragonese.

[15] Marañon, *Pérez* (Eng. ed.), p. 268.

of the skeptics. The present work is the first full-length treatment of the problem since Quinto's time. Substantive changes have been made in the evidence concerning the Oath, but a more important matter, I believe, is to reconsider the Oath in the light of its relevance for intellectual history. By now, the political significance of the Oath should have passed away, so that we can study the vagaries of Aragonese history (at least during the Renaissance) without having to identify ourselves with partisan issues.

The most obvious change that must be made in Quinto's thesis is to exculpate François Hotman. Quinto's belief that the Oath was invented in the 16th century remains tenable, but what is meant by "invention" should be considerably refined (as I shall point out shortly).

The False Fueros of Sobrarbe, long ago given "codified" status by Gerónimo Blancas, should be assigned a major role in preparing the way for the Oath. False Fueros I-IV originated in mediaeval legal codes which bear the label "Fueros of Sobrarbe." As early as the 13th century, according to many scholars, the legend had developed that Aragon originated in the primitive kingdom of Sobrarbe. But my researches have not confirmed this: the Sobrarbe legend enters the historiography of Aragon only in the 15th and 16th centuries.

False Fueros V-VI are the most important for the Oath, because their contents—the position of the Justice and the right to disavow the king—are the main points of the Oath. These two False Fueros arose from fanciful notions held by jurists about the contents of the Privileges of Union after 1348. Two hundred years later, those who believed in False Fueros V and VI had no idea that they derived from glosses on the Privileges of Union. False Fueros V and VI now kept company with False Fueros I-IV as supposed parts of the founding of the Aragonese nation—i.e., the kingdom of Sobrarbe.

The promulgation of a new compilation of the Fueros of Aragon in 1551 is an important event in the consolidation of the Renaissance legend about Aragon's early history. The new preface composed for this compilation sanctified the

idea that Aragon had originally been the kingdom of Sobrarbe, and that the laws of that kingdom (not spelled out,
however) were the first laws of Aragon. In addition, the
new compilation of law reaffirmed the two-hundred-year-
old edict prohibiting possession or knowledge of the Privileges of Union. The document was known to some scholars
in this period, however, and they were aware that its provisions about the Justice and the right to depose the king
must be related to False Fueros v and vi. Since the False
Fueros were believed to be much older, it was assumed that
they were partly the cause of the baronial revolt in 1287;
that is to say, scholars assumed that the barons who extracted the Privileges of Union from the king were asserting rights of resistance which they found in old law books
of their land. Thus it was that the Privileges of Union,
whose historical authenticity is unquestioned, came to be
viewed both as a product of the Fueros of Sobrarbe (via
their relation to False Fueros v and vi) and as proof of their
antiquity. Both these notions are wrong. Put briefly, the
condemnation and obliteration of the Privileges of Union
opened the way for historical myth by closing the door
upon historical truth; but Clio had her revenge when the
myth that grew up two hundred years later turned out to
be more pernicious to the royal cause than knowledge of
the Privileges of Union would have been.

If the Oath has any roots in actual ceremonial practices,
they are most likely to be in the royal jurisdictional oath.
This oath had special meaning for the Aragonese, first of
all, because it had to be taken in Zaragoza, reaffirming the
primacy of the capital city of Aragon even though Cortes
of the kingdom of Aragon were usually held elsewhere; and
secondly, because it was unilateral, representing a special
pronouncement by the king of his obligations, in contrast
to the reciprocal oaths of king and subjects in the Cortes.
In the times of the Habsburgs, the royal jurisdictional oath
became more jealously sustained in measure as the real
autonomy of Aragon became feebler. The oldest known
version of the Oath of the Aragonese, by Giovanni Soranzo,
refers to the "prince and heir"; the royal jurisdictional oath

was taken not only by the king but also by the "prince and heir," the primogenit; this coincidence is the strongest reason to believe that the actual royal oath is related to the fictitious one.

When all the elements mentioned above are synchronized, the period of the 1550's and the early 1560's seems to be the pregnant moment for the Oath of the Aragonese. The legend that Sobrarbe was proto-Aragon was fully attested; the False Fueros of Sobrarbe were at the penultimate stage of their codification; the Privileges of Union and the edict prohibiting them had worked their peculiar rôles in providing the internal substance and the external proof of the False Fueros; the Aragonese nation was at odds with Philip II, who had exercised jurisdiction properly as "prince and heir" since 1542, but disdained for several years after 1556, when he became king, to retake the oath as king.

The present study does not propose any answer to the question of who "invented" the Oath of the Aragonese. Documentary proof may appear some day which will indicate a definite person, but this is not very likely. For centuries now the Oath has been known to scholars of Spanish history. Some have made special searches for its origin, but their failure to discover it is even less telling than the absence of any report from the legion of scholars who have pored over Spanish sources while engaged in other studies. Most of them know about the Oath, would recognize it if they happened upon it, and would publicize any discovery of an early instance that would clarify its origins.

In terms of precise knowledge of the origins of the Oath of the Aragonese, therefore, the present work represents a retreat from the confident position established by Xavier de Quinto, and held by most scholars in the past century, that a particular individual invented the Oath. Having exculpated Hotman, I have not tried to find another culprit, although my conclusion that the Oath probably developed quickly in the period 1550-1565 should make the "single author" theory more attractive to me than the alternative hypothesis, the "oral tradition" theory. To make the "oral tradition" theory fit my chronology, I would have to make some convenient suppositions. One, for example, might be that the Oath had existed for a long time in some form different from the final product, and then was "Aragonized" after 1550 when the legend of Sobrarbe and its "Fueros" congealed very rapidly. A single person, of course, could have been responsible for this transformation. Another possibility (which would please the cynic who likes his history to reveal much ado about trivial things) could be that the Oath was contrived for a courtly or academic *divertissement* where the pridefulness of the Aragonese was satirized in an imaginary old formulary, which had been transmitted orally, with all its quaint phraseology: *Nos que valemos tanto come vos.* . . . Speculations like this could be multiplied easily enough, and I see no reason why one of them might not be nearer actuality than Quinto's theory that the Oath must have been the devilish contrivance of a single man. The "single author" theory does not have to presuppose a diabolical motivation, of course; but without it, it lacks allure.

A final word should also be said about the use of the philological method to discover the historical roots of various phrases and ideas in the Oath. This game is likely to go on and on; I have played it myself by quoting some suggestive passages from the writings of Francesch Eximeniç. If one supposes an invention by a single person, sitting in his study and cribbing from old books with no scruples about historical truth, then the possibilities of contrivance are numerous. But I say that none of them—not even the correct one, if it should be found—has any real historical interest. The philological method is useful in the history of ideas when one assumes that an author has used certain sources—whether deliberately or unconsciously—in an honest effort to advance the truth of his argument. If this intellectual honesty has not prevailed in the composition of the work being analyzed, then that work is not a genuine product within the realm of intellectual history, but a counterfeit. Now, for one thing, the Oath of the Aragonese as a whole is not true. Some parts of it may be true—e.g., the *Si no, no* phrase probably comes from the Isidorean dictum—in which case the rest is a forgery; or, all parts may be separately true to some historical saying or tradition, but some or all of them will have had to be twisted to some degree in order to make them blend in the formulary. Finally, we are not certain which, if any, of the four "primary" sources is close to the original; and the latest of the four to appear is the only one that has the one phrase, "*If not, not,*" which I have the greatest confidence can be located in earlier literature.

The combination of all these difficulties makes it seem vain to carry any further the piling up of literary analogues to the Oath out of mediaeval history and political thought. Until the time that one undeniably clear source can be shown, we have enough "suggested" sources.

Just how and by whom the Oath of the Aragonese was actually invented may long remain tantalizing questions, but in consequence of the present monograph, they may also become unimportant questions. The significant thing to me is not that the Oath is historically untrue, but that it was believed and bandied about at least from the 1560's onwards. It was evidently not an unnatural phenomenon in the intellectual milieu of those years, whether it was then new or old.

The writings of Gerónimo Blancas have provided almost all the clues necessary to "naturalize" the Oath in Aragonese thought of the second half of the 16th century: it has a home in the legend of Sobrarbe and its False Fueros. This is not a new discovery, although parts of the Sobrarbe legend have had to be reinterpreted. The chief novelty of the present work has been rather to present the legend, especially the parts which concern the Justice of Aragon, for the first time in a dynamic form. The main obstacle to a sure grasp of many Sobrarbe problems has been the lack of chronological reckoning of the stages by which the various parts of the legend grew. Even very careful scholars, who have been aware of the largely mythical character of Sobrarbe historiography, have unwittingly adopted anachronistic premises about the date when particulars of the myth originated. In my presentation I have paid particular attention to the stages required for the Sobrarbe legend to grow to maturity. Indeed, I have focused this study as much upon the legend-making process as upon the content of the legend.

Historiographical legends produced during the Renaissance have one regular difference from medieval legends about the origins of nations: they stress legal-constitutional bases of the nation as opposed to religious ones. This is most easily illustrated in France. The principal medieval legend concerned Clovis, the first Christian king, who was baptized by holy balm sent from heaven for the occasion and then used for all later French royal coronations. Contrasted to this, the Renaissance legend featured Pharamond, Clovis' pagan forbear who ordered the promulgation of the Salic Law which was believed to have controlled dynastic succession in France for a millennium. In brief, the consecrated Christian king is rivaled by the law-giving pagan king as the heroic founder of the nation.[16]

In Aragon, the parallel is found in the shift from the legend of the monks of San Juan de la Peña receiving refugees from the Muslim advance and counseling them on how to reestablish a Christian nation,[17] to the legend of Cerdan and others about the legal deliberations of the founding fathers. The new emphasis is upon strictly secular issues, even to the extent of allowing the accession of a pagan king if the Christian incumbent should violate the constitutional checks put upon him.

This French–Aragonese parallel has a flaw in its politics: the French example illustrates the blooming of absolutism by dint of dynastic right inherent in the Salic Law, while the Aragonese example constricts royal privilege due to the rôle of the Justice. This objection can be rebutted in kind, however, by adducing other examples that are politically harmonious, and can be dismissed outright by assuming a coign of vantage which makes political considerations irrelevant.

---

[16] For a discussion of this shift from Clovis to Pharamond, see my *Juristic Basis*, pp. 17-22.

[17] The story about the monks of San Juan de la Peña may be found, naturally, in the *Pinatense*, but also in other medieval chronicles.

The French historical work of the 16th century which is most harmonious with the political bent of the legend of Sobrarbe is Hotman's *Francogallia*. I view this work as a treatise on public law, an effort to discover the pristine constitution of France.[18] Hotman stressed those limitations upon the monarchy which, in his estimation, had been the mainstays of the Merovingian and Carolingian dynasties, as well as the Capetian until the later 15th century. On occasion he used comparative institutional examples to fortify his argument, and it was in this connection that the Oath of the Aragonese was cited. The Oath of the Aragonese is obviously compatible with the *Francogallia* insofar as it shows that limits to royal power existed at the very founding of the nation. Blancas, then, could be called an Aragonese Hotman. His *Commentarii rerum Aragonensium* is also an historical treatise, focused upon legal-constitutional issues, which establishes the limits to kingship set up at the founding of the nation. Blancas concentrates upon the power of the Justice of Aragon, Hotman upon baronial power located in the *Curia Franciae*.

The kind of "constitutional antiquarianism" in which Hotman and Blancas were engaged—and examples of it can be found in other European nations at this time[19]—has many political ramifications. It might well serve immediate political needs, as the *Francogallia* did for the religious wars in France, the *Commentarii* for the uprising of 1591-1592 in Aragon. On a higher plane, constitutional antiquarianism affected the "mode of legitimating" used in defending political systems. In the case at hand, this resulted in the proofs about a given nation's proper government shifting away from metaphysical and scriptural grounds onto historical grounds. For Hotman, as for Blancas, that which was established at the time of the founding of the nation must be upheld if the nation is to thrive. As is usually the case when

[18] See my "When and Why Hotman Wrote the *Francogallia*," *Bibliothèque d'Humanisme et Renaissance*, xxix (1967), esp. 608f.

[19] See the first chapter of J.G.A. Pocock, *The Ancient Constitution and the Feudal Law* (Cambridge, 1957), which treats Hotman at some length, and, on p. 16, n. 1, cites other national examples to which I would add Blancas.

appeal is made to the pristine past, the substantialistic fallacy takes command; so, both Hotman and Blancas believe that the institutions of their own times, or the very recent past, which they most admire must have been fully conceived and installed at the beginning of the nation.[20] Accordingly, their historical works can be severely criticized by modern standards.

There is a still loftier level from which we might view the work of scholarly legal historians such as Hotman and Blancas, so as to allow us to transcend the political nexus of their writings and even to nullify the feebleness of their scholarship. I refer to a general state of mind which grew up everywhere, and might be called "constitutional self-awareness." Legends such as we have been dealing with, along with the historical truths that emerged from the writings of people like Hotman and Blancas, fostered the concept of distinctive national constitutions. Political thought in the Middle Ages had tended to regard the problem of governance under general terms, so that notions about what characterized the well-ordered state were consistent, not relative. Constitutional antiquarianism in Renaissance times, on the other hand, brought to light the peculiarities of a given nation's original constitution, and thus stressed its difference from all other nations. Whether this was politically motivated to support or to attack royal absolutism was coincidental to the elementary purpose which both served, which was to instill a sense of the uniqueness of one's nation's legal character.

What I speak of falls well short of the kind of national self-consciousness associated with the French Revolution. For one thing, it had meaning—like most other things closely related to Renaissance humanism—only for those who were well educated. And it is not as broadly cultural as modern nationalism, but rather narrowly legal and constitutional. Against the legalism of the Middle Ages (upon which it builds, of course) constitutional self-awareness of Renaissance times thrives upon the things which history teaches

[20] I take the concept of the substantialistic fallacy from R. G. Collingwood, *The Idea of History* (Oxford, 1946), pp. 42-45.

us make nations different from each other. If it fails to evoke the kind of total emotional commitment to which Nicholas Chauvin gave his name, it is nonetheless a step in that direction.

Most parts of the legend of Sobrarbe were limned out during the 15th century, when Aragon was a European power, but the Oath of the Aragonese—the final flourish of the legend-making process, as it were—did not actually appear until after Aragon had ceased to be an independent nation. At least up through the 19th century the Aragonese remained keenly aware of the particular constitutional forms of their distant past, and they invoked them in the Cortes and the Academy. Indeed, for all we know the spirit of "If not, not" may surge up anew tomorrow in Spain.

APPENDIX I

The Four Primary Versions of the Fictitious Oath of the Aragonese[1]

Giovanni Soranzo *Relazione di Spagna*, 1565[2]	François Hotman *Francogallia*, 1573[3]	Gerónimo Blancas *Commentarii*, 1588[4]	Antonio Pérez *Relaciones*, 1598[5] [1593]
Noi, che valemo tanto come voi,	*Nos qui valemos tanto come vos,*	*Nos tan buenos como vos,*	*Nos, que valemos tanto como[6] vos*
che non valete piu di noi,	*y podemos mas que vos,*	*é que podemos más que vos,*	
giuriamo a voi[7] per principe ed erede del nostro regno,	*vos elegimos rey,*	*tomamos á vos por Rey,*	*os hazemos nuestro Rey, y Señor,*
con condizione che conserviate le nostre leggi e la nostra libertà,	*con estas y estas conditiones,*		*con tal que nos guardeys nuestros fueros, y libertades,*
	intra vos y nos, un que manda mas que vos.	*con que haya siempre entre vos, y nos un que mande más que vos.*	
e facendo voi altrimenti noi non vi giuriamo.			*y syno, No.*

[1] In Ch. II the reasons are given for this selection of "primary" versions, and references are made to others.

[2] See above, Ch. VI, n. 1, for the full context of Soranzo's presentation of the Oath.

[3] See above, Ch. VI, n. 3, for the full context of Hotman's presentation of the Oath, which I offer as representing all the French versions; Beza's is identical to Hotman's, and his or Hotman's was the basis for the other two French renditions, by Bodin and by the author of the *Vindiciae contra tyrannos* (see Ch. II, nn. 2-9; Ch. VI, n. 2).

[4] See above, Ch. V, n. 93, for the full context of Blancas' presentation of the Oath.

[5] See Ch. VI, n. 5, for the full context of Pérez' presentation of the Oath.

[6] *Come* in the first edition, 1593.

[7] The words "*giuriamo a voi*" actually come before and not after "*che non valete piu di noi*" in Soranzo's rendition; I have placed them in the order that similar words or thoughts come in the other versions in order to facilitate comparison.

APPENDIX II

Diagram of the "False Fueros of Sobrarbe"

False Fueros I-IV   False Fueros V-VI

1000

[True Fueros of Sobrarbe]

1100

FUERO of TUDELA

1200

FUERO of NAVARRE

Privileges of Union

1300

(*De prohibita unione*)
Martin SAGARRA

1400

Juan Jimenez CERDAN
[*FF* v only]

1450

Charles of VIANA   Antich de BAGES

Fabricio de VAGAD

1500

Miguel del MOLINO

Lucius MARINEUS

Joannes VASAEUS

1550

FUERO of ARAGON, *Nueva Compilación*

Pedro Antonio BEUTER [I-IV; v]

Gerónimo ZURITA [I-IV; v, VI]

GARIBAY y Zamalloa [I-IV; v, VI]

Gerónimo BLANCAS, *Commentarii* (1588)

FF I	*FF* II	*FF* III	*FF* IV	*FF* V	*FF* VI
Peace, justice, and rule by law.	Equal division of reconquered lands.	Rule with counsel of subjects.	Consent of elders in grave matters.	Creation of the Justice of Aragon.	Right to depose a lawbreaking ki

APPENDIX III

Fuero General de Navarra (Ed. Pamplona, 1869)

Título I. De Reyes et de huestes, et de cosas que taynnen á Reyes et á huestes.
Capítulo I.—Cómo deven levantar Rey en Espaynna, et cómo les deve eyll jurar.

E fué primerament establido por Fuero en Espaynna de Rey alzar por siempre, porque ningun Rey que iamas seria non lis podies ser malo, pues conceyllo zo es pueblo lo alzavan, et le davan lo que eyllos avian et ganavan de los moros:

[II] primero que les iuras, antes que lo alzassen sobre la cruz et los santos evangelios, que los toviess á drecho, et les mejoras siempre lures fueros, et non les apeyoras, et que les desfiziex las fuerzas,

Charles of Viana, *Crónica de Navarra* (Ed. Pamplona, 1843)

Cap. VI.—Este es el primer capítulo que los navarros é aragoneses establescieron en su fuero general.

Nos ricoshombres, caballeros é infanzones, é hombres de buenas villas de Navarra é Aragon, como aqueillos que siempre tovimos hermandat é buena compañia, establescemos primerament, por fuero de levantar rey para siempre; é por que ningun rey non nos pueda ser malo, pues que consejo, es á saber pueblo lo levanta é le damos de lo que tenemos é ganáremos de los moros.

Primerament que nos jure ante de lo alzar sobre cruz é sanctos evangelios que nos tendrá á derecho, é amejorará siempre nuestros fueros, é no los apeorará, é que desfará las fuerzas,

Blancas, *Commentarii* (1588): "De Antiquo Iure, Suprarbiensi Foro Nuncupato."

Uti futurus Rex, quandoquidem ad eum ultro, ac sponte Regnum iam é Mauris eripti, ac promoveri coeptum deferebatur, de legibus observandis, ac libertate Regni tuenda, tum iurisiurandi religione, tum etiam ipsarum legum vi, ac potestate premeretur. Ipsae vero leges huiusmodi fuere.

[I] IN. PACE. ET. IVSTITIA. REGNVM. REGITO. NOBISQ. FOROS. MELIORES. IRROGATO.

"Sagarra Story" from Miguel del Molino, *Repertorium* (1513)

Libertatum aragonensium origo in prima conquesta ab antiquis didici. Quod aragonenses de seipsis paribus et sociis in armis peditibus elegerunt in regem suum Enecum de Ariesta, alias secundum cronicam aragonum vocabatur don Garci Ximenez qui fuit de genere gotorum.

Fuero General de Navarra (Ed. Pamplona, 1869)	Charles of Viana, Crónica de Navarra (Ed. Pamplona, 1843)	Blancas, Commentarii (1588): "De Antiquo Iure, Suprarbiensi Foro Nuncupato."	"Sagarra Story" from Miguel del Molino, Repertorium (1513)
[III] et que parta el bien de cada tierra con los ombres de la tierra convenibles á richos ombres, á cavaylleros, á yfanzones, et á ombres bonos de las villas, et non con extranios de otra tierra.	é que partirá el bien de cada tierra con los hombres deilla, convenibles á los ricoshombres caballeros é infanzones é hombres de buenas villas, é non con estraños de otra tierra.	[III] E. MAVRIS. VINDICAB-VNDA. DIVIDVNTOR. INTER. RICOSHO-MINES. NONMODO. SED. ETIAM. INTER. MILITES. AC. INFAN-TIONES. PEREGRIN-VS. AVTEM. HOMO. NIHIL. INDE. CAPITO.	
Et si por aventura aviniesse cossa que fuesse Rey ombre de otra tierra, ó de estranio logar ó de estranio lengoage, que non lis adusiesse en essa tierra mas de V.º en vayllia, ni en servitio de Rey hombres estranios de otra tierra.	E si por aventura acontesciere que fuese rey hombre de otra tierra, ó de estraño logar, ó de estraña lengoa que no traya consigo mas de cinco, ni en valia ni en su servicio, hombres estraños de otra tierra.		
[III] Et que Rey ninguno que no oviesse poder de fazer Cort sin conseyo de los ricos ombres naturales del Regno,	E que rey nenguno haya poder nunca de facer corte sin consejo de sus ricos hombres naturales del regno,	[III] IVRA. DICERE. REGI. NEFAS. ESTO. NISI. ADHIBITO. SVBDI-TORVM. CONSILIO.	
[IV] ni con otro Rey ó Reyna, guerra ni paz, nin tregoa non faga, ni otro granado fecho ó embargamiento de Regno, sin conseyllo de XII ricos ombres ó XII de los más ancianos sabios de la tierra.	ni con otro rey ó reyna, guerra ó paz, nin tregoa, non fagua, ni otro granado fecho ó embargamiento del regno, sin consejo de doce ricoshombres ó doce de los mas ancianos sabios de la tierra.	[IV] BELLVM. AGGREDI. PACEM. INIRE. IN-DVCIAS. AGERE. REMVE. ALIAM. MAGNI. MOMENTI. PERTRACTARE. CAVETO. REX. PRAE-TERQVAM. SEN-TERQVAM.	

a vigil the night before. The day of the ceremonial he hears Mass. He is raised on a shield by the *ricoshombres*, who shout three times: REAL! REAL! REAL! The king issues a largess, and then he is girded with his sword. No other knight is made that day. The *ricoshombres* and other nobles in attendance then make their promise of fidelity to the king, and kiss his hand.]

[V] NE. QVID. AVTEM. DAMNI. DETRIMEN-TIVE. LEGES. AVT. LIBERTATES. NOS-TRAE. PATIANTVR. IVDEX. QVIDAM. MEDIVS. ADESTO. AD. QVEM. A. REGE. PRO-VOCARE. SI. ALI-QVEM. LAESERIT. IN-IVRIASQ. ARCERE. SI. QVAS. FORSAN. RE-IPVB. INTVLERIT. IVS. FASQ. ESTO.

[V] Et in eadem electione sive die elegerunt unum de seipsis in iusticiam aragoniae, qui esset iudex inter regem et subditos suos super omnibus hiis quae rex faceret vel peteret contra eos, vel econtra.

[VI] SI. CONTRA. FOROS. AVT. LIBERTATES. REGNVM. A. SE. PREMI. IN. FVTVRVM. CONTINGERET. AD. ALIVM. SIVE. FI-DELEM. SIVE. INFI-DELEM. REGEM. AD-SCISCENDVM. LIBER. IPSI. REGNO. ADITVS. PATERET.

[VI] Et condicionarunt potestatem regis quod nisi ipse et sui successores regerent iuxta foros datos et dandos quod possent sibi eligere regem etiam paganum,

et de hoc concessit privilegium aragonensibus quod tempore unitatis [read: unionis] ultime renunciatum extitit et cancellatum prehabito tractatu alias nolebant aragonenses renunciare.

Johannus Antich de Bages, *Glossae super Observantiae Martini Didaci Daux* [ca. 1445]; Gloss on Daux, Lib. vi, Tit. De priv. milit., § Item de omnibus causis.

> M=Biblioteca Nacional Madrid, ms 747, fol. 195[r-v] [anc. fol. 151[r-v]]
>
> Z=Biblioteca Universitaria de Zaragoza, ms 95, fols. 250[v]-51

N.B. A new paragraph has been begun at every point where Antich de Bages cites another passage from Martin Daux, in order to make perfectly clear what our manuscripts obfuscate, namely, the separateness of the parts of this particular gloss. Also, the words quoted by Antich from Daux, as keys to the gloss, have been italicized; they are often readable, as a whole, as the subject of one of Antich's sentences.

ITEM DE OMNIBUS CAUSIS[1] *contra regem* concordat cum alia observantia, "Item in Aragoniae quilibet qui querellam," infra, de interpretatione privilegii generalis [ad] libitum hoc.[(a)][2]

Et forum Exeae, in c. seu, § quinto, "Item in omnibus causis," lib. 8 fororum.[3]

Rex delegabit[(b)] *iudicem* concordat cum proxime dicta observantia "Item in Aragonia quilibet qui querellam," infra, de interpretatione privilegii generalis [ad] libitum hoc,[(c)] in fine ipsius observantiae, in qua hoc idem dicitur quod in praesenti.[4]

Iuxta foros antiquos[5] hoc fuit adquisitum regno per regnicolas tempore electionis Enneci Arista vulgariter dicti quinti regis Suprarbrii, Ripacurcii et Pampilonum, ut in genealogiae arbore regnum Aragonum dicitur;[6] et recitatur in glossa super foro primo libro decimo fororum ubi fuit abolitum et cissum[(d)] privilegium unionis;[7] et recitat etiam Martinus de Sagarra in suis observantiis et praticis in c. origo libertatum;[8] in quibus locis dicitur quod aragonenses ipsum jurarunt et crearunt ad[(e)] conditionem quod ipse et sui tenentur [f] creare, sic [g] fecit tunc in continenti, unum de ipsis in judicem qui judicaret et esset judex inter ipsum et eius vasallos et ille cognosceret et judicaret de quibuscumque causis et questionibus quae essent inter regem et eos, [Z:251] tam agendo quam defendendo, [h] et quod [i] ille rex servaret ipsi et suis successoribus [j] in perpetuum foros dantos, [k] et si non servaret quod ipsum possent privare et alium sibi eligere in regem etiam paganum;[9] et hoc erat privilegium unionis quod renunciarent tempore domini regis Petri [l] anno 1348, ut in dicto foro primo lib. 10,[10] et dicitur cuius loco successit et succedit inhibitio de facto jurisfirmae et manifestacio ut videtur quotidie, et dicitur in observantia [M:195ᵛ] dicti domini Martini de Sagarra quae est inserta per [m] glossam dicti primi fori lib. 10 fororum[11] quam diligenter lege et attende ubi maxima recitantur quae sunt libertates huius regni.

Appellari tamen potest de usu ad regem a sententia justiciae Aragoniae pro parte regis vel infancio, et rex delegabit [n] *judicem,* [o] et hoc tamquam ad superiorem in jurisdictione ordinaria ac suprema.

[a] M,Z: lib. hoc; [b] M,Z: delegabit; [c] ut supra; [d] Z: scissum; [e] Z, deleted, and in superscript by another hand: cum; [f] Z, superscript: tenerentur; [g] Z, added superscript: ut ipse (as Ximénez de Embún reads it); [h] Z, superscript, twice, of *in,* giving: tam in agendo quam in defendendo; [i] Z: per; [j] M,Z: sui successores; [k] M: daturos [?]; Z: datos (also superscript by another hand: et dandos); [l] M,Z: primi; Z, deleted and superscript by another hand: Petri 4; [m] Z, deleted, and in superscript by another hand: pro; [n] M,Z: delegavit; [o] M: judice.

---

[1] Z: in margin, "Justicia Arag. 12," which identifies the subject of this gloss, and numbers it as it is found in later editions of Martin Daux, as §12 of the title *De privilegiis militum.* The text of Daux's *Item de omnibus causis* itself is given above, Ch. IV, n. 21.

[2] A reference to Daux, *Observantiae,* Lib. VI, Tit. "Interpretationes qualiter, & in quibus intelligatur Privilegium Generale," § [10] Item, in Aragonia quilibet qui querelam. This observance is indeed relevant to our problem, and is short enough to be quoted in full: "*Item, in Aragonia quilibet qui querelam habet de domino Rege, sive personalis sit actio, sive realis, potest recurrere ad Iustitiam Aragonum, & Iustitia iudicabit inter Regem & querelatorem; et per hoc est statutum in novo foro, quod dominus Rex in Aragonia* [Antich, Glossa, MS M, fols. 182ᵛ-83 comments upon this] *semper habeat suum*

procuratorem fisci; appellare tamen potest procurator pro parte Regis a sentencia Iustitiae si voluerit, & Rex super appellatione Iudicem assignabit" (ed. 1624, fol. 27).

[3] *Fori Aragonum*, Lib. viii, c. Fori editi apud Exeam, § Item quod in omnibus causis. This is the fifth § of this statute, which begins with the word *Statuit*. In our text, therefore, the word *seu* should probably be read *statuit*. The text of this § reads: *"Item quod in omnibus causis que erunt inter ipsum regem vel successores suos et richos homines, filiosdalgos, et infanciones, quod iusticia aragonum iudicet cum consilio richorum homini et militum qui erunt in curia, dummodo non sint de partida. In omnibus aliis causis quae erunt inter richos homines, milites, et infanciones iudicet iusticia aragonum de ipsius regis consilio et de consilio richorum hominum, militum, et infancionum qui erunt in curia, dummodo non sint de partida ut dictum est"* (pre-1551 eds., fol. xxxvi^v).

[4] See n. 3.

[5] Z has in the margin this long note (in a different hand from the note cited in n. 8 below) which refers to the text's mention of Martin Sagarra: *"Nota enim ex testimonio M. Sagarra quatenus tempore electionis fuit statuta creatio magistratus Justiciae Aragonum. Istum autem M. Sagarra longe ante Salanovam Iusticam fuisse credo."* This note, it seems, made Ximénez de Embún say that "Z" was used by Blancas—see above, Ch. iv, n. 13.

[6] Note that Antich de Bages had himself composed a genealogy of the kings of Aragon; see above, Ch. iv, n. 14.

[7] *Fori Aragonum*, Lib. x, *De prohibita unione* (discussed at length above, pp. 90ff). In the manuscript of this work in the Bib. del Escorial (ms P. II. 3, fol. 96) there is a marginal note alongside *De prohibita unione* which is not easily read because of the tight binding; I reconstruct the first two-thirds of this note as follows: *"Origo libertatum Regni Antigui hunc in observantia Sagarra. . . ."* I am at least certain that the author of this note linked Sagarra's writings with the prohibited Privileges of Union.

[8] Z has a marginal note, which I read tentatively as: *"hic vult allegare glossam, sic ista sunt verba illius, non autem Sagarra."* This seems to imply that the gloss on Peter IV's *De prohibita unione* is not the same as Sagarra's, as Antich implies it is.

[9] Note that Blancas (ed. Schott, iii, 721) and Lasala and Ximénez de Embún end their quotation of Antich at this point.

[10] See above, n. 7.

[11] *Ibid.*

APPENDIX V

The Kings of Aragon

As explained in the text (above, p. 33), the kings of legendary Sobrarbe were actually the rulers of the kingdom of Pamplona (or Navarre). For the list below I have relied chiefly upon Sánchez-Albornoz, "Navarra del siglo IX," for the Arista family; Ibarra y Rodríquez, "Estados pirenaicos," for the Jimena family and the County of Aragon; and Ignacio Vincente Cascante, *Heraldica general y fuentes de las armas de España* (Barcelona, 1956), for the kingdom of Aragon.

Kingdom of Pamplona (Navarre)
Arista Family

Iñigo Arista	after 788-820
Fortún Iñíguez[1]	after 820-843
Iñigo Iñíguez[1]	820-852
Garcia Iñíguez	852-871[2]
Fortún Garsés	882-905

Jimena Family

Sancho Garcés (Garci Ximenez)	905-925
García Sánchez I	925-970
(930: Union with County of Aragon)	
Sancho Garcés II Abarca	970-994
García Sánchez II	994-1000
Sancho Garcés III (el mayor)	1000-1035

County of Aragon

Aznar Sánchez	833-836
Galindo Aznarez I	836
Aznar Galíndez II	X[3]-893
Galindo Aznarez II	892-930

[1] joint or alternating rulership.
[2] *terminus ad quem.*
[3] accession date uncertain.

Kingdom of Aragon
House of Navarre

Ramiro I	1035-1063
Sancho Ramírez	1063-1094
Peter I	1094-1104
Alfonso I	1104-1134
Ramiro II	1134-1137
Petronilla	1137-1162

Aragonese-Catalan Confederation

Alfonso II	1162-1196
Peter II	1196-1213
James I	1213-1276
Peter III	1276-1285
Alfonso III	1285-1291
James II	1291-1327
Alfonso IV	1327-1336
Peter IV	1336-1387
John I	1387-1395
Martin I	1395-1410
Interregnum	1410-1412

Compromise of Caspe
(Trastámara Family)

Ferdinand I	1412-1416
Alfonso V	1416-1458
John II	1458-1479
Ferdinand II	1479-1516

Union of Castile and Aragon
(Habsburg Family)

Joanna I and Charles I, jointly	1516-1555
Charles I alone	1555-1556
Philip II	1556-1598

Selected and
Indexed Bibliography

(The numbers at the end of entries—e.g., *I, 5*—refer to citations of chapters and footnotes in this work. Being listed in this Bibliography does not preclude another entry in the Index, especially with regard to mediaeval and Renaissance works.)

Aguado Bleye, Pedro. *Manual de historia de España.* Vol. I: 9th ed., Madrid, 1963. Vol. II: 8th ed., Madrid, 1959. *I*, 16; *III*, 1; *IV*, 39; *V*, 2.

Antich de Bages. *Glossa.* See Appendix IV; also *s.n.* in Index.

Anales de Aragon.

(a) Beginning to 1516: see under Zurita.

(b) . . . *desde el año 1516* [*hasta el de 1520*]. By Bartolomé Juan Leonardo y Argensola. Zaragoza, 1630. *VI*, 69-77, 79-81.

(c) . . . *desde el año de 1520 . . . hasta el de 1525.* By Francisco Diego de Sayas Rabanera y Ortubia. Zaragoza, 1666.

(d) . . . *desde el año 1525 . . . hasta el de 1540.* By Diego Josef Dormer. Zaragoza, 1697. *VI*, 69, 70, 74, 75, 81, 84.

(e) . . . *desde el año 1540 . . . hasta el año 1558.* By José Lupercio Panzano Ybañez de Aoyz. Zaragoza, 1705. *VI*, 85.

(Aragon, Kingdom). *Fori* [*et observantiae regni*] *Aragonum.* 2nd ed., Zaragoza, 1496. (1517, 1542, and other editions before 1551 preserve same pagination.) *III*, 17; *IV*, 9, 21, 28, 34, 35, 42, 44; *VI*, 47, 48, 51, 53, 57, 101; *VII*, 12; *Appendix IV*, 3, 4, 7.

―――. *Fueros, Observancias . . . de Aragón.* Ed. by Luis Parral y Cristobal. Zaragoza, 1907. 2 vols. [vol. I contains geographical and historical résumés of Aragon; vol. II, *Nueva Compilación*, Books I-IV only]. *III*, 47; *IV*, 21; *V*, 35, 36.

―――. *Nueva Compilación.* Zaragoza, 1552. (1576, 1624, and 1667 editions preserve same pagination.) *IV*, 6, 18; *V*, 18, 36, 37, 40, 41; *VI*, 47, 51, 53, 57, 86, 101; *VII*, 12; *Appendix II.*

Argensola, Bartolomé Juan Leonardo y. See *under Anales de Aragon.*

Argensola, Lupercio Leonardo de. *Informacion de los sucesos del reino de Aragon en los años de 1590 et 1591 . . . escrita por Lupercio Leonardo de Argensola . . . a instancia de los Diputados del Reino en este año de 1604.* Madrid, 1808. *VII,* 9, 12.

Arco, Ricardo del. *La erudición española en el siglo XVII y el cronista de Aragón, Andrés de Uztarroz.* Madrid, 1950. 2 vols. *VI,* 8.

Arco, Ricardo del. *Repertorio de manuscritos referentes a la historia de Aragón.* Madrid, 1942. *VI,* 8; *VII,* 9.

Balaguer, Victor. *Instituciones y Reyes de Aragón.* Madrid, 1896. *I,* 2, 17; *IV,* 49; *VII,* 1, 4. (*See also* Romero Ortiz.)

Ballesteros y Beretta, Antonio. *Historia de España.* Barcelona, 1918-1958. 12 vols. *III,* 1.

Beneyto Pérez, Juan. *Los orígenes de la ciencia política en España.* Madrid, 1949. *VI,* 9, 13.

———(ed.). *Textos políticos españoles de la baja edad media.* Madrid, 1944. *VI,* 9.

Beuter, Pedro Antonio. *Coronica general de toda España y especialmente del reyno de Valencia* [1546-1551]. Valencia, 1604. *V,* 27, 41-48, 87; *VI,* 26, 39, 56; *Appendix II.*

Beza, Theodore. *De iure magistratuum* [1573]. Lyon, 1580. *II,* 3, 4, 6, 7; *VI,* 2, 96.

Blancas y Tomás, Gerónimo de. *Comentarios de las cosas de Aragon.* Trans. (of *Arag. rer. comm.*) by P. Manuel Hernandez. Zaragoza, 1878. *I,* 18; *II,* 14, 15; *IV,* 20, 30, 31, 37, 38; *V,* 44, 62-66, 68, 69, 72, 73, 75-77, 79-82, 84-86, 89-93; *VI,* 42; *VII,* 12.

Blancas y Tomás, Gerónimo de. *Aragonensium rerum commentarii.* Zaragoza, 1588. Reprinted in Schott, *Hisp. illust.,* III, 366-839. *I,* 8, 9, 11-13; 15; *III,* 37, 42-47; *IV,* 4, 5, 12, 13, 20, 26, 37, 38, 42-44; *V,* 22, 44, 62, 64, 68, 69, 72-75, 77, 79-86, 89-93; *VI,* 21, 26, 27, 29, 93; *VII,* 9, 12; *Appendices I-III; Appendix IV,* 5, 9.

Blancas y Tomás, Gerónimo de. *Coronaciones de los serenissimos reyes de Aragon* [ca. 1585]. Ed. by Juan Fr. Andrés de Uztarroz. Zaragoza, 1641. *II*, 18; *III*, 18; *IV*, 14; *V*, 62; *VI*, 8, 9, 27, 50, 52, 55, 59, 61-64, 88.

———. *Modo de proceder en cortes de Aragon* [ca. 1585]. Ed. by Juan Fr. Andrés de Uztarroz. Zaragoza, 1641. *II*, 19; *VI*, 60, 84.

Blasco de Lanuza, Vincencio. *Historias ecclesiásticas y seculares de Aragon*. Zaragoza, 1619-1622. 2 vols. *VI*, 69, 70, 76, 87.

Bodin, Jean. *Les six livres de la republique* [1576]. Lyon, 1593. Latin trans. by Bodin: *De Republica libri sex* [1586]. Frankfort, 1641. *II*, 8, 9; *VI*, 98; *VII*, 9.

Briz Martínez, Juan. *Historia de la fundacion y antigüedades de San Juan de la Peña*. Zaragoza, 1620. *V*, 27, 40.

Cánovas del Castillo, Antonio. *Estudios Literarios*. Madrid, 1868. 2 vols. *I*, 6; *V*, 12.

Cerdan, Juan Jimenez. *Letra intimada por mossen Iohan Ximenez Cerdan, a mossen Martin Diez Daux, Justicia de Aragon* (1436). In *Fori Aragonum*, pre-1551 eds.; also in most later editions of the *Fueros de Aragon*. *IV*, 8, 9, 11, 34, 42; *V*, 2, 39, 53, 89; *VI*, 33; *Appendix II*.

Charles, Prince of Viana. *Crónica de los Reyes de Navarra* (ca. 1450). Ed. by José Yanguas y Miranda. Pamplona, 1843. *III*, 34, 36-38, 40; *IV*, 6; *V*, 27, 40, 42, 46, 83; *VI*, 25, 26; *Appendices II, III*.

Cirot, Georges. *Études sur l'historiographie espagnole. Les histoires générales d'Espagne entre Alphonse X et Philippe II (1284-1556)*. Bordeaux, 1904. *V*, 3, 4, 28, 29, 41, 42.

Cronicón villarense. See Villarense.

Danvila y Collado, Manuel. *Las Libertades de Aragon. Ensayo histórico, jurídico y político*. Madrid, 1881. *I*, 1, 7, 13, 17, 18; *IV*, 1, 4, 29-31, 35, 36, 40, 41; *V*, 88; *VII*, 1.

———. *El Poder Civil en Espagna*. Zaragoza, 1885-1887. 6 vols. *IV*, 2; *V*, 47, 88.

Daux, Martin Didaci. *Observantiae regni Aragoniae*. Always published together with *Fori Aragonum* (see Aragon, Kingdom). *III*, 9; *IV*, 7, 15, 18, 20, 21, 23; *VI*, 51; *Appendix IV*, throughout.

Dormer, Diego Josef. *Discurso Historico-Foral, juridico-politico, en orden el juramento que los supremos y soberanos senores Reyes de Aragon . . . deven prestar en el nuevo ingreso de su gobierno, y antes que puedar usar de alguna jurisdicion.* Zaragoza, 1676. [Title here as in Bib. Nac. MS. 7588 (verbatim extracts of about one-half the work) from which I quote; slightly different is Latassa², I, 406, No. 39.] *VI*, 88.

Dualde Serrano, Manuel. "Tres episodios zaragozanos de la lucha entre 'Pere el del Punyalet' y la Unión Aragonesa, relatados por el monarca a su tío Pedro, conde de Ribagorza," *Estudios de edad media de la corona de Aragón,* II (1946), 295-374. *I*, 18; *IV*, 33.

Escudero, Nicolás S. de Otto. *Especialidades políticas y civiles del antiguo reino de Aragón.* Barbastro, 1915. *I*, 22.

Eximeniç, Francesch. *Dotzen Libre* of the *Crestiá.* Known also as *Dotzé* and as *Regiment de princeps e de comunitats* [1380's]. Valencia, 1484. *VI*, 10, 12-20.

Fori Judicum. Ed. Real Academia Española. Madrid, 1815. Ed. *Los Codigos Españoles,* vol. I: Madrid, 1847. *VI*, 30; *VII*, 1, 3, 7.

Fuente, Vicente de la. *Estudios críticos sobre la historia y el derecho de Aragón.* Madrid, 1884-1886. 3 vols. *I*, 19; *III*, 38; *IV*, 4, 8, 10, 20, 35, 40; *V*, 39, 88.

Fuero Juzgo. Ed. Real Academia Española. Madrid, 1815. Ed. *Los Codigos Españoles,* vol. I: Madrid, 1847. *VII*, 1, 3.

Garibay y Zamalloa, Esteban de. *Los XL. libros d'el Compendio historial de las chronicas y universal Historia de todos los reynos de España.* Antwerp, 1571. 4 vols. *V*, 60, 61; *VI*, 56; *Appendix II.*

Giesey, Ralph E. *The Juristic Basis of Dynastic Right to the French Throne* (= Transactions of the American Philosophical Society, LI:5). Philadelphia, 1961. *VI*, 49, 54; *VII*, 16.

―――. "Nuevos puntos de vista sobre el juramento: 'Nos que valemos tanto como vos,'" *BRAH,* CLX, 209-21. *I*, 23.

Giménez Soler, Andrés. *La edad media en la corona de Aragón.* Barcelona, 1930.

Giménez Soler, Andrés. "El Justicia de Aragón, Juan Giménez Cerdán," *RABM*, 3rd ser., ɪ (1897), 337-48. *IV*, 8.

Giménez Soler, Andrés. "El Justicia de Aragón, Martin Diez de Aux," *RABM*, 3rd ser., ɪɪɪ (1899), 385-91. *IV*, 18.

Giménez Soler, Andrés. "Las libertades aragonesas," *Boletín de la Real academia de buenas letras de Barcelona*, ɪ (1901), 25-38. *IV*, 4.

Giménez Soler, Andrés. "El poder judicial en la corona de Aragón," *Memorias de la Real academia de buenas letras de Barcelona*, ᴠɪɪɪ (1906), 33-112. *IV*, 2.

Gurrea y Aragón, Francisco de, Conde de Luna. *Comentarios de los sucesos de Aragón en los años 1591 y 1592*. Ed. by Marcelino de Aragón y Azlor Duque de Villahermosa. Madrid, 1888. *VII*, 9.

Haebler, Konrad. "Los fueros de Sobrarbe," *AHDE*, xɪɪɪ (1936/41), 5-35. *I*, 10, 22; *III*, 3, 10, 17, 18; *IV*, 6.

Hernandez. *See under* Blancas, *Comentarios*.

Hinojosa y Naveros, Eduardo de. *Influencia que tuvieron en el derecho público de su patria . . . los filósofos y teólogos españoles anteriores á nuestro siglo*. Madrid, 1890. *VI*, 11.

Hotman, François. *Francogallia*. Geneva, 1573. 2nd ed., Cologne, 1576. 3rd ed., Frankfort, 1586. *I*, 15; *II*, 1, 3, 6, 7, 10, 11; *V*, 94; *VI*, 3, 7, 9, 21, 29, 38, 97, 99, 101; *VII*, 6, 7, 9; *Appendix I*.

Ibarra y Rodríquez, Eduardo. "La reconquista de los Estados pirenaicos, hasta la muerte de don Sancho el Mayor (1035)," *Hispania*, ɪɪ (1942), 3-63. *III*, 1; *Appendix V*.

Ilarregui. *See under* Navarre, Kingdom.

Inventorio. *See* Madrid, Biblioteca Nacional.

Kern, Fritz. *Gottesgnadentum und Widerstandsrecht im früheren Mittelalter*. Leipzig, 1914. 2nd ed., by Rudolf Buchner, Münster, 1954. *I*, 21; *VI*, 10; *VII*, 1, 2.

Lacarra y de Miguel, José María. "Aragon en el Pasado," in vol. ɪ of *Aragón: Cuatro Ensayos*. Zaragoza; Banco de Aragon, 1960. *V*, 70, 71.

Lacarra y de Miguel, José María. "Notas para la formación

de las familias de Fueros Navarros," *AHDE*, x (1933), 203-72. *III*, 5, 6, 9, 11, 16, 17.

Lalinde Abadía, Jesús. *La gobernación general en la corona de Aragón.* Madrid, 1963. *VI*, 50.

Lasala, Manuel. *Exámen histórico-foral de la Constitución Aragonesa.* Madrid, 1868-1871. 3 vols. *I*, 10, 12, 22; *IV*, 6, 26, 35; *V*, 39, 93; *Appendix IV*, 9.

Latassa y Ortín, Félix de. *Bibliotecas antigua y nueva de escritores aragoneses, de Latassa.* 1st ed., 1796-1802; 2nd ed., [my Latassa²] by Miguel Gomez Uriel, Zaragoza, 1884-1886. 3 vols. *I*, 4; *IV*, 12, 14, 15, 20, 40; *V*, 27, 52; *VI*, 8; *VII*, 12.

Lea, Henry Charles. *A History of the Inquisition of Spain.* New York, 1906-1907. 4 vols. *I*, 21; *II*, 1; *IV*, 2; *VII*, 14.

Lévi-Provençal, E. "Du nouveau sur le royaume de Pamplune au IXᵉ siècle," *Bulletin Hispanique*, lv (1953), 5-22. *III*, 1.

López de Haro, Carlos. *La Constitución y libertades de Aragón y el justicia mayor.* Madrid, 1926. *I*, 10, 22; *II*, 16; *III*, 27, 46; *IV*, 2, 4; *V*, 17; *VII*, 1, 11.

López-Amo y Marín, Angel. "El pensamiento politico de Eximeniç en su tratado de 'Regiment de Princeps,'" *AHDE*, xvii (1946), 5-139. *VI*, 11, 12-17, 20.

Luna, Conde de. *See* Gurrea y Aragón.

Madrid, Biblioteca Nacional. *Inventorio general de manuscritos de la Biblioteca nacional.* Madrid, 1953ff. 8 vols. (through 1965). *III*, 18; *V*, 2.

Marañon, Gregorio. *Antonio Pérez.* Buenos Aires, 1947. English trans. by C. D. Ley: New York, 1955. *VII*, 10, 14, 15.

Marichalar. *See* Montesa.

Marineus, Lucius. *De rebus Hispaniae memorabilibus opus.* In Schott, *Hisp. Illus.*, i, 291-518. *II*, 10; *V*, 27, 28, 30, 33, 48; *VI*, 29, 38; *Appendix II*.

Marongiu, Antonio. "L'avvento al trono nella monarchia aragonese," *Clio*, xxix (1966), 181-200. *I*, 23.

Marongiu, Antonio. "Geronimo Zurita e 'Las Cortes' d'Aragona," *VII Congreso de historia de la Corona de Aragón.* Barcelona, 1962. ii, 83-97. *I*, 23.

Marongiu, Antonio. "Nos qui valemos tanto como vos . . . ," *Homenaje a Jaime Vicens Vives*. Barcelona, 1965. I, 543-50. *I*, 23.

Mayer, Ernst. *Historia de la instituciones sociales y políticas de España y Portugal durante los siglos V a XIV*. Madrid, 1925-1926. 2 vols. *VI*, 47.

——. "Studien zur spanischen Rechtsgeschichte, I. Der Fuero de Sobrarbe," *Zeitschrift der Savigny-Stiftung für Rechtsgeschichte*, germ. Abt., XL (1919), 236-72. *III*, 2, 18.

Mayerne, Louis Turquet de. *Histoire generale d'Espagne*. Paris, 1608. Trans. as *The generall historie of Spaine*; London, 1612. *II*, 17.

Meijers, Eduard M. "Los Fueros de Huesca y Sobrarbe," *AHDE*, XVIII (1947), 35-60. Repr. in Meijers' *Études d'histoire du droit, I: Histoire du droit español*. Leyden, 1956, pp. 267-86. *III*, 5.

Merriman, Roger B. *The Rise of the Spanish Empire in the Old World and the New*. New York, 1918-1934. 4 vols. *I*, 21; *IV*, 2, 3; *VI*, 65, 66.

Migne, J. P. *Patrologiae cursus completus . . . series latina*. Paris, 1844-1864. 221 vols. *VII*, 1, 2.

Molho, Mauricio (ed.). *El Fuero de Jaca*. Zaragoza, 1964. *III*, 11.

Molino, Miguel del. *Repertorium fororum et observantiarum regni Aragonum* [1513]. Zaragoza, 1533. *IV*, 44; *V*, 18-22, 24-26, 39, 59, 87, 89; *VI*, 33, 38, 79; *VII*, 11, 12; *Appendices II, III*.

Montesa, Amalio Marichalar, Marqués de, and Cayetano Manrique. *Historia de la legislación y recitaciones del derecho civil de España*. Madrid, 1861-1872. 9 vols. *I*, 13; *III*, 11, 27; *IV*, 32, 41; *V*, 88; *VI*, 101.

Moreri, Louis. *Le Grand dictionnaire historique*. Lyon, 1674. *II*, 17.

Morlanes, Diego de. *Alegaciones . . . en favor del Reyno de Aragón, en la cause de Virrey estrangero*. Zaragoza, 1591. *II*, 11, 13; *V*, 40, 94; *VII*, 9.

Mornay, Philippe de. *Vindiciae contra tyrannos*. Edimburg, 1579. *II*, 7; *VI*, 96, 101.

Muñoz y Romero, Tomás. *Coleccion de fueros municipales y cartas pueblas de . . . Castilla, Leon, corona de Aragón y Navarra.* Madrid, 1847. Vol I (only vol. published). *III,* 6, 7, 8; *VII,* 11.

Näf, Werner. "Die aragonischen Privilegien von 1283 und 1287," *Herrschaftsverträge des Spätmittelalters,* pp. 17-44 (= Quellen zur neueren Geschichte, 17). Bern, 1951. *IV,* 30, 31, 40.

(Navarre, Kingdom.) *Fuero General de Navarra.* Ed. by P. Ilarregui and S. Lapuerta. Pamplona, 1869. *III,* 17, 19-24, 31-33, 40; *IV,* 6; *VI,* 25, 27; *Appendices II, III.*

Nueva Compilación. See under Aragon, Kingdom.

Observantiae (regni Aragoniae). See Daux, Martin Didaci.

Oliver y Esteller, Bienvenido. *Análisis y crítica por historiadores y jurisconsultos nacionales y extranjeros de las obras de D. Bienvenido Oliver y Estellar.* Madrid, 1907. *I,* 20.

Oliver y Esteller, Bienvenido. *La Nación y la Realeza en los Estados de la Corona de Aragón.* Madrid, 1884. *I,* 20; *VI,* 17.

Pérez, Antonio. *Relaciones de Antonio Pérez* [1593]. Paris, 1598; Geneva, 1654. *I,* 2, 3; *II,* 12; *VI,* 5-7, 21, 100, 102; *VII,* 4, 12; *Appendix I.*

Pidal, Pedro Jose, Marqués de. *Historia de las Alteraciones de Aragon en el reinado de Felipe II.* Madrid, 1862-1863. 3 vols. French trans. by J. G. Magnabal: *Philippe II, Antonio Perez et le royaume d'Aragon.* Paris, 1867. 2 vols. *IV,* 1; *VII,* 9, 10, 11, 12, 14.

Pinatense. Historia de la Corona de Aragón (la más antigua de que se tiene noticia), conocida generalmente con el nombre de "Crónica de San Juan de la Peña. Zaragoza, 1876. *III,* 35, 38; *V,* 24, 27; *VII,* 17.

Portolés, Jerónimo. *Scholia, sive adnotationes ad repertorium M. Molini, super foris . . . regni Aragonum.* Zaragoza, 1588-1592. 4 pts. *II,* 11; *V,* 94; *VI,* 7.

Prescott, William H. *History of the Reign of Ferdinand and Isabella the Catholic* [1836]. 3rd ed., Chicago, 1841. *I,* 21; *VI,* 102.

Quinto, Xavier de. *Del juramento politico de los antiguos reyes de Aragon* (= Discursos politicos sobre la legislacion y la historia del antiguo reino de Aragon, 2). Madrid, 1848. *I*, 4-6; *II*, 1, 2, 11, 17, 18; *III*, 46; *V*, 12, 36, 54, 88, 94; *VI*, 9, 21, 27, 29-37, 52, 59, 61, 64, 80, 85, 87, 101; *VII*, 1, 7.

Ramos y Loscertales, José María. "Los fueros de Sobrarbe," *CHE*, vii (1947), 35-66. *III*, 4, 8, 11, 16, 17.

Ramos y Loscertales, José María. *El Reino de Aragón bajo la dinastía pamplonesa* (= Acta Salmanticensia, xv:2). Salamanca, 1961. *III*, 1.

Ramos y Loscertales, José María. *Fuero de Jaca*. Barcelona, 1927. *III*, 4.

Robertson, William. *The History of the Reign of the Emperor Charles V*. London, 1769. *II*, 17.

Romero Ortiz, Antonio and Victor Balaguer. *Las cosas de Aragón. Discursos leidos en la real academia de la historia . . . el dia 30 de Enero de 1881*. Zaragoza, 1881. Ortiz' *Discurso de ingreso*, pp. 5-34; Balaguer's *Contestación*, pp. 35-57. *I*, 17; *VII*, 4.

Rubió y Lluch, Antoni. *Documents per l'historia de la cultura catalana mig-eval*. Barcelona, 1908-1921. 2 vols. *IV*, 44.

Sagarra, Martin. *See* Index.

Sánchez, Juan Manuel. *Bibliografía aragonesa del siglo XVI*. Madrid, 1913-1914. 2 vols. *IV*, 12; *V*, 18, 28, 52, 64; *VII*, 9.

Sánchez-Albornoz, Claudio. "La *Ordinatio Principis* en la España goda y postvisigoda," *CHE*, xxxv-xxxvi, 5-36. *VI*, 25, 47.

Sánchez-Albornoz, Claudio. "Problemas de la historia navarra del siglo IX," *CHE*, xxv-xxvi (1957), 5-82. *III*, 1; *Appendix V*.

Sánchez Alonso, Benito. *Historia de la historiografía española*. Madrid, 1941-1950. 3 vols. *III*, 35; *V*, 3, 4, 27, 28, 29, 51, 60.

Sánchez Alonso, Benito. *Fuentes de la historia española*. 3rd ed., Madrid, 1952. *V*, 2, 3, 4, 27, 42.

Schott[us], Andreas. *Hispaniae illustratae*. Frankfort, 1603-1608. 4 vols. *See under* individual authors.

Schramm, Percy Ernst. "Der König von Aragon. Seine Stellung im Staatsrecht (1276-1410)," *Historisches Jahrbuch*, LXXIV (1955), 99-123. *VI*, 48, 49.

————. "Die Krönung im katalanisch-aragonesischen Königreich," *Homenatge a D. Antoni Rubió y Lluch*, III, 577-98. (= Estudis Universitaris Catalans, XXII). Barcelona, 1937. *VI*, 8, 9, 27, 56, 57; *VII*, 6.

————. "Der König von Navarra (1035-1512)," *Zeitschrift der Savigny–Stiftung für Rechtsgeschichte*, germ. Abt., LXVIII (1951), 110-210. *III*, 17; *VI*, 27; *VII*, 6.

Serrano y Sanz, Manuel. *Noticias y documentos históricos del contado de Ribagorza hasta la muerte de Sancho Garcés III (año 1035)*. Madrid, 1912. *III*, 1, 38, 39. (*See also Villarense.*)

Shneidman, J. Lee. "Political Theory and Reality in Thirteenth Century Aragon," *Hispania*, XXII (1962), 171-85. *VI*, 31.

Sobieski, Wacław. "Si non jurabis, non regnabis: Spór o przysięgę królewską," *Reformacja w Polsce*, II (1922), 54-70; *VII*, 8.

Soranzo, Giovanni. *Relazione di Spagna di Giovanni Soranzo, 1565*. Ed. by Eugenio Albèri in *Relazioni degli ambasciatori veneti al Senato*. Ser. I, vol. V: Florence, 1861. *II*, 1; *V*, 1; *VI*, 1, 45, 88, 89; *VII*, 14; *Appendix I.*

Tomic Cauller, Pedro. *Historias e conquestas dels . . . reys de Arago* [written in 1438; publ. in 1495]. Barcelona, 1886. *V*, 3, 5, 6, 37.

Tudela, Fuero of. *See* Index.

Ureña y Smenjaud, Rafael de. "Las ediciones de los Fueros y Observancias del Reino de Aragón anteriores á la compilación ordenada por las Cortes de Monzón de 1547 é impresa en 1552," *RABM*, 3rd ser., IV (1900), 201-36. *IV*, 8, 18.

Uriel, Miguel Gomez. *See* Latassa y Ortín.

Uztarroz. *See under* Blancas, *Coronaciones* and *Cortes.*

Vagad, Gauberte Fabricio de. *Corónica de Aragón*. Zaragoza, 1499. *V*, 4, 9-13, 15-17, 24, 32, 37, 44, 82; *VI*, 34, 39; *Appendix II.*

Vasaeus, Joannes. *Rerum Hispanicarum Chronicon.* In Schott, *Hisp. illus.*, ɪ, 572-727. *II*, 10; *V*, 27, 29, 31, 34; *VI*, 38; *Appendix II.*

Vicens Vives, Jaime. *Juan II de Aragón, 1398-1469.* Barcelona, 1953. *VI*, 22, 23, 59.

Villarense. Ed. by Manuel Serrano y Sanz, "Cronicón villarense (Liber Regum)," *BRAE*, ᴠɪ (1919), 192-220 [text and commentary]; ᴠɪɪɪ (1921), 367-82 [more commentary]. *III*, 26, 27.

Vindiciae contra tyrannos. See under Mornay.

Wolzendorff, Kurt. *Staatsrecht und Naturrecht in der Lehre vom Widerstandsrecht des Volkes gegen rechtswidrige Ausübung der Staatsgewalt* (= Untersuchungen zur deutschen Staats- und Rechtsgeschichte, 126). Breslau, 1916. *I*, 21; *VI*, 10.

Ximénez de Embún y Val, Tomás. *Ensayo histórico acerca de los orígenes de Aragón y Navarra.* Zaragoza, 1878. *I*, 14-16; *III*, 1, 19, 20, 38; *IV*, 13, 14, 26, 44; *V*, 27, 42, 93; *VII*, 9; *Appendix IV*, 5, 9.

Ximenez de Rada, Rodrigo (Archbishop of Toledo, d. 1247). *Historia Gothica o Rerum in Hispania Gestarum Chronicon.* In Schott, *Hisp. illus.*, ɪɪ, 121-246. *III*, 35, 39; *VI*, 19.

Yanguas y Miranda, José María. *Diccionario de antiguidades del reino de Navarra.* Pamplona, 1840ff. 4 vols.

Zurita, Gerónimo. *Anales de la corona de Aragon.* Zaragoza, 1562-1580. 6 vols. [Up to 1516; for continuations, *see Anales de Aragon.*] *IV*, 36, 39; *V*, 50, 52-56, 59; *VI*, 31, 34, 38, 44, 61; *Appendix II.*

Zurita, Gerónimo. *Indices rerum ab Aragoniae Regibus gestarum ab initiis regni ad annum MCDX.* Zaragoza, 1578. *II*, 10; *IV*, 36; *V*, 52, 57-59; *VI*, 29, 38.

Index

Italicized page numbers indicate entries in the bibliography, where additional references to footnotes will usually be found.

Academy of History (Madrid), 6, 7, 9, 13, 95

Aclot, 117n

Ainsa, 40, 46, 50n, 55, 121

Albear, Sancho, 116n

Alfonso I (el Batallador), 35, 37, 234n, 256

Alfonso III, 66, 86, 87, 90, 99, 106, 109, 178, 194n, 202n, 256

Alfonso V, 77n, 78, 192n, 256

Alla van leyes o quieren [mandan] reyes, see Maxims

Alonso de Venero, 116n

alzar el rey, 44, 174-75, 177, 251

Andreas of Isernia, 82n

Andrés de Bobadilla (Archbishop of Zaragoza), 139

Antich de Bages, Johan, 64, 65, 89n, 101, 105 (work on Aragonese genealogy), 108n, 110, 111, 114, 115, 248, 252-54 (*Glossa* on Daux); version of Sagarra Story, 76-87, 97ff, 254ff; source for Blancas, 142-43, 149ff, 151n

Antich de Bages, Johan (son of previous), 77

Apostóligo Aldebano, see Popes

Arabs, *see under* Moors

Aragon:
    founding and early history, 12n, 14, 32ff, 52, 60, 71, 104, 110n, 144, 164, 226 (cf. Sobrarbe, Navarre, Iñigo Arista, Garci Ximenez); County of Aragon, 119, 148, 255; Crown of Aragon, 164, 165, 171, 195n, 197-98, 201, 209-10, 213 (*see also* Barcelona, Catalonia, Valencia); Council of Aragon, 139, 140, 160; Deputies of Aragon, 139n, 192, 195, 210, 213; revolt of 1458-1461, 172, 196n; revolt of 1591-1592, 17, 68, 232-37 (*see also* Cortes, Historiography)

Fueros of Aragon (before 1551): 69n (Vidal Mayor's redaction), 81-82 (Fuero of Exea), 92n (Book X and the Liberties of Aragon, *q.v.*), 110n (identical pagination of eds.), 113n (power of Justice), 120-21 (history, 13th-16th centuries), 123, 125 (Compilation of Huesca), 198, 248, 254n; confusion with Sobrarbe laws, 33, 123f, 125, 129-30; Cerdan's *Letra* (*q.v.*), 71, 111; Book X, Fuero 1, *see below, De prohibita unione; re* royal inaugurations, 203, 205, 209. *257*

    Individual laws: *Coram quibus* (1461), 192-200 *passim,* 213; *Cum secundum forum* (1364), 190n; *De his quae dominus rex* (1348), 187-91, 194-95, 213; *De iure coronationis* (1461), 195n; *De prohibita unione* (1348), 8, 83-87, 90ff, 96-99, 115, 157, 183-84, 187, 188, 218, 254n; *Quod primogenitus* (1366), 188, 190-93

    Nueva Compilación (1551), 79n, 110n, 248; Commission for, 110n, 120-21, 126n, 214; renewal of *De prohibita unione,* 94n, 183, 184; Prologue (citing Fueros of Sobrarbe), 119, 120-25, 130, 146, 153, 238-39; "laws before kings," 69n, 122ff, 153. *257*

    Liberties of Aragon, 57, 68n, 100n, 183, 236; in 19th-century debate, 6, 9, 11, 13-14, 15n; in Fueros of Aragon, 66, 92n, 132n; in Sagarra Story, 83, 86, 87n, 97, 99; in Molino, 111ff; in Blancas, 147n, 151; in Charles I's oath, 203, 209

Arista dynasty, 33, 255; *see also* Iñigo Arista

Aristotle, 108n

Artasona, Pedro Martinez, 75n

Asturias, 48n, 49, 56; *see also* Don Pelayo, León

Augustin, Antonio, 68n, 139

St. Augustine, 227n

Aznar, Count of Aragon, 127, 255

Bages, *see* Antich de Bages

Balaguer, Victor, 3, 5, 6, 8n, 12, 13. 258, 265

Baldus de Ubaldis, 188n

Barbastro, Fuero of, 37n

Barcelona, 165, 168n, 171; *see also* Catalonia

Basques, 33

Bernat Boades, 103n

Bertran de Born, 100n

Beuter, Pedro Antonio, 119, 125-30, 136, 148, 150, 194n, 248. 258

Beuther, Michael, 194n

Beza, Theodore, 20-24, 26, 158-62, 181, 218, 220, 221, 225, 230, 231, 247. 258

Biondo, Flavio, 117

Blancas, Gerónimo, 54n, 126n, 135, 138n (*Effigies et Inscriptiones*), 175n, 199 (royal jurisdictional oath), 236 (Pérez affair), 245; on fictitious Oath, 9, 26-27, 140, 154-57, 158-63 *passim*, 171n, 181-82, 220, 222, 225, 242, 244, 247; on Fueros of Sobrarbe, 10-11, 12, 15, 31, 57ff (comparison with Charles of Viana), 60-63 (False Fueros I-IV), 64, 68-69 (False Fuero V), 102, 104n, 116, 125, 136-57 *passim*, 174-77 *passim*, 218, 238, 242, 248, 249ff; on Privileges of Union, 11, 93-97, 140, 143-44, 147, 152, 184n, 224-25; his *Commentarii* (esp. *re* Justice of Aragon), 18, 127n, 136-57, 232; on Sagarra Story, 75-76, 142-43, 149-50, 254n; as royal historiographer, 131, 138n, 139, 236. 258

Bodin, Jean, 20, 23, 181, 218, 220, 221, 230-32, 247. 259

Bracton, Henry of, 150

Briz Martínez, Juan, 116n, 125. 259

Caesar, 149n

Calatayud, 205n, 212n; *see also under* Cortes

Cáncer, Martin Cleriguech de, 103n

Canon Law, 188n

Cánovas del Castillo, Antonio, 8, 107n. 259

Carbonell, Pedro Miguel, 116n

Castile, 49, 68 (Castilianization of Aragon), 89n (*Fuero Viejo*), 164, 199-208 *passim* (Charles I's accession), 234; *see also* Asturias, León, Don Pelayo

Catalanes, 117n

Catalonia, Catalans, 164, 171ff (revolt in 1461), 196-97 (*idem*), 200; *see also* Barcelona

Cerdan, Juan Jiminez, 64, 96n, 101; *Letra intimada* on Justice's origins, 49n, 70-75, 84, 107, 111, 124, 132, 134, 135, 142, 143, 146, 151, 178n, 179n, 243, 248. 259

Cervera, 35

Champagne, Counts of, 42n

Chancellor of Aragon, 190

Charles I of Spain, 200; accession in Aragon in 1518, 199, 200-13, 214, 217, 219, 223, 229, 231, 256

Charles of Viana, 110n, 116n, 125n, 123-25 (source for *Nueva Compilación*), 126-30 (comparison with Beuter); claim to Aragonese crown, 172, 196; *Crónica* on founding of Navarre-Aragon and False Fueros I-IV, 52-57, 105, 114, 117, 119, 133, 248, 249ff; source for Blancas, 57-63, 102, 142, 146, 148, 249ff. 259

Chauvin, Nicholas, 246

Cicero, 108n, 149n

Clovis, 243

Compact theory of government, 51, 57, 74, 167, 222; *see also* "laws before kings"

Coronations, 51 (*FN* ɪ, 1, 1 as *ordo*), 191-95 (royal jurisdictional oath); actual Aragonese practice, 163n, 185, 191-95, esp. 194n; supposed Aragonese practice, 159-62, 219-24; *see also alzar el rey*

Coronista de los Reyes Catolicos, 117n

Cortes:

Aragonese generally, 19, 29, 94n (mentioned in Privileges of Union, *q.v.*), 108n, 120, 162n (bibliography), 168, 222, 239; Spanish Constituent C. in 1868-1869, 3-12 *passim*, 232; Castilian, 19, 201, 207, 214; Valencian, 165; Catalonian, 171, 200n

oaths in Aragonese C.: actual oaths, 194-98, 212; fictitious Oath, 159-61, 185, 220

particular Aragonese C.: Huesca in 1247, 123, 125; Exea in 1265, 66; Zaragoza in 1283, 66; Aragon in 1286, 194n; Zaragoza in 1300, 235n; Zaragoza in 1348, 67, 90, 96n, 132n, 187, 209, 214n; Zaragoza in 1364, 191n; Calatayud in 1366, 188, 191n, 214n; Calatayud in 1461, 192, 195n, 196-98, 199, 209, 214n; Aragon in 1481, 199; Zaragoza in 1498, 199; Zaragoza in 1502, 200; Zaragoza in 1518, 201-08 *passim*; Aragon in 1533, 120; Monzon in 1542, 120, 213; Monzon in 1563-1564, 19, 159, 215, 217, 234n, 237n; Monzon in 1584, 234n; Tarazona in 1592, 232n

Cynus of Pistoia, 82n

Danvila y Collado, Manuel, 13. 259

Dauphin of France, 190n

Daux, Martin Didaci, 70-71, 191n; his *Observantiae* and the Fueros of Aragon, 120, 143; *Observantiae* and Antich's *Glossa*, 77-86, 97, 252-54. 259

Diego de Monreal, Canon of Zaragoza, 139n

DuMoulin, Charles, 189n

dynastic right, *see under* succession

England, 154, 164, 188n, 193, 194n

Ephors of Sparta, 72, 74, 107-08, 134-35, 234

Epila, battle of, 90

Exea, Fuero of, 81-82

Eximeniç, Francesch, 164n, 165-71, 173, 241. 260

Ferdinand I, 195n, 256

Ferdinand II (the Catholic), 120, 172, 189n, 196, 197n, 198-201 *passim*, 203, 256

Fernando de Aragon, Archbishop of Zaragoza, 116n

fianza de derecho, 67n, 88n, 89n

firmas de derecho, 67, 69, 83, 98, 151, 237n

Fori Judicum (Fuero Juzgo), 177, 179, 227, 228n, 229n, 230n, 231. 260

Fortun Ahe, 75n

Franks, France, 46, 73, 123, 128, 136, 155, 164, 167n, 188n, 193, 194n

Fuente, Vincente de la, 13. 260

Fueros, early Spanish, 35, 41ff, 46; *see also under* Aragon, Barbastro, Navarre, Sobrarbe, Tudela

Galacin de Tarba, 96n

Gallipienzo, 36

Garci Ximenez, 56, 57, 58, 105, 106ff, 109n, 110n, 112ff, 116n, 119, 123n, 126ff, 132, 136, 142, 148, 182n, 255

Garibay y Zamalloa, Esteban de, 135f, 145, 194n, 248. 260

Gauls, 155; *see also* Franks

General Privilege (1283), 87n, 92n, 235n, 252n

Geneva Town Council, 21-22

Germans, 154, 164

Gerona, Duke of (title), 190n

Gondiçalvus, 169, 170n

Gonzalo de Illescas, 116n

Gonzalvo de Hinojosa, 169, 170n

Goths, 14n ("Gothic liberties"); *see also* Visigoths

Governor General of Aragon, 190, 191, 200, 204, 213, 214
Gregory VII, see Popes
Guerau Alemany de Cervelló, 172, 173n
Guillen del Sesmero, 138

Habsburgs, 120, 198, 210, 239, 256
Hadrian I, see Popes
Henry of Valois (later Henry III of France), 231n
Hilpranco, see Popes
Historiography: in the Renaissance, 17, 44, 56 (a Renaissance forgery), 57, 104 (Tomic & Vagad), 105, 117 (Marineus & Vasaeus), 119, 165 (Valencia), 173, 238-46 (esp. 243-45, comparing France & Aragon); concerning Fueros of Sobrarbe (q.v.), 31 34, 181, 226, 238; royal historiographer in Aragon, 104n, 131, 138n (see Blancas, Zurita); concerning fictitious Oath, 171, 216, 229
Horace, 227n
Hotman, François, 7-8, 12n, 18, 20-28 passim, 154, 158, 160, 162, 163n, 171n, 175-81 passim, 189n, 194n, 218, 221ff, 225, 230-31, 238, 240, 244-45, 247. 261

Iñigo Arista: in actuality, 33, 255; in Sobrarbe legend, 49n, 55ff (Charles of Viana), 57 & 69 & 142-57 passim, & 163 (Blancas), 75 & 82ff (Antich de Bages), 105-08 & 182n (Vagad), 108n (as Count of Bigorra), 112ff (Molino), 116n, 118f (Marineus & Vasaeus), 123n (Nueva Compilación), 126 & 129 (Beuter), 132ff (Zurita), 135-36 (Garibay), 180 (Quinto)
Inquisition, 19, 215, 236, 237n
Inquisition of the Office of Justice of Aragon, 68n
Isabella of Castile, 198; see also Ferdinand II
Isabella of Portugal, 199
Isabella II of Spain, 3

Isidore of Seville, 227, 229n, 231, 241

James I, 66, 75n, 106n, 120, 121, 123, 178n, 202, 256
James II, 90, 235n, 256
Jean d'Albret, K. of Navarre, 175
Jimena dynasty, 33, 255; see also Garci Ximenez
Joanna, Queen of Spain, 198, 200, 201, 202, 204, 206-07, 210n, 230, 256
John I, 189, 190n, 256
John II, 120, 172, 192, 196, 199, 256
John, son of Ferdinand and Isabella, 199
Juan de Lanuza IV, 138n, 139
jurisdictional oath, see under oaths
Jurors of Zaragoza, 192, 195, 210, 213
Justice of Aragon: 91, 204;
    actual history, 24, 64, 65-69, 96n, 97, 138, 131-52 (Blancas' Commentarii), 200-05 passim (regental powers, 1516-1518), 232-37 (Pérez affair, 1590-1592) (see also Cerdan, Daux, Juan Lanuza IV, manifestación, firmas de derecho)
    legendary history, 71-74 (in Cerdan), 82-84 (in Antich), 97-101 (in Sagarra), 107-08 (in Vagad), 111-15 (in Molino), 118-19 (in Marineus and Vasaeus), 129-30 (in Beuter), 132-35 (in Zurita), 136-52 (in Blancas), 156 (idem), 177n, 178n, 225 (in Pérez), 238-39, 242, 243, 244, 252-54 (in Antich's Glossa) (see also Sobrarbe [False Fuero V] Sagarra Story)
    jurisdictional oath ceremonial rôle, 185, 187, 191-98 (before Charles I), 203, 208-12 (Charles I in 1518), 215 (Philip II in 1562), 219 (Charles I), 223 (idem)
    fictitious oath ceremonial rôle, 22, 25 218ff, 219-20 (Soranzo), 220-21 (Beza, Hot-

man, and Bodin), 222ff (Pérez)
    powers in Privileges of Un-
    ion, 88-89, 94n, 239
    powers in fictitious oath, 27,
    169, 174, 177n, 179, 182, 218ff
Justice of the Mountains, 65n
Justiciar of England, 66n

king beneath the law, *see* Maxims,
    rex Sub lege

Languet, Hubert, 22n
Lasala, Manuel, 8-11 *passim. 262*
"laws before kings," 49 (Fuero of
    Tudela), 58, 69 & 124 (Navarre-
    Viana tradition), 74 & 124 (Cer-
    dan), 122ff (*Nueva Compila-
    ción, q.v.*), 153 (Blancas)
León, 49, 169; *see also* Don
    Pelayo, Asturias, Alfonso IX
lex regia, 124n
Liber Regum, see *Villarense*
Liberties of Aragon, *see under*
    Aragon
Lieutenant General of Aragon,
    192
Lieutenant Justice, 76, 80, 98n,
    190
Lombards, 46, 48, 59, 73, 123,
    128, 136

Majorca, 164
Manifestación, 5, 67, 69, 83, 98,
    140, 151, 233-36; prison of,
    67n, 233-36
Manuscripts: Academia de la
    Historia [Madrid] MS 107
    (Fuero of Tudela), 39n, 40n,
    41n, 45n, 48n, 50n; *idem* MS
    139 (Privileges of Union), 9n,
    13n, 92-95, 96n; Archivio Gen-
    eral de Navarra [Pamplona]
    MS of Tudela charter of 1117,
    36n; Archivo de la Corona de
    Aragón [Barcelona] MS 75
    (Privileges of Union) 95n; Bib-
    lioteca del Escorial MS Lat. P.
    II. 3 (Fueros of Aragon), 87n,
    162n; Biblioteca Nacional [Ma-
    drid] MSS on Fueros of So-
    brarbe, 42n; *idem* MS 747
    (Antich's *Glossa*), 79n, 252ff;
    idem MS 901 (see Cáncer);

idem MS 6742 (Martinez'
    Anales), 126n; *idem* MS 7391
    (Vidal Mayor), 69n; *idem* MS
    7588 (Dormer), 215n, 216n;
    Biblioteca Universitaria de Za-
    ragoza MS 95, 78n, 79n, 252ff;
    Danish Royal Library [Copen-
    hagen] MS Thott 328² (Fuero
    of Tudela), 39n, 40n, 41n,
    45n, 48n, 50n; Facultad de
    Derecho de Madrid MS of
    Fuero of Tudela, 39n, 40n,
    41n, 45n, 48n, 50n
Maria of Castile, 78
Mariana, Juan de, 68n
Marineus, Lucius, 117ff, 129, 135,
    248. *262*
Martin I, 190n, 256
Martinez, Pedro Luis, 126n
Maxims:
    *Alla van leyes o quieren [man-
        dan] reyes,* 124n, 169, 170
    *Primero huvo Leyes que Reyes
        (en Aragon),* 122ff (*see*
        "laws before kings")
    Reges a recte agendo, 227n,
        228n
    Rex eris si recte facies, 227n,
        228n
    Rex sub lege, 70, 90, 221n
Mayerne, Louis Turquet de, 28n
Miguel, son of Isabella of Portu-
    gal, 200n
Molino, Miguel del, 117, 121n,
    135n, 178n, 180n; version of
    Sagarra Story, 76, 108n, 110-
    16, 248ff (text of); source for
    others, 118 (Marineus and
    Vasaeus), 133 (Zurita), 142-
    43 & 149ff (Blancas), 209
    (Charles I's jurisdictional oath).
    263
Monsoriu, Bernardo de, 76n, 110n
Moors, Moorish (Arabic) con-
    quest, 38, 40, 44, 46-47, 56,
    58, 65n, 121, 151; *see also*
    Sobrarbe legend and Prologues
    to Fueros of Tudela, Navarre,
    and Aragon (*Nueva Compila-
    ción*)
Morales, Ambrosio de, 116n
Moreri, Louis, 28. *263*
Morlanes, Diego de: cites Hot-

man's version of oath, 25n, 26n, 156n, 232n; author of work on oaths, 162n. *263*

Mornay, Phillipe de, *see Vindiciae contra tyrannos*

Navarre, 42, 43, 45-46, 89n (Privilege of 1270), 165, 174 (*alzar el rey, q.v.*), 175-76 (coronation Jean d'Albret); early history, 12n, 32ff (and Sobrarbe, *q.v.*), 52, 56n, 60, 103, 110n, 118, 136, 164; *see also* Pamplona
Fuero General de Navarra, 34, 41-45, 57, 122-23, 124, 125, 146, 148, 176, 229n, 248; its epigraph, 31, 44ff, 49, 55, 123, 133; its prologue, 31, 46-49, 51, 69, 73, 74, 100, 105, 117, 123, 126, 133, 177; *FN* I, 1, 1, 31, 44, 49-57, 60-63, 119, 129, 130, 145, 174, 175n, 177, 249-51 (text of). *264*
Netherlands, 200, 201, 208

Oaths:
in general and outside Aragon, 163n (mediaeval Spain), 167 (Valencia), 175-76 (Navarre), 188n (France, England, Canon Law); dynastic oath in Cortes of Aragon, 188-91, 195, 196, 197-200, 213; royal jurisdictional oath in *La Seo*, 29, 30, 164, 186-216 *in extenso*, 217ff, 239
Oath of the Aragonese: Beza's version, 20-23, 26, 159, 160, 162, 218, 220-21, 225, 247n; Blancas' version, 247 (text of), 9, 11, 26ff, 137n, 140, 148, 154-57, 158, 162-63, 171n, 181-82, 218-19, 220, 222, 242; Bodin's version, 23-24, 218, 220-21, 247n; Hotman's version, 247 (text of), 7, 20-27, 158-59, 160, 162, 171n, 175, 177, 178, 218, 220-21, 222, 225, 230n, 244; Pérez's version, 247 (text of), 6, 7, 24ff, 27, 161-62, 171n, 175, 218, 220, 222-26, 230-31; So-

ranzo's version, 247 (text of), 19-20, 26, 27, 159, 160, 162, 186-87, 217, 218, 219-20, 225, 230-31, 239-40; other versions, 21n, 23 (*Vindiciae contra tyrannos*), 24n, 27-28, 162 (Portolés), 232n (Morlanes), 247n; Quinto's views, 7ff, 12, 18, 95, 176-81, 230n, 237-38, 240-41; others' views, 4ff (Balaguer), 8 (Cánovas), 8-11 *passim* (Lasala), 12-13 (Balaguer), 13-14 (Oliver y Esteller), 71n, 148 (language of), 164, 169 (cf. with Eximeniç), 170n, 171n (language of), 173, (cf. with Catalan "oath"), 224n, 237 (in revolt of 1591-1592), 237-46 (summary); relation to Privileges of Union, 9-17 *passim*, 30, 178, 183-86, 225, 229, 238-39; relation to Fueros of Sobrarbe, 10-17 *passim*, 30, 64, 70, 102, 155-56, 158, 163, 174, 179ff, 181ff, 218-19, 225, 229, 232, 234n, 238ff, 242-43, 246; relation to royal jurisdictional oath, 209, 212, 216-19, 223-24, 229, 239-40; ritual circumstances generally, 22n, 23n, 25, 28, 159-63; as a Cortes ceremony, 29, 158-63, 185, 220-21, 222, 246; as a royal inaugural ceremony, 28-29, 158-63, 170-71, 174ff (Navarre), 177, 185, 212, 219, 222ff; "If Not, Not" as a separate idea, 4-5 (Constituent Assembly, 1869), 25, 179, 225-26, 227-32, 231n, (Polish analogy), 241

Oliver y Esteller, Bienvenido, 14. *264*
Olózaga, Salustiano, 4-5
Ortiz, Antonio Romero, 13

Pamplona: kingdom of, 32n, 33, 83, 128, 133, 134, 151, 255; city of, 51n
Parlement of France, 67, 194
Pelayo, Don, 47, 48-49, 50n, 52, 55-56, 59, 73, 122, 123, 126ff, 148
Pérez, Antonio: version of the

Oath, 247 (text of), 5*n*, 7, 18, 24-27, 157, 158, 161-62, 171*n*, 175, 179, 218, 220, 222-26, 229*n*, 230-31; "Pérez affair" of 1590's, 7, 232-37 *in extenso*. *264*

Peter I, 37*n*, 194*n*, 224*n*, 256

Peter III, 66, 256

Peter IV: authorship of *Pinatense*, 53*n*; crushes baronial Union, 83, 87, 88*n*; issues *De prohibita unione* (*q.v.*), 85, 88*n*, 90ff, 96, 98, 100, 115, 135*n*, 157, 183, 185*n*, 187, 254*n*; other legislation, 67, 135*n*, 187-91 (*De his quae dominus rex* and *Quod primogenitus, qq.v.*, under Aragon), 224*n*; 256

Peter Martyr of Anghiera, 202, 203, 208*n*

Petronilla, 199, 256

Pharamond, 243

Philip II of Spain, 25, 43*n*, 121, 213-14 (primogenitary oath), 232*n* (oath at Cortes of 1592), 233-37 ("Pérez affair"); relations to Aragon, 68, 240; alters Blancas' work, 139-40, 157; royal jurisdictional oath, 19, 215-18

Philip, Duke of Burgundy, 200

Pillars, 32

Pinatense (Chronicle of San Juan de la Peña), 53, 56, 104-05, 113, 132. *264*

Pliny: 224*n*

Polish coronation of 1574, 231*n*

Pope (in prologues to Fueros of Tudela, Navarre, and Aragon), 59, 73, 123, 136, 153; *Apostóligo Aldebano*, 46, 48, 52; Hadrian I, 54*n*; Hadrian II, 54*n*, 128; Hildebrand (Gregory VII), 48

Portolés, Jerónimo, 25*n*, 156*n*, 162*n*. *264*

Prescott, William H., 145*n*. *264*

primogenit, 189-99 *passim*, 208 (Charles V), 213ff (Philip II), 240; *see also* Prince and heir

Prince and heir: in Soranzo's Oath, 186, 239-40; Charles V called, 202-03, 217; Philip II

as, 217-18; *see also* primogenit

Privilege, General (1283), *see under* General Privilege

Privileges of Union, 109, 115, 133, 157, 180*n*, 218, 240, 248, 254*n*; in 19th-century debates, 8-16 *passim*, 94-95, 184; manuscripts of, 9, 92-97 *passim*, 137*n*, 239; related to Fuero of Sobrarbe, 10-11, 99, 100, 112, 133 (Zurita), 143-44 (Blancas), 152 (*idem*), 238-39; related to Oath of the Aragonese, 10-11, 12, 14, 30, 183, 222-25 (Pérez), 229; issuance in 1287, 66-67, 85-86, 87-90 (text on 88, 89), 99, 147 (Blancas); abolition, *see* Aragon (Fueros), *De prohibita unione*; *see also* Union

Procurator General, 189

Quinto, Xavier de: place in 19th-century debate, 7ff, 12, 95, 107*n*; works other than *Juramento*, 7*n*, 189*n*; attack on Hotman, 7-8, 18, 20, 176-81 *passim*, 240; attack on others who record the Oath, 20, 22, 25; explanation of the Oath, 176-81 *in extenso*, 182, 237-38. *265*

Ramiro I, 106, 107, 119, 194*n*, 256

Regency in Aragon, 1516-1518, 201, 203, 208*n*, 209*n*, 210

Reges a recte agendo, see Maxims

resistance right, 151, 167, 168, 180*n*, 222, 237; *see also* Sobrarbe, False Fuero VI

Rex eris si recte facies, see Maxims

Ribagorza, 32, 83, 88, 105, 109*n*, 128, 234*n*

ricoshombres, 54, 62, 63, 143, 147, 178; *see also* Sobrarbe, False Fueros II and IV

Risco, Juan Luis Lopez de Tarba, Marqués de, 94, 95*n*

Robertson, William, 28. *265*

Roig y Jalpi, 104*n*

Roman Law, 120 (model for *Nueva Compilación*), 121, 124

(*Lex regia*), 150 (*Dig.* 1,1,10), 193

Sagarra, Bartomeu, 98*n*
Sagarra, Berengarius, 98*n*
Sagarra, Martin: the man, 64, 74, 75-76, 80, 97ff, 101, 248; "Sagarra Story," 31, 64, 65, 70, 75-87 *passim* (Antich's version—text in Appendix IV), 100, 102, 104, 108*n*, 111-15 (Molino's version—text in Appendix III), 119, 124*n*, 133ff (Zurita), 142-57 *passim* (Blancas), 177*n* & 180*n* (Hotman), 179*n*, 182, 184, 248, 249ff (Molino's text), 252ff (Antich's text); *see also* Sobrarbe, False Fueros V-VI
Salanova, 75*n*, 76*n*, 254*n*
Salic law, 243
Sallust, 149*n*
San Juan de la Peña, 243; *see also Pinatense*
Sanchez Abarca, 147, 148*n*, 255
Sancho Mayor, 32, 255
Santisteban, José Morales, 189*n*
Scripture, 71 (I Samuel 8)
Senatus consultum ultimum, 149-50
Sicily, 164
Sobrarbe:
   actual history, 32-33; True Fueros of Sobrarbe, 15, 31, 33-41
   legendary Sobrarbe, 12, 14, 33 (same as Kingdom of Pamplona), 34, 63, 69*n*, 70, 102 103*n*, 116, 131, 158 (and Oath), 168*n*, 174-75 (dissociated from *alzar el rey*), 216*n* (in 17th century), 218 (in 1550's), 228*n* (and Councils of Toledo), 232*n* (and revolt of 1591-1592), 238-46 (summary), 244 (parallel with *Francogallia*), 255 ("Sobrarbe" dynasties); cross-above-tree etymology, 118, 127 (esp. n. 44), 128; in Bernat Boades, 104*n*; in Beuter, 126-30; in Blancas, 60, 110*n*, 136, 141-57 *passim*, 174, 181f, 238, 242; in Cerdan,

71-73; in Charles of Viana, 53-57, 123-24, 128-29; in Fueros of Aragon, 119, 121-25, 238-39; in Fuero of Navarre, 41-52, 124; in Fuero of Tudela, 39-41, 44; in Garibay, 135-36; in Marineus, 118-19; in Pérez, 225-26; in Quinto, 176-81; in Tomic, 104-05; in Vagad, 104, 105-10; in Vasaeus, 118-19; in Zurita, 135-36
   False Fueros of Sobrarbe (text, 249-51): in Blancas, 57-59, 102, 136-37, 142-49, 153; in others and in general, 10ff, 15-16, 30, 31, 32, 34, 41ff, 44-48 (Fuero of Navarre introduction), 49-52 (Fuero of Navarre i,1,1), 52-57 (Charles of Viana), 61-62 (Twelve Tables style), 71, 73*n*, 85, 104*n*, 107 (Vagad), 116, 119-25 (*Nueva Compilación*), 128-30 (Beuter), 131, 132-35 (Zurita), 135-36 (Garibay), 157, 158, 163, 165, 174 (and Oath), 175*n* (*alzar el rey*), 176-81 (Quinto), 216*n* (Dormer), 222ff (Pérez), 232 (revolt of 1591-1592), 234*n*, 237, 238-42 *passim* (summary of influence), 248; False Fueros I-IV in particular (cf. Ch. III), 34, 44 (=*FN* i,1,1, *q.v.*), 60-63 (Blancas' formulation), 64, 129-30 (Beuter), 134, 136 (Zurita), 142 & 145 & 148-52 (Blancas), 174, 238, 248 (*see also* Charles of Viana); False Fuero V in particular (cf. Ch. IV), 68ff & 149-50 (Blancas), 71-74 (Cerdan's *Letra intimada, q.v.*), 108 (Vagad) (*see* Justice of Aragon [legendary history], *also* next entry); Fueros V and VI together (cf. Chs. IV, V), 75-87 (Sagarra Story, *q.v.*), 107ff (Vagad), 110-16 (Molino), 132ff (Zurita), 135-36 (Garibay), 135*n*, 174 (suit the Oath), 219 (suit jurisdictional oath), 238-39 (summary of), 248 (*see* preceding and succeeding entries); False Fuero

VI in particular (cf. Chs. IV, V), 75-87 (Sagarra Story, *q.v.*), 100*n*, 108 (Vagad), 112ff (Molino), 133ff (Zurita), 151ff (Blancas), 180-84 (relationship to Oath), 222-23 (Pérez), 229 (Oath), 248; "False Fuero VII" (Oath of the Aragonese as), 156, 163
Soranzo, Giovanni, 18, 19-20, 181, 182, 215*n*, 216, 237*n*; wording of Oath (text, 247), 19-20, 22, 24, 26, 27, 186-87, 217-18, 225-26, 230-31, 239; Oath ceremonial, 158-59, 162, 186-87, 217-18, 219-20. *266*
Sparta, Spartans, 72, 107, 154; *see also* Ephors
Succession, 167 (Eximeniç), 177 (Sobrarbe-Aragon), 188-200 *passim* (Aragon), 193-94 (France and England), 255-56 (Aragonese dynasties), *see also* royal jurisdictional oath, primogenit

Tarafa, Francisco, 166*n*
Terre Rouge, Jean de, 189*n*
Theopompos, 72, 74, 107
Toledo, Councils of, 177, 180*n*, 228*n*, 229*n*
Tomic Cauller, Pedro, 103-06. *266*
Trajan, 224*n*
Trastámara dynasty, 190*n*, 256
Tribune of Rome, 68*n*, 135
Tudela: city of, 34, 35-39; charter of 1117, 35ff, 38-39; edict of 1330, 36-39; Fuero de Tudela, 34-41 *in extenso* (see 39*n* for MSS), 42-52 *passim* (cf. with Fuero of Navarre), 53, 89*n*, 145, 148, 175*n*, 229*n*, 248
Twelve Tables (*XII Tabulae*): 61-62, 149
"Twenty" (*La Veinte*), 234*n*

Union, baronial, 66-67, 88*n*, 90, 112, 147, 178, 183; *see also* Privileges of Union
Universal Empire, 166, 167*n*

Uztarroz, Juan Fr. Andres de, 137*n*. *259* (under Blancas)

Vagad, Gauberte Fabricio de 103-10, 114, 117, 118, 147, 248. *266*
Valdes, Jacobus, 194*n*
Valencia, 88, 164, 165ff (Eximeniç), 168*n*, 172, 197
Valerius Maximus, 72
Valladolid, 203, 205*n*, 207
Vasaeus, Joannes, 177ff, 136, 248. *267*
Viana, *see* Charles of Viana
Vice-Chancellor of Aragon, 190
Viceroy of Aragon (*virey extranjero*), 62*n*, 234-35
Viciana, Martin, 166*n*
Vidal Mayor, 69*n*
Villalba, Diego Franco de, 224*n*
Villarense (*Liber Regum*), 47-48. *267*
Vindiciae contra tyrannos, 20, 23, 160*n*, 220*n*, 224*n*, 247. *263*
Visigoths, Visigothic kingdom, 121, 123, 132, 174*n*, 176, 177, 179, 229*n*

Wales, Prince of, 190*n*

Ximenes, Cardinal, 201
Ximénez de Embún y Val, Tomás, 12, 13, 16. *267*
Ximenez de Rada, Rodrigo, 53, 56, 105, 132, 169*n*, 170*n*. *267*

Zaragoza, 62, 88, 147 (reconquest of, 1118), 206 (Aljaferia), 233ff ("Pérez affair"), 234*n* (Privilege of the Twenty); *La Seo*, 192, 200*n*, 206, 210-11, 212*n*, 215; locus of jurisdictional oath, 191-92, 196-97, 203-12 *passim* (Charles V), 213-16 (Philip II), 217-18 (*idem*), 239; *see also various* Cortes
Zurita, Gerónimo: royal historiographer, 104*n*, 131, 139; records Privileges of Union, 92-95, 184, 185, 224; source for later writers, 136, 178, 224; version of Sobrarbe legend, 131-35, 145, 182-83, 248. *267*